# ROME & THE SWORD

# ROME
# & THE SWORD

## SIMON JAMES

### HOW WARRIORS
### & WEAPONS
### SHAPED
### ROMAN HISTORY

116 illustrations, 13 in color

Thames & Hudson

*For Jill and Tom and in memory of my grandfather, Ernest Sinclair James (1894–1969), who was proud to be an 'Old Contemptible'*

*88907 L/c James, E.S., 1/8 Bn. D.L.I., formerly S/32334, 17 F. Bky. A.S.C.*

Frontispiece: The tombstone of Insus (see Pl. ɪᴠ), as found.

First published in 2011 in hardcover in the United States of America by Thames & Hudson Inc., 500 Fifth Avenue, New York, New York 10110

thamesandhudsonusa.com

Library of Congress Catalog Card Number 2011922630

ɪsʙɴ 978-0-500-25182-9

Designed and typeset by Fred Birdsall Studio
Printed in China by Toppan Leefung

# Contents

# Preface

This book finds its genesis in the Aisne valley of France. In 1980, as a graduate student, I found myself on a summer excavation, digging buildings raised on the gravel river terraces by early German settlers who, in the fifth century AD, were taking Gaul from Roman rule. These remains were themselves disturbed by evidence of much more recent 'Germanic occupation'; the site was pock-marked with shell-holes, and bisected by the trenches of what for much of World War I had been the German front line. Only years later, by an eerie coincidence, did I discover that I had a very personal connection with this later phase of the war-torn history of the Aisne valley. At the time, as a budding military archae-ologist, I was intrigued to learn that our dig was also on a much earlier battlefield.

Here, one morning in 57 BC, at the place now called Mauchamp, Julius Caesar and his legions stood facing a vast army of Belgic Gaulish warriors intent on killing or expelling the Roman invaders.[1] Caesar fortified his camp and dug entrenchments to ensure that his massively outnumbered force was not out-flanked. Thus prepared, Caesar's soldiers formed line, challenging the Gauls to attack. The ensuing battle of the Aisne was just one of a series of major clashes marking the conquest of Gaul, among hundreds punctuating the history of Roman imperial power. Alongside such great set-pieces were thousands of smaller-scale raids, skirmishes and punitive actions, and millions of other occa-sions on which Roman soldiers inflicted death or injury in war, during military occupations, as juridical retribution, or for their own ends.

'The Roman Army' continues to fascinate, its remarkable organization and spectacular sustained success in war unequalled in the ancient West.[2] It is often regarded as the prototype for modern Western armies. Rome has also given us many of our historically important concepts, terms and values, including 'con-stitution', and 'republic'. 'Patriotism' comes from the Latin *patria*, 'fatherland'. 'Army' derives from the verb *armare*, to take up arms, and 'military' from the adjective *militaris*, pertaining to soldiers, *milites*. 'Soldier' is a medieval word derived from *solidus*, a Roman gold coin minted to pay *milites*.[3]

Rome's military was not only the instrument of imperial conquest: through the booty it seized, it became the engine of the republican Roman economy (especially from the third century BC) and, when expansion slowed in imperial times (after *c.* 30 BC), it became the greatest consumer of tax revenue and resources. It was the largest single organization in the ancient Western world. During the main period of focus of this book, between Rome's rise to world power status soon after 300 BC and the aftermath of the collapse of the western empire during the fifth century AD, something like ten million men served in its ranks. And of course these soldiers touched the lives of uncounted millions of others, whether direct victims of war, enslavement or military occupation, or merely grumbling tax-payers, or families who depended on soldiers for their daily bread. Soldiers' actions, their very presence, profoundly shaped not only politics and war, but also the societies and economies of the Roman era. If soldiers considered glorious victory in battle their greatest ambition, the actual impact of the military, violent and otherwise, stretched far beyond campaigning, or even warfare.

It makes little sense, then, that the 'Roman Army' is so frequently considered in isolation from the rest of Roman society, or from its enemies: Carthaginians and Celtiberians, Greeks and Macedonians, Celtic Gauls, Britons and early Germans, Sarmatian nomads, Parthians and Sasanians, and not least the ancient Jews. For as is the case with modern armies, Roman military organization, equipment and practice were all shaped by interactions with specific foes, and cannot be properly comprehended without considering them as well.

So, to understand the profoundly important martial aspect of the Roman era we need to consider it holistically, for each aspect affected the others. For example, few historians would argue that Rome's spectacularly rapid conquest of Gaul in the 50s BC could have happened as it did without the unique genius of Caesar as commander. However, they would also admit that Caesar's military adventure was prompted by the climate of cut-throat competition for glory, wealth and power in the dying Roman republic. Equally, the course of the conquest was profoundly shaped by the nature and responses of the Gaulish societies and leaders Caesar befriended or fought. And they would accept that, for all Caesar's personal genius, his Gallic triumph was only conceivable because of the resources of men and materiel on which he could draw, and the military traditions of Rome. These provided him with an army and the means to sustain it, a formidable force of ferocious men with high morale, unsurpassed expertise in the arts of war and excellent equipment – not least, famously deadly swords. It was a combination that proved too much even for the enormous manpower and military prowess of the Gauls.

Our understanding of the martial aspect of Rome came first from surviving ancient literary texts. Yet these largely focus on officers and commanders; ordinary soldiers are usually treated as anonymous masses, 'barbarian' enemies as stereotypical sword-fodder. Modern historians of the ancient world have not always struggled very hard to overcome the limitations of the top-down perspective of ancient writers, often gentlemen comfortably ensconced far from the frontiers. Certainly, study of inscriptions left by Roman soldiers, and archaeological exploration of imperial frontier systems, have added major dimensions to our understanding of the military. However, much of this work seems curiously sanitized, worrying away at details of organization and structure, rarely dealing with the brutal realities of ancient soldiering. Even archaeological study of arms and equipment remains mostly focused on typology and chronology of arms, rather than what they did. Only recently have some ancient historians turned their attention to the mechanics of battle. Many popular treatments draw on these academic traditions and developments, offering views of the Roman military which tend to remain top-down representations of a pseudo-modern force.

There is a need for a new and different approach to what Romans called *res militaris*, 'military affairs'. Instead of the familiar perspective from the apex of Roman society, the viewpoint of Scipio, Caesar, Trajan and their fellow aristocrats, I emphasize the literal cutting edge of Roman power: physical acts of soldierly violence, the weapons with which they were inflicted and the hands that wielded them – the soldiers and warriors on whom military hierarchies were built. My case for this is simple. In contrast to modern mechanized, anonymized mass slaughter at a distance, ancient military force was delivered by hand, by individuals, using muscle-powered weapons – *par excellence*, the sword itself – against the bodies of other individuals. The results of battles, campaigns, wars and imperial rule were the cumulative results of myriad individual acts of mayhem. Swords, soldiers and their victims are central to this study, not minor or peripheral details. Bringing them into the foreground creates a picture very different from the familiar image of the 'Roman Army at war'. It shifts the focus from the internal dynamics of Rome – too often considered in virtual isolation when discussing *res militaris* – to the interactions between Romans and others: to what went on at the boundaries with other polities, and between conquerors and conquered.

Focusing on the sword also re-emphasizes the suffering, carnage and glorification of lethal violence at the heart of *res militaris*, which the Romans themselves celebrated in triumphal processions,[4] and reproduced in quasi-theatrical form through ritualized slaughter in the arena. It brings in the direct human experience, and something of the horror, of building and maintaining the empire. This kind of bottom-up perspective also has another distinct advantage over conventional treatments. It is much closer to how most Romans saw these matters for themselves.

I offer a new sketch of the history of Rome and the sword from this unconventional standpoint, aiming to cover new ground, and to explore familiar themes from different angles, as far as possible through new or unfamiliar examples, especially from archaeology. Few societies of the era other than the Romans themselves have left us written accounts, but most have left archaeological remains, helping us to put into the picture Rome's antagonists, allies and subjects, giving them a voice (of a kind) and allowing us to see them as factors in Rome's story. *Rome and the Sword* weaves together a number of strands of my work as an archaeologist. It is about what material remains (especially the portable artefacts I have long studied, such as swords and saddles, clothing and coins) can tell us about our prehistoric and early historic past. Besides studying ancient martial culture, I have also long been interested in the nature of group identities, such as 'Romans', 'Celts', 'Germans' and 'Parthians'. Identities were, and are, about insiders and outsiders, about boundaries and (with grim frequency) violent conflict. Culture and violence are intimately connected, producing those specialized artefacts that are used to wage war and, often, to help construct identities.

There is also the visual representation of the past. Many ancient objects and places are best understood through pictures, while much of our evidence for the past comes from images made by ancient peoples themselves. This book is largely illustrated with my own line drawings, computer graphics and photographs of ancient artefacts, images and sites. These comprise an extra dimension of information and interpretation expanding on the textual narrative, and – I hope – enriching the sense I have sought to convey of what the Roman era was really like, and how it evolved.

This is not a monograph on Roman swords, nor is it a detailed anatomy of the Roman military; space precludes repeating what is ably presented elsewhere.[5] Neither will I much discuss that other staple of 'Roman Army' books, forts and frontier systems.[6] Likewise, I must largely pass over themes such as naval warfare (a fascinating field yet one which was almost always secondary and subordinate to land conflict), generalship, or intelligence, on which specialist studies are available.[7] Rather, I seek to show how the Big Picture of society in the Roman era is inseparably bound up with the microscale of people and the artefacts they used both in routine life and dramatic events, and in so doing I also hope to help move the military aspect further back into the mainstream of discourse on Antiquity. To keep the endnotes in bounds, I have referenced primary ancient sources and key syntheses with a selection of harder-to-trace and recent scholarship used.

General works on 'the Roman Army' tend to be sanitized or celebratory about the martial side of Roman antiquity. This study aims to avoid either, and to deal directly with the violent reality. Perhaps especially in Europe, violence has become taboo in polite discourse, like sex in Victorian times. While some (especially young males) can't get enough of it, others (especially scholars) regard such work with grave reservations, and are as likely to suspect the motives of researchers as to consider the value or implications of their work. Can the study of violence do more than satisfy the prurience of modern military fantasists?

Academic justification for such study is actually simple. Scholarship takes all human experience as its domain, and few would dispute that warfare and armed violence have constituted one of the principal themes of human history. To seek to comprehend martial violence is not to condone it, any more than forensic pathology validates murder.

An explanation of how and why I came to this perspective should be offered, so that readers can better judge the ideas and conclusions presented. Fascinated by the Romans since childhood, I became an archaeologist, special-izing in the study of ancient fighting men, Romans and their contemporaries, through their arms and equipment, and traces of ancient battles. When in 1980, already a Roman military specialist, I went to excavate in the Aisne valley, it was not the nearby Caesarean battlefield which impressed me most. Indeed, that engagement proved relatively indecisive. The Gauls attacked inconclusively, then ran out of supplies, got hungry and dispersed. Caesar pursued, and fought a far more decisive battle on the Sambre soon after.[8] I became more intrigued by the tangible remains of the German trenches across our excavation area, for I was strongly aware that my paternal grandfather had served on the Western Front. Subsequently, I learned that this culminated in the Aisne valley.

In 1997, when due to return to the Aisne to help survey Gaulish sites roughly of Caesar's time, I was astonished to discover that on my previous visit I had been digging just an hour's walk from where my grandfather had narrowly escaped death in 1918. The World War I front line snaked across the Aisne basin, through places branded on the hearts of a generation of the French: the Chemin des Dames, and the shattered village of Craonne. During the last German offen-sive of spring 1918, British troops were placed under French command and sent to shore up the Aisne front. They included 1/8 Battalion, Durham Light Infantry, into which Lance Corporal Ernie James had recently been transferred. A pre-war regular soldier-tradesman and one of the few survivors of 'England's contemptible little army', the original British Expeditionary Force of 1914, he now found himself in the front line just east of ruined Craonne. On 27 May 1918 he was lucky to survive one of the most ferocious bombardments of the war. Afterwards, while shooting on the fire-step, he was luckier still not to be bayo-neted by the big German who surprised him when the Durhams were outflanked. Lifted out of the trench by his helmet strap, he was led into captiv-ity where, during the winter of 1918–19, he survived surgery without anaesthetic, and nearly starved to death.

From the stories he told me in childhood, I gained powerful impressions of the twin Janus-faces of soldiering and war. On the one hand, there was the glorious aspect, the visceral appeal of uniforms, glittering weapons and the thrill of martial music and drill epitomized in military displays such as Trooping the Colour. Books and films offered tales of heroism and self-sacrifice, the com-radeship of the peculiar society of soldiers, and the warrior ethos. But the other, grim visage was also ever present in my family's memory: suffering, death, destruction, fear, horror and privation, acknowledged, albeit in sanitized form, in the sombreness and reverence of Remembrance Sunday. These first impressions left me with the fascination for, yet deep ambivalence about, soldiers, which is, I think, the deepest of the many roots of this book.

My grandfather died as I was entering my impressionable teens, when two other conflicts were under way. In Vietnam, the confused nature of guerrilla warfare and the slaughter of women and children, seen daily on TV, put paid to any surviving easy illusions of good guys and bad guys, or unalloyed military glory. US soldiers came to be represented less as heroes, and more as victims crippled by Post-Traumatic Stress Disorder, or butchers, such as at My Lai. Their status as guardians of society was also shattered by the shooting of students at Kent State University, Ohio, in 1970.

In Northern Ireland the 'Troubles' flared, with Republican and Loyalist terrorists, paramilitary police and British troops fighting for control. The beatings, bombings and shootings gave me a growing realization of the ambiguity of the boundaries of soldiering and war not immediately apparent from representations of the World Wars. One person's war for liberation was another's criminal violence. Then, in 1972, Bloody Sunday saw British troops shooting British citizens. When I went under-age drinking in my home city, Guildford, I saw soldiers from the nearby army town of Aldershot fighting locals, and each other, outside the pubs; on duty or off, 'our boys' could be dangerous. In 1974 the Provisional IRA paid a visit to town, bombing two soldiers' pubs and splattering human flesh on the walls of the public library across the street from what was left of the Horse and Groom. War had come close to home. For this atrocity four innocent Irishmen subsequently spent years in jail; armed conflict compromised civil justice too.

These experiences and impressions shaped the kinds of questions I subsequently brought to the study of soldiers, warriors and war in antiquity, inclining me to seek the viewpoints of soldiers and their victims more than generals and politicians, and to regard 'armies and warfare' as an inadequate characterization of the subject matter: what soldiers do has always extended far beyond war.

# Acknowledgments

The bulk of the writing for this book was originally undertaken in 2006–7 during a semester of research leave granted by the University of Leicester, and a second funded by the Arts and Humanities Research Council. I am grateful to both institutions.

Any work of synthesis such as this draws on the work, expertise and inspiration of many other people, over many years. Mark Hassall originally fostered my interest in the Roman military, John Wilkes and the late Margaret Roxan first introduced me to the method and rigour of German-style scholarship, while Richard Reece taught me not to be afraid to ask awkward questions about antiquity. My rough contemporary Martin Millett has always been a priceless source of encouragement, advice and support.

The present volume draws on the work of the community of Roman military scholars. Among these special thanks are due to Ian Haynes and Adrian Goldsworthy, who helped kick-start new understandings of the Roman military, more recently particularly enriched for me by the work of Ted Lendon. I also rely on the achievements of other colleagues working on weapons and armour, especially Mike Bishop, Jon Coulston and Peter Connolly, who have built so well on the foundation of scholarship laid by the late H. Russell Robinson. It is also appropriate to mention here my debt to Chris Haines and other friends in the Ermine Street Guard, whose recreations of Roman arms and military practices are of such great value to specialists like me.

This book relies equally on the perspectives of scholars in areas outside Roman military studies, some working in overlapping areas, notably Nicola Terrenato for showing me a radically new understanding of the nature of early Rome completely different from the one I learned at university. Others belong to different fields entirely, from prehistory to medieval and early modern archaeology. My understanding of the peoples Rome encountered in Europe was transformed by scholars like J. D. Hill, Colin Haselgrove and Peter Wells. I owe a profound debt to Matthew Johnson, for opening my eyes to archaeological theory, and to my former colleagues at Durham, Sam Lucy, Pam Graves and Margarita Diaz Andreu, for helping me understand the archaeology of identity.

Similarly, my present colleagues at the University of Leicester, particularly David Mattingly, have provided invaluable support and encouragement.

I am also grateful to former colleagues at the British Museum, Ralph Jackson, Paul Roberts and Dyfri Williams, for access to some key examples of Roman swords, and stimulating discussions about them, and to Janet Lang for her expertise on Roman blade manufacture. Fraser Hunter generously provided information on the Newstead swords. I would also like to thank Bob Savage and his colleagues at the Royal Armouries, Leeds, for access to the 'Pompeii' sword in their collections, and valuable discussion of edged weapons in general. Special thanks also go to Paul Binns for his demonstration of hammer welding and discussion of pattern welding techniques. Many others also kindly helped in various ways, providing information and references, assisting with provision of images or answering my questions, and I thank them here: Colin Adams, Lindsay Allason-Jones, Claus von Carnap-Bornheim, Elly Cowan, Simon Esmonde Cleary, Megan Doyon, Carol Van Driel-Murray, Iain Ferris, Peter Heather, Jørgen Ilkjær, Peter Johnsson, Simon Keay, Ernst Künzl, Andy Merrills (not least for prompting me to focus more on metaphor), Aubrey Newman, Rebecca Redfern, Achim Rost and Susanne Wilbers-Rost, Graham Shipley, and Guy Stiebel. I am also grateful to the publisher's anonymous reader for constructive comments on an earlier draft. At Thames & Hudson, I again benefited greatly from the experience of Colin Ridler, who guided me gently and with good humour through the prolonged creation of this book, and am also very grateful to Fred Birdsall, Celia Falconer and, above all, Carolyn Jones for her efficiency in copyediting and the subsequent production stages. I apologize if I have inadvertently overlooked anyone, and must add the conventional disclaimer that none of these can be held responsible for what I have made of the ideas I have drawn from them.

For their support and forbearance during the prolonged gestation of this volume, I owe a special debt of gratitude to my wife Jill, and to my son Tom. I fervently hope that he, and his children, will never get closer to these things than books and news media. I dedicate this book to Jill and Tom, and to the memory of my grandfather Ernest James.

If we don't find anything agreeable, we will at least find something new.
VOLTAIRE, *CANDIDE*, CHAPTER 17

# Introduction
## Swords and Soldiers

### The inescapable sword

*Arma virumque cano, Troiae qui primus ab oris*
*Italiam, fato profugus, Laviniaque venit*
*litora, multum ille et terris iactatus et alto*
*vi superum saevae memorem Iunonis ob iram;*
*multa quoque et bello passus, dum conderet urbem,*
*inferretque deos Latio, genus unde Latinum,*
*Albanique patres, atque altae moenia Romae.*
VIRGIL, AENEID 1.1–7


Arms, and the man I sing, who, forc'd by fate,
And haughty Juno's unrelenting hate,
Expell'd and exil'd, left the Trojan shore.
Long labors, both by sea and land, he bore,
And in the doubtful war, before he won
The Latian realm, and built the destin'd town;
His banish'd gods restor'd to rites divine,
And settled sure succession in his line,
From whence the race of Alban fathers come,
And the long glories of majestic Rome.
JOHN DRYDEN'S TRANSLATION[1]

Thus begins the *Aeneid*, tale of Aeneas, son of Venus, Prince of Troy, who escaped Greek vengeance in the flaming ruins of his native city to embark on divinely guided wanderings. Coming at last to the shores of Italy, in Latin lands he would establish a line leading to Romulus, founder of Rome (Fig. 1). The first word of this, imperial Rome's national epic, is *arma*: weapons and armour. Virgil's great poem also culminates in a duel, decided by a fatal sword-thrust. The sword – usually referred to as the *gladius*, conceptualized as a short, thrusting weapon belonging to the early imperial legionary – stands as an archetypal symbol of Rome, and provides a central metaphor for her power.

For centuries Rome ruled lands now divided among more than thirty nation-states on three continents washed by the Mediterranean, and directly affected peoples far beyond, to Biscay, the North Sea, Baltic, Black Sea and Caspian, the Persian Gulf and Sudan. Her vast empire was, literally and figuratively, carved out primarily by the sword.

1. Aeneas escapes from Troy, carrying his aged father Anchises, and an ancient statue of Athena to the future site of Rome. Silver *denarius* of Caesar, who claimed descent from Aeneas, and his mother, Venus.

Because Westerners still often identify with Rome, its martial aspect is frequently seen in strongly positive terms or, paradoxically, is equally fervently played down. Many popular treatments, and some academic works, celebrate the Roman military as the greatest of Western antiquity. Alexander of Macedon may have conquered more territory more quickly, but Rome's armed might proved far more durable, and it is her legions, rather than Alexander's phalanx (see p. 87), which are often seen today as the inspiration for modern armies. In this view the almost invincible legions of 'The Roman Army' (at least implicitly capitalized) constituted a glittering 'war machine' of unprecedented effectiveness. After conquering the Mediterranean world and most of western Europe in a series of admittedly very bloody wars, this military juggernaut thereafter established fixed frontiers, where it stood as an unblinking sentinel, defending demilitarized provinces from the barbarians that threatened them.

Popular books and television may dwell with relish on the nature of Roman warfare, but little modern academic writing discusses the realities of war directly. The horrors of conquest are often skated over with haste to reach the more comfortable ground of provincial development and 'Romanization'. Insofar as the military is discussed thereafter, emphasis is often placed on its achievement in establishing the *pax Romana*, the 'Roman peace', creating the environment for the greatest imperial achievement of all: a brilliant flowering of Greco-Roman urban civilization in the civil provinces, vaunted by some in Roman times,[2] and celebrated by Gibbon as the zenith from which Rome subsequently declined and fell.

This view of Rome is still deeply ingrained in the modern West. After the initial conquests, outside the special and horribly fascinating context of the gladiatorial arena, violence of any kind is rarely discussed as a factor in provincial life. Emphasis is placed on the collaborative nature of developing the empire, through foundation of cities, building communications and international trade, driven by the convergence of provincial ruling classes sharing the values and trappings of Greco-Roman civilization.[3] Under the *pax Romana* military violence, in particular, is seen as banished to the frontiers, except for occasional revolts or inter-army civil wars. According to this view, the military was an outer protective shield, in all senses peripheral to the 'real' story of Roman civilization. However, others – the Jewish tradition, early Christian writers, people in modern Arab countries once part of the empire, and modern Europeans who prefer to identify with the so-called barbarians – take much more hostile positions on the Roman military, seeing its actions in terms of perpetration rather than achievement.[4] From this perspective, integration among the powerful and privileged was underpinned by fear of the legions, by violent coercion, oppression or enslavement of the majority. Rome became a society obsessed with dominating and subjugating the rest of the world. Her armies destroyed Jerusalem and the Second Temple, slaughtering perhaps a million Jews,[5] then (allegedly) expelling the rest from Judea, which the emperor Hadrian renamed 'Palestine'. These actions still resonate today. Roman soldiers crucified Jesus, and arrested, tortured and executed early Christian martyrs and saints. Roman troops destroyed the oasis city-state of Palmyra, which many Syrians regard as an early, pre-Islamic flowering of Arab civilization. Roman armies also repeatedly devastated – but could not hold – what is now Iraq. At the other end of the former Roman empire, some blame the Romans for the destruction of 'Celtic'[6] culture in most of Continental Europe and what would subsequently become England.

From such viewpoints the Roman military was an alien conqueror, an oppressive army of occupation, destroyer of indigenous cultures and sometimes an instrument of genocide. Emphasis is placed much more on the bloody reality of military power and imperialism: of heartless foreign soldiers hideously torturing and butchering defenceless civilians in the streets of burning cities, as archaeology confirms Pompey's soldiers did at Valencia (p. 100). Men who could do such things are frequently labelled inhuman, and can easily be seen as brutal unthinking cogs of a soulless war machine.

We will examine the recurrent image of the 'Roman war machine' later. The Romans and many contemporaries certainly used machines in war, and even knew about automata; and many of the accoutrements of war were also used in symbolic and metaphorical ways in antiquity. Especially important, then as now, was the sword itself.

## Sword as artefact and metaphor

> The Gaul … held out his shield … to meet his adversary's blows and aimed a tremendous cut downwards with his sword. [Manlius] evaded the blow, and pushing aside the bottom of the Gaul's shield with his own, he slipped under it close up to the Gaul, too near for him to get at him with his sword. Then turning the point of his blade upwards, he gave two rapid thrusts in succession and stabbed the Gaul in the belly and the groin, laying his enemy prostrate... He left the body of his fallen foe undespoiled with the exception of his torque, which though smeared with blood he placed round his own neck.
>
> T. MANLIUS WINS THE SURNAME 'TORQUATUS', 360 BC: LIVY 7.10[7]

In this book, the Roman sword is explored both as a material instrument of physical violence, and as a metaphor for thinking about the actions of armed men in Roman times.[8] Warfare and especially battle itself were, of course, central to this – not least in the self-images of warriors and soldiers – but there was much more to it besides.

Millions served in the armies of the Roman era, and hundreds of thousands were slain on the battlefield, some dying bravely, selling their lives dearly for their own honour and in defence of their homes and families, some butchered while begging for mercy. Romans, like Gauls and others, preferred close-quarter killing over arrows or other missile weapons, and especially favoured swords: many fell to their blades, whether combatants or the defenceless like Archimedes, killed by a legionary in the sack of Syracuse.[9] Men at war also sometimes directed their violence against themselves. The death of Ajax by impaling himself on his own sword was a famous incident of the Trojan War. Suicide by falling on one's sword, aiming at a quick death by running the point under the rib-cage into the heart, was an honourable exit for Roman generals defeated in civil war, although Mark Antony famously botched it, dying slowly in the arms of Cleopatra.[10] Mass suicides, as a last desperate act of defiance and as escape from the humiliations of defeat, are also attested. The most famous example is perhaps that of the defenders of Masada, last stronghold of the first Jewish Revolt.[11] Roman soldiers did it too; the survivors of those defeated by the Gallic Eburones chose suicide over surrender.[12]

However, the violence of fighting men was by no means confined to war. Roman soldiers, in particular, used the sword to suppress civilian unrest, and were detailed to execute criminals. They also engaged in much freelance violence of their own volition against civilians: enemy non-combatants, but also Rome's subjects, allies and even fellow Romans. Indeed, it may be that they maimed and killed more off the battlefield than on it.

The broad term 'martial violence' best encompasses all these brutal activities. 'Martial' is doubly fitting, deriving from the name of the Roman war-god, and also because it refers to both soldiers and warriors, whereas 'military' tends to connote regular armies alone. 'Martial violence' also distinguishes the actions of soldiers and warriors from other forms of armed mayhem, for, as we shall see, many other groups (and not just gladiators) also used weapons, legally or otherwise. Further, 'armed violence' does not encompass all the brutality committed by soldiers, much of which was inflicted by means other than weapons of war. In English, 'violence'[13] retains the pejorative undertone connoted by its Latin root, *vis*, meaning excessive, and especially socially unsanctioned, force. Many of the activities discussed here are now seen – and were perceived at the time – as negative, illegitimate or reprehensible, and not only by their intended victims. Hence 'violence' is preferred to the potentially more positive-sounding 'force'.

Alongside assaults intended to kill, many violent acts perpetrated by soldiers, official (for example, juridical punishment) or unofficial (for example, roughing up civilians), were inflicted without lethal intent – although many died as a result. Such violence was dealt with fists (and Roman soldiers wore metal rings), hob-nail boots and various kinds of cudgel, leading to concussion, broken bones, lost eyes and teeth.[14] Roman whips included the flesh-ripping metal-tipped *flagellum*,[15] which was far from the most extreme form of torture. Many war captives suffered and died simply as a result of overworking or wilful neglect. And not the least significant instrument of violence was the phallus: rape was, and is, a common phenomenon in encounters with soldiery. Sub-lethal tactics operated not just by physical suffering, but by humiliation and terror.

Indeed, the effectiveness of martial violence in the Roman era reached far beyond its direct victims, arguably working as much by the fear it engendered in witnesses, undiminished in the telling.[16] Rome in particular engaged in high-profile acts of savagery appalling even by ancient standards, both to punish 'wrongdoers', and as a deterrent. The sheathed, but deliberately visible, sword worn by Roman soldiers and other fighting men constituted a deadly threat, and constant source of terror. Maintaining the credibility of this threat also necessitated actually drawing the sword on a regular basis.

The sword['s] … terror and majesty are greater than those of all other weapons. It is for this reason that when a Kingdom has been taken by force of arms, it is said to have been taken by the sword.

FAKHR-I-MUDABBIR, IN A THIRTEENTH-CENTURY INDIAN
MILITARY MANUAL[17]

Since pre-Roman times swords have held special symbolic value in many cultures, in East and West. Mechanized armies still use crossed swords in their badges.[18] Metaphors depend for their effectiveness on the power of one idea to express another; the source needs to carry a potent meaning already for it to provide a compelling image. Why has the sword commonly fulfilled this role, and not other weapons? It has not always and everywhere been the supreme symbol of military power. Among ancient peoples in Central Asia, horse-archery was the principal martial skill, expressing both horsemanship and proficiency at arms. The bow symbolized warrior prowess and, for the Huns, royal authority (p. 267). However, while Parthians favoured horse-archers they also used cataphracts (lance-armed, armoured shock-cavalry), while Huns used sword as well as bow. Although Roman soldiers likewise made use of the full range of projectile weapons and spears, the sword was the weapon of choice when battle-lines collided. Similar tastes were shared by many contemporary societies, such as the Gauls.

Among pre-gunpowder weapons of offence, arms such as the axe, spear, javelin, bow or sling had origins or alternative uses as tools or hunting equipment. The sword was different. From its Bronze Age invention it was a specialized instrument for killing people.[19] Further, while weapons such as the powerful composite bow, shooting iron-tipped arrows, rival it in lethality, the sword demands that its wielder approach a foe closely; it is a murderous extension of the fist, yet also puts the wielder in reach of a similarly armed opponent. *Par excellence* it connotes both aggression and courage, and an especially personalized source of terror quite distinct from the danger of a distant, semi-anonymous bowman. For, instead of the relatively small puncture wounds of arrows (lethal though they may be), it threatens cloven skulls, dismemberment or disembowelling, injuries more devastating and hideous to behold than those inflicted by most other hand-wielded weapons. Of all common arms, it offers the highest likelihood of instantly killing, or at least incapacitating, foe or victim.[20]

Swords were also prized because, of all elements of the pre-gunpowder panoply,[21] with the possible exception of the composite bow, they were the most technically demanding to make, with consequent expense in materials, expertise and time. In thrusting or slashing, a blade must withstand huge mechanical stresses, flexing to a degree yet not bending or snapping, while retaining sharpness of edge. By comparison the spear, itself a fearsome weapon, was simple and cheap to produce.

The sword enjoyed another important advantage over bow or spear: it could and did become an item of regular dress. Scabbard, hilt and belt provided eye-catching fields for decorative display,[22] connoting taste, wealth and above all the personal autonomy, courage, or sanction of higher authority openly to wear a lethal weapon. It was a warning, challenge or threat, symbolizing status, rank, or profession as a fighting man. Here we move beyond mere functional considerations to the symbolic value and meaning of the sword. Highly prized material objects of great physical and symbolic power, swords were widely selected for religious offerings in ancient Europe (a key reason we now have so many in our museums).[23] In particular, they were deposited in watery places,[24] inspiring the legend of Excalibur. It is hardly surprising, then, that the sword was also widely used as a metaphor in antiquity, not least by the warlike Romans themselves.

In Roman writings, the primary metaphorical meanings of the sword were war between peoples, conquest and military power in general. A celebrated case of an actual sword symbolizing military conquest occurs in the story of the Senonian Gaulish sack of Rome in 387 BC, a disaster which left the Romans with an abiding *terror Gallicus*. The Romans agreed to buy the Senones off, but when they complained about the weights used to measure out the bullion, the Gallic chief Brennus threw his sword onto the scales, declaring '*vae victis*', 'woe to the conquered!'[25] Others also used sword metaphors, including Jews and early Christians. Including the New Testament, the sword is mentioned more than 500 times in the Bible, mostly figuratively for warfare.[26]

The image was also used of threats to the internal order of societies and regimes. Another famous example of a sword as both material object and metaphor occurs in a Greek story retold in Latin by the famous orator Cicero. He describes how the powerful fourth-century BC tyrant of Syracuse, Dionysius I, was dining with his court:

> When Damocles, one of his flatterers, was dilating in conversation on his forces, his wealth, the greatness of his power, the plenty he enjoyed, the grandeur of his royal palaces, and maintaining that no one was ever happier, [Dionysius asked him] 'Have you an inclination…Damocles, as this kind of life pleases you, to have a taste of it yourself, and to make a trial of the good fortune that attends me?'

Damocles was seated on a couch covered with gold and embroideries, surrounded by gold and silver vessels, and handsome youths ready to do his bidding.

> … Damocles thought himself very happy. In the midst of this apparatus, Dionysius ordered a bright sword (*fulgentem gladium*), to be let down from the ceiling, suspended by a single horse-hair, so as to hang over the head of that happy man. After which he neither cast his eye on those handsome waiters, nor on the well-wrought plate; nor touched any of the provisions… At last he entreated the tyrant to give him leave to go, for that now he had no desire to be happy.
> CICERO, *TUSCULAN DISPUTATIONS* 5.20.60–62[27]

In this parable, the deadly artefact literally embodies the threat of violent death, by war or assassination, hanging over the powerful.

The sword was also used figuratively to express the power of the state in the maintenance of order and the rule of law – or at least enforcement of the will of regimes, naked or under the guise of justice. While the Roman world is notorious for hideous forms of execution such as crucifixion, the honourable mode of capital punishment was condemnation to beheading by the sword (*damnatio ad gladium*).[28] The capacity to order capital punishment was expressed in the legal terms *ius gladii* ('justice of the sword') or *potestas gladii* ('power of the sword'). This juridical power of life and death was possessed by holders of *imperium* (supreme executive authority) such as republican consuls, or later emperors who delegated it to their appointed provincial governors and army commanders.[29] The sword also became a material symbol of investment with imperial power: when Vitellius was declared emperor in AD 69, he was paraded around holding a sword allegedly once belonging to Caesar, taken from a nearby temple where it had been dedicated.[30]

Further, the sword symbolized other forms of armed violence waged by individuals or groups unsanctioned by society, which the state sought to suppress. These comprised armed criminal violence (*vis*), or activities so treated, some of which we might characterize as armed strife within the Roman state, such as the faction fighting of the later republic, or political resistance to imperial power. Throughout the era – even under the famed *pax Romana* – armed robbery, murder, banditry and brigandage were endemic, sometimes reaching a scale that the state was obliged to treat as warfare, and requiring formal military campaigns to suppress. *Gladius* could be used to mean a dangerous armed man (like a 'hired gun'), while the word *gladiator* literally means 'swordsman'.[31]

By imperial times, the elaborate spectacle of gladiatorial shows had itself evolved into a kind of allegory of military and judicial power. Gladiator types were named after defeated nations ('Samnites', 'Gauls'), and their combats – some of which were full-scale battles – brought performances of now-distant wars, with real blood, into the heart of Rome. These 'games' also symbolized the triumph of Roman law and order: gladiators and other arena victims were mostly prisoners of war or condemned criminals, whose deaths reasserted the cosmic order in a way that reassured everyone watching. Even the poorest could feel superior to the aliens and outcasts dying under their gaze.[32]

And, unsurprisingly in a world that barely distinguished between sex and violent force,[33] the sword also provided a slang term for the phallus. In Plautus' comedy *Pseudolus* a Greek term for a sword, *machaera*, and the Latin for a scabbard, *vagina*, are used in sexual innuendo to stand for phallus and male anus.[34] (The extension of *vagina* as a term for the female sexual organ arose later, in medical terminology.) Correspondingly, the orientation of inlaid figures on middle imperial blades show that (in contrast to the tip-downward way blades are shown here and in other modern publications) Romans envisioned the sword as it was when held in the hand, the blade tip upwards and outwards, phallus-like, being inverted when in the scabbard.

Roman uses of the image of the sword point up both similarities, and particularly striking differences, between the ways in which Romans thought about their world, and those in which we think about our own – and theirs. This divergence is seen especially strongly between modern understandings of the Roman military, and how the Romans themselves conceptualized it.

## 'The Roman army: war machine'?

Today, Rome's military is commonly represented as an entity called 'The Roman Army', implying a monolithic state institution essentially like the modern US Army or British Army. In its operation, it is further often characterized as a 'war machine', a metaphor paradoxically frequently shared by otherwise diametrically opposed views of Roman imperialism; the 'machine' may be admired for its power and apparent efficiency, or regarded with horror for its perceived unthinking, unmerciful relentlessness. Unsurprisingly, it is a favourite image of many popular books and television presentations.[35] Yet both images, monolith and machine, are seriously misleading, indeed pernicious anachronisms.[36] 'The Roman Army: war machine' ignores, indeed contradicts, the ways in which the Romans thought about their own military; and as we shall see, in consequence it seriously misrepresents how it actually operated. It turns out the Romans thought primarily in terms of *people*, not an institution, let alone a machine. Startlingly, the Romans had no term equivalent to our phrase 'The Roman Army', because no such entity or concept existed.

We think of a state creating a centralized army, with a unified, inverted-tree-like hierarchy of subdivisions such as corps, divisions, brigades, regiments, battalions, companies and platoons down to sections, nested boxes into which soldiers are slotted. This top-down conceptualization emphasizes command and organizational structures. The Romans' conception of their own military, originating in the republic but still underpinning thinking during the empire, was the precise opposite: it was bottom up, starting from the existence within the citizen body of a pool of free men able and willing when called upon to perform military service (*militia*) for the state as soldiers (*miles* singular; *milites* plural).[37] When war loomed in republican times, eligible men were selected from this pool, and organized into *legiones* (singular: *legio*). Alongside contingents of allies, legions were brigaded into armies (*exercitus* singular; *exercitūs* plural).[38] Armies were almost always multiple, to serve the specific current needs of the state. Under the emperors, the now-professional soldiers continued to be brigaded into multiple armies, now territorially based standing forces attached to particular provinces.[39] Hence the Roman forces at the disposal of the governor of Syria comprised the *exercitus Syriacae* (Fig. 2).

During republic and empire, to describe their armed forces Romans normally spoke of 'the armies', (*exercitūs*), or 'the legions', in plurals.[40] Significantly, just as Americans often talk about 'our troops' instead of 'the Army' or 'Marine Corps', Romans also commonly spoke of *milites*, 'the soldiers', of men rather than institutional collectives.

Above these multiple armies, under neither republic nor empire was there any single central military command structure analogous to a modern general staff or 'ministry of defence'. Individual army commanders, themselves for most of Roman history senior politicians who were part-time rather than professional

2. Bronze *sestertius* coins of Hadrian commemorated the various armies, including the *exercitus Britannicus* (left), and the *exercitus Syriacus* (right).

soldiers, were directly responsible to the senatorial government in Rome or, later, to the emperor. The late imperial period saw more unified and centralized command hierarchies – but these still almost always remained plural, since there were usually multiple emperors and armies in a segmented empire.

Even with the institution of a standing, professional force of permanent regiments under the empire, the reality of multiple armies persisted, while the notion of 'the soldiers' as a class of people became, if anything, stronger, as *milites* became a distinctive and increasingly self-aware identity group. In emphasizing groups of *people*, Roman understanding of their own military reflected the reality of the social and political importance of soldiers. This underlines a fundamental practical and ideological distinction within the Roman military. On the one hand there were the institutional structures created by the state, and controlled by rulers and aristocrats (units, armies and command). On the other there were the *milites* serving within them who, as we will see, evolved in imperial times into a class of self-aware and strongly opinionated human beings, an 'imagined community', i.e. a far-flung identity group real in the minds of its members, even though they only ever encountered some of their fellows.[41]

Looking at the Roman military through Roman, rather than modern, eyes in this way, it becomes apparent that 'The Roman Army' as widely imagined today quite literally did not exist. Here, then, following Roman terminology and concepts, I will write instead of 'the soldiers' as a class of men, of units, of plural armies, and, to cover the whole martial aspect of Rome from institutions to the men in the ranks, of 'the Roman military'.[42]

To its contemporaries, Rome's military carefully cultivated an image of irresistible invincibility. When discussing it we naturally reach for metaphors familiar from our own time to convey this quality, including (as mentioned above) the modern idea of 'army as war-machine', regularly applied to the Nazi Wehrmacht or the Red Army. This image derives its power from the seductive analogy of the anatomy of a modern 'high-tech' army with the machines it uses. The top-down, monolithic conception of a modern army is readily compared to a military vehicle and its subsystems. From the top (general, tank commander, pilot) instructions – orders, electronic impulses – are fed downwards; relays, servos and gears automatically obey, engines roar, weapons fire. Soldiers may be thought of as cogs in the war-machine, pawns in the giant chess-sets of military formations. Modern expectations of unquestioning obedience, strict discipline and precise parade-ground drill all contribute to an image of soldier as automaton.[43] However, vivid though this is, it provides a very poor model for understanding the Roman military.

Certainly, Romans were expert with early war machines in sieges, and some cavalrymen wore impassive face-masks, making them resemble cyborgs to modern eyes. Classical times saw the first real automata,[44] and Romans went further than any contemporaries in dehumanizing people, writing of agricultural slaves as perambulating implements to be used and discarded.[45] However, they also feared these supposedly passive 'possessions', giving the lie to their own rhetoric. And there was no question of thinking of 'the soldiers' in such terms while armies were seen as collectivities consisting of 'some of *us*'. To contemporaries, masked cavalrymen resembled not machines, but statues of heroes (p. 224). Robots and chess-pieces do not succumb to demoralization, exhaustion, sickness or panic. Besides showing icy ruthlessness, Roman soldiers could also be overcome by sentimentality,[46] or frightened out of their wits by a comet or a surprise attack. Sometimes they ran away, if less often than their foes. Further, cogs are not wilfully disobedient; it frequently comes as a shock to discover just how unruly Roman soldiers regularly were. *Milites* were active, self-aware human beings, not robotic instruments of the state – and, as we will see, from the poorest slave to the emperor, didn't the Romans know it.[47]

### Eagles or wolves? The double-edged Roman sword

> All the hostility and quarrelsomeness [the Romans] had formerly entertained towards other nations was now being turned against themselves; the wolves were blinded with mad rage at one another...
> LIVY 3.66[48]

The Romans themselves associated many symbols and powers with their state and its military. Not the least was the soaring imperial eagle (*aquila*), most majestic of sky-borne predators, symbol of Jupiter Best and Greatest, principal deity of the state. During the late republic the eagle came to be intimately identified with the military, especially through the precious-metal statuette mounted on a thunderbolt, which was not simply the standard of each legion, but a holy object and its very soul, a material artefact of extraordinary value and power.[49] Imperial legionaries followed Jupiter's eagles, and had eagle's wings and thunderbolts emblazoned on their shields. Loss of a legionary *aquila* was the ultimate disgrace. In 55 BC it was only fear for their standard that persuaded Caesar's legionaries to leap from their ships into the waves and follow their eagle-bearer up the beach to face the waiting Britons.[50] (Fig. 3)

Another major deity of special relevance to soldiers was naturally Mars, god of war, whose totemic animal was the wolf. Alongside Jupiter's eagle and thunderbolt the legendary *lupa*, the she-wolf, constituted a central symbol of Rome, suckling Mars' semi-divine twin sons Romulus and Remus, saving them from death in the Tiber so that Rome itself might be born. The image of the she-wolf and twins thus stood for the divinely inspired origins of the Roman people. The wolf appeared on coins minted to pay the troops (Fig. 4); it was also used

3. The earliest known representation of the legionary *aquila* (eagle standard), on a silver *denarius* of 82 BC.

4. The she-wolf suckles the semi-divine twins Romulus and Remus. Republican silver *denarius*.

as an early legionary standard and embellished soldiers' equipment down to the late empire. Some republican *velites* (young, light-armed legionaries) wore wolf-skins.[51]

The wolf is another symbol of strength, speed, power and savagery appropriate to the ideology of soldiers, and was used in this sense.[52] However, it is a more ambivalent image than that of the distant, soaring eagle, majestic yet little direct threat to human society. Wolves were a real menace to communities in ancient Italy; living in mountain and forest at the edge of civilization, especially in the hungry times of winter they were a constant danger, and not just to people. Wolves sometimes tear each other to pieces.

The potential ambivalence of the image of *miles* as wolf of Mars was not lost on the Romans. An alternative tradition held that the she-wolf who suckled Romulus and Remus was no divinely enchanted quadruped but a more earthly variety: *lupa* was also slang for a whore.[53] Throughout their history Romans were acutely aware that besides the threat of foreign enemies, their own soldiers, especially loose in packs, posed a deadly potential threat to the well-being of the community. Fear of internal conflict was ever present in a society whose founding moment was, according to legend, marked by fratricide when Romulus encompassed the death of his twin.[54] No one could be sure when a soldier might turn into a wolf – or worse. In the *Satyricon*, Petronius describes how, at night among the graves outside a town, to the terror of his companion, a soldier metamorphosed into a werewolf.[55] Tiberius, Rome's second emperor, famously described ruling the state as 'holding the wolf by the ears'; he had in mind lethal threats both from fellow aristocrats, and from his own soldiers.[56] As a veteran general he knew what he was talking about, and on his accession in AD 14 had faced major military mutinies over service conditions.

Like other ancient warriors and soldiers,[57] Roman *milites* were startlingly far from the modern ideal – or fantasy – of soldiers as unquestioningly obedient automata. Despite the undoubted facts that they were intensively trained and ferociously disciplined, one of the most underappreciated, astonishing and glaringly 'un-cog-like' features of Roman *milites* in republic or empire is their sheer unruliness. Roman culture was intensely competitive, and nowhere more so than on the battlefield; in stark contrast to the team ethic of modern armies, *milites* strove to outdo each other in feats of arms.[58] Far from silent in the ranks, these touchy warriors regularly shouted their approval or their anger at their commanders.[59] Prone to mutiny, from the later republic they sometimes fought each other, and under the empire on occasion killed generals, officials and emperors. They were always likely to abuse and kill civilians (including other Romans), whether ordered or forbidden to do so. Their commanders had to exhort, plead, flatter and sometimes shame their soldiers into obedience as much as compel them. *Milites* were often feared and despised by other Romans more than admired as 'our boys'.[60] Eagles, then, provide a metaphor for men under command in the service of their country, and wolves for the constant threat they posed to each other, to their officers, and to wider society.

The eagle and the wolf were the two sides of the coin of Roman military power, opposites but inseparable, like the twin faces of the god Janus, gazing simultaneously in opposite directions (Fig. 5). He was god of gateways and of changes of state – above all the transition between peace and war. The doors of his shrine in the Roman forum stood open when the state was anywhere at war.[61] Their closure, symbolizing peace throughout Rome's dominions, was a rarity worthy of celebration on coins (Fig. 6). The twin faces of Janus may also serve here to symbolize the binary nature of much of our subject matter: its contrasts and contradictions, and the opposing perspectives from which it may be seen. Considering these together often proves much more informative than examining matters from a single viewpoint.

For example, we tend often to separate, and treat as irreconcilable opposites, those aspects we think of as 'positive' in society – especially mutual assistance, friendship and

5. The two-faced god Janus, on a republican silver coin.

6. The temple of Janus, on a bronze coin of Nero. Its doors are closed, indicating peace throughout Rome's dominions – a condition rare enough to be worthy of commemoration.

love – from those we regard as most negative: violence, killing and the infliction of suffering. Yet in reality, they may be inseparably linked, especially in the domain of Mars. For some of the greatest, and most emotionally engaging of all cooperative human enterprises occur in pairs: we call them wars. At the individual level, those who have served as soldiers frequently report that there are no closer or more intense bonds of friendship and love than those between people who have fought side by side and faced death together. These are important and often uncomfortable truths to bear in mind.

Another basic yet frequently neglected truth is that it takes two sides to make a fight. Even if our aim is simply to understand the Roman military, we must also look at Rome's foes, and their interactions in war.[62] Vast attention has been lavished on the internal organization of the imperial armies, and on the details of frontier systems such as Hadrian's Wall, but many researchers still show curiously little interest in the societies these organizations and systems were chiefly designed to deal with; the success of the Roman military is still largely explained in terms of its internal qualities, real or imagined. In part, this may be because Rome's opponents have left fewer traces for us to study, but often it is because we have not looked at them as hard as we have at the Roman side. The shape of Rome's armies, the equipment its soldiers used and the men who were to be found in its ranks, were all as much the result of the nature and characteristics of the peoples Rome faced, as of her own internal history. They, too, are a vital aspect of the picture.

A further Janus-like aspect of Rome's military is that the gaze of the armies on the imperial frontiers was directed into the empire as well as towards outsiders, for one fundamental use of the sword was intimidation and repression of provincial populations. However, even this was characterized by ambivalence.

Rome's provinces were held together by the threat of violence, but equally important were 'glues' actively binding them: positive, convergent, integrative forces. Among the most powerful was service in the military itself. At the height of the empire, roughly half Rome's soldiers were themselves provincials, acquiring Roman citizenship through service, making the armies major engines of integration, creating an intensely felt, military-flavoured, frontier-focused 'Romanness' forged from remarkable ethnic diversity.

Another profound ambivalence already touched on was Rome's attitude to her own soldiers. Ancient societies generally regarded martial violence as at least necessary and inevitable, and often positively as a source of power, wealth and glory. Roman opinion regarded war as necessary to the health and vigour of society. However, from the early republic the Romans took extraordinary steps to keep the sword out of politics, for they never forgot that it was double-edged: one clove enemies, enriching and empowering the state, senators and soldiers, but the other always faced back at Roman society itself. Roman and most contemporary sword types were literally double-edged, and this term was used allegorically, for example *Revelations* 1.16: 'And he had in his right hand seven stars: and out of his mouth went a sharp two-edged sword (*rhomphaia distomos*) …'.[63] The double-edged nature of the sword is something we must also examine to deepen our understanding of the Roman military.

### Cold steel: swords themselves

Many types of sword belonging to the Romans, their allies and foes are attested through hundreds of archaeological finds, and various kinds are described in surviving texts.[64] Swords can be optimized for cutting or thrusting although, as we shall see, most Roman-era weapons could be used in either mode, even if one may have been preferred. Almost all swords appear to have been wielded in one hand, as they were normally used in combination with a shield. Apart from a small number of early Iron Age European weapons perhaps for ritual duelling, there were no swords resembling the very narrow rapiers of recent centuries. Most known types were straight, symmetrical, flattish and double-edged, the general form which later evolved into weapons like the medieval broadsword. There were exceptions, such as the asymmetric single-edged swords used from Spain to the Middle East and apparently known to the Greeks by the names of *machaera* or *kopis*. I say 'apparently', because although there are hundreds of references to Roman and other swords in Classical literature, the problem is confidently relating textual terms to archaeological types, not least for Roman swords themselves.

The Latin term *gladius* is today commonly understood to refer to the stereo-typical two-edged short, stabbing sword of the early empire. Unfortunately, the Romans were not consistent in their usage of *gladius* (or indeed other military terms) in surviving texts, many of which are literary rather than military or tech-nical works. So *gladius*, which Varro derived from *clades*, 'slaughter', was used generically for any sword.[65] Particular types might be qualified, for example *gladius Hispaniensis*, 'the Spanish [or Hispanic] sword'. Some other foreign sword types retained their native names in Latin usage, for example, the Greek *machaera*. *Gladius* might also be used on its own more specifically, for a type, or at least class, of sword.

A passage from Tacitus' *Annals* seems to offer important information about different types of Roman sword, and who used which. It describes how, in Britain in AD 51, the troops of the rebel Caratacus were 'caught between the *gladii* and javelins of the legionaries, and the *spathae* and thrusting-spears of the auxil-iaries'.[66] However, this neat division is not a technical description, but a carefully crafted literary contrast.[67] It does, at least, prove that by the time Tacitus was writing (*c.* AD 100), Romans were distinguishing between two classes of sword, and that the term *spatha* was sufficiently established to need no explanation, implying it had been current for some time. This is, incidentally, the earliest known use of *spatha* for a kind of sword, usually interpreted as 'a long slashing sword' ascribed to early imperial auxiliary cavalry. *Spatha* was originally a Latinized Greek word for a flat stirrer,[68] and was evidently applied to a new class of weapon in Roman use by the later first century AD, initially as slang (a con-temptuous reference to its length and primary mode of use, 'stirring' the air in contrast to a 'manly Roman' thrust?). Tacitus' usage does not, of course, prove that either the weapon or the name were really current as early as the 50s. However, whatever cavalry may have been using, the artificiality of Tacitus' dis-tinction is underlined by the fact that first-century auxiliary *infantry* tombstones show them with short swords – Tacitus' *gladii* rather than his *spathae*.

During the second century AD, the relationship between the terms *gladius* and *spatha* apparently changed, perhaps because the short, supposedly stabbing sword went out of widespread use. *Gladius* continued as a generic term for swords, although all military weapons may now have been referred to as *spathae*. Hence Apuleius, in his later second-century novel *The Golden Ass*, describes a soldier (arm of service unspecified) as wearing a *spatha*, but elsewhere distin-guishes another sword as *equestrem spatham praeacutam*, an 'extremely sharp cavalry *spatha*', the 'cavalry' qualification presumably emphasizing that it was a particularly long sword, here used by a street performer.[69] By implication, then, there were also shorter infantry *spathae* – at least in the usage of gentleman writers.

We do not know how far even Roman soldiers used precise and consistent technical terminology. Terentianus, an Egyptian-born serviceman in the early second century AD, wrote to his father requesting various items including a 'battle sword' (*gladius pugnatorius*), presumably emphasizing that he did not mean a double-weight training sword, but was no more specific.[70] A military writing tablet of the later first century AD from Carlisle mentions 'regulation swords' (*gladia instituta*), but gives no indication of what that meant.[71] It is interesting that *gladius* is here used of the swords of cavalrymen – which are supposed to have been long, and called *spathae*, by this time. Perhaps here *gladius* is employed in its generic sense of 'sword', or was the official name for what a trooper now nicknamed his *spatha*…

Confused? This is why military equipment specialists tend to avoid such inconsistently used, meaning-shifting or downright obscure Latin terms (what was the distinction between Vegetius' *spatha* and *semispatha*, and to what period was he referring?).[72] Alternative, more descriptive terms sometimes used (like 'broadsword' or 'rapier') convey more idea of the weapon's form, but are anachronistic transferrals from much later, quite different weapons, and potentially mislead because they may prejudge mode of use (the so-called 'short, Roman thrusting sword' was actually also good for cutting). Specialists often employ less ambiguous terms for types defined and described from actual examples of Roman-era swords. Some are self-explanatory, for example the 'ring-pommel sword' (*Ringknaufschwert*: p. 186). However, most archaeological names are based on the sites where the type was first definitively described, for example 'Mainz type', 'Pompeii type' or the 'Straubing-Nydam' and 'Lauriácum-Hromówka' types. Such names are more precise, but often triumphantly clumsy and unmemorable. The prize perhaps goes to the eye-crossingly confusing '"spatha"-type *gladius*, "Straubing" variant'. It is all very unsatisfactory.

The hundreds of known archaeological examples of Roman swords have recently been catalogued, and the development of these weapons is examined in more detail throughout this book.[73] However, a brief introductory sketch of their development is in order here. For, like the Roman military and wider society as a whole, Roman swords actually underwent major changes over time (Fig. 7), and often there were multiple types at any given period.

We now know that the weapon that conquered the Mediterranean during the latter half of the republican era was distinctly different in form from the long-familiar, supposedly archetypal Roman short swords now classified as the Mainz and Pompeii types of the early imperial era (below). They were descendants of the republican sword, appearing only in early imperial times. Scipio's and Caesar's legionaries carried weapons which were significantly longer (p. 80). This is apparently the real weapon known as the *gladius Hispaniensis*. However, even that was only introduced to Roman service after the unification of Italy. The sword used during the first two centuries of the republic was almost certainly the Greek hoplite's *xiphos*, a waisted two-edged weapon of variable length with a well-defined point (p. 48).

The short, often broad, long-pointed Mainz-type sword, introduced in the last decades BC (p. 122), was replaced a single lifetime later by the generally narrower, parallel-edged, short-pointed Pompeii type (p. 150). It also now seems that while this change was occurring, a new category of longer sword was being introduced to Roman service, exemplified at Newstead in Scotland, presumed

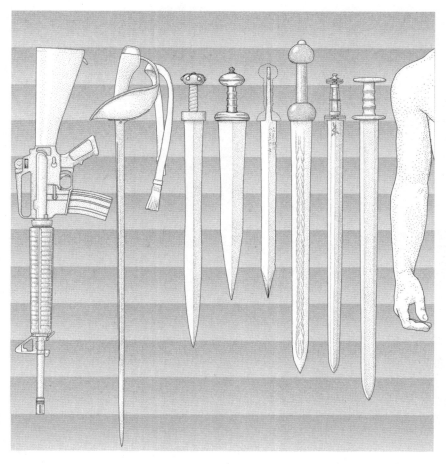

7. A selection of Roman swords reproduced to the same scale (1:10) with, for comparison, a modern American M16 rifle (conveniently 1,000 mm long); a Pattern 1908 trooper's sword, reputedly in both senses the ultimate British cavalry sword; and the human arm, which wielded such weapons, after Polykleitos. The Roman swords are (left to right) a republican *gladius Hispaniensis*, an early imperial Mainz type and a Pompeii type, a second-century pattern-welded sword, a third-century Straubing-Nydam type, and a fourth-century Illerup-Wyhl weapon. The background is graduated in 100 mm (*c.* 4 in) bands.

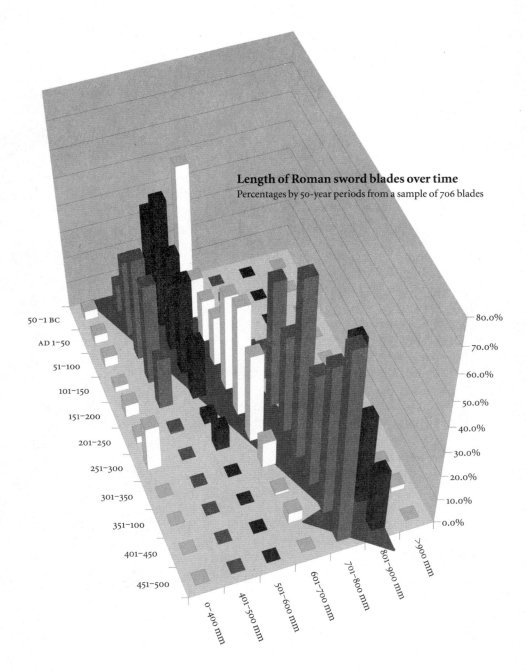

**Length of Roman sword blades over time**
Percentages by 50-year periods from a sample of 706 blades

8. Average lengths of Roman sword blades over time (after Miks 2007). The marked, sustained trend towards longer and longer weapons is clear. The graph collates measurements taken from archaeological finds (N = 706). This shows the percentages of blades falling into 100 mm bands, by fifty-year periods, from when our data becomes plentiful enough to measure meaningfully (as republic turned to empire) to when it currently runs out (around the time of the fall of the western empire).

initially to have been (logically enough) a cavalry weapon (p. 151). This was presumably Tacitus' '*spatha*'.

During the mid-second century AD, the repertoire of Roman swords underwent further major changes, which we are beginning to understand. Types and manufacturing techniques changed radically. The later second century also saw the brief florescence of swords with all-iron hilt assemblies, comprising a bar-shaped guard and a ring pommel that gives the type its modern name (*Ringknaufschwert*). This was a short-lived addition to the Roman tradition of sub-spherical pommels and deep, usually ovoid guards, which prevailed before and after. Some of these weapons (p. 186), had blades of 'Pompeii' size and proportions. But during the second century the Pompeii type went out of use, and although some small – occasionally remarkably small – swords were still made, the age of the 'short, stabbing sword' was coming to an end. From the second century the average length of Roman swords grew significantly (Fig. 8).

Henceforth many blades had shallow grooves, or fullers, known luridly in German as *Blutrinnen*, 'blood-channels', speculated to reduce wound-suction and so ease weapon withdrawal,[74] but certainly enhancing rigidity and saving weight. An elaborate new blade-making technology, 'pattern welding', became widespread by AD 200 (p. 184). Generally blades grew significantly longer, '*spathae*' becoming standard for infantry and cavalry alike. The new forms included relatively wide 'broadswords' and longer, slenderer 'rapiers'. Most retained a usable point, and could have been employed to cut or thrust. Longer swords thereafter remained dominant in Roman usage into the fifth century AD – far longer than the reign of the 'short, stabbing sword'.

Other types of sword existed in the Roman world. Emperors are depicted with eagle-head-hilted weapons (Fig. 82), of which a single actual example is known.[75] Soldiers also used wooden training swords.[76] Gladiatorial equipment included specialized swords and sword-like arms, and a symbolic wooden sword was used to release gladiators from service.[77]

Until the second century AD, most Roman soldiers wore their swords on the right, like Gauls, but contrary to subsequent Roman and later Western practice (see Fig. 51). Although it looks odd to modern eyes, in fact it is easy to draw even quite a long weapon worn on the right; the hand can be reversed and the blade pulled upwards or forwards from the scabbard. It is unclear why Romans and Gauls wore their swords on the right. Perhaps on the left the scabbard tended to clash with the tightly curved Roman body shield of the era. If there had once been a practical reason, by the imperial period it may have been simply a hallowed tradition. Centurions always wore the sword on the left, and by AD 200 all soldiers did so.

We cannot recover the fine details of Roman-era sword-fighting techniques the way we know Renaissance swordsmanship, but we can say something about them from descriptions and depictions of combat (specifically, foot-combat), and the weapons themselves. Roman swordsmanship was very different from post-medieval styles, because Romans would normally expect to wield sword in conjunction with shield. A later European unshielded swordsman or fencer would lead with the weapon, right leg advanced, but if a shield is used it is the left arm and leg which lead, the sword reserved for thrust or cut.[78] Roman shields, with their single central grip covered by a metal boss, were not just for parrying blows, but for striking, to unbalance the foe or push his shield aside to expose him to the sword. If obliged to fight shieldless, Romans improvised defence for the left hand with their cloaks.[79]

Weapons themselves provide some pointers to the nature of Roman swordsmanship. Roman swords, like most of any era, were not very heavy. The blade of a Pompeii-type weapon weighed about 0.5 kg (c. 1 lb), later Roman longsword blades rarely reaching 1 kg (2.2 lb). Most of the energy in a thrust or cut would come from active muscular driving of such relatively light blades, rather than the mass and momentum of a blow from an end-heavy axe or pickaxe. However, their construction and form meant that they behaved differently from more recent European swords.

Some sword grips seem remarkably short, fitting the weapon very tightly into the hand; military weapons occasionally imitated gladiatorial practice in having a wrist-chain or cord to prevent dropping. Although pommels were often large, and suitable for reverse blows, like the rest of the hilt assembly they were usually of organic materials, and so added little weight. This contrasts with many medieval weapons, which boasted heavy metal pommels partially counter-balancing the weight of the blade, facilitating its manipulation about the wrist. Although great attention was paid to the distribution of metal along the blade (for example, through tapering of the outline of many longer 'spathae', while not thinning the blade), Roman swords were less well balanced, and so perhaps more demanding to wield, than many later weapons.

From Polybius and Vegetius right through to modern times, writers discussing swordsmanship have debated the relative advantages of cutting and thrusting. Cutting actions can comprise simple axe-like chopping at arm's length, but may be more effective if the sword is used to slash, i.e. angled backwards at the wrist in a slicing action; however, this reduces reach (Fig. 9). The most powerful cuts, downward from over the head, also tend to expose the right armpit to a thrust from the foe.[80] Cuts also give more warning than thrusts, which were better at overcoming the foe's first line of defence – the senses, especially vision. A thrust darting from behind the shield is faster and far harder to see coming than a long slashing stroke ponderously swung round it, across the antagonist's field of vision. In 48 BC, against some especially effective Pompeian cavalry,

9. Cutting with a sword: axe-like chopping (left) and slicing (right) actions.

Caesar ordered his soldiers to jab their swords at the faces and eyes of the enemy, successfully forcing them to retire.[81] Roman-era opinion is often perceived as decisively in favour of thrusting over cutting.

A number of passages in Greco-Roman literature contrast Roman tactics of thrusting, particularly at torso or groin, with Gallic or other barbarian preference for cutting with a long blade, especially at the head. Greco-Roman writers suggested this was already so in the fourth century BC, as in Livy's account of the duel fought by T. Manlius Torquatus around 360 BC (p. 16). Similarly, Dionysius of Halicarnassus records that in 387 BC, while the Gauls:

> ...were still raising their swords aloft, [Camillus' Romans] would duck under their arms, holding up their shields, and then, stooping and crouching low, they would render vain and useless the blows of the others, which were aimed too high, while for their own part, holding their swords straight out, they would strike their opponents in the groins, pierce their sides, and drive their blows through their breasts into their vitals.
> DIONYSIUS OF HALICARNASSUS 14.10.17–18[82]

However, these accounts, which deeply colour modern perceptions, were written centuries after the alleged events. Could they be other than fictionalized at such a remove, literary set-pieces, a standard *topos* of agile Roman versus lumbering barbarian? Archaeology confirms they are at best anachronistic: fourth-century Gallic swords were not yet especially long, and had distinct points for thrusting as well. Nevertheless, such accounts plausibly reflect the ways in which late republican and early imperial Romans were taught to deal with the long Gaulish slashing swords, which archaeology confirms were common in the last century BC and some of which indeed lacked points (Fig. 35).

The Greek soldier/historian Polybius provides more convincing accounts of middle republican swordsmanship. He described the Romans' battle with the Gauls at Telamon in 225 BC, then still just in living memory. He notes that Gauls fought with great courage:

10. *Denarius* of 41 BC commemorating an otherwise-forgotten feat of arms of a senatorial ancestor, C. Numonius, on the defences (*vallum*) of an enemy camp, which earned him and his descendants the surname Va(a)la. Note the crouched stance and low sword-thrust under the raised shield.

In spite of the fact that man for man as well as collec tively they were inferior to the Romans in point of arms. The shields and swords of the latter were proved to be mani-festly superior for defence and attack…[because the Gaulish swords] could only give one downward cut with any effect but after this the edges were so turned and the blade so bent that unless they had time to straighten them out with their foot against the ground, they could not deliver a second blow…their blade has no point.

On the other hand, 'the Romans, having excellent points to their swords, *used them not to cut but to thrust…*' (my emphases).[83] However, this account still simplifies and stereotypes. For example, metallographic study of Gallic blades confirms that some were indeed so soft that they would have been prone to bending, as Polybius describes – but most were better made, and many did have thrusting points (Fig. 11).[84] It is also significant that, elsewhere, Poly-bius emphasizes that the Roman sword was as excellent for cutting as for thrusting, implying an all-round weapon, not a dedicated thrusting sword.[85] Rather it is clear that, when facing longsword-armed foes, Romans made a tac-tical choice to concentrate on thrusting – which may also have become a cultural preference (p. 49). However, Roman cavalry apparently used the same weapon to slash, to gruesome effect (p. 38).

Mode of use is not necessarily rigidly related to form or length of blade. Slashing does not demand a long weapon, nor thrusting a short one; blades of some early modern rapiers – principally thrusting swords – were over 1 m (39 in) long. Still, even if Romans did have an overwhelming preference – practical or cultural – for thrusting with the sword, this would not automatically demand especially short weapons.

A practical reason why republican Romans perhaps preferred shorter swords may have been the risk of longer blades bending, which imperial-era technological developments reduced. However, as will be argued below, it is likely that the appearance of the 'classic' short-sword types of early imperial times may well have resulted from a combination of tactical practicalities and military ideology. It may also have resulted from emergent specialization in Roman infantry and cavalry swords. The foregoing presumes foot combat, but mounted sword-fighting has its own dynamics, with added momentum from the mount, but less agility to dodge blows in a melée: hence an increase in limb protection, and the use of face-masks.

One special Roman (or Italian) sword thrust, facilitated by shorter blades, appears recurrently in depictions of martial violence from *c.* 300 BC to the later second century AD, when such blades declined in use (Fig. 58). This was an execution or *coup-de-grâce* thrust, used to kill an unresisting victim, with sword reversed in the right hand and plunged downwards, dagger-like, between throat and clavicle, into the heart.[86]

To us looking back, Roman soldiers and their famed swords are familiar and enduring features of Western history, yet Rome's rise to military domination of the known world was both astonishingly swift and unforeseen. To the Greek states of the eastern Mediterranean, especially the great Hellenistic kingdoms (heirs of Alexander's Macedonian empire, who considered themselves the superpowers of the era), upstart Rome's eruption onto the world stage came as a shattering shock.

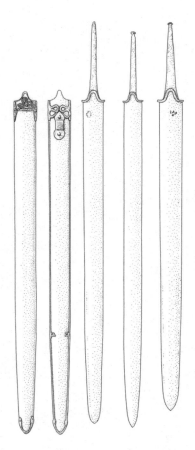

11. Gaulish swords, later third century BC, from La Tène, Lake Neuchâtel, Switzerland. That on the left is shown with the two sides of its scabbard, with the typical Gallic suspension loop on the back. These examples show that while some Gallic swords lacked points as Classical authors describe, others were also designed for thrusting. (Scale 1:8)

# Prelude
## Shock and Awe | The Unexpected Rise of Rome

In 146 BC, Roman soldiers sacked and destroyed two of the most famous cities of the ancient world. In desperate house-to-house fighting, legionaries took the great Phoenician colony of Carthage in North Africa, centre of a powerful trade-based maritime empire in the western Mediterranean. They completely obliterated this 'Venice of Antiquity', ploughing the site with salt, ending a century of terrible wars between them. The First Punic War[1] (264–241 BC) brought Rome her first overseas territories, but led to the terrible ordeal of Hannibal's unstoppable rampages through Italy during the Second Punic War (218–201 BC). Rome finally beat Hannibal, but her vengeful paranoia drove broken Carthage to a suicidal third conflict, ending in massacre in 146 BC. In that same year on another continent, a second Roman army took once-mighty Corinth, at the heart of old Greece, stripping it of its treasures, slaughtering its male population and enslaving the rest. Obliteration of this great Classical city was an act of calculated terror designed to show the unruly Aegean Greeks once and for all who was now master.[2]

This symbolic double atrocity stunned a Mediterranean world still reeling from the sudden rise of the Italian city-state of Rome to superpower status. The critical period spanned roughly 270–190 BC, encompassing the First Punic War, the struggle with Hannibal, and its fallout, which drew Rome into clashes with the successors of Alexander's Macedonian empire, the Hellenistic Greek kingdoms then dominating the eastern half of the known world. During these decades the Romans mastered naval warfare. They also learned how to defeat soldiers equipped, trained and led according to the latest Greek and Macedonian ideas, refinements of the art of war as Alexander had waged it to conquer Persia. Roman armies defeated the famed Macedonian phalanx of dense-packed pike-men in 197 BC, and definitively destroyed it at Pydna in 168 BC. By then, the other Hellenistic states, Ptolemaic Egypt and Seleucid Asia, were also cowed. In roughly a human lifespan, then, Rome rose from mere top dog in Italy to peerless superpower, fielding armies on three continents.

Sudden acquisition of invincible military hegemony encouraged astonishing Roman arrogance, exemplified soon after Pydna when C. Popillius Laenas drew a circle in the sand around the Seleucid king Antiochus IV, demanding an answer to Rome's requirement for Antiochus' withdrawal from Egypt before he stepped out of it.[3] Rome was arbiter of the Mediterranean, and the fates of Carthage and Corinth were not lost on contemporaries. In 133 BC Attalus III of Pergamon bequeathed his entire kingdom to Rome in hopes that his people would thus escape Roman violence and rapacity.

Their world turned upside down in the second century BC, bewildered Greeks asked themselves how this situation had come about. What was the secret of Roman power? Why was it so successful? These questions have exercised minds ever since. Unsurprisingly, attention has often focused on the nature and special characteristics of Rome's soldiers, armies and warfare.[4]

Roman military success around 200 BC was not, for the most part, due to exceptional generalship; indeed the senatorial elite was suspicious of brilliant individuals. Scipio Africanus, Rome's first world-class general and the conqueror of Hannibal, died in exile. Roman command became competent in strategy and tactics, but excelled in other regards, notably in securing and maintaining a vast resource base and in exploiting it efficiently through skilled logistics – keeping men and materiel flowing to maintain multiple, large, composite armies of Romans and allies in the field.[5]

However, what impressed Greeks most directly were material and moral factors. Rome seemed to have an inexhaustible supply of soldiers, quantity matched by quality. Equally impressive were the determination and aggressiveness of Roman soldiers, and the effectiveness of their arms, jointly exemplified by what *milites* could perpetrate with their 'Spanish swords'. In 200 BC, when Rome turned her attention from defeated Hannibal to his Macedonian allies, Philip V of Macedon got his first taste of Roman land warfare when his men recovered their dead from an otherwise indecisive cavalry fight:

> Philip['s soldiers] had seen the wounds dealt by javelins and arrows and occasionally by lances, since they were used to fighting with the Greeks and Illyrians, [but] when they had seen bodies chopped to pieces by the Spanish sword, arms torn away, shoulders and all, or heads separated from bodies…or vitals laid open, and the other fearful wounds, realized in a general panic with what weapons and what men they had to fight. Fear seized the king as well, who had never met the Romans in ordered combat.
> LIVY 31.34.4–5[6]

Roman armies did not win every battle during this era, but established a grim reputation for ferocity, ruthlessness, implacable determination and – equally important – possessing vast resources to back these up, ensuring ultimate victory. How did they get to this position? Was it down to traits that the Romans possessed from the start, which inevitably destined them to dominate?

In seeking to explain republican Rome's rise, it seems reasonable to assume that there was something inherently special about her. After all, it was Rome that dominated Italy from *c.* 300 BC, not Etruscan Capua nor Greek Naples, nor any outsider ambitious for empire such as Pyrrhus of Epirus (who tried) nor, as had recently happened in the east, a king of Macedon. Can Rome's secret have been the sword alone? It is tempting to see her ascent simply as a story of violent aggression, explained above all in terms of her martial specialness.[7]

One event, centuries earlier, apparently foreshadows the doom of Carthage and Corinth: the destruction and depopulation of Rome's neighbour, the major Etruscan city of Veii, in 396 BC. By the standards of contemporary Italian warfare, this was a stunning military feat and exceptional event: major cities were not often captured by their enemies, and rarely obliterated. The destruction of Veii was later seen by Romans as the symbolic start of Rome's rise to greatness, a precocious manifestation of those martial talents which two centuries later would overwhelm every other Mediterranean power, to create a lasting empire.

Indeed, Romans of imperial times liked to believe that their imperial destiny was divinely ordained from the outset and had been achieved primarily by the sword. Livy has Romulus say:

Go…tell the Romans that it is the will of heaven that my Rome should be the head of all the world. Let them henceforth cultivate the arts of war, and let them know assuredly, and hand down the knowledge to posterity, that no human might can withstand Roman arms.[8]

However, if from the start the gods really intended Rome to dominate the known world, it took her a long time to get into her stride. By the end of the sixth century BC, when the last king was expelled and Rome became an aristocratic republic, she was already one of the biggest city-states of the peninsula – but as yet showed no obvious exceptional military capabilities. Indeed, the fragmentary historical record suggests that during the fifth century BC, while the Greeks were defeating Persia and the Athenian democracy was at its zenith, Rome was struggling to maintain herself against her powerful Etruscan neighbours to the north, and to gain ascendancy over the smaller Latin city-states to the south. She only finally achieved the latter in 338 BC, just before the reign of Alexander the Great. This makes the destruction of Veii look all the more impressive – or anomalous.

There is actually reason to doubt whether the fate of Veii was a precocious sign of exceptional Roman military virtuosity, although it certainly indicates considerable abilities. If Rome was already so good, it is hard to explain the disasters that soon followed, when she faced her first encounter with non-Italian 'barbarians', picking a fight with marauding Gaulish Senones. At the battle of the Allia (390 BC) her soldiers panicked and fled at the sight of the Gallic army, which looted Rome and had to be paid to go away, engendering an enduring

Roman *terror Gallicus*. Rome survived her humiliation, but took time to recover power and prestige.

In fact, the destruction of Veii was not what it seems. As the Italian archaeologist Nicola Terrenato argues,[9] it may have been more shotgun marriage than assassination. The two major cities were simply too close to each other for regional resources to sustain both and, in stark contrast to Rome's treatment of Carthage or Corinth, the result was partly merger rather than conquest. Significantly, Veii's goddess Juno was adopted as one of the three principal deities of the Roman state,[10] some Veientine families subsequently reappear as Romans, and the victors even discussed moving Rome to the site of Veii. This example, and much other evidence, suggests that the processes resulting in Rome's phenomenal military power during the second century BC were more complex and subtle than is often portrayed – and not wholly military.

Livy and other early historians present Rome's rise as a seemingly endless catalogue of wars, triumphs and conquests. The sword was certainly central, but it is clear that it was only part of the picture, as Polybius (*c.* 200–*c.* 120 BC), a Greek soldier and politician, knew well. He saw the Romans erupt into the Hellenistic world, fought them and subsequently spent years as their hostage-cum-guest, witnessing their wars in Spain, and was present at the death of Carthage.[11] He wrote his *History* to try to explain Rome's rise to his fellow Greeks.[12] Taking a holistic approach, he attributed Roman success to a combination of factors, including the design of Roman swords, the qualities of the soldiers who wielded them, the motivations of these men and their generals and the special characteristics of the Roman state. We are well advised to follow Polybius in taking such a broad view, indeed to go further than he usually did, especially by including Rome's allies as well as her foes as important factors in the equation, and not just as 'spear carriers' or 'sword-fodder'.

Sheer martial might is, then, inadequate to explain the phenomenal rise of Rome, or its long-term sustainability. Regimes that rule solely by force and terror rarely last long. In the great struggle with Carthage, most of Rome's subjects and allies chose to stick with her even when Hannibal gave them a real opportunity to break Roman power, proving that their loyalty depended on more than fear of the sword. Clearly, there was also some positive attraction.[13] As we shall see, Rome succeeded through developing a uniquely effective combination of martial aggression and political negotiating tactics, the carrot as well as the stick – or the sword and the open hand.[14]

To explore how the Roman republic found itself poised to achieve superpower status during the third century BC, we will begin with a snapshot of her on the cusp of empire, at the moment when she was becoming the first power ever to unify the peoples of Italy, and was about to find herself in direct conflict with the world-class armies of the Hellenistic Mediterranean, and the naval superpower, Carthage.

# Forging the Roman Sword
## The Republic to 270 BC

### Rome on the ascendant: the battle of Sentinum

In 295 BC, at Sentinum in Umbria, an army of Romans and Italian allies faced a dangerous confederation of enemies who had joined in a determined effort to stop Rome achieving complete domination of Italy. The ensuing clash, memorably described by Livy, was the decisive battle of the last Samnite War.[1] Rome fought three exhausting wars (343–290 BC) to subdue the Samnites, tough warriors from the un-urbanized uplands of southern Italy. Despite humiliating defeat at the Caudine Forks (321 BC), Rome gradually hemmed in the Samnites with military colonies. In 295 the Romans were simultaneously fighting the Etruscans to their north as well as the Samnites to the south. These peoples made common cause with the Umbrians and Gauls from the Po valley[2] in a joint, last-ditch effort to maintain their autonomy.

The Samnites, Etruscans and Gauls sent armies to mass in Umbria. To counter this, the Romans despatched a 'federal' force, comprising the then-standard core of four citizen legions, with a strong force of Roman cavalry, with which operated a thousand Campanian horse and infantry formations from the allies and Latins, which outnumbered the legions. This army was jointly commanded by the patrician consul Q. Fabius Maximus Rullianus and his plebeian colleague P. Decius Mus.[3] Two smaller armies, probably based around a single legion, each doubtless backed as usual by comparable numbers of allied troops, were stationed near Rome facing Etruria, while a fourth army, centred on legions II and IV, was operating under a proconsul in Samnium.[4]

The main consular army contacted the enemy near Sentinum, just south of the modern Sassoferrato, 170 km (106 miles) north of Rome. The armies bivouacked 6 km (4 miles) apart, Rome's foes keeping separate camps. It was agreed that the Samnites should operate with the Gauls and the Etruscans with the Umbrians. The Samnites and Gauls were to attack the Romans, while the Etruscans and Umbrians assaulted their camp.[5] However, Etruscan deserters betrayed these intentions. The Romans set about dividing the coalition, to defeat it in detail. They drew off the Etruscans and Umbrians by ravaging their lands, aiming to bring on a battle with the Gauls and Samnites while they were away.

Skirmishing led on the third day to both armies drawing up to fight, as Livy describes:

> As they stood arrayed for battle, a hind, pursued by a wolf that had chased it down from the mountains, fled across the plain and ran between the two lines. They then turned in opposite directions, the hind towards the Gauls, the wolf towards the Romans. For the wolf a passage was opened between the ranks but the hind was killed by the Gauls. Then one of the front-rankers on the Roman side called out, 'That way flight and slaughter have shaped their course, where you see the beast lie slain that is sacred to Diana; on this side the Wolf of Mars, unhurt and sound, has reminded us of the Martian race and of our Founder.'[6]

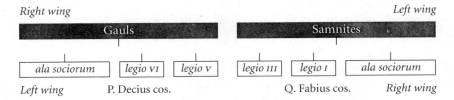

12. Diagram of the disposition of the confronting armies at the battle of Sentinum, partly conjectural: the order of legions shown is based on the fact that the right was the post of honour and went to the senior legion present.

The Gauls faced the Roman left wing composed of legions v and vi under Decius, while the Samnites formed up facing the Roman right, legions i and iii under Fabius (Fig. 12). Livy omits to mention deployment of the major Latin and allied contingents of infantry and cavalry, but they presumably formed 'wings' (*alae sociorum*) flanking the legions in the then-usual way. At first, the battle hung in the balance; Livy reports that the Romans would have been overwhelmed had the Etruscans and Umbrians still been present:

> But, though so far it was a doubtful battle and Fortune had given no indication where she intended to bestow her might, the fighting was very different on the right wing from what it was on the left. The Romans with Fabius were rather defending themselves than attacking, and were trying to prolong the struggle to as late an hour in the day as possible. This was because their general was persuaded that both Samnites and Gauls fought fiercely at the outset of an engagement, but only needed to be withstood; when a struggle was prolonged, little by little the spirits of the Samnites flagged, while the physical prowess of the Gauls, who could least of all men put up with heat and labour, ebbed away, and, whereas in the early stages

of their battles they were more than men, they ended with being less than women. So until the time should come when the enemy were wont to fail, he was keeping his men as fresh as he could contrive to do. But Decius, with the greater impetuosity of his youth and spirits, expended all the strength he could muster in the first encounter. And because the fighting of the infantry seemed to languish, he called on the cavalry to attack, and attaching himself to the bravest squadron of troopers besought the youthful nobles to join him in a charge. Theirs, he said, would be a double share of glory, if victory should come first to the left wing and to the cavalry. Twice they drove the Gallic cavalry back. The second time they were carried on for a considerable distance and soon found themselves in the midst of the companies of infantry, when they were subjected to a new and terrifying kind of assault; for, standing erect in chariots and waggons, armed enemies came rushing upon them with a mighty clattering of hooves and wheels, frightening the horses of the Romans with their unfamiliar din. Thus the victorious cavalry were scattered, as if by a panic fit of madness, and, suddenly fleeing, were overthrown, both horse and rider. From them the disorder was communicated to the standards of the legions, and many of the first line were trodden underfoot, as horses and chariots swept through their ranks. No sooner did the Gallic infantry perceive the confusion of their enemies than they charged, without leaving them a moment to recover or regain their breath.

Decius cried out to them to tell him whither they were fleeing, or what hope they had in flight; he endeavoured to stop them as they broke and ran, and to call them back; then, his exertions proving powerless to stay their rout, he cried aloud on the name of his father P.[ublius] Decius. 'Why,' he asked, 'do I seek any longer to postpone the doom of our house? It is the privilege of our family that we should be sacrificed to avert the nation's perils. Now will I offer up the legions of the enemy, to be slain with myself as victims to Earth and the *Manes*.'

On going down into the field of battle he had ordered M.[arcus] Livius the *pontifex* not to leave his side. He now commanded this man to recite before him the words with which he proposed to devote himself and the enemy's legions in behalf of the Roman people, the *Quirites*. He was then devoted with the same form of prayer and in the same habit his father, P. Decius, had commanded to be used, when he was devoted at the Veseris, in the Latin War[7] and having added to the usual prayers that he was driving before him fear and panic, blood and carnage, and the wrath of gods celestial and gods infernal, and should blight with a curse the standards, weapons and armour of the enemy, and that one and the same place should witness his own destruction and that of the Gauls and Samnites...he spurred his charger against the Gallic lines, where he saw that they were thickest, and hurling himself against the weapons of the enemy met his death.

From that moment the battle seemed scarce to depend on human efforts. The Romans, after losing their general – an occurrence that is wont to inspire terror – fled no longer, but sought to redeem the field; the Gauls, and especially the press about the body of the consul, as though deprived of reason, were darting their javelins at random and without effect, while some were in a daze, and could neither fight nor run away. But in the other army the *pontifex* Livius, to whom Decius had handed over his lictors, bidding him act as propraetor, cried aloud that the Romans had won the victory, being quit of all danger by the consul's doom. The Gauls, he said, and the Samnites were made over to Mother Earth and to the *Manes*; Decius was haling after him their devoted host and calling it to join him, and with the enemy all was madness and despair. While the Romans were restoring the battle, up came L.[ucius] Cornelius Scipio and C.[aius] Marcius, whom Q.[uintus] Fabius the consul had ordered to take reserves from the rearmost line and go to his colleague's support. There they learned of Decius' death, a great incentive to dare everything for the republic. And so, though the Gauls stood crowded together with their shields interlocked in front of them, and it looked no easy battle at close quarters, the lieutenants [*legati*] bade their men gather up the javelins that were scattered about on the ground between the hostile lines and cast them against the *testudo* of their enemies; and as many of these missiles stuck fast in the shields and now and then one penetrated a soldier's body, their phalanx was broken up – many falling, though unwounded, as if they had been stunned. Such were the shifts of fortune on the Roman left.[8]

Meanwhile, on the right, once the force of the Samnite attack abated, Fabius sent his cavalry to attack their flank, with a simultaneous push from the legions. The Samnites broke and:

> ...fled in confusion past the Gallic line itself, abandoning their comrades in the midst of the fighting and seeking refuge in their camp. The Gauls had formed a *testudo* and stood closely packed together. Then Fabius, who had learned of his colleague's death, commanded the squadron of Campanians, about five hundred lances, to withdraw from the line, and fetching a compass, assail the Gallic infantry in the rear; these the *principes*, or middle line, of the third legion were to follow, and, pushing in where they saw that the cavalry charge had disordered the enemy's formation, made havoc of them in their panic. He himself, after vowing a temple and the enemy's spoils to Jupiter Victor, kept on to the Samnite camp, whither the whole affrighted throng was being driven...[9]

The camp fell, and the Gauls were defeated:

> There were slain that day twenty-five thousand of the enemy, and eight thousand were captured; nor was it a bloodless victory; for of the army of P. Decius seven thousand were slain and seventeen hundred of the army of Fabius. Fabius sent out men to search for the body of his colleague, and, piling up the spoils of the enemy, burned them in sacrifice to Jupiter the Victor...

In the aftermath of the battle, says Livy:

> Quintus Fabius, leaving the Decian army on guard over Etruria, led down his own legions to Rome and triumphed over the Gauls, the Etruscans, and the Samnites. The soldiers followed his triumphal chariot and in their rude verses celebrated no less the glorious death of Publius Decius than the victory of Fabius...Every soldier received from the spoils a present of eighty-two *asses* of bronze, with a cloak and tunic, a reward for military service in those days far from contemptible.[10]

This is a striking account, but how much of it can we believe? Much of the detail – and not just the implausible symbolic role of the wolf and the hind – is likely to be later invention. No topographic features such as rivers or hills are mentioned.[11] Livy himself notes major discrepancies, flat contradictions, exaggerations and distortions in his sources for these events centuries earlier.[12] In particular, the father of Decius Mus also reputedly 'devoted' himself in battle against the Latins near Vesuvius in 340; these accounts may be garbled duplication of a single incident.[13]

However, subsequent history supports its general correctness, in terms of preceding strategy, outcome and consequences of the battle. Much of the detail of the fighting is also generally plausible in terms of practice and expectations of the period.

Literary set-piece with exemplary purpose though it is, this 'battle-piece',[14] like many others, does portray the way Romans had long understood war, as something depending on getting many things right at once: enough well-armed, well-trained, well-motivated soldiers, with high morale; competent command; effective logistics; better strategy than the foe; superior diplomatic and political skills, especially in maintaining a strong network of allies and dependants; and by no means least, ensuring the favour of the gods.

First, arms. How were the combatants actually equipped at Sentinum? While nothing is (yet) known from the battlefield, Italy has produced a rich archaeological record of weapons of the era, and a remarkable body of roughly contemporary paintings and sculptures has also survived, representing warriors and combat (albeit duels rather than battles) (Fig. 13). This evidence pertains almost entirely to Etruscans, Greeks and Samnites rather than Romans. Unlike some of their foes, Romans did not bury arms with their dead. They did paint scenes of war for triumphs and tombs, and dedicated them in temples, but hardly any survive because of endless subsequent rebuilding of the city's fabric.

However, as half their fighting strength routinely came from other Italian peoples (like the Campanians at Sentinum), Roman armies will have sported a wide range of equipment prevalent in Italy. But what of the Romans themselves?

13. Painting of a duel between warriors from a tomb at Paestum, in southern Italy. Such single combats at funerary games appear to have been the origin of gladiatorial displays.

Reportedly, Roman kit was also deliberately less gorgeous than that of peoples like the Samnites, who invested heavily in showy armour; certainly, later *milites* regarded plainness in dress, linked to their willingness to toil and sweat for their country on dusty roads and digging entrenchments, as things distinguishing Roman *virtus* from gaudy and effeminate foreign equipment. Texts indicate that by 295 BC most legionaries were helmeted, apparently already had their great body shields, and wore metal chest-protectors common at the time. However, it seems that Roman soldiers came to dominate Italy without other key items of equipment now considered Roman icons. They were yet to acquire mail, apparently invented in the decades preceding Sentinum by the Gauls, who probably sported examples at the battle. As yet Romans made limited use of the *pilum* (the heavy javelin), and the Hellenistic Greeks were only just developing torsion artillery (twisted-spring catapults). Not least, legionaries did not yet have the famous *gladius Hispaniensis*.

Certainly, Romans were already adopting foreign equipment: legionaries widely wore the 'Montefortino'-type helmet of Gallic origin (Fig. 14). While a

propensity to adapt others' equipment became a Roman hallmark, it was a development of a long-standing and widespread Italian tradition of adopting foreign, especially Greek, arms and styles of armour, adapted to local needs. Through this route the Greek two-edged hoplite sword, usually known as the *xiphos*, became common in Italy as Rome became a republic, and it seems that versions of this weapon were used by Roman soldiers into the third century (Fig. 15).[15] It had a characteristic hilt-guard, the blade leaf-shaped, with more weight near the tip, but also a businesslike point, and so suitable for cut or thrust. Known examples from Italy and Greece dating from the sixth to later third century BC vary greatly in length and breadth, with blade lengths (excluding tang)[16] from 350 mm (14 in) to 650 mm (26 in), with most between *c.* 400 mm (16 in) and *c.* 550 mm (22 in) (Fig. 16). The longest examples may have been specialized cavalry variants.

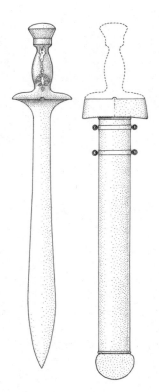

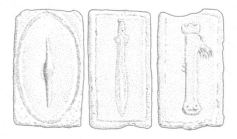

14. *Above left.* A Campanian cavalryman, wearing a bronze 'Montefortino' helmet of Gaulish form, to which Italian-style cheekpieces have been added. The 'horn' crests (probably thin flat plates) exaggerate his height. Tomb painting from Nola, Italy, late fourth century BC.

15. *Left.* Restoration of a fine example of a common Greek sword type, the *xiphos*, from Beroia, Greece. Its scabbard, unusually, has the ring suspension also adopted by the Romans. (Scale 1:8)

16. *Above.* Early Roman money-bars (*aes signatum*), *c.* 300 BC, featuring a Greek-style *xiphos*, matching scabbard, and front view of a large oval shield with central boss covering the single handle.

If Roman troops were indeed using such a weapon with the big and cumbersome body shield (see Fig. 31), it may well be that they had already developed their later preference for the darting thrust around, under or over the shield, and so were predisposed to seize on the 'Spanish sword' when they subsequently encountered it (p. 79). Indeed, Italians as a whole may already have shared not only a particular taste for sword-combat,[17] but a cultural preference for thrust over cut as well. The later fourth-century Etruscan paintings from the François tomb at Vulci show incidents from the *Iliad* and Romano-Etruscan mythical history, with figures sporting contemporary arms including *xiphos* swords.[18] One is being used to cut the bonds on a prisoner; four others are being used to kill, all by thrusts to thorax or neck (one reversed for a downward stab: Fig. 17).

17. Detail of Etruscan paintings, late fourth century BC, from the François tomb, Vulci. The protagonists use *xiphoi*, employing a straight thrust (left), and reverse-handed downward blow (centre). Right, a thrust pierces a bronze breastplate.

Only after the era of Sentinum did the Romans acquire the 'Spanish sword', during the course of their collision with Carthage (according to Polybius, not until the end of the third century BC), and mail shirts from the Gauls during the same period. These changes marked significant enhancements to Roman offensive and defensive arms, the new sword especially magnifying the impact of the soldiers' ferocity. Yet, without these, the Romans had confronted and defeated all the Italian peoples, withstood a state-of-the-art Hellenistic army under Pyrrhus of Epirus (p. 66) and defeated Carthage in the First Punic War. Roman arms, then, were clearly already highly effective by 300 BC, functionally neither obviously inferior nor superior to – because not very different from – those of other Italian peoples. Adequate arms and fighting skills were a prerequisite for victory at battles such as Sentinum, but between peoples who were, by and large, similarly armed and also familiar with each other's style of fighting, they were not decisive. So why did Rome win at Sentinum?

†

Among the European 'barbarians', notably the Iberian peoples and the Gauls, weapon manufacture was developed to a degree at least as technologically sophisticated as that of Rome; and in the case of mail and iron helmets, the Gauls led the field. How their industry was organized is unknown. Many aspects were relatively portable, and the equipment needed quite simple; it was the technological expertise that was critical. Items such as bronze horse-harness fittings, even elaborately enamelled examples, could be produced relatively easily by a skilled smith almost anywhere.[19]

Among the urbanized societies of the Mediterranean world, arms were probably an established part of the repertoire of the smiths of most cities, not necessarily of specialized armourers, although the finest sword blades may have been the work of dedicated swordsmiths. In times of war, the best craftsmen might be hired or pressed into service, supplemented by other more or less skilled labour, to churn out large quantities of equipment quickly to arm or rearm a fighting force, as both Carthage, and the Romans in Spain, did during their long struggle.[20] During the later republic, Rome procured the arms she needed through these means, or through contractors.[21] What we do not seem to have before the fourth century AD is anything resembling large-scale, centrally organized arms factories. At least outside the mass-production potteries of Roman Gaul and naval shipyards, the ancient world lacked anything much resembling modern factory-scale production.

There was another especially important military artefact which all armies shared, yet which Rome developed further than any other, and which was certainly part of the secret of her success. This was the nightly camp of armies in the field. The Romans developed this into an exceptionally rigorous system, unmatched in sophistication and complexity even by Hellenistic armies: the 'marching camp', routinely provided with a defensive rampart (perhaps strengthened if battle was imminent) and gates surrounding a standard layout of streets, tent-lines, command locations, horse-lines and service facilities. Echoing the regular street grids of many cities, marching camps subsequently became elaborated into more substantial siege camps and winter quarters. The latter eventually evolved into the permanent military bases familiar from imperial times. It is unclear when Roman marching camps developed, although they were in use by the Punic Wars, and perhaps were evolving long before Sentinum.[22]

Marching camps became themselves vital accoutrements of Roman warfare, practically and in less tangible ways. When campaigning in hostile territory, most soldiers could sleep in relative security in their tents, surrounded by a broad swathe of open ground with a constantly patrolled rampart beyond, safe from surprise assaults or random missiles. This formidable 'mobile city' will also have made a daunting impression on watching foes.[23] Polybius marvelled at it, describing it in detail.[24] In battle, a well-built camp to the rear offered sanctuary to many a hard-pressed Roman army, staving off rout. The predictable layout, even when the camp's site moved miles each day, was itself reassuring in its familiarity, and its regularity physically expressed the order and discipline of the army, which impressed foes and the soldiers themselves. Marching camps were, then, valuable to morale. But equally they facilitated surveillance and control of the soldiers, especially vital when Rome routinely fielded composite armies including many non-Roman contingents. They also made straggling and desertion more difficult, and seditious gatherings hard to hide. Indeed, these disciplinary considerations may have been at least as important in driving development of the marching camp as its effectiveness in the face of the enemy.

There is some reason to believe that part of Rome's edge at this period was her superiority in tactics, at least over some of her major foes in Italy. To be sure, the Roman system had its weaknesses: two consuls sharing authority could lead to disastrously divided command on the battlefield.[25] However, if at Sentinum one wing really did save the other from collapse before turning the tide towards Roman victory, then in whichever way this feat was achieved, it implies an ability to respond mid-battle to dangers and opportunities by moving contingents to different parts of the field, tactical flexibility not shown by Rome's foes who appear still simply to form line and charge. The Romans were certainly using such tactical redeployments a century later. Legions were organized in small subunits (maniples, 'handfuls' of $c.$ 120 men), and also may have been practising already a tactical manoeuvre highly important in subsequent times: 'battlefield reliefs', i.e. periodically withdrawing to the rear sub-units in hand-to-hand combat with the enemy, confronting tiring foes with fresh soldiers. Romans were acutely aware of stamina as a factor in battle, as witnessed by both battlefield reliefs and the intensity of training, at least in later times. Stamina was also used as an overt weapon against the Gauls, whose first onset, the Romans knew by long experience, was often ferocious, but also rarely sustained for long.[26] It is plausible that Fabius did indeed decide to defeat the Gauls by letting them exhaust themselves first while his men stood on the defensive. However, that he could do this in turn implies high morale, good training and great steadfastness on behalf of his soldiers – and mutual trust between commander and men.

So, was Roman victory at Sentinum down to superior Roman morale and fighting spirit? The fact that some Roman soldiers, as well as Samnites, broke and ran at Sentinum, and also that Roman allies were instrumental in the victory, all suggest that, in reality, there was no vast disparity of warlike spirit between the contingents on the field. All Italian warriors prized fame and glory, and competed to win renown.

However, that the Romans could go in for complex manoeuvres at Sentinum, while their enemies apparently did not, suggests levels of discipline and training on the Roman side above the Italian norm. Rome knew how to coordinate allied armies of considerable size and heterogeneity – something borne out by their ability soon after to take on a professional Hellenistic army and emerge victorious (p. 69).

The run-up to Sentinum also highlights superior Roman vision and capability at the strategic level. During this campaign Rome was able to organize four separate armies, and field them on three fronts, containing other enemies while dividing and reducing the main threat; she successfully drew off the Umbrians and Etruscans by attacking their homelands, greatly improving the odds at Sentinum by halving the army she faced.

The fact that the Romans were able to maintain several scattered armies also implies sophisticated logistic capabilities, and illustrates the scale of resources of soldiers and materiel on which she could draw, from her own territories and those of her allies. Rome's Latin and other Italian allies comprised more than half her force at Sentinum. Coming from outlying territories and forming the flanks of Roman armies in battle, the allies are often ignored or treated as peripheral, yet they were absolutely crucial to Roman success.

Both sides at Sentinum were able to draw on large reserves of manpower, reflecting the general rise in the population of Italy during this era, which subsequently would underpin Roman military might. However, beyond mere numbers, and the fact that both armies at Sentinum were coalitions of allies, striking contrasts are apparent.

Roman strategic success in splitting the enemy army exploited the weaknesses of the anti-Roman coalition. It was symptomatic that the coalition's contingents kept separate camps, perhaps on grounds of sheer numbers but probably also due to limited mutual trust, and lack of experience in coordinating with each other. The Roman-led force was far better integrated, sharing a single camp and a unified command structure (so long as the two consuls in joint command worked in harmony). This marks a political as well as a military contrast. Rome's alliance network was far more cohesive, with clear leadership providing coordinated strategy, doggedly pursued. Her enemies in 295 BC proved unable to sustain the joint military effort to defeat Rome in the face of dangers to their several homelands. At Sentinum, Rome successfully divided them, and conquered them piecemeal. It was a weakness Rome would not exhibit in her own crisis, a lifetime later, when she sent armies to fight in Spain even with Hannibal at the gates.

This, then, was the position Rome had achieved by the early third century BC, as she was about to face her first direct military clash with a major power from beyond Italy: King Pyrrhus of Epirus, one of many talented Hellenistic Greek soldier-rulers somewhat resembling the *condottieri* of the Italian Renaissance. She already had loyal and well-integrated allies like the Campanians at Sentinum. Over the following centuries she also managed to integrate the peoples she faced on that field, turning them all, ultimately including Samnites and even 'barbarian' Gauls, into Roman soldiers. To understand how such things could be possible it is necessary first to look even further back, to Italy in the earlier first millennium BC, at the dawn of history.

## Warlike Rome in warlike Italy

Italy enters the light of history not long after the establishment of Rome (traditionally 753 BC),[27] first through the literature of the Greeks who, during this era, were colonizing the southern coasts of the peninsula. Greeks were settling because the fertility and natural resources of Italy were capable of much greater economic output and of sustaining larger populations than the Aegean lands.

At the time the cultural and political map of Italy was complex, with diverse language groups and many ethnicities. Populations were divided by the mountainous spine of the peninsula, and subdivided into tribal or clan-based communities, many already dominated by aristocrats whose power and status derived in significant measure from 'heroic' warfare later remembered in tales such as those surrounding Aeneas.

The Greeks found the Italian 'barbarians' bellicose even by their own warlike standards. Where did this propensity come from? Archaeology and myth agree that Italy had partaken of the wider processes across Late Bronze Age Europe, which saw the appearance of specialized weapons, and then armour, for combat and with it, apparently, the establishment of the notion of the 'warrior' (Fig. 18).[28] We don't – yet – know why archaic Italian societies became and remained strongly inclined to martial violence; the question lies beyond the boundaries of the present study, yet this background comprises a crucial starting point for understanding the rise of Rome.

Rome was born, then, into a world of clans and warriors, and chronic insecurity. In the pre-state era, there was no general 'peace' as we understand it, a condition that needs to be maintained and enforced. Armed violence was endemic, from duelling and raiding to seasonal small-scale warfare.[29] Wealth and prestige depended on free males displaying the ability to acquire and to hold onto prized property, which was largely portable: cattle, horses, arms and fine artefacts. It was honourable to acquire these, and to seize women and slaves, through armed violence, and honour demanded that they should be defended

by the same means. In the first instance, free mature men (women, the young, the elderly and the servile depending on them) had to look to their own safety and survival through bearing arms. We are dealing with touchy 'honour cultures' like those seen more recently in the Mediterranean,[30] writ large by Homer as Rome was being born: the Trojan War was fought over honour, and possession of Helen. It was a world punctuated by violence, but not utter unrestrained carnage, for warrior masculinity can only thrive if it does not annihilate society, and itself. A central purpose of arms and armour, of strutting and boasting one's prowess, is deterrence of challenges, or intimidating a foe into running away. However, deterrence relies on the credibility of the threat, and this demands that violence is sometimes, perhaps frequently, inflicted. This was a world in which actual mayhem was important, but so were mutual threat and mutual fear.

18. A bronze Antenna sword from Fermo, Italy, the kind of weapon current in the centuries during which Rome developed. (Scale 1:8)

It was never Thomas Hobbes' 'war of all [individuals] against all'. While all competed for honour, those in danger of attack could also call on kin connections for support, although this, in honour societies, has always been a two-edged sword. Involving family or wider clan can improve deterrence, or lead to escalation; it is the basis for vendetta.[31] In the case of Italy (and indeed Greece and other regions), kin-based violence stood at the beginning of a general long-term trend towards more effective forms of restraint within groups as they coalesced into larger polities, perhaps resulting in generally lower levels of mayhem. However, when it erupted, armed violence tended to be on an ever larger and more devastating scale, as raids and vendettas became wars between clans,[32] then states, then alliance networks, then empires.

Societies develop other means of regulating the potential damage of clashes arising from honour codes. Infliction of a minor wound in combat, shedding some blood, may result in agreement that 'honour is satisfied', a practice reaching a height of ritualization in nineteenth-century German duelling clubs. However, there is little sign of such methods of 'conflict resolution' in Iron Age Italy, where our evidence suggests that, if it came to sword-play, the stakes were high: death or enslavement for the losers, glory and the losers' arms for the victors.

In archaic Italy, then, capacity for armed violence was vital to notions of free manhood. In such a world, those especially skilled at fighting, and at leading other warriors, could accumulate wealth, followers and power. Such men became aristocrats. The vulnerable might place themselves under their dubious and domineering protection, shading into less voluntary 'protection rackets'. 'Tribal' entities comprising clans of propertied free men under emergent aristocracies, for whom martial action, display and success were a central part of their identity, were emerging before the establishment of Rome and other city-states.

Through the seventh and sixth centuries BC many such multi-clan, tribal polities developed into city-states, which in part served as a means of internal 'conflict resolution', as the new states developed spaces, institutions, rituals and procedures through which clans could compete and negotiate without resorting to internecine bloodshed, while better resisting outsiders.[33] Nevertheless, much of the old clan-based warrior structure became embedded in the new city-states, with citizenries and nobilities defined at least in part by the possession of arms and the right, or duty, to use them on behalf of the state.

This process, partly influenced by the proximity of new Greek colonies around the southern coasts and contacts with other urban societies such as the Phoenicians, affected some (such as the Etruscans and the Latins, on whose shared frontier Rome developed) more than others. Notably, the Samnites of the southern Apennines retained their earlier, clan-based social organization.

By the time Rome became a republic in 509 BC, much of Italy was a mosaic of fiercely independent city-states, and Rome was already one of the largest. For military, religious, marriage, trading and political purposes, city-states tended to form ethnically based leagues (for example the Latin League to which Rome belonged). However, such links were relatively loose, and communities often fought within, as well as across, ethnic boundaries (Fig. 19). The default state between polities was 'cold war': straying across frontiers risked death or enslavement, and cross-border cattle- or slave-taking might be endemic. From this chronic condition of interstate insecurity, 'hot' war between cities had to be ritually declared, or fully peaceful friendly relations formally established by treaty. Martial violence, then, from raiding to pitched battles between city-state armies, was a routine experience, as it was among contemporary Greek city-states.

With the establishment of city-states, all did not suddenly change from private vendetta and clan skirmishing to a state monopoly on the right to deploy violent force, and warfare between centralized polities that were internally peaceful and stable. Transfer of the right to inflict armed violence from the individual and his clan to the twin arms of the state – judicial system and military – was only ever partial, and went nowhere near as far as in modern Western states.[34] In ancient Italy, there was always a tense and potentially unstable balance between individual rights and the law. Free males obsessed with personal honour and prowess would resist 'excessive' encroachment on their right to bear and use arms in their personal interests. The need – and the right – to defend one's honour, life and property by armed force continued into the empire; self-defence and 'self-help' (for example in the pursuit, arrest and prosecution of felons) remained the norm.[35] In Rome, state institutions only ever developed limited

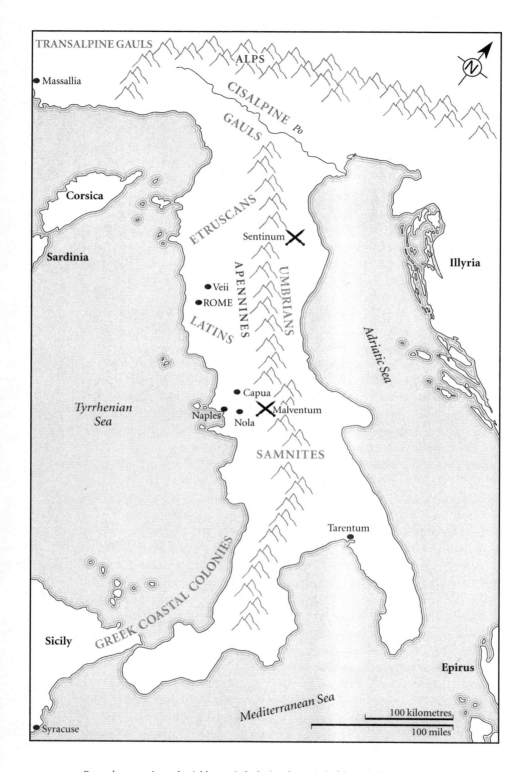

TRANSALPINE GAULS

ALPS

• Massallia

CISALPINE GAULS

Po

Corsica

ETRUSCANS

Sentinum ✕

Illyria

Sardinia

APENNINES

• Veii
• ROME

UMBRIANS

Adriatic Sea

LATINS

Tyrrhenian
Sea

• Capua

✕ Malventum
Naples • • Nola

SAMNITES

Tarentum

GREEK COASTAL COLONIES

Sicily

Epirus

Mediterranean Sea

100 kilometres

100 miles

Syracuse

19. Rome, her enemies and neighbours. Italy during the period of the rise of the Roman republic.

policing, detection and arrest powers, primarily because these would have been seen as tyrannous by the powerful males who made the rules.

Possession of arms and credible ability to use them remained a central pillar of masculinity throughout the republican era, which states certainly did not seek to eradicate. In societies where it was the norm for the army to comprise the free citizenry mustered bearing their own arms, its continuation was seen as essential to collective security, and to the honour and prestige of the state. Rather, leaders sought to control use of the sword among their own people – and to direct it outwards.

States, therefore, needed at least to suppress private and clan war, which imperilled internal stability or, waged across their borders, threatened to trigger unwanted full-scale wars. They gradually moved to achieve this as Italy was becoming unified and internal borders vanished, not least through redefining as criminal many hitherto honourable practices such as raiding to kill and to seize goods, women and cattle; these became treated as murder, theft, kidnapping and brigandage.[36]

A particular reason for the limited transfer of control of violence to the state lay in the notably touchy honour of the aristocratic clans, which came to dominate many of the new city-states. There remained a profound tension between great families' desire to retain their power and autonomy, and the need for state control over their actions. At Rome, from the start controlled by great clans, this was achieved by mutual surveillance, and effective sharing of the opportunities for honour and glory offered through fierce but regulated competition for prestige via service to the state, through magistracies and military commands. Yet this system of regulation was never perfect or complete. Clans and prominent individuals long retained their propensity for private violence. The early republic apparently saw some nobles acting as *condottieri* with warbands more or less independent of the state.[37] The famous case of the Fabian clan 'subcontracting' the conflict with Veii on behalf of Rome is little distinguishable from private war.[38] Autonomy of great men was something the Roman republic always struggled to control, ultimately failing when the senatorial warlords of the late republic such as Marius, Sulla, Pompey and Caesar waged war and foreign policy to suit themselves – and turned against their own state. Romans had feared this ever since the exiled Coriolanus led a Volscian army against his own city in the early fifth century BC.[39]

The possibility of misuse of the sword, by individuals, criminal gangs or – worse – political factions, remained a permanent threat to the internal peace and stability of societies dominated by weapons-bearing males, mostly led by proud aristocrats who professed patriotism but, if pressed, often put personal and family honour above the interests of the state. Alongside endemic inter-state warfare, the picture of early Italian states given by ancient writers was one of frequent internal strife, even civil wars. The seriousness with which Romans regarded these internal threats, which several times endangered the earlier republic, and the extraordinary measures they took to contain them, are discussed below. However, overall she was able to weather her own crises, while also learning to exploit those threatening other societies. This proved key to Rome's rise to dominion.

Martial violence and armed masculinity were certainly central to Roman culture, the ideology of war pervading the lives of her citizens, and monuments of victory dominating the City of Rome, to an extent unmatched elsewhere in the Classical world. Unmatched, but far from unparalleled; for if she went further than others in the degree of her obsession with the sword, in kind Rome was not exceptional, but fundamentally similar to her neighbours.[40] For none of the Italian peoples, northern Gauls or Greek colonists were easy sword-fodder. Indeed they often outdid Rome in aggression and violent tastes. It was not only Gaulish warriors who took boastful pride in the spoils of naked aggression (p. 20), while the origins of gladiatorial combat attest the bloodthirstiness of other Italians; often thought of as archetypally Roman, gladiators were actually invented in Etruscan and Samnite Campania (Fig. 13). Gladiatorial contests derived from single combats at funerals of the great, themselves perhaps developed from human sacrifices. Even Greeks, often misconceived as pacific by comparison with the bellicose Romans, were not at all squeamish about annexing land 'won with the spear'.[41]

By comparison, republican Romans could appear surprisingly circumspect about the ethics of violence. Among many peoples, war required appropriate rituals to gain the support of the gods. However, Romans regarded themselves as the most pious and just of peoples, with very elaborate rituals surrounding warmaking.[42] To gain divine sanction a war had to be 'just' (*bellum iustum*), which meant it had to be at least technically defensive, of state interests if not territory. This was simply established when facing foreign invasion, but often meant manoeuvring a hapless target into, at best, a ritually plausible state of transgression of Rome's rules of war, peace and relations between peoples. Romans could then attack, either with a genuine sense of self-righteousness or at least a legalistic pretext, and expect divine support.[43] Romans certainly manipulated this system to facilitate aggression, but it does suggest rather more moral qualms than were exhibited by some of her foes, who retained a simpler warrior ethic.

Especially for the earlier republic, the similarities in martial values between Romans and other Italians were clearly as important as any Roman peculiarities, for the fundamental reason that half – at Sentinum, more than half – the soldiers she fielded were non-Romans. This suggests that, alongside her martial qualities, vital though they always remained and impressive as they were becoming, Rome's unexpected rise to dominion over Italy depended equally on another, very different ability. If Rome truly possessed a special quality that explains her rise, this lay, paradoxically, in her unique skills in the arts not of war, but of diplomacy and politics.[44] The following draws especially on the ideas of Nicola Terrenato.[45]

Arguably, the decisive moment in Rome's rise to hegemony in Italy was the Latin War (340–338 BC) – or, more specifically, the settlement that followed it. By the 350s, Rome was dominating the other, smaller city-states of the nominally federal Latin League, which in 340 demanded restoration of equal status in a joint republic. Roman refusal led to war, and defeat for the Latins. The settlement Rome imposed would have tremendous consequences. The Latin League was replaced by a new system in which each Latin state was linked to Rome but not to the others, replacing the old alliance network with a new radial structure, which Rome controlled. But the Latins were not reduced to vassal status. The Romans developed a solution that involved genuine, if usually partial and conditional, incorporation of the vanquished, rather than simple domination by the sword. Some communities, like Tusculum, were given full Roman citizenship. Others were given a lesser form of citizenship, minus the vote (so-called 'Latin rights'). None of these states was required to pay tribute, but all had to furnish soldiers for wars decided upon and led by Rome. Thus, the Romans did not destroy or humiliate the defeated but rather harnessed them in ways which, even though they had lost their autonomy, allowed them to save face, and even to profit. Supplying troops to Rome offered the prospect of a share of booty and glory. Rome had also set the precedent that loyalty might lead to full integration into the expanding Roman polity. This clever solution, which provided powerful incentives to loyalty, was initially applied to peoples with whom Rome had profound and longstanding links, but would subsequently be extended to many other Italian states, and form the template of empire.

Rome's policy towards the defeated after 338 BC was novel, and proved spectacularly successful in building and sustaining her power. Its secret depended as much on what Rome held in common with other Italian societies as on her own special characteristics, and its success arose from interplay of the two. It relied both on shared bellicosity, and also similar political cultures. Although some Greek colonies were democracies, most Italian states and societies, including Rome herself, were oligarchies, in which aristocracies dominated citizenries but could not completely control or ignore them, especially since they depended on them – primarily on the mass of lesser landowners – to take up arms in war.

In many Mediterranean city-states, aristocrats – individuals, families, clans – jostled for personal power and glory, allying, competing and clashing with their peers to secure civil magistracies or military commands to lead their people in battle against armies of other states (also led by aristocrats). In practice the biggest threats to such elites often lay not on the battlefield but came from within. All nobles felt potentially threatened by rival aristocratic factions and by social subordinates: the mass of ordinary citizens, and slaves. It was common for city-states to be torn by internal conflict between aristocratic factions or between nobles and commons, resulting in what Greeks called *stasis*. This could involve coups, assassinations, even civil wars. Such crises might result in the flight of the losers into exile. The supposedly simultaneous expulsions of the Tarquins from Rome and the Pesistratids from Athens provide famous examples.

Despite – indeed, largely because of – the fact that aristocrats led their peoples in war and peace, their common interests meant that, even across ethnic boundaries, nobles often had more in common with each other than with their own social inferiors. Mutual contacts – developed through diplomacy, residence as diplomatic hostages and intermarriage – all helped foster a shared 'international' aristocratic culture, based largely on that of the Greeks. This was analogous to that shared by the nobilities and royal houses of medieval Europe, which fought each other, but also intermarried and copied each other's ways, through a common chivalric code, French song or Italian fashion. Through personal contacts, and entirely separate from formal treaty relations between states, aristocratic families established and maintained friendships, virtual private alliances, with families in other states, even across ethnic boundaries. Such links, which doubtless existed before states evolved, were especially valuable in time of crisis, when nobles fell foul of rival factions or popular unrest. They provided the possibility of appealing for foreign aid, as Rome's exiled last king Tarquin the Proud did to Lars Porsenna of Clusium. Failing that, it might provide an escape route into temporary exile, or a permanent move to another state, as when the entire Sabine *gens Claudia* migrated to Rome, or Coriolanus fled Rome to the Volscians.[46]

Cases such as these provide striking examples of mobility among the aristocracy, and not least of how personal honour could override loyalty to native community. Though we take 'patriotism' from Rome, national identity as we understand it was weakly developed. Great men in Rome and other Italian states putting their personal and class interests above those of their *patriae* (whether or not they deluded themselves about their real motives) was a theme recurrent in the history of the period.

The private networks of friendship between aristocrats spanning Italy could also be useful to states in providing informal channels for diplomatic contacts. This web certainly incorporated Roman noble families. Consequently, the senatorial aristocracy already maintained links with noble factions inclined to be well disposed towards Rome in many other Italian states, even if their ruling regimes were hostile.[47] In Nicola Terrenato's view, the channels of diplomatic communication and private conspiracy provided by these contacts proved as important to the unification of Italy as the swords of the soldiers.[48]

From the start of the republic Rome was powerful, so it is easy to see why aristocrats in other cities might find rapprochement with Roman noble families especially attractive. If through their personal links they could foster alliance between their own state and Rome, it would bring far greater personal security at home, against other noble factions or against popular risings, since Rome could send 'federal' troops in support of her friends, as in the case of Ardea in 442 BC.[49] For the ambitious aristocrat, there was also the glittering prospect of a 'slice of the action' through serving in the allied contingents of Roman armies in further wars of expansion. They could even aspire to become Romans themselves.[50]

The last point highlights another truly exceptional Roman trait, which gave Rome a real edge in accreting allies and retaining their loyalty. This was her exceptional openness, at all levels, to inclusion of others. The roots of this lay deep in the self-image of the Roman people. They did not see themselves as a 'pure-blooded' descent group, but as a mixed community from the start. Their foundation myths and early historical legends conceived of Rome, located on the boundary between Latium and Etruria, as forged from fugitive or migrant Trojans, Latins and Sabines, Etruscans and others. While the USA offers a notable modern parallel, Rome was perhaps then unique in this 'mongrel' self-image, which made it easy to accept that almost anyone might *become* Roman in the right circumstances. This forms a striking contrast with, for example, Greek cities, notoriously reluctant to extend their citizenship to outsiders, no matter how deserving. To the amazement and horror of Greeks, access to Roman citizenship was even extended to freed slaves. It was certainly offered to 'deserving' friendly Italian aristocrats from an early date, gradually extending to elites across the peninsula. This relatively open access to her citizenship was a key reason why Rome, rather than (say) Capua or some other major city, came to dominate Italy.

For me, Nicola Terrenato's view constitutes a major insight into the origins of Roman power, highlighting processes that, as we will see, also make sense of later phases of Rome's imperial expansion. Although it has often been neglected, clear evidence has always existed that Rome's rise in Italy was not solely due to the sword. Some of Rome's major allies were acquired through entirely voluntary negotiation, based on shared or complementary interests, as in the case of Greek Neapolis (Naples), with which Rome had a *foedus aequum*, an alliance between nominal equals. Others joined with Rome willingly, as the perceived lesser of two evils: the Samnite Wars began when Campanians and Capuans appealed to Rome for alliance and protection in the face of Samnite threat.[51] Rome acquired her allies, then, through a variety of mechanisms ranging from shared interests to intimidation or defeat. In the long term even most of the defeated were, like the Latins in 338 BC, treated as subordinate allies rather than subjects, required to furnish soldiers for Rome's future wars rather than tribute, an obligation with profound consequences.

Terrenato also notes that Rome tended to clash especially with democratic regimes like that of Greek Tarentum (Taranto), replacing them with oligarchies wherever she encountered them. On this view, some of the fighting involved in Roman expansionism may have been token resistance by covertly pro-Roman regimes to save face and honour, or the last gasp of the opponents (noble or democratic) of pro-Roman elite factions. However, Terrenato's model focuses very strongly on elites, who may have been the key players, but were by no means the only people on the pitch.

Rapprochement with Rome by ruling cliques of nobles also required at least the acquiescence of non-aristocrats, especially the citizen-soldier class. The courage they normally showed as Rome's allies suggests that the Roman connection also held positive attractions for them as well. For it allowed free citizens as well as nobles to continue to do what they had been brought up to do. Rather than paying tribute as subjects, they could continue fighting for their own ideals of manhood, for their own cities, and for potential personal profit as part of an ever-expanding victorious alliance. Allied contingents shared the booty. Despite their losses and complaints of unequal burdens, the attractions (on average) outweighed the costs. Ultimately, the possibility of full Roman citizenship also became an attractive long-term prospect to the mass of allied soldiers who constituted half of Rome's armies. Pressure to deliver this complete integration became violent towards the end of the republic.

Even if rapprochement with Rome proved so attractive to many Italian nobles and citizen-soldiers, for their states the price of alliance was subordination to Roman hegemony and Roman policy. This is evident in the structure of Rome's alliance system, which since the Latin War was no longer a network nominally of mutually supporting equals, but strictly radial, with Rome at the hub; her allies were kept separate, and linked only through her. It was a proto-empire.

The unification of Italy under Roman hegemony was certainly substantially achieved by direct use of the sword, against cities like Veii and Tarentum, and against peoples like the Samnites (Fig. 20). Still, Nicola Terrenato argues that, if we look past later rhetoric and back-projection of the ways Rome behaved subsequently, examples like Neapolis prove that it was to a significant extent also a process of voluntary federation. However, while Veii may have been absorbed as much as destroyed, there was a war, and ancient writers did not wholly fabricate the endless catalogue of carnage marking Rome's ascent. Numerous triumphs attest vast bloodshed, not least in the Samnite Wars. Terrenato himself concedes that 'elite negotiation' did not really work with groups apparently weakly linked into existing 'elite networks', such as the little-urbanized Samnites, or not integrated at all, such as the 'barbarian' Gauls of the Po valley (an area not considered part of Italy in republican times). These peoples were incorporated – or destroyed – primarily by force of arms. In summary, Rome came to unite Italy through a remarkably effective combination of the sword and the open hand.

This was made possible by the particular social and political conditions which had developed in archaic Italy, in which she was embedded, and her own peculiar origins and values. Her characteristically Janus-like mix of violence and conciliation was expressed in her very foundation myths: Romulus killed his twin Remus even as he marked out the ritual boundary of the City of Rome, and established unity with the Sabines as a result of forcible abduction of their daughters. Alongside the threat of martial violence, Rome's openness, and the prospects of glory and profit through participation in the military campaigns she launched, provided the positive attraction that bound the burgeoning Roman 'federation' together. This helps to explain how it could be that, even after Hannibal had annihilated several major Roman/Italian armies and camped before the City itself, so few of Rome's Italian allies took the opportunity to desert her.

20. A Campanian soldier in a tomb painting of *c.* 330 BC, from Nola, Italy. He wears a Samnite bronze chest-protector and waist belt. He has recently won a single combat and despoiled his vanquished foe, whose tunic and belt now hang from his javelins.

## The sword in the republic

Rome was by no means immune to the internal stresses that racked many city-states. Indeed, her rise placed strains on her domestic order more tremendous than those faced by any other society. The wonder is that she did not implode in chaos until long after the unification of Italy. However, Rome successfully avoided serious political violence or outright civil war until the later second century BC, when the republic began to fall apart under the distorting weight of empire, ultimately leading to its replacement by imperial monarchy. How did she manage to maintain internal peace so long? We are well placed to answer since, as ultimate victor, Rome's history was documented in unusual detail.

Rome was always much less egalitarian in ideology than Greek states like democratic Athens. Yet strongly hierarchical though it was, Roman society was no beehive of obedient drones. While ordinary Romans may have resented domination by great senatorial families, sometimes vocally, they were also accustomed to it, and expected their leaders to adhere to mutual obligations established by tradition, whether as civil magistrates in the forum or as commanders in camp. Deference was important, but citizens also knew their rights. Internal tensions and processes of negotiation are reflected in the role of the tribunes of the plebs, and seen in the efforts made to curry favour with the masses as well as to repress them. This situation was the result of crises in the early Roman state.

Sixth-century struggles at the top led to the expulsion of the kings and the establishment of a republic. Subsequent monopolization of offices of state and military commands by a closed circle of old patrician families, and aristocratic high-handedness, led to further crises known as the 'Struggle of the Orders'. This was no simple clash of nobles and masses, since the 'plebeians' included rich and powerful families in the senate who felt disadvantaged by the exclusivity of the clans of the patriciate, which monopolized the sacral life of Rome, including matters relating to war. Before battle only patricians had the authority to take the auspices, ensuring divine approval. They used their privileges to dominate society. Ensuing tensions threatened the republic with catastrophic disruption. Many of the most dramatic events were played out in relation to raising armies and campaigning. For example, the several 'Secessions of the Plebs' during and after the fifth century BC, in which the commoners withdrew to the Sacred Mount outside Rome, were actually general strikes or mass mutinies in which the plebs refused military service to force concessions from the patriciate. These actions led to the establishment of the popular tribunate, an important civil magistracy thereafter; to protect them, serving tribunes were personally sacrosanct.[52] On such occasions the plebs flexed the political muscle provided by their vital role as soldiers, resisting patrician commanders' attempts to control them via war alarms and getting them under military oaths of obedience enforceable by the death penalty.[53] In 358 BC, emotions ran high enough for soldiers to murder their commander.[54]

Virtue was by no means solely on one side in these struggles. Roman soldiers were already wolflike. Those wintering in allied Capua in 342 BC plotted to seize the rich city, but were thwarted by their commander, who dismissed the conspirators. However, they organized themselves into an illegal army and supposedly started to march on Rome. Their aims, and the course of events, are obscure. Livy reports that the danger was great enough for Rome to appoint a dictator and assemble another army to confront them, although he notes other differing accounts existed. However, the crisis was somehow averted without civil war.[55]

In the earlier republic, then, Romans were politically active as soldiers as well as citizens in togas, and under arms could already pose a threat to the state. The patricians were understandably anxious to control the people under arms, and Romans at large considered it in their interests to keep the sword out of politics. But how to achieve this as, with the growth of Roman wealth and power, the stakes rose ever higher?

Mutual fear played a central role, not least in constraining the behaviour of nobles. The plebs could and did force some into exile and, as we saw, occasionally resorted to assassination. Aristocrats also policed each other. There was a fine line between vigorous pursuit of honour and glory in the intensely competitive arena of service to the state that channelled heroic aristocratic violence, and becoming an over-mighty individual whose ambitions were deemed to threaten the *status quo* (especially through demagoguery). Such men faced exile (like Scipio Africanus) or later, death by assassination or more or less legal execution, the fate of the Gracchi, Catiline and finally Caesar, whose murder brought down the republic.

Romans treated armed violence like a potential contagion, or rather as Westerners have treated nuclear power: as a source of potential benefit if used properly (preferably a long way away), but a possibly lethal domestic peril. Later in the republic, laws were increasingly used to control *vis* – unsanctioned and excessive violence – especially *vis publica*, collective violence regarded as armed sedition.[56] These measures were intended to thwart over-ambitious aristocrats, armed gangs or, worse, combinations of both. However, from early times, religion and ritual were central to keeping the sword out of the city. Romans regarded armed violence as so dangerous a threat to state and society that it was hedged around with extraordinarily elaborate systems of divinely underpinned sanctions, rituals and taboos.

If passion for the sword was integral to the ideology of Roman males and the state, fear of its misuse was built into the symbolic, sacred and ritual topography of the City. Romans divided the world into two domains called, significantly, *domi* and *militiae*. *Domi* – from *domus*, 'house(hold)' – was the world of Romans at home, of families, the civil community and peaceful internal civic life. *Militiae* was the realm of the community under arms, facing its enemies. Remarkably, the boundary between the domains of sword and civil community was not simply conceptual; it was materially demarcated by a ritual boundary, the *pomerium*, a strip of land roughly corresponding to the line of the city defences and occasionally extended with the growth of the city and its territory.[57] The *pomerium* was not just about regulating war, but creating a sacrosanct space immune from armed violence of any kind, especially internal private war.

It is difficult to overstate the ritual and practical significance of this boundary during the republic. It was not just about the sword; it also marked the symbolic boundary between the urban world and agriculture/wilderness beyond, between 'us' and foreigners, and not least between the living and the dead, who had to be buried outside the *pomerium*. Sub-lethal violence as such was not forbidden within the city; people could beat subordinates inside, but killing of slaves and state executions were normally conducted beyond the boundary. Executioners and butchers had to live outside it. Yet much of its significance was specifically in relation to war and other collective armed violence. These were, quite literally, placed beyond the bounds of the civil community.

Meetings of the senate to debate war, or to receive emissaries from foreign powers with whom no treaty existed (and therefore by default technically enemies), were held in the Temple of Bellona, goddess of battle-frenzy, beyond the *pomerium*.[58] A fetial (one of the special college of priests concerned with matters relating to diplomacy, peace and war) originally declared war by approaching the enemy's frontier, making a ritual denunciation and hurling a ceremonial spear across it. As frontiers receded this became impractical, so the ritually prescribed physical act was fulfilled by hurling a spear into an area designated 'enemy territory' for sacral purposes, outside the *pomerium*.

Military training and mustering of soldiers also took place outside it, on the adjacent *campus martius*, the Field of Mars. Roman soldiers could not legally cross the *pomerium* in arms except in the special, divinely sanctioned transgression of a formal triumph – and only then by a special gate. Commanders took up and relinquished command of armies by crossing the *pomerium*, switching between civil and military dress as they did so. A serving general crossing it into the city automatically extinguished his supreme authority (*imperium*). This had real practical and political consequences down to the end of the republic. In 60 BC it forced Caesar to choose between a triumph for his victories, or a consulship. To get the triumph, he had to stay outside the city as a serving general until the day of the procession; but if he crossed the *pomerium* to campaign for election, his military command would lapse, and with it went the opportunity to triumph. (He opted for the consulship, anticipating more triumphs later.)

To stop martial violence being turned on the body politic, it was kept firmly beyond the *pomerium*, and directed outwards. However, the sword was not literally excluded. Since, until the state started issuing them late in the republic, weapons were the personal property of citizens and kept at home, they must have been carried over the *pomerium*. Sacral state regulation of this is seen in special festivals for purifying arms and trumpets, ritually commissioning them at the start of the campaigning season in March, month of the war-god, and decommissioning them at its end in October.[59]

## Pyrrhus and the proving of Roman power

While Philip II of Macedon was overwhelming Greece and Alexander was conquering Persia, Rome rose from mistress of the Tiber valley to arbiter of Italy. Her military and political power rapidly expanded over the entire peninsula, from the northern fringes of the Apennines, through Etruria and Campania to the southern coasts. Despite later, retrospective assertions of divinely ordained destiny, it is unlikely that Rome initially had ambitions beyond the regional, or simply winning the next war. However, she learnt incrementally from her successes and errors, and during the course of the fourth century BC, her ruling class will have realized that domination of the entire peninsula was becoming a feasible ambition. Her rise culminated in definitive defeat of the powerful Samnites of the southern highlands, and hegemony over the great Greek coastal colonies through alliance or the sword. It was the resistance of one major Greek city, Tarentum (Taranto) that precipitated Rome's first clash with a major extra-Italian military power: Epirus, under its Hellenistic *condottiere*-king, Pyrrhus. In the face of Roman threat, the Tarantines appealed for Pyrrhus' help. Sensing the chance of creating an empire in Italy on the model of the successor-states carved from Alexander's conquests, in 280 BC Pyrrhus shipped over his powerful, highly trained army.

Pyrrhus expected to fight barbarians, and got a shock. Even facing a state-of-the-art Hellenistic army, complete with Macedonian-style phalanx and war elephants (Fig. 21) under the best general of his generation, the Romans finally prevailed. In three battles they were unable to beat Pyrrhus outright, but their armies (which doubtless included grizzled centurions who, as young legionaries, had also served at Sentinum) fought him to a bloody standstill. Despite appalling losses, Rome kept coming back for more, whilst inflicting terrible damage on the invader who, significantly, was joined by few other Italians. Pyrrhus' clearest success over the Romans at Ausculum in 279 was so costly to him in experienced soldiers and officers that it gave us the expression 'Pyrrhic victory'. The third great battle of the Pyrrhic War was fought at Malventum in 275. The fighting on the field was indecisive, but the Romans were able to claim victory, because Pyrrhus conceded strategic defeat by withdrawing from Italy.[60] This finally confirmed Roman mastery over the peninsula, including the remaining Greek cities of the southern coasts.

21. A model of a war-elephant with 'castle', like those used in Italy by Pyrrhus. Terracotta from Pompeii.

The struggle with Pyrrhus shows that key capabilities and characteristics, which Rome soon after exhibited against Carthage, and later against the Hellenistic world, were already in place. Certainly, on the battlefield Pyrrhus exposed the limitations of Roman tactics and generalship. Yet, if not especially well led by Hellenistic standards, Roman *milites* showed great discipline, courage, ferocity and superior staying power. These were a result of ideological motivation of the soldiers, combined with Rome's command of reserves of manpower, materiel and money permitting the fielding of multiple large armies, and the organizational abilities to wield and maintain them. All this gave Rome the material and moral capacity to absorb enormous losses and keep fighting to outlast the enemy. Strategically if not tactically, they had defeated a major Hellenistic army. Rome had graduated from leading Italian power to a player on the Mediterranean scale.

†

> ...by the time that they met Pyrrhus [the Romans] had become perfectly trained athletes in war. POLYBIUS 2.20[61]

The clash with Pyrrhus revealed the vast manpower and sheer ferocity that the republic would later unleash on the Greek world, and which would prove lasting hallmarks of the Roman military. However, both factors were matters of degree, not special kind, and both may actually have been quite new phenomena when Pyrrhus came up against them. They represent twin, mutually supporting outcomes of wielding the sword and offering the open hand.

The manpower Rome deployed to achieve hegemony over the Mediterranean in the third and second centuries BC was, then and later, presented by commentators as 'Roman', although it was actually an equal mix of Italians and Romans – many of whom were very new Romans. In scale and composition, it was largely a product of Rome's open hand. Just as Italy's developing city-states had faced the dilemma of how to ensure that the martial violence of their own citizen-soldiers would not tear them apart, so Rome, by unifying Italy, created a potentially far more intractable problem: how to prevent hundreds of thousands of bellicose males disrupting the Roman-dominated federation by doing what they had been raised to do – fighting each other. In the third century BC demilitarization was literally unthinkable for Romans or other Italians, especially when other predatory powers, Greek and 'barbarian', were circling nearby, in Sicily, North Africa, Greece and Gaul.

In fact, Rome achieved increasing (if imperfect and interrupted) internal stability in Italy by extending to her federation the same methods she used with relative success at home – and which had contributed to her military prowess. The ideologies and practices behind martial violence were not to be suppressed. Far from it: they were encouraged and celebrated more than ever. As we have seen, Rome did not tax wealth out of her *de facto* subjects, but required them to supply the sinews of war: soldiers and their courage. The trick, just as it had been within Rome itself, proved to be synchronizing their martial energies and directing them outwards, away from the commonwealth, towards mutually satisfactory goals: foreign wars. Here there were opportunities for Italian aristocrats and soldiers alike to display prowess, and to win glory and booty. Rome orchestrated and exported the violence of Italian males, in a process finding a contemporary parallel in Alexander and his successors providing an outlet for Macedonian and Greek martial energies in the east. Here is an important sense in which Rome's rise in Italy was a process of unification rather than oppressive conquest; Rome did not suppress, but accommodated and encouraged the martial pride of allies and subjects.

Wars beyond Italy offered other domestic political benefits. Sharing military service against common foes bonded Romans and Italians, promoting integration and making refragmentation increasingly unthinkable. The policy proved highly successful; later in the republic, resentment grew among the allies that they were bearing too much of the burden of Roman-led wars and not being properly rewarded. This led eventually to fighting in Italy (the 'Social War', i.e. the war with the *socii*, the allies: p. 98), but tellingly the aim of the allies, apart from some die-hard Samnites, was not independence, but final, full integration as equal Roman citizens; they fought to get further in, not out.

We have seen how military service and, specifically, showing courage on the battlefield, were central to Roman notions of *virtus*, manliness (emphasizing physical courage). The intensity of indoctrination in these traditional masculine values evident through the republic goes a long way to explaining Roman morale and ferocity on fields such as Sentinum. Roman commanders and soldiers alike showed deep – even fanatical – ideological commitment to patriotism and demonstrating their *virtus*, aggressively competing for *gloria* and *laus* (fame). But Rome would rise to dominate the Mediterranean not because the other Italian peoples had been militarily weak, but because they, too, had been so bellicose. Martial aggressiveness was actually a general Italian trait of the era.

After decades of escalating struggle in a hard shared school of mutually reinforcing savagery, Rome's allies and enemies at Sentinum were all similarly motivated to fight for manhood and country, and consequently were as fierce in battle as the Romans themselves; as we have seen, Rome's ultimate domination was largely the result of her special political talents, not innate martial superiority.[62] If subsequently Roman/Italian armies shocked the Greek world by the extent of their inclination to torture, mutilate and kill prisoners of war, slaves and criminals,[63] this was not a specifically Roman trait either. Deepening mutual brutalization during the crescendo of the struggle for Italy around 300 BC likely marked the first forging of that ruthless ferocity which would be fire-hardened by Roman Italy's subsequent death-struggle with Carthage. Ensuing clashes with the Hellenistic powers, highly bellicose themselves, would simply serve to sharpen its razor edge.

# 2 Obsessed with Victory
## The Imperial Republic 270–30 BC

### From arbiter of Italy to sole superpower 270–167 BC

> Can anyone be so indifferent or idle as not to care to know by what
> means, and under what kind of polity, almost the whole inhabited
> world was conquered and brought under the dominion of the single
> city of Rome…?
> POLYBIUS, 1.1[1]

Having driven off Pyrrhus, the Romans consolidated their grip on Italy. With
remarkable speed – in barely a decade – they took decisions that would embroil
them in a series of even greater wars, ranging far beyond Italy. In 264 BC Rome
clashed over Sicily with the North African-based Phoenician colony of Carthage,
the greatest naval and maritime trading power of the age, like Rome an aristocratic republic but one based on commerce, prefiguring Venice. The First and
Second Punic (Phoenician) Wars were the predominant military events of the
remainder of the third century BC, totalling some forty years of fighting (Fig.
22). Rome was ultimately triumphant in both, winning her first overseas territories, and Carthage was permanently crippled. However, the wider fallout of
the Second Punic War brought Roman armies into collision once again with
those of the Hellenistic world, this time on Greek rather than Italian soil.

In a single generation, from around 200 to 167 BC, the Romans turned
upside-down the world of the old Greek states and of Alexander's successors.
Long accustomed to thinking of themselves as the pinnacle of human civilization, and the most sophisticated military powers, the Hellenistic states suddenly
found themselves defeated by upstart Italian 'barbarians'. This was all the more
astonishing because, just a few years before Rome began to batter the Hellenistic world, at Hannibal's hands she herself had sustained a series of shocks so
tremendous that her hold on Italy itself seemed to be loosening. The greatest of
these blows came on the field of Cannae.

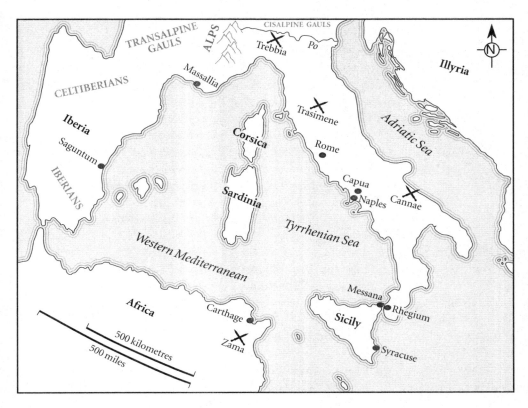

22. The theatre of the Punic Wars, with peoples, regions and places mentioned in the text.

## Two duels with Carthage, 264–202 BC

In 218 BC Hannibal made the famous march from his base in Spain over the Alps and into the Po valley, proceeding to smash major Roman armies at the River Trebbia and Lake Trasimene. He ranged south through Italy, seeking to prise Rome's allies and subjects away from her. In 216 BC, having already lost tens of thousands of soldiers killed or captured, Roman commanders determined to confront him head-on once more, and drawing on their own and their allies' vast reserves of manpower, assembled yet another huge army.

Hannibal, his 40,000-strong army outnumbered by the Romans who had perhaps 50,000 men, offered battle at Cannae in Apulia. Here, the deep Roman formation charged into a deliberately thin Carthaginian centre, which was under instructions to fall back, luring the Romans and their allies into envelopment by the stronger Carthaginian wings of foot and horse. Audaciously, the smaller army enveloped the larger. The result was the most notorious of all Roman military disasters. Trapped and herded so tightly they could not fight, legionaries and allies were slaughtered; few escaped. Hannibal effectively annihilated Rome's great army, losing 'only' 6,000 men himself.[2] But what was Hannibal doing in Italy at all? The answer lies in the First Punic War, and how Rome had won that vast struggle.

Carthage was a major Phoenician maritime trading colony in North Africa, with extensive interests and possessions in the western Mediterranean, and a powerful fleet to protect them. Significantly, the First Punic War was triggered in 264 BC by Roman intervention on behalf of a group of mercenaries, the 'Mamertines', who held Messana in part-Carthaginian Sicily, on the straits facing Italy. During the 280s, a body of the mercenaries from many nations who found plenty of employment in the Hellenistic era had been placed in garrison there. They called themselves Mamertines, from Mamers, the Samnite name for Mars, suggesting they were mostly south Italians. Their conduct in Messana had been less than honourable. They seized the city for themselves, killing the men, taking the women and dividing the land.[3] In the face of Carthaginian threats they appealed for Roman help. Rome used this as a pretext to invade Sicily.

Early Roman land successes caused them to decide on conquest of the island. This effectively obliged the Romans to take to the sea for the first time on a major scale. They built a fleet to face Carthage, employing a novel spiked boarding-bridge (*corvus*), which allowed the skills of the legionaries to overmatch Carthaginian naval prowess.

The ensuing two-decade war was fought across vast areas on a scale that amazed even the powerful Hellenistic kingdoms to the east. Both powers controlled enormous resource bases, exhibited in construction and manning of huge fleets of major warships, and the ability to replace vast losses, mainly inflicted by storms. Polybius calculated that during the war the Romans lost 700 quinquiremes (large oared warships), and Carthage 500, in the biggest naval conflict of Classical antiquity (Fig. 23). However, ultimately Rome's resources proved greater. She also showed her boldness, copying the successful strategy of a ruler of Syracuse fifty years earlier by deciding to attack the heart of the Carthaginian empire, invading Africa directly. Brilliant initial success ended in disaster in 255 BC when the Carthaginian force, under another Greek, the Spartan mercenary-general Xanthippus, pinned the Roman centre with his infantry and enveloped them with his horse; Hannibal's later tactics at Cannae were not invented from thin air. The war dragged on until 241 when Rome gained final victory in Sicily. As with their strategic victory over Pyrrhus, the Romans' success was largely a result of outlasting the enemy in aggressive commitment, and of the greater strategic resources and manpower of Italy. Her soldiers had won Rome her first overseas province. During Carthage's subsequent vicious war with her own mercenaries (which outdid Roman cruelty), Rome took the opportunity to seize Sardinia and Corsica too.

23. Roman republican coin (one *as* piece) depicting the prow of a warship, complete with ram.

To avenge their defeat, some Carthaginians realized that they would need to do as Rome had done: take the war to the gates of the enemy. Carthage had to destroy Rome, or at least to cripple her by breaking up her alliance system. For this, Carthage needed a major land army with a substantial resource base of men and materiel. She found both by colonial expansion in the Iberian peninsula (Spain/Portugal), an effort led by the Barcid family, into which Hannibal was born. The Barcids came to be famed for their enmity with Rome, leading Carthaginian efforts against her on behalf of the state. They roughly parallel great Roman senatorial families with particular political/strategic interests, such as the Fabii who faced Veii. The Barcids forged a formidable new army, drawing especially on the martial traditions of the Iberians and Celtiberians, who provided excellent mercenaries.

The inevitable renewed struggle with Rome also began in Iberia, when Hannibal conquered Saguntum, a Roman 'friend'; Rome's political network already extended to Spain and Greece. The Second Punic War, the greatest and most deadly foreign war the republic ever faced, began in 218 BC. From the start it was on a Mediterranean scale.

The Romans planned to face Hannibal in Spain, but he intended to do what the Romans had done in the first conflict: take war to the enemy's heartland. Crossing the Alps complete with war elephants, Hannibal descended on the new Roman possessions in the Po valley. At the River Trebbia, the Romans lost 75 per cent of their *c.* 40,000 men, and the local Gauls flocked to join the invader. Another Roman army of similar size was annihilated at Lake Trasimene in Etruria the next year. Rome itself now appeared to be at Hannibal's mercy, except for one remarkable fact. Even now, Italy remained entirely loyal to the Romans.[4]

Denied a base and source of supply, with limited manpower and unable to secure reinforcements, Hannibal could not besiege Rome. He needed to turn some Roman dependants if he was to win. He decided his best chance lay to the south, among Rome's bitterest former foes, such as the Samnites. The Romans knew they could not yet face Hannibal again in the field, and so Fabius Maximus 'the Delayer' shadowed him to track and constrain his movements, while the state gathered another huge army of Romans and allies. In 216 BC, the Romans were intent on destroying Hannibal by sheer weight of numbers. They had learned nothing from the previous disasters.

The slaughter at Cannae was a stunning blow to Rome, the nadir of the two wars she had fought with Carthage in half a century. Cannae became a byword for military disaster. Worse, this was on top of the two other major disasters at the Trebbia and Trasimene.

Cannae seemed to bring Hannibal what he sought. Rome's tentacles of control over Italy started to snap. Unsurprisingly, some of her allies, notably powerful Capua, judged this series of shocks to Roman prestige mortal to her hegemony, and threw off their allegiance. It began to look as though Rome's recently acquired domination of Italy, and first forays as a Mediterranean power, might prove short-lived. Yet despite the desperation of her plight, most of Rome's allies stayed loyal, encouraged by the Romans themselves, who refused to capitulate or even to treat so long as foreign invaders remained on Italian soil.

The Romans rose to the occasion, showing remarkable – fanatical – determination. Despite losing three armies, there was no 'peace party'. This was Rome's finest hour, showing the senate and people at their most courageous. By 212, pressing almost every able-bodied man into service, the Romans were fielding twenty-five new legions. Such astonishing resolution and national sacrifice successfully kept the many remaining allies loyal and contributing soldiers. Conversely, Hannibal, despite his new territorial base, proved unable to recruit many Italian troops, and the Romans successfully prevented him receiving reinforcements from Iberia or the Gauls of the Po valley.

Despite significant defections, Rome's alliance network proved strong enough to sustain an astonishing recovery, ultimately leading to victory. Romans and their Italian allies proved able to: withstand a series of shattering defeats and losses of perhaps 100,000 men; contain Hannibal in Italy and gradually erode his position; prevent reinforcements reaching him; conquer his Iberian base by 206; maintain naval superiority; fight in Sicily; wage a war on Greek soil to prevent Philip v of Macedon joining Hannibal in Italy; and, finally, repeat the invasion of Africa.

Carthage blinked first. Hannibal was finally recalled to defend his homeland, escaping from Italy with 15,000 veterans. The showdown at Zama in 202 BC saw a weakened Carthaginian force facing battle-hardened Roman troops. This time it was the Roman cavalry that was victorious, and fell on the Carthaginian rear: Scipio's soldiers 'Cannae'd' Hannibal's, their general winning the honorific surname Africanus. Carthage now lay vulnerable to Roman siege, yet Scipio decided to negotiate. The peace terms stripped the defeated of power and possessions, and imposed massive financial reparations. Carthage capitulated, permanently crippled. Hannibal went into exile.

The battles of the Trebbia, Trasimene and especially Cannae brutally confirmed what the struggle with Pyrrhus had suggested: that the fine weapons, courage and aggression of Roman and Italian soldiers were fearsome, but not enough on their own to defeat the invaders. Hannibal certainly did not enjoy any significant advantage in armaments; he rapidly re-equipped many of his men from the vast stocks of captured Roman arms, implying that the reverse was true.[5]

At Cannae, Roman and allied soldiers were defeated by a smaller number of courageous foes, following superior 'higher-level' tactics assigning different contingents to distinct pre-planned battlefield roles: containing, outflanking and enveloping.[6] They were also defeated by superior training, especially at unit level: moving large parts of armies around the battlefield in a coordinated manner during the fighting, without dissolving into chaos, required practice and skill. This is seen, above all, in the actions of the Carthaginian cavalry. These men had the double task of defeating the flanking Roman horse, and then, while the Numidian horse pursued the Roman/Italian cavalry off the field, Hannibal's Celtic and Iberian horse had to disengage, reform, wheel and fall on the rear of the legions, completing the envelopment.

On average, Roman and Italian soldiers may well have been fiercer individual fighters with greater stamina than the Africans, Gauls and Iberians they faced, but the high-quality tactical training and discipline in action that Hannibal's troops exhibited in their serial victories in Italy, including annihilating a bigger Roman army, show that the Carthaginian's men were, at the time, the better soldiers. They possessed this superiority due to stark contrasts in the quality and methods of generalship, and consequent conceptions of training and tactics.

On entering Italy, Hannibal's soldiers already comprised a well-established, battle-hardened army, combining experienced warriors displaying high morale, with a brilliant general well versed in sophisticated Hellenistic strategy and tactics. Hannibal and his soldiers knew each other well and displayed fierce mutual loyalty, bonds fostered by continuity and consistency of command under one charismatic individual. The result was one of the finest armies of antiquity, an achievement all the greater because it demanded the welding together of contingents even more ethnically diverse than those comprising Roman/Italian armies.

In contrast, Roman commanders were normally appointed for much shorter terms, leading Roman and Italian soldiers who remained essentially city militiamen, periodically mustered for war, lacking the continuity of professional service enjoyed by Hannibal's soldiers. The state's main army was usually led by the two consuls for the year. These magistrates changed annually and, if in the field together, shared or rotated command, a recipe for trouble if they disagreed – which, as political rivals, was likely. Senatorial competition bred jealousy and mutual suspicion, militating against development or promotion of exceptional military talent. It was extremely difficult for exceptional generals to appear, or to flourish. Given aristocrats' emphasis on the ways of their ancestors, and the contempt they publicly expressed for the corruption of eastern potentates, it is unsurprising that Roman generals did not keep up with Hellenistic military developments in their approaches to waging battles, or in training their men accordingly. The results could be catastrophic, in terms of tactics and also of intelligence failures: Trasimene was a vast ambush, which the Romans failed to detect.

✝

If Hannibal repeatedly exhibited such superiority on the battlefield, why did he lose the war? While individual generalship is vital to success in war, it is only one of many factors, all of which need to be in place, especially in a prolonged death-struggle such as the Second Punic War.

Polybius argued that Hannibal was only successful against Rome so long as the Romans had no comparable general.[7] In Scipio, afterwards surnamed Africanus, Rome found one. However, by the time the two great generals actually faced each other at Zama, Rome had already virtually won the war. She had destroyed the Carthaginian empire in Spain, eroded Hannibal's strength in Italy, forced his withdrawal by invading Africa, and obliged him to stand and fight with a much weakened army. Scipio's victory at Zama was a great achievement, but was the *coup de grâce* completing a triumph largely achieved by a combination of factors and means in addition to his generalship.

Scipio had certainly masterminded Rome's conquest of Carthaginian Spain on the ground, but was implementing senatorial strategy. Both sides, drawing lessons from their previous war, exhibited grand strategic vision, projecting armies on other continents, seeking to destroy the enemy's capacity and will to fight. However, in the long term Rome proved more capable of putting her plans into effect, and achieving her goals. Hannibal was able to get into Italy, but Carthage proved unable to reinforce him; Rome achieved command of the sea and of the land routes between Iberia and Italy (preventing Hannibal receiving reinforcements from Spain or the Po valley), and conquered Carthage's Iberian resource base, ultimately forcing Hannibal's withdrawal by counter-invading Africa again.

The Romans were able to achieve all this because of excellent logistical skills, in turn underpinned by a vast resource base, which, in a renewed war of attrition, they proved able to protect where the Carthaginians failed to defend their own. Even with an enemy rampaging past their gates and through the territories that provided their soldiers and sinews of war, the Romans remained able not only to keep most of their allies loyal, but to project armies in distant lands. This contrast highlights Roman superiority in determination. As their physical training brought them exceptional physical stamina for battle, so intensive ideological indoctrination gave Romans the psychological stamina to endure long wars, and to withstand reverses which would break others. Polybius remarked on the Romans' invincible self-belief, and determination that once they had decided to do something, no power on earth would stop them –

qualities that often brought spectacular success, but could equally lead to utter disaster.[8]

Before the clash with Carthage, Romans were obsessed not just with war, but with successful war – with Victory, personified as an oft-depicted goddess bearing the victor's laurel crown to give to the next senatorial general overcoming a foreign foe (Fig. 24). During the middle republic Rome saw innumerable triumphal processions parading the spoils of war through her streets; such spoils were then used to bedeck private senatorial mansions and public buildings such as the *rostra*, the public-speaking stage named after the warship rams mounted on it. Yet more booty went to finance construction of the 'manubial' temples – shrines dedicated in thanks for success in battle – which sprang up in ever-increasing numbers. The very

24. Roman *Victoriatus* coin minted in Spain in 211 BC, showing the goddess Victoria placing a laurel crown on a battle-trophy made of captured enemy arms.

urban landscape of the city became one vast celebration of Roman victory. Having Hannibal loose in Italy further intensified Roman determination to the point of fanaticism.

The Romans – senators, the people in general and fighting men in particular – refused to admit defeat. In a famous exhibition of steadfastness, while Hannibal sat before the walls of Rome (too big for his army to besiege), the land on which he was camped was sold for the normal peacetime price.[9] However, Roman determination was underpinned by a calculus of fear. They simply had to gamble on ultimate victory, remaining defiant; to negotiate would be a public admission of weakness, risking collapse of their power in Italy, and almost certain destruction of the City. Yet maintaining resolve while fearful *is* real courage.

Hannibal failed in part because he could not force the Romans to negotiate, let alone admit they were beaten. Refusing to concede defeat was an open secret of war of which Romans remained acutely aware in later centuries. Hannibal also failed to suborn enough of Rome's allies – and from those he did 'turn', he could not extract enough men to join him in the field. Given their own fierce pride, it is likely that an important reason that most Italians stayed loyal was that they resented foreign invasion as much as they feared or loved the Romans, and wanted vengeance for their own dead.

Despite appalling losses and humiliating tactical defeats at Hannibal's hands, the Romans demonstrated sustained superiority in all other areas of warfare and politics, from the fielding of fierce soldiers with fine arms and adaptable fighting techniques, to logistics and grand strategy. With all else in place, the Romans were able to sustain the war until they found a world-class general, who understood complex tactics and could train his troops to execute them – someone who could lead his soldiers to face Hannibal and his veterans on the battlefield with a real chance of winning.

In the struggle with Rome, great were the achievements of Hannibal, his family the Barcids and Carthage. Yet Carthage had only one Hannibal; Rome needed only to find one Scipio, to lead her fine and innumerable soldiers. Rome rapidly recovered from Cannae; Carthage never recovered from Zama. Polybius divided the credit for Roman victory at Zama between Scipio and his men, 'the steadiness of their ranks and the superiority of their weapons'.[10]

## Consequences of the Second Punic War

After Zama, victorious Rome projected her power beyond Italy and the islands to western Europe, North Africa, the Aegean and western Asia. Suddenly she was a major force on three continents, an emergent superpower. Perhaps most surprising is that Rome did not destroy Carthage immediately, although she permanently crippled her, removing her military capacities, seizing her empire in Spain and loading her with vast war indemnities.

However, if Rome emerged more powerful than ever, she was both damaged and transformed by the struggle with Hannibal. While the devastation of Italy was materially compensated by wealth seized overseas, and manpower losses eventually replaced, the collective shock at prolonged invasion, and private grief over tens of thousands of dead, had a major impact on the Roman/Italian psyche. Roman elation at their victory was largely a reaction to deeply ingrained fear, having had *Hannibal ad portas*, 'Hannibal at the gates'. Fear of outsiders, not least *terror Gallicus*, had long underpinned Roman aggression ('do unto others before they do unto you'). Zama left Carthage a broken reed, yet Rome remained deeply paranoid about the Punic bogeyman during the following decades, epitomized by the statesman Cato the Elder endlessly intoning 'Carthage must be destroyed' in senate speeches. Rome ultimately drove its old enemy to a third war (149–146 BC) widely regarded as shameful. Despite her status as sole superpower, ploughing the ruins of Carthage with salt did not end Roman paranoia. Not least, the Gauls still lurked beyond the Alps.

Rome also imitated and learned much from the Carthaginians and their allies. Most grimly, the Punic Wars saw Carthage and Rome refine each other's ruthlessness to the highest pitch. Voltaire, satirizing the scandalous shooting for alleged cowardice of the British admiral George Byng in 1757, scathingly observed how 'in this country, it is good to kill an admiral from time to time, to encourage the others'.[11] The Carthaginians pursued a similar policy, crucifying generals considered not to have tried hard enough. Rome probably adopted this gruesome judicial punishment from Carthage. Carthage offered Rome other lessons in brutality, as though they were needed, not least in the savagery of the Truceless War (241–237 BC) that she fought against her own mercenaries after the First Punic War.

Important martial exchanges between the two states went much further than Scipio imitating Hannibal's tactics. Among the most significant areas of mutual influence was weaponry.

Exchanges in military technology and technique were a two-way street. Hannibal's soldiers adopted Roman arms, but the Romans proved far keener to innovate during this era, copying enemy equipment, adapting and sometimes improving it. In describing how, soon after Zama, the Romans copied Greek cavalry spears and shields as soon as they realized they were superior, Polybius noted that '...no nation has ever surpassed them in readiness to adopt new fashions from other people, and to imitate what they see is better in others than themselves'.[12] Notably, naval warfare and complex sieges were whole new arenas of martial technique and technology that Roman soldiers and commanders mastered during this period.

In the First Punic War, Rome realized that, in fighting for domination of Sicily, she would have to take on the powerful Carthaginian fleet, despite having effectively no tradition or experience of naval warfare. She could draw on the expertise of her Italian maritime allies, but none of these possessed quin-quiremes, the large state-of-the-art warships used by Carthage and Hellenistic fleets. The Romans boldly resolved that problem when the fortunes of war gave them a beached Carthaginian quinquireme; they studied it and rapidly built 100 copies.[13] Adapting the warships to suit their own style by adding the *corvus* (boarding bridge), through their inventiveness the Romans beat the Carthaginians at their own game.

During the Second Punic War, Marcellus' legions besieging Syracuse in 212 BC were thoroughly demoralized by elaborate defences and ingenious weapons invented by Archimedes, brilliant Hellenistic scientist and military engineer. (The Romans eventually took the city by surprise assault.) Just as they had quickly mastered naval warfare in the third century BC, so during the second the Romans would adopt Hellenistic torsion artillery and siege tactics.

It was also during the first two Punic Wars, and the intervening conquest of the Gauls of the Po valley, that Roman legionaries – and their Italian allies – acquired key items of the 'classic' panoply which they used to conquer the Mediterranean, and which Polybius described. To the big body shield and the *pilum* – the heavy shield- and-armour-piercing, charge-disrupting javelin already carried by some legionaries – were added mail shirts copied and adapted from the Gauls. Perhaps the most important Roman innovation of the Punic Wars, symbolically and practically, was the adoption of a new kind of sword.

Romans and their Italian allies went into the Punic Wars without the *gladius Hispaniensis*, the famed 'Spanish sword' of the later republic. Polybius placed its adoption as a consequence of the war with Hannibal – which makes sense, since this was the first period in which Romans came into intensive contact with

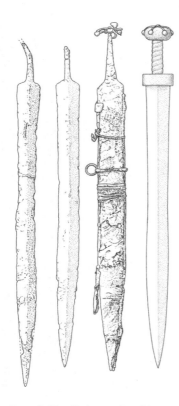

troops from Iberia.[14] During the sack of Syracuse, Archimedes fell victim to the sword of a common Roman soldier; perhaps he had the dubious honour of being among the first of the many thousands who would die by the new Roman weapon. By the end of the Second Punic War it appears to have been in general use among infantry and cavalry alike.

This was the most famous example of Roman adoption and adaptation of enemy military technology. Only in the last twenty years have we identified actual examples of such weapons.[15] These have proved surprisingly different from the long-known Mainz-type swords that succeeded them in early imperial times. As yet, we have no third-century examples showing exactly what the earliest Roman versions of the 'Spanish sword' were like. However, several weapons believed to be later republican examples have recently been identified from second and earlier first century BC contexts (Fig. 25). One, complete with a frame-scabbard and suspension rings prefiguring early imperial weapons, was found on the island of Delos. Apparently buried as a result of fighting in 69 BC, it has given its name to the type. Among the oldest examples yet identified are blades from Šmihel, Croatia, deposited with other Roman arms as the result of an unknown mid-second-century siege.[16] Now we know what they look like,

25. Recently identified examples of the famed republican *gladius Hispaniensis*: two from Šmihel, Croatia and another still in its ring-mounted scabbard from Delos, Greece, together with a reconstruction. (Scale 1:8)

others have been identified, and more will follow.[17]

These weapons had two-edged blades, quite slender and generally of diamond section. Most were slightly waisted or 'leaf-shaped', with a long tapering point. The Delos example had a blade *c.* 625 mm (2 ft 1 in) long, *c.* 48 mm (2 in) wide, the Šmihel blades 622–661 mm (25–27 in) long, and 40–45 mm (1.5–1.8 in) wide.[18] Hilts are not yet well attested, but traces on the Delos sword, and one depicted on the 'Altar of Domitius Ahenobarbus', suggest it was already the three-part assembly of wood or perhaps other materials seen in imperial times. The Delos pommel was studded with rivets. This sword was still in its scabbard, suspended via two rings on either side, prefiguring early imperial scabbards. It may be that all four rings were never used at once; the arrangement may have been to allow the scabbard to be worn face-outwards on either left or right.[19] Monuments of the later republic show the sword was worn on a waist belt.

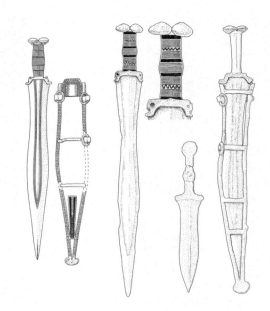

26. The Iberian ancestry of the Roman 'Spanish sword' and accompanying dagger, the *pugio*. Left, short sword and ring-mounted frame scabbard from a grave at Altillo del Cerropozo, Guadalajara. Centre, a weapon from Monreal de Ariza, Zaragoza, with enlargement (not to scale) of the two-colour inlay to the grip, also seen on scabbards. Right, sword and accompanying dagger from a grave at Osma, Soria. All date from around the third century BC. (Scale 1:8)

In what sense was the new sword 'Spanish'? In the Iberian peninsula, suitable precursors for the general form of the sword blade are waisted double-edged weapons, known from the fifth century BC to the crucial third century (Fig. 26). Many come from cemeteries of Celtiberians and related peoples of the interior (distinct from the ethnic Iberians towards the Mediterranean, although henceforth I use 'Iberian' in its ancient geographic sense of the Iberian peninsula, modern Spain and Portugal). However, the putative third-century peninsular precursors diverge significantly from the newly identified Roman swords, in having a completely different form of hilt, and especially in length.

Iberian blades were significantly shorter, some only *c*. 300 mm (1 ft) long, but most 400–500 mm (16–20 in).[20] If Romans were using *xiphoi* hitherto, then known examples suggest that they were accustomed to blades more in the 450–550 mm (18–22 in) range or longer, and this is one important aspect in which they are likely to have adapted Iberian designs rather than simply adopted them. Another major element of Spanish design they abandoned completely. In contrast to the all-iron Iberian hilts, Roman weapons had a wood or bone assembly of quite different form, probably already comprising the separate guard, grip and pommel familiar from imperial times. In blade shape, the second-century Roman swords are similar to the Iberian weapons, in that they are double-edged and tend to be waisted, but then so were *xiphoi*; however, it may have been especially significant that the Roman blades are more like the Iberian in tending to have proportionately longer, narrower points.

In summary, the unsheathed Roman weapon did not look very obviously 'Spanish'. On the other hand, in its scabbard and hanging from its belt, it looked unmistakably Iberian to contemporaries. The ring-mounted frame scabbard (see Fig. 25) confirms the literary tradition of the weapon's Iberian origins,[21] something underlined by the unambiguously Iberian type of dagger, the *pugio*, worn with it. The Romans took the *pugio* almost unaltered from its Iberian prototypes, retaining for centuries the blade shape, complex layered grip, ring-mounted metal frame scabbard and contrasting inlaid decoration (see Fig. 26).

The 'Spanish sword' did not have to be adopted along with the frame scabbard or ring mounts, let alone the accompanying *pugio*. After all, the Romans abandoned a hilt design that did not suit. These other elements seem to have been adopted for reasons connected with visual display. It was important not only to possess a sword that was in some sense 'Spanish', but (especially as it now lacked an Iberian hilt) also for its accoutrements to advertise the origin and special deadliness of the sheathed blade. To achieve this, along with the sword itself the Romans adopted with limited modification a complete material package of Iberian 'sword culture'.

So, in what sense, apart from associations conjured by sight of its accoutrements, was the Roman *gladius Hispaniensis* 'Spanish'? A fragment from an otherwise-lost section of Polybius preserved in a Byzantine source provides important clues:

> The Celtiberians differ greatly from others in their manufacture of swords (*machairai*). For it [sic] has an effective point, and a down-strike that is powerful from both hands. Whereby the Romans, putting away their ancestral swords as a result of the affairs involving Hannibal, adopted instead those of the Iberians [sic]. And while they took over its manufacture, they are [sic] no way capable of imitating the very excellence of the iron and the rest of the *epimeleia*.[22]

The last word translates as 'careful attention', or better in this context 'elaborate finishing', which likely refers to the simpler hilts of known Roman examples, and lack of the fine working of the blade surface seen on Iberian weapons. Overall, the passage suggests that the Romans imitated both the general form and especially the fundamental manufacturing techniques used in these Hispanic swords, even if they could not quite match the quality of the steel produced (which may have depended on ores available in Spain as much as on the skills of craftsmen in smelting and treating metal from them), and did not master – more likely, opted not to bother with – many details of finishing or embellishment. Their focus was on acquiring desired mechanical traits, adaptation rather than slavish copying. They will have learned these from Iberian swordsmiths recruited or captured in war.

In the absence (yet) of metallurgical analysis, my view is that this, and another passage in Polybius (below), together suggest that the main special qualities of Iberian swords that caught the Romans' attention were in part the form of the blade, which suited Roman fighting tastes in shape (longer, narrower point) if not size. However, a relatively modest change of shape from the *xiphos* was hardly revolutionary. Rather, the secret lay in the combination of form with superior methods of manufacture, resulting in a sword which was deadlier both because of improved shape, and because it was markedly stronger than previous Roman weapons. Elsewhere, in discussing the fighting excellence of Roman legionaries, Polybius highlights the confidence engendered in them by their large body shields and the strength of their swords, which could withstand repeated blows.[23] Here, and in a further famous passage describing legionaries' arms,[24] he emphasizes the strength of the blade, which by implication was less likely to bend or break, and perhaps retained its edge and point better, than other weapons during the intensive sword-fighting Romans preferred. The 'Spanish-ness' of the 'Spanish sword', then, probably lay mainly in the technology of its manufacture. Therefore its nature, disguised by a non-Iberian hilt, had to be advertised by Spanish-looking accoutrements. There is a direct analogy here with the reputation of 'Toledo blades' of later centuries, a byword for excellence in swordsmithing. Morphologically it is perhaps best to think of the new Roman *gladius Hispaniensis* as an evolved hybrid of Iberian weapons and *xiphoi*.

What has surprised observers is the length of Delos-type weapons, significantly greater than the familiar early imperial 'short stabbing swords': they are as long as some imperial '*spathae*'. If, as is fairly certain, such blades do represent the *gladius Hispaniensis*, then – given its wicked point – it is wholly believable that it was a devastating thrusting weapon. Indeed, there is specific literary evidence that the Romans were taught to thrust with the sword in combat. In battle against the Gallic Insubres in 223 BC (and so, incidentally, according to Polybius before they adopted the 'Spanish sword'), Polybius reports:

> The Romans…having excellent points to their swords, used them not to cut but to thrust: and by thus repeatedly hitting the breasts and faces of the enemy, they eventually killed the greater number of them.[25]

However, Polybius explains that this was the result of specific instructions on fighting techniques and general tactics given to the troops by the tribunes before the battle. These tactical instructions were customized on the spot for fighting Gauls equipped with long slashing swords, and Roman victory was credited to these fighting techniques, for the Roman general Flaminius had made an error in drawing up his troops where the maniples would not be able to perform a standard Roman tactic, of limited withdrawal (i.e. battlefield reliefs). The implication of all this is that thrusting with the sword was perhaps a standard, but not necessarily universal, practice for Roman soldiers. And indeed, elsewhere Polybius emphasized that Romans used their swords for both thrust *and* cut.[26]

He also noted the versatility in both modes of the swords of Hannibal's Spanish troops at Cannae.[27] The length of the blades thought to be later republican *gladii Hispanienses*, and their slight waisting (putting more mass towards the tip), are consistent with a weapon also intended to slash. Suited to foot combat, it was a practical cavalry weapon too, capable of inflicting the injuries which so shocked Philip v of Macedon, many of which were clearly cuts, not thrust-wounds (p. 39).

## The perils of military success

It was not just in arms and fighting techniques that Romans and Italians learned hard lessons about war during the third century bc. It was also Hannibal's sophisticated Hellenistic-style approach to warfare. This proved the most diffi-cult aspect for the Romans to adapt to. It required new, 'higher-level' tactics involving complex battlefield manoeuvres of different formations beyond those familiar to the Romans, and their traditional political system made command-ers resistant to it. While they showed political and strategic skill, they also exhibited shortcomings arising from their constitution as a city-state built around the rivalries of competing aristocratic clans. If their 'grand strategy' was relatively ambitious in fielding armies on multiple fronts, and their logistics com-petent in enabling this, their approach to battle was relatively simple. Even if, as Sentinum suggests, the flexible manipular legion established a structure capable of complex manoeuvres over and above simple 'battlefield reliefs', most Roman generals were more accustomed simply to deploying their men in traditional formation, exhorting them and leading them forward bravely; this, and little more, was thought to be their legitimate role. Hannibal was able to take advan-tage of this lack of imagination to trap and destroy brave but lumbering and predictable Roman armies. Their traditional career structure also made it diffi-cult for most senators to accrue much command experience before leading armies as consuls. Mutual surveillance of rival senators, keen to ensure that com-mands and glory were shared out and should not accrue too much to any individual, made them highly suspicious of exceptional talent. If both consuls took the field together, shared command often resulted in friction, even dan-gerous paralysis. These could prove disastrous limitations when facing experienced, tested, professional generals like Hannibal. However, eventually Scipio showed that a Roman general could learn Hellenistic tactics, and equally important, train his men to carry them out.

The rise of Scipio was, in a sense, another example of imitating foreign ways: promoting precocious military talent. Young Scipio developed a reputa-tion for exemplary courage and leadership, which, in the crisis of Hannibal's invasion, gave him command of Rome's army in Spain when, by normal rules, he was far too junior. This, precipitated only by the depth of the military crisis, threatened the traditional structure of Roman government – marked by turn-taking at commands, and progression by seniority rather than ability – and it was vigorously resisted. Scipio long overrode such resistance due to popular pressure during extraordinary crisis.

It is significant that, made consul for 205 BC on the prestige of his success in conquering Carthaginian Spain, Scipio went over the heads of the senate to appeal to the people – effectively, to the soldiers – to support his plan to invade Africa. Popular hatred and fear of Carthage and a desire for revenge carried Scipio and his army to Africa, and smouldered in Roman public opinion thereafter until Carthage was finally subjected. However, such unorthodoxy inflamed senatorial suspicion and jealousy, with a sad outcome for Scipio. Senatorial competition had constrained even Scipio, after Zama. It was plausibly suggested that after his victory he chose to negotiate with Carthage partly because he knew how prolonged and bitterly fought a siege would be, but especially because he feared being robbed of final glory over the Carthaginians if (as was likely) he was replaced as commander by a senatorial rival before the city fell.[28]

Scipio's career proved an innovation too far for Rome's suspicious aristocratic traditionalists. Like Hannibal, the over-successful senator ended his days in exile. Subsequent Roman commanders often remained more concerned with their status among their peers and the gaze of their forefathers, than with contemporary military science or the capabilities of the enemy. Divided command, and bitter rivalry, long resulted in further military disasters, for example at Arausio in 105 BC, when two consular commanders failed to cooperate, and their armies were smashed piecemeal by the migrating Cimbri and Teutones, who threatened Italy.[29] However, subsequent events would also show that senators feared the rise of over-mighty generals with good reason. Ambitious men seeking to outdo Scipio in the burgeoning empire became a central, increasingly deadly internal threat to the later republic. The Cimbri and Teutones were eventually annihilated by the upstart general Gaius Marius, whose tradition-breaking career resulted in civil war (p. 97).

More to the taste of traditionalists was M. Claudius Marcellus, a figure seen as an old-style republican hero (Fig. 27). Winner of the greatest and rarest of all battlefield honours, the *spolia opima* (bestowed on a commander who personally killed and despoiled the enemy general in combat),[30] he also conveniently met a warrior's end in battle. Rather than surviving too long to wield vast personal prestige to the chagrin of his peers, he became a safely departed model of ancient *virtus* to emulate. Yet, like Scipio, Marcellus' actions also pointed to the future.

Conqueror of Syracuse, he paraded through Rome the fabulous riches seized from the city, not least many superb Greek statues. This display apparently changed Roman

27. A later republican silver *denarius* commemorating Marcellus' dedication of his *spolia opima* in the Temple of Capitoline Jupiter at Rome.

attitudes to Greek culture,[31] awakening a taste for Hellenistic splendour, which became a thirst satiated by sacking more Greek cities. Marcellus also dedicated a 'manubial' temple (i.e. funded by the spoils), itself a traditional action, but its double dedication to *honos* and *virtus* (honour and manliness), was a controversial innovation. In addition, he commissioned the first *fabula praetexta*, a drama celebrating his own military exploits, Nevius' *Clastidium*.[32]

Senators were understandably concerned if any one of their number achieved too much military glory. This destabilized the tradition of power-sharing, while a very successful general might also be tempted to misuse for personal gain his influence not only over Rome's citizens under arms, but also her allies. It raised the prospect of treason. Roman commanders were now players in the world of Hellenistic *condottieri* and kings whose power was personal, absolute and rested prominently on their soldiers and personal military prowess. These offered dangerous examples for ambitious Roman generals. Little wonder, then, that the senate reacted with alarm to the rise of Scipio, especially when they saw how closely his soldiers were attached to him. Allegedly, some of his foreign allied troops wanted to bestow on him the title of king, anathema to senators, and indeed probably to Scipio himself. He supposedly suggested a less provocative alternative, and so his men proclaimed him *imperator*, meaning victorious general.[33] Thus was born a new and lasting honorific, which subsequent generals sought to earn from their *milites*. It was a mark of the growing direct rapprochement between generals and soldiers, which bypassed the senate. And thus, also, was born the title which would later evolve in meaning to give us the English word 'emperor'.

Besides too-powerful peers, senators also continued to have reason to watch the ordinary *milites*. The sustained self-motivation of Roman troops, invaluable when unleashed on the battlefield, had its alternate Janus-face in the problem of controlling them the rest of the time. Even Scipio could lose the loyalty of his men: in Spain in 206 BC part of his army, disgruntled at the perceived lack of reward for their achievements, 'seceded' and built their own camp, chose their own centurions and officers, and took new military oaths, in effect illegally 'firing' their general.[34]

Rogue *milites* would become a standing peril, and this was already an issue before the Punic Wars, as shocking events at Rhegium had demonstrated. During the war against Pyrrhus Rome sent 4,000 soldiers, under 'one Decius, a native of Campania' who had apparently won Roman citizenship, to protect the friendly city of Rhegium on the toe of Italy.[35] Rhegium lay almost opposite Sicilian Messana, then in the hands of the Mamertines (p. 72). The example of those renegade mercenaries and the wealth of Rhegium proved too tempting for the Roman garrison, which probably included Italians who, when not called up for 'federal' service, perhaps freelanced as mercenaries themselves. Like the Mamertines, they violently seized the place they were sent to protect. The Roman government acted with extreme force against this rogue contingent, sending an army to retake the city in 270 BC. In the ensuing siege most of the rebel soldiers fought to the death against their compatriots, knowing their fate if captured. Still some 300 prisoners were returned to Rome, flogged and beheaded.

The Romans had to make an example of these men, to safeguard military discipline, and to restore their good name among the allies. Doubtless they were also anxious to protect their self-image as god-fearing, just and trustworthy. However, the garrison of Rhegium simply achieved what an earlier Roman garrison had plotted to do in Capua (p. 64). Whatever the austere values of senatorial commanders may have been, their troops were always looking for opportunities to indulge their violence and rapacity. Roman and Italian soldiers garrisoned in rich Greek cities were like kids in a candy store, with a sweet tooth – and a switchblade.

## Humbling Alexander's successors, 200–167 BC

> The progress of the Romans was not due to chance and was not
> involuntary, as some among the Greeks choose to think, but…by
> schooling themselves in such vast and perilous enterprises it was
> perfectly natural that they not only gained the courage to aim at
> universal dominion, but executed their purpose.
> POLYBIUS 1.63[36]

Having vanquished Carthage and established mastery of the western Mediterranean, Rome now faced the great, established powers that ruled the eastern half of the common sea. Alexander's empire had fragmented into three successor states comprising, in addition to the original Macedonian kingdom that continued to dominate Greece, the vast Seleucid empire reaching from the Mediterranean to Afghanistan, and fabulously wealthy Ptolemaic Egypt (Fig. 28).

Even before Zama, Rome had clashed indecisively with Macedon, which had, in normal opportunistic fashion, allied with Hannibal in hopes of exploiting Rome's weakness, compelling pre-emptive Roman action. In the circumstances of the era, sooner or later major wars between the new Roman power and the Hellenistic states were inevitable. The question was, could the Romans defeat the descendants of Alexander's soldiers, who had conquered the Persian empire? In particular, could they face the terrifying Macedonian-style phalanx perfected by Philip II and Alexander the Great, a tight-packed formation of infantry soldiers that bristled with row upon row of long pikes reaching several metres beyond its front? The phalanx dominated the battlefield for nearly two centuries.

The Hellenistic world was both rich and highly cultured but, as in Italy, glory was prized by its many soldiers, generals, *condottieri* and kings; wars were frequent and often ferocious.[37] Warfare was professionalized, fought largely by career soldiers, especially Greeks and Macedonians who served in the phalanx, and contingents of mercenaries such as Gauls and Thracians supplemented with exotica such as war elephants and scythed chariots. Commanded by professional generals, the large, sophisticated and innovatory Hellenistic armies expected to make mincemeat of barbarians, including the upstart Romans.

Probably during the Hannibalic War Rome developed the legionary organization soon to be famously described by Polybius. He states that a legion nominally comprised 4,200 infantry, in three main lines: ten 120-man maniples of younger *hastati* ('spearmen') at the front, then a similar line of experienced

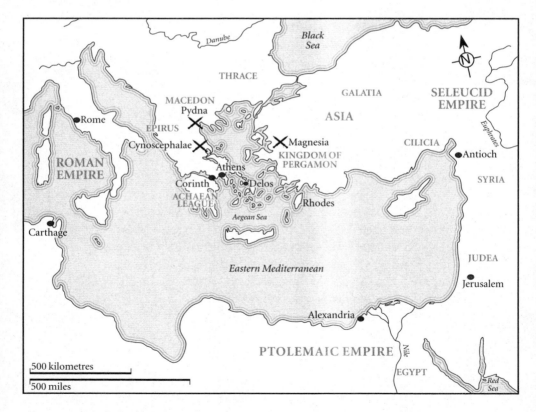

28. The Hellenistic east, showing the peoples, states and places mentioned in the text.

*principes* ('chief men'), and a rear line of 600 *triarii* ('third line men'), the oldest soldiers, presumably in ten small maniples of sixty each (perhaps due to attrition of older age-sets by death and invaliding). All were armed with the 'Spanish sword', long oval body-shield (*scutum*) and bronze helmet, the *hastati* and *principes* carrying *pila* (heavy javelins), the *triarii* retaining thrusting spears. Armour comprised a bronze chest-protector, or coat of iron mail for the wealthier men (one of the last vestiges of organization according to wealth, now largely superseded by age and experience, although soldiers were still recruited from propertied citizens). The three lines were screened by the youngest and poorest soldiers, unarmoured, javelin-armed *velites* ('cloak men'), 1,200 by simple arithmetic. The legion also possessed 300 cavalry.[38]

If the Roman people were for taking the sword to Africa in 205 BC because of their hatred and fear of Carthage, by 200, with Hannibal humbled, they were also tired enough of war to resist another against Macedon. Yet opinion in the senate, encouraged by appeals from the Greeks for help, was for supposedly 'pre-emptive' action against Macedon, which had allied with Hannibal, and against Antiochus of the Seleucid empire, who gave sanctuary to Rome's exiled nemesis.

At Cynoscephalae in 197 BC the Roman legions shocked the Greek world by defeating the legendary Macedonian phalanx, through tactical flexibility and a measure of luck.[39] Seleucid interference in Greece, with Hannibal's presence at the Seleucid court fuelling Roman fears, led to another major Roman victory over a Hellenistic army at Magnesia in Anatolia in 190 BC, leaving Rome dominant in the Aegean and Anatolia and the Ptolemies of Egypt seeking her friendship. That their previous victories were no flukes was confirmed at Pydna in 168 BC when, for the second and final time, Roman soldiers took on the Macedonian phalanx, and destroyed it (Fig. 29).

29. Some of the earliest surviving representations of *milites* in combat. These scenes appear on surviving fragments of the monument set up at Delphi in Greece to commemorate Aemilius Paullus' defeat of the Macedonian phalanx at Pydna in 168 BC.

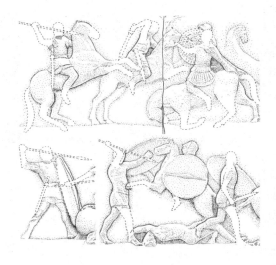

How did the Romans achieve this series of earth-shaking military victories? Polybius describes the organization of the phalanx, and also its weakness; it required unobstructed flat ground to operate.[40] If it became disrupted, or was outflanked, the phalangites would be slaughtered. At Cynoscephalae the Romans did outflank part of the Macedonian phalanx, and caught the rest not yet in battle formation. At Pydna the flexibly organized legionaries were able to exploit gaps in the phalanx caused by rough ground to get in among the otherwise lightly armoured phalangites, who, once their rigid formation was disrupted, entangled in their mass of pikestaffs, were almost helpless. Destruction of the phalanx at Pydna was as much down to the weapons, training, fighting techniques and 'low-level' tactics of the ordinary Roman and Italian soldiers as to generals and strategy, aspects all emphasized by Polybius.

At the end of his account of Zama, Polybius reflected on how Roman soldiers fought, an account doubtless coloured by his later eyewitness observations, during Rome's humbling of the Hellenistic world:

> The order of a Roman force in battle makes it very difficult to break through, for without any change it enables every man individually and in common with his fellows to present a front in any direction, the maniples which are nearest to the danger turning themselves by a single movement to face it. Their arms also give the men both protection and confidence owing to the size of the shield and owing to the sword being strong enough to endure repeated blows. So that for these reasons they are formidable antagonists very difficult to overcome.[41]

Comparing Roman tactics with the rigidly organized Hellenistic phalanx, he notes:

> With the Romans each soldier in full armour also occupies a space three feet wide. However, according to the Roman methods of fighting each man makes his movements individually: not only does he defend his body with his long shield, constantly moving it to meet the threatened blow, but he uses his sword both for cutting and for thrusting…[42]

Polybius directly links Rome's battlefield success to the quality of Roman arms, which also contributed to the high morale of *milites*. Through their series of earth-shattering victories Roman soldiers established a moral ascendancy over the Hellenistic kingdoms, despite their abandonment of the phalanx and reform of their armies to imitate Roman arms and tactics (Fig. 30).[43] Henceforth, Roman generals and armies came to expect to win, and many enemies at least half anticipated defeat before battle was engaged.[44] Rome was now a world-class imperial power, whose dominance was underlined by the double atrocity of Carthage and Corinth in 146 BC (p. 38).

30. Later Hellenistic soldiers –
Ptolemaic, Seleucid, or
mercenaries – probably second
century BC, from painted funeral
*stelae* found at Sidon, Lebanon.
Salmas (left) has a Roman-style
mail shirt and shield.
Dioskourides of Balboura
(right) wields a sword of
uncertain type.

In seeking to understand the phenomenon of Roman power, it is instructive to consider it in relation to what was happening in adjacent regions at the time. While the Middle East had known major empires for many centuries, the Aegean and Italy had not. However, Rome's ascent in Italy was roughly contemporaneous with the rise of empires elsewhere in the Classical world. This was no coincidence. The rise of the Classical world appears to correlate with changes in the long-term climatic cycle, which brought better conditions for agriculture, certainly to Europe and probably to adjacent regions, during the later first millennium BC and lasting through the early centuries AD.[45] This probably facilitated the markedly increased settlement and population density seen in the Greek world and Italy, and also elsewhere in Europe from Iberia and Gaul to Britain, reflecting economic growth that permitted (or obliged) Iron Age peoples to move at varying speeds towards state formation and urbanization.

As soon as city-states appeared in the Aegean and central Mediterranean, they displayed a tendency to accrete into larger groupings, forming multi-state leagues and empires. The attraction of larger blocs – not least in terms of collective military power – was considerable, especially for those who controlled them. Among the Greeks, there were some voluntary federations, such as Polybius' own Achaean league.[46] However, most were dominated by one especially powerful state. During the fifth and fourth centuries BC, Athens, Sparta and Thebes at various times dominated Greece, with constellations of more-or-less willing allies or subjects. Then the Aegean Greeks were all incorporated into the new Macedonian empire of Philip II and Alexander, leading swiftly to a devastating assault on the Achaemenid Persian empire. Rome's rise may be seen as the outcome of parallel processes occurring simultaneously in Italy.

As around the Aegean, in Italy too, growing populations, wealth and increasing political experience made larger political units and structures imaginable and practicable, perhaps inevitable. Had it not been for Rome, Italy would eventually have agglomerated into one or more larger states, perhaps around existing 'ethnic' leagues or, most likely, under some ambitious Hellenistic ruler such as Pyrrhus or Dionysius I of Syracuse; perhaps even Alexander himself, had he lived.[47]

Alexander's boundless ambition and brilliant generalship depended for success on the fighting qualities of the Macedonian army – and of the Greeks who fought alongside them. The Macedonians did not suppress Greek military traditions, but instead directed the martial proclivities of both Greeks and Macedonians against Persia, rather than each other. Alexander's imperial adventure simultaneously harnessed these ideologies and energies to mutually beneficial ends, simultaneously helping pacify Macedonian-ruled Greece. Macedon, then, provides a parallel and precedent for a 'semi-barbarian' state on the edge of the Greek world, which unified its neighbours to unleash world-conquering military power, through marshalling their aggression, and directing it outwards.

As we saw, the fact that Italy would turn out to be led by Rome only became apparent during the fourth century BC. However, Rome's peculiar dynamics took this further than any other state could have, and proved more durable; witness the rapid fragmentation of Alexander's sprawling empire. Counterfactual history – in which Rome was destroyed or permanently crippled by the Senones in 387 BC, or by Hannibal later – would probably have resulted in a patchwork of smaller kingdoms and empires, and no political unification for western Europe and the Mediterranean, a unique anomaly in long-term history.

## Masters of the known world 167–44 BC

After Pydna, having survived and beaten Hannibal, and having defeated or cowed all the other great empires of the Mediterranean, the Romans decided the fate of the known world. Greeks reflected that the name *Roma* sounded like a word meaning 'to force'.[48] Reflecting on their dramatic rise to unchallenged dominance, Romans came to believe, as imperialists often do, that such success 'obviously' must be divinely sanctioned; their 'manifest destiny' was to be *imperium sine fine* – empire without limit.

However, Rome's sole-superpower status did not result in rapid, systematic establishment of direct rule over the Mediterranean world. Complete reduction to provinces took about two centuries, a prolonged period of instability for the region and internally for Rome itself. Long before the process was complete, and as a direct consequence of empire, Rome was convulsed by civil wars, and emperors replaced the republic.

There were complex causes and consequences of Rome's hesitant consolidation of territorial empire, after her spectacular ascent to military dominance. The Roman general Flamininus' famous declaration of 'Freedom for the Greeks' (i.e. for the Aegean Greeks, from the rule either of Hellenistic kings or Rome: 196 BC), reflected touchy Roman self-consciousness in the presence of the acknowledged cultural leaders of their world.[49] But it also expressed Rome's long-held general wariness of the political and military commitments of direct rule overseas, especially over such quarrelsome city-states as those of old Greece. Engaged in apparently endless wars around their new provinces in Hispania, the Romans were also now dealing with peoples they saw as increasingly alien to Italian values: effete eastern Greeks, shifty orientals, and uncouth barbarians, all best kept at arms' length. So the Romans sought military hegemony instead of direct rule in the east, extending their alliance system to include powers great and small, like Rhodes, Pergamon and Ptolemaic Egypt, waging mostly cold war against the Seleucids, rattling the sword to get their way, and not hesitating to wield it when they were not obeyed.

Rome was wielding power without taking responsibility, an unstable situation with serious deleterious effects. Repeatedly Greek states appealed for Roman support against rivals, while others long hoped that Rome's dominance might yet be broken. This was how Corinth met her fate, after joining the Achaean League in a war against Roman hegemony. Rome limited potential rivals' naval power without projecting her own, resulting in a rise in large-scale piracy.

Unbridled power encouraged callousness, leading to atrocities and extreme treatment of subjects. Roman pretexts for attacks on cities and states became thinner, and looked increasingly driven by greed for material wealth and slaves. In 167 BC, with negligible justification, the Romans attacked Epirus and enslaved 150,000 people, an index of brutalization and rapacity foreshadowing the fates of Corinth and Carthage. The Hellenistic world maintained a busy slave trade, but Rome's wars flooded the market. Delos was said to be able to process thousands of slaves a day.[50] Mass importation of agricultural slaves amounted to large-scale forced migration, changing the demography of Italy.

Nevertheless, gradually Rome did eventually annexe the Mediterranean. Having seized Sicily, Sardinia and Corsica as consequences of the First Punic War, Rome's assault on Hannibal's resource-base in the Second resulted in new Roman provinces in the Iberian peninsula. Rome had already seized the Po valley from Gallic control, and increasingly interfered in the coastal strip of southern Gaul linking Italy with Spain, creating a territorial province there in the later second century BC. This, in turn, would prove the springboard for Rome's first ventures into transalpine Europe, notably Caesar's conquest of the rest of *Gallia Comata* ('Hairy Gaul') to the Rhine, and raids into Germany and Britain during the 50s BC. The years 167 to 44 BC would see annexation of almost all Europe west of the Rhine, huge regions with 'barbarian' populations. By the end of the period, Macedon, much of the Aegean and Asia Minor also comprised Roman provinces, as did parts of Africa and Syria; Rome had extinguished the rump of the Seleucid empire, too, which was simultaneously being overrun from the east by the Parthians. The rest of the Mediterranean littoral was reduced to client status. Ptolemaic Egypt was less a Roman ally than a protectorate. The course of expansion shows Roman imperialism lacked any systematic plan or continuity of policy. Conversion into territorial provinces was fitful, and, as we will see, largely unplanned by central government. Sometimes Rome acted out of necessity: for example, Macedon proved too troublesome to leave even nominally independent. Other major annexations, including Syria and Gaul between Provence and the Rhine, were personal initiatives of Roman governor/commanders seeking glory and wealth for themselves. Such actions, especially Caesar's aggression in Gaul, were fiercely denounced by some senators. These events were a result of the way Roman traditional politics were transfigured and increasingly destabilized, as Rome became a superpower.

And while the world suffered, without power to resist or prospect of redress, Rome and Italy were transformed by the fabulous booty of victory over the east. Traditionally austere Roman aristocratic behaviour was changed by the adoption of Hellenistic luxury lifestyles, resulting from greater exposure to them, and increased opportunity and inclination simply to seize their trappings as spoils of war: the general Mummius at Corinth showed sharp awareness of the monetary value of the Greek artworks he looted, but betrayed little interest in, or understanding of, their qualities or meanings. Contemporaries bewailed loss of traditional Roman morality, corrupted by riches and exposure to exotic foreign practices. The political and military consequences of the rapid, vast additional enrichment of the political elite were profound; we will return to these below. However, the impact of empire on lesser Romans and Italians who served as soldiers was equally far-reaching.

Roman commanders employed foreign mercenaries, but their own *milites* and Italian allies still formed the core of their armies and shared the booty, even if the lion's share went to the generals and the state. These men were instruments of Roman power, but as the second century BC wore on, the classes liable for military service also came to be seen as victims of its consequences. As they shed their blood for Rome, a perception arose that self-sufficient citizen-smallholders, traditional backbone of Rome's legions, were being forced off their lands by the rich. On the other hand, landless citizens yearned for a chance to make their fortunes soldiering, but remained excluded from service, feeding back into a looming recruitment crisis. At the same time, there was growing unrest among the Italian allies at being taken for granted in war, and denied full participation in the state. Deadly internal resentments were building.

### Soldiers and change in the later republic

In contrast to many of her foes, and paradoxically given her military dominance, republican Rome never formally retained professional soldiers, permanent regiments or armies. Nevertheless, the realities of distant, multi-year wars and the need for overseas garrisons made for increasing *de facto* continuity of military formations over periods of years. The traditional citizen militia was evolving towards a force of long-service quasi-professionals.

Soldiers of the middle republic continue to be anonymous to us. Although we have a few second-century reliefs showing groups of soldiers (see Figs 29 and 31), we have nothing like the military tombstones and hand-written records of imperial times. One *miles*, however, we do know something about. Livy preserves details of the remarkable career of Spurius Ligustinus, legionary and centurion. He was over fifty in 171 BC when he intervened in a dispute about legionary recruitment at Rome, citing his own record of service to the state.[51] Of Sabine stock, born shortly before Hannibal's invasion, he inherited a smallholding, and his unnamed wife bore him two daughters and six sons; all apparently survived childhood. He enlisted in 200 BC, and served two years in the ranks in Macedonia. For his courage the general Flamininus, who defeated Macedon and liberated Greece (for a while), promoted him junior centurion in his third year of service. On discharge in 195 he immediately volunteered for Spain, where his conduct attracted the consul Cato's notice, resulting in a more senior centurionate. He volunteered again to fight the Seleucids in 191, and was appointed first centurion of the *principes*. Discharged after Antiochus' defeat at Thermopylae, he served two more single campaigning seasons, followed by two further campaigns in Spain (182–80). This list does not account for all the twenty-two years' service he claimed. He had been chief centurion for four years, and received thirty-four awards for bravery, including six civic crowns. At the time these details were recorded, he was about to be made chief centurion of the First Legion in yet another campaign.

Such a career, recorded as an exemplar, was clearly exceptional. Ligustinus was the Roman ideal of a soldier, a respectable propertied citizen who could provide his own arms, with a smallholding on which he raised more sons for the legions. His wife must have been equally tough and resourceful, since her husband was away in the military for more than two-thirds of their marriage.

31. Relief from the so-called altar of Domitius Ahenobarbus, set up on the Campus Martius at Rome in the late second century BC and now in the Louvre, Paris. It shows the regular military census listing citizens liable to military service.

During these years, as the children grew they will have provided the labour to keep the farm going. Ligustinus' tiny plot – one *jugerum*, roughly half an acre or *c.* 0.25 hectares – was inadequate to sustain a family of ten. This is probably why he repeatedly volunteered for military service, for pay and booty. However, it also seems he enjoyed soldiering; he was clearly very good at it. Such a career shows that, if the Roman military remained formally a citizen militia from which armies were raised and disbanded as needed, wars were now so many, so large and so prolonged that professional soldiers were appearing in practice if not name. With ten campaigns remaining the tariff for aristocrats seeking a political career,[52] the Roman citizen body – and the Italian communities that still furnished half the armies – remained intensely militarized.

Yet few men were as fortunate as Ligustinus. Of course, most did not make the centurionate. Few will have seen their wives survive so many pregnancies, and so many children grow to adulthood. Those who died overseas of wounds or disease often left their families in financial crisis. During the lifetimes of Ligustinus' children, the Roman countryside slid into crisis.

The traditional view envisages Rome's domination of the Greek world bringing vast quantities of booty and enormous numbers of slaves into Italy, most going to make the powerful richer still, corrupting traditionally austere Roman *mores*, and altering the demography of the peninsula. The disasters inflicted by Hannibal, and the endless Mediterranean-wide wars of the following decades, placed a terrible strain on the old citizen militia system. The propertied smallholders who had traditionally formed the core of the legions found service ever harder, requiring absence from their farms not, as in early times, just for the summer months, but for years at a stretch, leaving their families to cope as best they could. Many fell into debt and had to sell up to rich men (especially senators) employing expendable chain-gangs of war slaves, who toiled and died in unimaginable privation on the expanding great estates.

This long-established interpretation has been challenged. The perceived shortage of soldiers may have arisen from growing reluctance to enlist for lengthening, more distant service, offering declining rewards (especially in the endless Spanish wars, where fighting barbarians offered little prospect of booty), rather than any great decline of the propertied classes liable to serve. The historian Nathan Rosenstein argues that the second-century wars may not have driven smallholders to the wall, but constant demands for military service may have made it hard for them to prosper. More may have become impoverished, while populations were also rising fast, despite military mortality.[53] Indeed, archaeological survey suggests that decline of small farms and the rise of vast slave-estates has been greatly exaggerated.[54] Paradoxically, given the scale of wars, the free rural population may even have expanded, leading to overpopulation. The result would have been growth in the numbers of landless citizens (how did Ligustinus' many sons cope after his death?).

The 'headcount' (landless citizens), too poor to provide their own arms, were not considered stakeholders in the state and were traditionally excluded from the privilege of serving in the armies. This exacerbated the long-lasting struggle for control of *ager publicus* – state-owned land in Italy, taken in war and disproportionately controlled by great senatorial families. Whatever the real dynamics of change, there was a powerful political perception of crisis, and pressure for land reform.

Attempts were made by the brothers Tiberius and Gaius Gracchus – grandsons of Scipio Africanus – to assuage popular land-hunger by redistributing public lands in Italy, or by establishing overseas colonies (a Greek idea, new to Rome, although the Romans had long planted colonies inside Italy, for military and political purposes). These initiatives were violently resisted by the nobility. Tiberius perished with 300 supporters in 133 BC; Gaius' death in 122 was followed by the summary execution of 3,000. Under the strains of adapting to imperial power, the republic began to unravel in bloodshed.

Soon after these events, military reforms created a key factor contributing to subsequent destruction of the republic. The state was gradually forced to recognize that it could no longer man the legions from propertied smallholders. It would have to do something hitherto only resorted to in dire emergencies like the aftermath of Cannae: open the ranks to landless citizens.

Pressures on recruitment and tactical developments led to a series of significant military reforms at the end of the second century BC, traditionally attributed to the populist 'new man', Gaius Marius. These were hastened by the huge migration of the Cimbri and Teutones from northern Europe towards the Mediterranean, which in 105 BC saw destruction of two Roman armies at Arausio (Orange) in Gaul, with casualties rivalling Cannae.[55] Terror of a massive barbarian invasion of Italy triggered important innovations, such as the consul Rutilius Rufus bringing in professional gladiator trainers to improve the swordsmanship of his troops.[56] However, it was Marius, already a war hero in Africa, who followed in Scipio's footsteps, winning an exceptional series of consecutive consulships during which his army destroyed the invaders in two major battles.

In working up his army for these campaigns, to make up the numbers of his propertied legionaries, Marius is also credited with opening the ranks to the unpropertied 'headcount', equipping them with arms furnished by the state.[57] This emergency measure rapidly became established practice, with far-reaching consequences (below). Simultaneous with abolition (more likely, quiet abandonment) of the property distinction which hitherto had determined the right to serve, was eradication of the age/wealth classes that marked out the different kinds of troops in the 'Polybian' legion. Henceforth all legionaries were equipped alike with mail, helmet, body shield, two *pila* and 'Spanish sword'. Marius was also credited with getting soldiers to carry more of their own kit on the march, earning them the nickname 'Marius' mules'. The legion's organization was also simplified now or soon after, certainly by the time of Caesar. Soldiers were henceforth organized into centuries of eighty men,[58] six of which formed a *cohors*, a formation apparently hitherto used by Roman allied contingents. Ten identical and interchangeable cohorts formed the new tactical subunits of the legion, larger, fewer and so more controllable than the many maniples of the old system. The result was an even more tactically flexible legion. From this time on, the eagle was the principal legionary standard.[59]

The new, perhaps somewhat more proletarian, soldiers of the reformed legions proved to be as good as the propertied men who still formed, perhaps, the majority of legionaries, but with a major and ominous difference. Undoubtedly, they fought well as proud Romans, but as a reward for their service to the state many hoped to get land to call their own. Unsurprisingly, they looked to their generals to act as their patrons in support of land grants for veterans. These ambitions, manipulated by commanders for their own reasons, became a significant factor in politics and civil war.

In the decades following the Marian reforms, which saw homogenization of the legions in arms and tactics, the other major traditional division within Roman armies – that between Romans and Italian allies – also disappeared. However, this was only achieved through the return of war to Italian soil.

During the second century BC, Rome's armies continued to include major contingents from the Italian allies. This fact had important domestic consequences, positive and negative. It continued to provide a shared outlet for the martial values and ambitions of Italian males, and thereby helped consolidate the Roman peace in Italy. Further, shared service with Romans in foreign wars helped deepen the sense of common bonds, while a share of the loot of empire also accrued to these men and their officers. However, many of the allies felt strongly that their efforts and sacrifice were not fairly rewarded by a Roman government dominated by arrogant and selfish grandees. They became increasingly bitter that, as generation on generation they shed their blood in Rome's wars, they were still excluded from full participation in the state. For the vested interests in the senate resisting land reform also resisted further extension of Roman citizenship to the Italian allies.

In the winter of 91–90 BC, the Italian allies prepared to fight for the franchise – an extraordinary example of peoples going to war not for independence, but for full integration (although some diehard Samnites did seek autonomy). During the Social War, Romans fought veteran comrades-in-arms.[60] Bitter fighting led Rome to make concessions, granting full citizenship to those who had not rebelled, and later to those who laid down their arms. The struggle lasted several years, resulting in great loss of life, but at last all Italians were fully

Romans, their soldiers henceforth serving in the reformed legions.[61] Yet there was little respite; much of the following fifty years would be torn by internal violence, sometime full-scale civil wars, culminating in the death of the republic.

As old distinctions between Roman soldiers, and between Romans and their Italian allies, were abolished, so a new cleavage, destined to become enormous, was already opening within Roman society. Military service, now often undertaken overseas for years at a stretch, was no longer part of the shared annual cycle of city-state life, but was increasingly the special experience of that fraction of the citizenry under arms. *Milites* became an increasingly distinct social group, which had its own experiences, perspectives and values. In the first century BC a declining proportion of Rome's soldiers were drawn from the propertied citizens of the city or its surroundings. Increasingly they were recruited not only from the hitherto marginalized 'head-count', but from the new citizens of outlying parts of Italy, and from settler-families in Gallia Cisalpina (the Po valley) and soon even further afield. Simultaneously with the drift of propertied citizens towards civilian rather than military careers, many aristocrats became less interested in martial affairs, concentrating more on civil politics, the law and making money; and when they commanded armies, many were less inclined to lead from the front.[62]

On the other hand, certainly during the era of civil wars and perhaps earlier, Roman commanders could no longer simply behave as awe-inspiring wielders of *imperium*, or even paternalistically as aristocratic patrons who valued the men they led. As soldiers increasingly perceived that some haughty aristocrats actually disdained them, their citizen pride became increasingly touchy. Soldiers knew their generals relied on their loyalty, above all in civil war, and more and more they had to be wooed as well as commanded and coerced. Some generals chose, and others were sometimes obliged, to be seen to share the routines, toils and dangers of the ordinary soldier, establishing personal *virtus*, setting an example and proving they did not despise their men. The young Marius led bravely from the front and ostentatiously lived like an ordinary *miles*.[63] Soldiers appreciated their leaders identifying with them symbolically, in deed and in word: many commanders, not least Caesar, addressed their men not distantly as *milites*, but much more familiarly as *commilitones* ('fellow soldiers', 'comrades'),[64] 'thereby heightening their zest for battle by the term's equality of honour'.[65] Such 'chumminess' had to be carefully judged; overdoing it undermined soldiers' respect for their officers, who were still expected to be proper gentlemen.[66] Nevertheless, such practices reflect the real power of the soldiers, in a period when the nature of their relations with the senators who commanded them was undergoing profound change.

Traditional bonds between *milites* and senatorial commanders, sanctified by military oaths and cemented by shared experience – preferably profitable, victorious campaigning – had, at least in theory, articulated loyalty to an individual as an office-holder appointed by the state. But with the state in factions and senatorial warlords increasingly raising effectively private armies to fight each other, the relationships between general and soldiers became increasingly personal, and would quickly evolve into dynastic loyalties.

Consequently, many Roman aristocrats and wealthier citizens no longer saw soldiers as Us under arms, but increasingly as Them, quasi-mercenaries whose loyalty to the state, as opposed to their generals, was unclear. This induced fear which became too often based on experience as the last century BC wore on, when the wolves really turned. The fateful divergence between Roman civilians and Roman *milites* had begun – and soon saw soldiers butchering fellow-Romans as well as enemies and subjects.

Excavations at Valencia in Spain have provided grim archaeological testimony of post-Marian *milites* in action. Roman troops sacked and burned the city, subjecting its hapless inhabitants not just to massacre, but (in some cases) to hideous torture in the process. A number of the victims have been found still lying where they were butchered, amid the debris of destruction. What happened is clear enough from the disposition of the bodies and their gross injuries.[67] One had had a *pilum* inserted into his rectum and driven lengthways up his body, and his legs hacked off, doubtless with the 'Spanish sword'. The horrific testimony of Valencia fits more with the sadism of soldiers out of control than with calculated 'slaughter before you loot' orders (Fig. 32).

We can identify the historical context of this atrocity with confidence. It corresponds to the historically attested sack of the town in 75 BC by soldiers of Gnaeus Pompeius, surnamed Magnus (Pompey the Great), during the Sertorian War (see p. 102).[68] At the time, Hispania was still not completely under Roman power; however, Valencia had long been a provincial city. This was not an act of aggression against barbarians. The unfortunate Valencians were victims of a Roman civil war, one of many from the 90s to the 30s BC that racked the Roman world.

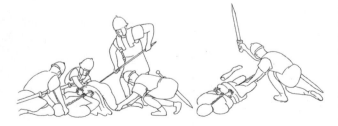

32. Archaeological testimony of atrocities committed by Roman soldiers is rarely found, but excavations at Valencia, Spain, uncovered gruesome evidence of torture and mutilation meted out by Pompey's *milites* during their sack of the city.

## Enemies and internal strife

Causes of war from the middle republic onwards have been characterized as fear, greed and glory.[69] Romans had genuine cause, from time to time, to fear foreign foes. Their continued dread of broken Carthage had been paranoid, if comprehensible. However, the vast and mysterious invasion of the Cimbri and Teutones erupting out of northern Europe in 113 BC posed a real danger to Italy, and destroyed badly led Roman armies, before Marius smashed the invaders to win multiple consulships and unrivalled glory.

Nevertheless, most of the time, Rome's greatest sources of fear were internal. Not least, the threat of risings among the millions of foreign war slaves in Italy gave all Romans nightmares, which sometimes became reality, most famously with the revolt of the Thracian gladiator Spartacus (73–71 BC).[70] His rebel slave force beat several Roman armies sent against him before their defeat and the mass crucifixion of the 6,000 survivors, on crosses set up along the whole road from Capua to Rome.[71]

Roman senators also feared the swelling urban proletariat. Despite general acceptance of traditional government by aristocrats who were as hostile to democracy as they were to kingship, popular pressure had always been significant in Roman politics, and was now increasingly supplemented by outright mob violence. Even if politicians wooed the masses through public munificence or manipulated them by bribery, they could not entirely control them. Yet most of all, senators feared each other.

In the last century BC, Rome was still trying to control a vast empire with the political institutions of an Italian city-state, run by a group of competing senatorial families, whose inner circle expected their scions to take turns at magistracies and military commands, with their opportunities for winning glory. The vast war-booty brought back to Italy enormously raised the stakes of political competition for office and military commands. The wealth now available to some senators to spend on public spectacles and, increasingly, outright bribery to get elected to magistracies and commands, inflated to perilous levels the tariff for everyone wanting to compete. To stand a chance of winning, candidates needed very deep pockets, or had to incur vast debts, which, if the borrowers could not honour them, would at best lead to ruination and exile. Winning military commands gave the coveted opportunity for glory, as valuable as ever for gaining prestige in the state and standing in the senate.[72] They also provided opportunities to replenish coffers, at the expense of provincials or foreign foes. Competitive greed for glory and gold drove systematic rape of the provinces and expansionist wars. In later times, the Romans would extend the open hand to the landowning classes of the east (especially Greeks), and even to Iberians and Gauls, just as they had to Italians. But during the later republic, the Hellenistic world was mainly subject to the sword, and one of the greatest, most prolonged armed robberies in history.

To protect his people from the horrors of conquest, the last king of Perga-mon had bequeathed his kingdom to the Roman people in 133 BC. Still, even directly ruled provinces were treated by senatorial governors as private milch-cows, for extortion or overt looting. Provincials could prosecute them for misgovernment at Rome, and sometimes won – the Sicilians, with Cicero's help, got Verres condemned and exiled in 70 BC – but not often. Notoriously, in this era it was said that a governor needed to make three fortunes from his province: one to pay off debts incurred in bribery to get elected, one for the legal costs of his trial for misgovernment, and one for his old age. Senatorial competition, tra-ditionally fierce, became cut-throat, almost literally. Consequent jealousies and anxieties could still sometimes be resolved by driving rivals into exile; but increasingly, they led to political violence, assassinations and finally civil wars.

Marius became a special hate-figure for senatorial conservatives. Another war hero, like Scipio he challenged the traditional rules of the senatorial game on the basis of exceptional personal military success and his popularity with the masses. Worse, he was a 'new man', a senator of obscure family from backwater Italy. Antagonism between his supporters and his enemies in the senate erupted into bloodshed. Neither law nor custom was any longer enough to contain vio-lence within the state: repeatedly, armed men crossed the *pomerium*, and blood flowed on the streets.

The early rounds of civil war, intertwined with the Social War, saw the pop-ulist Marius clash with senatorial reactionaries championed by Sulla. Both massacred their enemies in brutal purges. As political rivals resorted to the sword, politics came to be dominated by the most powerful senatorial generals – who increasingly broke free of collective senatorial control – and their soldiers. The historian Arthur Keaveney has recently argued that it was Sulla who first politi-cized Rome's soldiers, in his struggle with the Marians teaching them that enemies could lie within as well as without. Thereafter, as the *milites* became increasingly aware that they, rather than the state, were now the real source of a warlord's power, so they began to be more demanding on their own account.[73]

As the state progressively lost authority over its own armies, foreign policy and war fell more and more into the hands of these warlords, and the old oli-garchy was reduced to trying to play them off against each other.

The Sertorian War, in which the hapless citizens of Valencia were massacred, was fallout from the struggle between Marius and Sulla. With the latter's triumph at Rome, the Marian senator Q. Sertorius, a provincial governor in Hispania, found himself an enemy of the state. He gathered Roman exiles and also successfully wooed indigenous peoples, especially Lusitanians, who provided him with fine soldiers. Sertorius' strength derived from combined political and military skills:

he was a talented general who earned the personal loyalty of Iberian leaders and soldiers, and encouraged rapprochement of Romans and indigenes. He established an Ibero-Roman 'state' to which many anti-Sullan senators fled, constituting a rival Roman government-in-exile.[74]

Trying to suppress Sertorius were two Roman armies, one led by Pompey. His father had been another 'new man', from back-country Picenum, who had made a fortune and reached the consulship. Pompey inherited his father's money, estates and, significantly, the loyalty of his veterans: soldiers of the new, more proletarian armies often behaved more as loyal clients of their general and his heirs than as servants of the Roman state, since they depended on him for their well-being and fortune. During the violent 80s BC, at the age of twenty-three, Pompey privately raised three legions of his father's veterans to aid Sulla (an index of the scale to which individual senatorial fortunes had grown). This earned the gratitude of the reactionary dictator. Though Pompey was far too young for normal military commands, in civil war such niceties were ignored, and Sulla made Pompey one of his generals. His savagery against the Marians in Sicily earned him the nickname 'teenage butcher'. Sulla hailed him, probably ironically, as *Magnus*, 'the Great'. Indeed, Pompey was reminiscent of Plautus' *miles gloriosus*, 'the swaggering solder'; his puffed-up pride and vanity masked insecurity over humble origins looked down on by senatorial blue-bloods (including Sulla). This drove him to try to outdo them all in his quest for personal glory.

When Sertorius proved hard to suppress, Pompey, back in Italy with his legions, demanded the senate assign him the task. They prevaricated; he refused to disband his soldiers; the senate capitulated at the implicit threat. Pompey was becoming dangerous, although his political judgment proved shaky, and his generalship was not as good as he thought; he couldn't beat Sertorius, who was instead assassinated in 72 BC.

After Sulla's death Pompey became Rome's most famous *condottiere*, extorting from the senate two extraordinary commands during the 60s BC. The first was to suppress the pirates plaguing the Mediterranean sometimes in fleet strength, themselves a side-effect of Roman expansion (p. 93). In a few months during 67 BC, Pompey swept the seas clear, destroying pirate lairs in Cilicia, and slaughtering, enslaving or (interestingly) peacefully resettling the pirates themselves.

Pompey's career climaxed in the mid-60s, with a second great proconsular command in which he careered around the eastern Mediterranean and, by the sword or intimidation, settled affairs according to his own whims. He reinforced Roman hegemony over Anatolia and Egypt, and extended it over Judea. He snuffed out the rump of the old Seleucid state in Syria, reducing it into a directly ruled province, soon kingpin of Roman power in the Levant, which directly confronted the Parthian empire on the Euphrates. His exploits were phenomenally profitable, allegedly increasing Roman state revenues by two-thirds overnight, besides the riches he took for himself. In 61 BC he celebrated a stupendous triumph at Rome. However, the senate sought to undermine him by blocking land grants to his veterans, seeking to strike at the root of his soldiers' loyalty to him: his ability to look after them in war and retirement. The result was an opportunistic private pact of mutual support between Pompey and two rival, ambitious senators: the fabulously rich M. Licinius Crassus, and the scion of an obscure blue-blood family and kinsman of Marius by marriage, Gaius Julius Caesar. As consul Caesar was able to help Pompey settle his veterans, and Crassus was able to assist Caesar by keeping his creditors at bay (Caesar had run up vast debts to launch his own political career), allowing him to take up his allotted governorship of the Po valley and Mediterranean Gaul.

## Conquering the Gauls 58–50 BC

Despite – in part because of – violent internal struggles, Roman power continued to expand, through bullying diplomacy and the sword. One of the most famous of all Roman conquests occurred during the 50s BC, Caesar's spectacularly rapid annexation of *Gallia Comata* ('Hairy Gaul'), between Pyrenees and Rhine, which also saw Rome's first incursions into Germany and Britain. The Romans had made Mediterranean Gaul a province in the second century BC, and it was as its governor that Caesar launched his assault on free Gaul to the north. Famously divided into three, Aquitania, Celtica and Belgica, it covered a vast area, its population numbering millions (Fig. 33). Its conquest has been regarded as one of the great military achievements – or brutally effective acts of aggression – of all time. Even though his army was vastly outnumbered by the Gauls, Caesar's victory was spectacularly rapid, due to his famous audacity and speed of action (*celeritas Caesariana*), and the unique brilliance of his leadership – of highly motivated, aggressive, loyal, well-trained, battle-hardened and well-equipped soldiers, with whom he had deep personal bonds of trust and affection. It was an invincible combination.

The fame of the conquest arose partly because Caesar was also an enormously effective self-publicist, conquering Gaul not least for the prestige it would bring him at home. Yet its public impact was so dramatic because it truly was an epic achievement, with deep emotional resonances for Romans. For centuries the Gauls had been a by-word for barbarism, terrifying hordes with a taste for head-hunting and human sacrifice, lurking beyond the Alps. Several times they had surged into Italy and had outdone even Hannibal by actually sacking Rome (p. 20). Fear of these alien marauders lingered long in their wake. Caesar's achievement in so rapidly conquering them looked stunning, especially by comparison with Rome's record in similarly sized Hispania, still not completely subdued 150 years after Scipio. It took Caesar just a few campaigns to crush Gallic resistance, climaxing in the famed besieging of the Gauls' war-leader Vercingetorix at Alesia, and the defeat of an enormous Gaulish relief army – although it

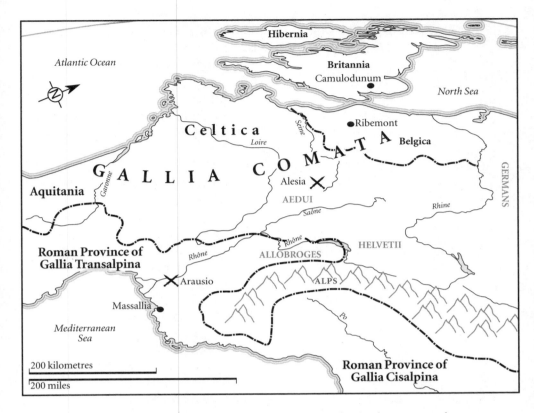

33. Transalpine Gaul in the decades leading up to Caesar's conquests, showing the groups, peoples and places mentioned in the text.

has recently become apparent that the Romans had to maintain heavy military control of Gaul longer than once believed.[75] It was to remain a Roman possession for 500 years.

The annexation of Gaul involved horrors to match any in Roman history. Reportedly, Caesar's troops killed a million Gauls, and enslaved a million more.[76] His famed mercy was a political tactic primarily aimed at disarming fellow Romans, though it was granted to potentially useful Gauls as well. He also ordered equally calculated atrocities; at Uxellodunum in 51 BC he ordered his soldiers to hack off the hands of those who had opposed him in arms, and freed them to spread terror.[77] Caesar even destroyed entire peoples. In 53 BC, in revenge for their massacre of Roman troops trapped in winter quarters, he subjected the Eburones to systematic slaughter and destruction of their territory, with such thoroughness that the name of the tribe was expunged from the map: 'ethnocide' (destruction of the identity group) if not thoroughgoing literal genocide.[78]

And what of Caesar's antagonists? Were they just hapless primitives, plucky but doomed sword-fodder for Caesar's glory? His own account makes clear that, he did not conquer the Gauls by sheer force of Roman arms and terror alone; this was beyond even him. The evidence suggests something more interesting.

✝

The stereotypical view of the barbaric Gauls in battle was, and remains, one of crowds of brave, impetuous warriors who, having worked themselves into a battle-frenzy with the din of war-cries and fearsome animal-headed war-trumpets (Fig. 34), rushed into hand-to-hand combat, competing for personal glory. Their ferocious first onset was terrifying, but the Romans came to believe they lacked discipline and staying power. There is no doubt that the Gaulish peoples were warlike among themselves, putting much of their formidable metalworking skill and artistic abilities into producing fine weapons; they had already given the Romans helmet designs and mail shirts. Among the Gauls, the sword, as both instrument of violence and symbol of masculinity, was even more prominent than among the Romans. Many Gaulish swords of Caesar's era had become enormously long, and while some retained thrusting points (perhaps optimized for the cavalry which had become important in Gaulish warfare following abandonment of chariots in the second century BC) others lacked any point at all; these were indeed dedicated slashing weapons (Fig. 35).[79]

The Gaulish warrior image is epitomized by a silver coin of Dumnorix, a nobleman of the Aedui of central Gaul, showing him with a wild boar for feasting and a war-trumpet, while wearing a mail shirt, and a long sword which he has presumably used to sever the head which hangs from his left hand (Fig. 36). He looks the epitome of heroic barbarism. The Gauls' bellicose reputation is also confirmed by archaeology, at sites like the shrine at Ribemont in northern France, where in the third century BC the bodies of the defeated from some unknown battle were hung on wooden racks as though standing, still with their weapons – but minus their heads.[80]

Some Gallic responses and failures in the face of Caesar's invasion also fitted the blundering barbarian stereotype. The Romans had long experience of vast, sustained, multi-front, multi-year wars, but the Gauls had not, and lacked the institutional structures for complex logistics. Despite outnumbering Caesar on the Aisne, the great Belgic army, lacking experience of feeding so many men at once, got hungry and dispersed.[81]

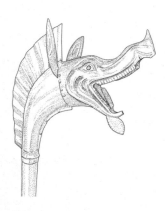

34. Reconstruction of a fearsome-looking Gallic bronze war-trumpet (*carnyx*), based on one of a group of recent finds of late Iron Age date from Tintignac, France.

However, Caesar's own account shows that the Gauls were far from timeless primitives. He reports their rapidly learning the new realities of war with Rome, even copying Roman siege techniques; some may have watched, even participated, in Roman siege warfare elsewhere. Further, except in siege warfare, his men enjoyed no qualitative technological advantage over these 'barbarians'. Indeed, rather the opposite. Many Gauls had arms at least as good as those of the Romans, and some of their new-type iron helmets were superior; within decades, Gallic smiths would be adapting these designs for the legions. Likewise, Gauls were superior to Romans in cavalry: Caesar relied on Gallic allied and German mercenary horse. Rome's material advantage was rather quantitative, man-for-man: from a resource base vaster and richer even than that of the teeming Gauls, all of Caesar's legionaries were equipped just about as well as any Gallic chieftain; but most Gaulish warriors lacked helmets or body armour.

In technology, economy or social organization, the Gauls were no more 'timeless' than the Romans, and many Gallic peoples had been undergoing especially rapid and profound changes over recent generations, changes which made Caesar's conquest feasible.

If Caesar's army had formidable logistical expertise to move the food and other materiel it needed, once it left the Rhône basin and the navigable rivers connecting with the Mediterranean, to keep its soldiers able to fight it had to secure more local sources of supply, especially of bulky grain. Caesar's *milites* could and did seize stores from their foes, but for permanent garrisons they needed access to regular food production. Even before he invaded, Caesar knew enough about the Gauls to be confident that they would be perfectly capable of providing this support, and that some at least would be willing to do so.

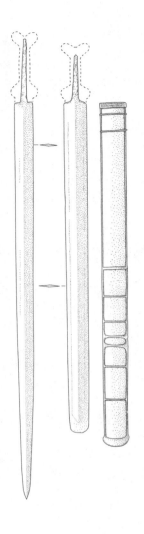

35. *Above right.* Later Gaulish blades: while some were indeed literally pointless dedicated slashing weapons (right: for foot combat?), others had effective points, like the very long weapon on the left (probably for cavalry use). Restorations of weapons preserved as water offerings at Port-Nidau, Switzerland. (Scale 1:8)

36. *Right.* Dumnorix the Aeduan, every inch the Gallic warrior noble, with mail shirt and sword, war-trumpet and wild boar for feasting in one hand, and an enemy's severed head in the other. But he is shown on a Roman-style silver coin with Latin letters. Dumnorix held much in common with senatorial warlords such as Caesar.

During the last centuries BC, Transalpine Gaul, like Italy, had seen expanding populations, rising agricultural surpluses and material wealth, and major political changes. Many of its larger tribal units (much more populous than typical Classical city-states) appear to have developed well-defined, dominant aristocracies, and had begun processes of state formation and urbanization; significantly, Caesar used the term *civitas*, 'city-state', to describe the Gaulish polities. Such developments were driven largely by local conditions, but it is noteworthy that the Gaulish *civitates* that changed most were situated around the Rhône basin, with easy communications to Greek Massalia (Marseilles) and the Mediterranean world. Besides a thirst for Italian wine (Gaul was full of Roman merchants when Caesar invaded), Gaulish mercenaries serving across the Mediterranean also provided their peoples with knowledge of Classical precedents for nascent states seeking to develop effective institutions of government. Coinage was an idea adopted from the Greco-Roman world and, for all its barbaric imagery, Dumnorix's coin is inscribed in Latin characters. Caesar encountered huge settlements that he described as *oppida* (towns), and indeed a number of these major Iron Age centres would develop directly into Gallo-Roman cities. Some *oppida* formed the centres of states under kings or elected magistrates, with developing legal institutions and tax systems. Dumnorix's own power rested on his warrior reputation, but also on his control of Aeduan tax revenues.[82]

In the last century BC Gaul was characterized by multiple, often warring systems of alliance and dominance centred on the most powerful *civitates*, whose political connections reached into Britain, across the Rhine to the Germans, and to Rome itself. Gaul was part of a wider network of interconnected aristocracies from southern Britain to Bohemia. This was largely separate from, but in important respects similar to, the aristocratic network seen among the states of Italy and across the Greek world, which had facilitated Roman expansion. Its connectedness was largely expressed through common heroic warrior culture seen in the weapons, horse-harness and feasting gear characteristic of 'Celtic'[83] metalwork, which fulfilled the role provided by Greek-style artefacts among the networks of the Mediterranean. The Aedui, especially, were long friendly with Rome, originally on the time-honoured basis of 'my enemy's enemy is my friend': both they and the Romans had fought other major Gallic *civitates* like the Allobroges, considered by the Romans a threat to their established hold on Mediterranean Gaul.

Many of these Gallic inter-state connections were personal, involving alliances and plots between factions within different states. Dumnorix was an ambitious warrior-aristocrat who intrigued with nobles of other Gallic peoples, against his own state. His brother, Diviciacus, was a friend to Rome, and had even addressed the senate. This shows factions within the Aeduan aristocracy – even within families – analogous to those that Rome had exploited in Italy.

Dumnorix, an over-mighty noble out of control, resembles contemporaries at Rome, not least Caesar himself.

The similarities between Roman Italy and many of the Gallic *civitates* were, then, as significant as the differences, and would facilitate subsequent integration of Gaul into the empire. Some Gallic societies and individual nobles would resist to the death, but many others would prove amenable to what Rome could offer them – and some were already doing so before Caesar.

Indeed, it was these pre-existing political connections that provided Caesar with the plausible pretext he needed to represent his advance from his territorial province in southern Gaul as *bellum iustum* (p. 58). Ostensibly he was protecting the interests of Roman allies against the migration of the Gaulish Helvetii, and then against German mercenaries who had turned on their Gallic paymasters. It was only when Caesar kept going after smashing both Helvetii and Germans that the Gauls realized he was bent not just on interference, but full conquest.

Similarities between Gaul and Roman Italy were, then, fundamental to Caesar's success. He conquered Gaul not because it was primitive, but because, in terms of political organization and governance, much of it had already become sufficiently like Italy for successful application of the tested twin-track method of Roman expansionism, martial violence and deals with amenable leaders: the sword and the open hand.

The Romans, then, successfully adapted their customary methods of annexation, developed in dealings with city-states, to barbarians in Gaul. Incorrigibly hostile Gallic aristocrats were eliminated, if they didn't flee into exile in Britain. Dumnorix was eventually killed by Caesar's soldiers. Just as in Italy, Rome would support and reward amenable local leaders, offering them integration. Alongside the attractions of the Greco-Roman civil lifestyle, which would soon see new cities and villas dot Gallic landscapes, the Romans provided attractive opportunities to Gaulish warriors and aristocrats for the traditional pursuit of military glory on a global stage already familiar from mercenary service. Gallic martial ideologies were largely compatible with that of the Romans. As happened with the peoples of Italy, Gaulish military power was not destroyed but harnessed, and turned against other enemies of Rome. Wars between Gauls, intolerable under provincial rule, were forbidden, and risks of internal trouble minimized by the same methods developed in Italy: providing an outlet for Gallic martial energies elsewhere, where they could be used to the mutual benefit of the imperial power, and of the Gauls themselves. Gallic nobles, like the Treverans Julius Indus and his son-in-law C. Julius Alpinus Classicianus, rapidly acquired Roman citizenship, and even equestrian status (the order below the rank of senator), through military and governmental service.[84] A few even became senators. More important in the long term, over the coming centuries, Gaul would furnish hundreds of thousands of fine soldiers, initially as allies and auxiliaries, then increasingly as legionaries for the northern armies.

These would be the consequences of Caesar's conquest of the Gauls. Given Rome's trajectory of expansion, and the fact that she had already annexed Mediterranean Gaul, attempts at northward expansion would doubtless have been made regardless of Caesar. Yet it remains a central fact that the vast wars that carried Roman arms to the shores of Brittany and the banks of the Rhine were not the result of Roman government policy. They were entirely at the personal initiative of Caesar. Indeed, his political enemies in Rome professed outrage at his unwarranted aggression, and denounced his actions as war crimes.

Why did Caesar really conquer the Gauls? Given Roman power, they no longer constituted the potential danger they once had. In the long term, even if traditional Italian distrust of the Gauls was seemingly justified by later events (p. 156), Caesar's decision to incorporate them into the empire was broadly vindicated, since they developed into good provincials and provided a major source of military manpower. However, his primary reasons for conquest were more immediate. Having survived decades of political violence, and now competing with the likes of Pompey and Crassus, Caesar needed martial glory to boost his prestige at home. He also had another compelling reason. He was vastly in debt, owing to the cost of getting himself elected *pontifex maximus* (highest state priest) and consul. He needed enormous sums to settle these debts or face ruin, exile, or worse; and he required even more riches to finance future political plans. Since the rich east was Pompey's, what better way to fulfil these aims than by conquering and plundering a feared and wealthy western barbarian enemy? A successful war of conquest would also provide him with another vital asset, since he would doubtless soon have to fight one rival or another: loyal, battle-hardened soldiers of his own, and the money to pay them. The Gauls paid for Caesar's ambitions, both in blood and gold.

## Warlords, soldiers and the death of the republic

Pompey, Caesar and his lieutenant Mark Antony are larger-than-life figures who have caught the Western imagination, not least through Shakespeare's plays.[85] If its course was shaped by these titans, the crisis of the republic obviously also involved many other players, no mere spear-carriers on the historical stage, but active participants with their own objectives who created the environment in which the rogue generals operated. Ordinary soldiers of this era remain largely anonymous, as the military tombstones which tell us so much about individual *milites* mostly belong to subsequent centuries, but an early example, commemorating the centurion Minucius in Padua, may represent one of Caesar's many recruits from Gallia Cisalpina, who rose to the centurionate in Caesar's service during the civil wars (Fig. 37).[86] Throughout the death-struggle of republican Rome, men like Minucius, the soldiers and veterans of the various warlords, comprised players as vital to the game as senators. If *milites* lacked the education, access to information and power of aristocrats, their emotions and ambitions enabled, constrained, guided and sometimes drove what their generals did. Relations between soldiers and their commanders were as crucial at the time as rivalries and alliances between warlords.

Doubtless *milites* of the last century BC considered themselves Roman patriots, and in battle against foreign foes were still fired by the tales and examples of old Roman heroes soon to be set in the literary forms familiar to us: Livy and Virgil were born during this period. However, as we saw, they were becoming a distinct group within Roman society, rather more proletarian, and increasingly professionalized. During the civil wars units often became quasi-permanent formations, such as Caesar's beloved tenth legion.[87] Patterns of loyalty among late republican *milites* were significantly different from those of their middle republican forerunners.

37. A civil war soldier: the tombstone of the centurion Minucius, probably of Caesar's *legio Martia*, buried at Padua *c.* 40s BC. It is likely that he was recruited from the Po valley, where Caesar raised many troops. The vine-staff and left-mounted sword mark him as a centurion. Unusually, his Spanish dagger is worn horizontally.

*Milites* had traditionally looked to their general to take care of their interests (pay, supplies, a chance of booty), in return for the personal oath of loyalty and obedience they gave to him as legally appointed representative of the state. This mutual obligation was a vital source of military cohesion, and an asset to Rome – provided the commander was legitimately appointed, and so long as the demands of the soldiers did not clash with the interests of the government. In the post-Marian era, the bond between commander and *milites* took on an ever more patron/client-like character, since soldiers increasingly expected not just pay, glory and booty, but (as many were landless) grants of farmland on discharge as a reward for service. They looked first to their general to secure these ambitions. These pressures were now more than reciprocal moral obligations; commanders felt increasingly under threat if they failed to satisfy their men.

Later republican troops, like those before and after them, were unruly and often mutinous.[88] This arose from Rome's ancient traditions of citizen-soldiers expressing their feelings and resisting oppression, which had long tended to spill over into violent unruliness. Such tendencies were also seen in the parallel warrior cultures of other Italian peoples now fully integrated into the legions. Soldiers asserted their power to pressurize their commanders. Mid-second century *milites* – those seen and described by Polybius – were, in a time of recruitment difficulty, already using their muscle to extract concessions from commanders regarding leave of absence, and some relaxations of discipline that scandalized traditionalists. In conditions of civil war, when generals needed their men to battle fellow-Romans, maintaining military discipline became especially difficult. Commanders had to watch their own soldiers more anxiously than ever, trying to strike a delicate balance, maintaining fighting efficiency while not antagonizing them lest they be tempted to desert (vanishing homewards or, worse, joining a rival warlord) or to mutiny, and even to assassinate their leaders.

During the civil wars, generals and their soldiers were bound even closer in mutual interests, in an embrace that could become a stranglehold if expectations were not fulfilled. Securing land for their veterans became imperative to the emergent warlords. The problem was where to find the land, since soldiers wanted to settle in Italy. If this could be achieved, it would benefit the warlords; veterans and their sons settled close at hand provided military reserves against future eventualities, as Pompey's early career demonstrated. Failure to deliver land grants would be disastrous. Obstructing such grants was a tactic their enemies used to try to weaken them, and drove Pompey into alliance with Crassus and Caesar. Satisfying their veterans encouraged warlords to liquidate rivals. It became doubly convenient to eliminate opposition through violent purges, exiling or murdering political enemies, or even the non-partisan simply for their property; veterans could then be settled on their confiscated lands.

The civil wars saw Rome's *milites* deeply factionalized, segmented into multiple armies, partisan groupings which fought each other but which might also change allegiance. When fighting for their generals against other Roman armies, *milites* might tell themselves that the government had been hijacked by malevolent men (senatorial oligarchs, rival warlords) intent on cheating them of their rights or destroying them; but the fact remained, they faced battle against fellow Roman soldiers. They were not always enthusiastic about it, as embittering, demoralizing conflicts raged for years. They would sometimes change sides, abandoning a less-loved commander for a more famous one, rather than fight his men (as when Lepidus' legions simply abandoned him for Octavian).[89] The civil wars led to desperate strains within as well as between factions, manifested in mutinies which commanders – even Caesar – constantly risked and could rarely simply crush. As the historian Stefan Chrissanthos has commented, 'of the thirty mutinies during the last fifty years of the Republic', that staged by

Caesar's legions at Placentia in 49 BC 'was…one of only three in which a commander was able to impose any real punishment'.[90] Caesar threatened the Placentia mutineers with decimation (killing one man in ten), actually executing a dozen ringleaders.[91] In 47, he faced a far more serious mutiny in Campania involving his veteran Gallic legions, famously scotching it by addressing them not as *commilitones* but as *Quirites* – '[civilian] citizens', shaming them back to their duty.[92] Or did he? Chrissanthos argues that this tale, part of Caesar's legend, disguises a very different reality. Caesar had been unable to pay his troops properly. His veterans had fought for years, many just wanting discharge; others resented prospects of yet more war against fellow Romans. Many were simply using the leverage they knew they had: Caesar was powerless without their support. In reality he had to capitulate, discharging veteran legions, and did not dare attack the ringleaders; hence the bloodless outcome.[93] However, Caesar's death in 44 BC fired up his soldiers and veterans for bloody vengeance against the assassins.

Traditions of patronage by great families, fundamental to Roman society, were evolving into dynastic loyalties among the soldiers. *Milites* were faithful to particular warlords and their families. As we saw, Pompey's career was launched by the veteran legionaries he 'inherited' from his father. Even more momentous were the events following the assassination of Caesar, whose veterans flocked to support his adoptive son, Octavian – destined to become Rome's first emperor.

When Crassus, Pompey and Caesar banded together, the senate was powerless. However, this 'First Triumvirate' was riven with distrust and continued rivalry. Crassus attempted to outdo the past military achievements of Pompey, and Caesar's still-continuing conquest of Gaul, by an attack on Parthia. Rome's new neighbour on the Euphrates, where they met as a result of their recent joint dismemberment of the Seleucid state from opposite directions, seemed a glittering prize. Parthia was the only major neighbouring state still outside the Roman orbit, and as yet untested in battle against the legions. The catastrophic slaughter of Crassus' soldiers at Carrhae in 53 BC, in which he himself perished,[94] left Pompey and Caesar to fight for supremacy. Civil war raged from Spain to North Africa, Greece and Egypt. Caesar was victorious, Pompey murdered in Egypt. Caesar was famously merciful to the Pompeians and his other senatorial rivals, but their resentment simmered as he made himself dictator. This was a respected ancient Roman office used briefly in times of military emergency, but Caesar made himself dictator for life, king in all but name. He was about to embark on his own Parthian War in vengeance for Carrhae when he was assassinated in 44 BC.

The assassins were senators who issued coins proclaiming liberty from the tyranny of Caesar's quasi-royal rule, symbolized by a freedman's cap flanked by

38. Silver *denarius* minted by the senatorial assassins of Julius Caesar in 44 BC. It features the cap of liberty, worn by freed slaves, flanked by Spanish-style Roman military daggers.

Spanish-style military daggers (Fig. 38). But the republic was finished. Yet more civil wars followed, which first saw Caesar's loyalists destroy his killers, and ended with his great-nephew and adoptive heir Octavian, and his former chief lieutenant Mark Antony, fighting for supreme power. Octavian was based in Italy, Antony in Egypt with his consort the Ptolemaic queen Cleopatra. The showdown at Actium in 31 BC drove Antony and Cleopatra to suicide and led to Roman annexation of Egypt. Young Octavian was last warlord standing. Warweary contemporaries doubtless looked around nervously to see who next would rise to challenge him, unleashing yet more violence.

It is a remarkable index of how far Roman domination already seemed unchallengeable that, even as the republican regime was tearing itself to pieces, Roman power over the Mediterranean neither collapsed nor fragmented. The precedent of the fate of Alexander's empire suggests Rome's could have shattered into successor states, for example with someone like Mark Antony, based in wealthy Egypt, deciding to follow the precedent of Ptolemy, the Macedonian general who, on Alexander's death, had seized the Nile kingdom and founded his own independent dynasty. Yet few of Rome's subjects took the opportunity to try to throw off her hegemony. Rather they were forced into dangerous gambles on which Romans would win and rule thereafter. For ultimately the imperial centre prevailed, and between bouts of civil war the empire continued rapid and aggressive expansion, for example annexing Syria in the 60s BC, and Gaul in the 50s and Egypt itself, the greatest prize of all, in 30.

In part, the warlords who brought down the republic were like Hellenistic Greek *condottieri* and soldier-kings. They operated on a Hellenistic stage (Pompey affected hair like Alexander the Great). Still, they were also very Roman figures. Over-mighty warrior-nobles, who prized their personal honour and ambition above loyalty to the state, were in a sense throwbacks to the early republic, to men such as Coriolanus (p. 57). Quintus Labienus, son of Caesar's former lieutenant-turned-enemy Titus Labienus, ended in exile among the Parthians, even leading them against Antony in a briefly successful invasion of the Roman east. He managed to turn some Roman garrisons to his cause, which then saw allied Parthian and Roman troops fighting other Romans, a bizarre illustration of the confused loyalties of the civil wars. Mark Antony was an even greater example, basing his power in Cleopatra's Egypt to fight for his honour and standing at Rome. Too much of the ancient honour-culture of archaic Italy had survived among the oligarchy, and broke loose anew to destroy the republic.

Yet if it bore echoes of Rome's remote past and Hellenistic present, Antony's career – and that of Sertorius and his Hispano-Roman 'state' – also foreshadowed the future, marking the 'globalization' of Roman imperial power, which need no longer be based in the City itself.[95] There are hints that similar processes were also already affecting Rome's soldiers. During the civil wars, in Egypt Caesar had to fight the *Gabiniani*, several legions whom the general Gabinius had left in Egypt in 55 BC to protect Rome's client king there. After a decade they had 'gone native', raising local families and becoming soldiers of Egypt more than of Rome.[96] This evidence of separation of the Roman sword from the City prefigures the profound 'provincialization' of the Roman armies of the imperial period, which would prove as important as the 'Romanization' of the conquered peoples. With most *milites* henceforth permanently in distant frontier provinces, expatriate soldierly Romanness would grow increasingly distinct, and regionalized, generating multiple and sometimes warring Roman armies.

# 3    'Our Weapons and Armour'
## The Earlier Empire 30 BC – AD 167

## Under the first emperors

In AD 9, Roman armies had been overrunning Germany between the Rhine and Elbe for some years (Fig. 39). Rome's first emperor, Augustus (formerly Octavian, heir of Julius Caesar) believed his soldiers had subdued or befriended enough of the Germans to begin establishing civil government, as had been successfully achieved in Gaul. Alongside major military bases, the Romans had even started founding towns.[1]

P. Quinctilius, newly appointed governor of Germania, was leading *legiones* *XVII*, *XVIII* and *XIX*, with their auxiliaries and thousands of civilians, through his province in a column miles long. In the Teutoburg forest, the Romans thought they were in friendly territory, and so were probably marching helmetless, even unarmoured. Suddenly, they were attacked by the Germans. Taken completely by surprise, they were slaughtered. Varus fell on his own sword to escape capture. Prisoners became human sacrifices, and the victorious Germans made off with the three holy legionary eagles. Only a handful of Romans escaped to tell the tale. The actual site of the battle was located near modern Kalkriese, Germany in 1987. Scatters of military equipment and artefacts, and pits containing the collected bones of the slaughtered, have now been revealed. A tactical earthwork built by the Germans at the edge of the wood has been excavated, the body of a pack-mule, still wearing its bell, lying beside it. The numbers of the ill-fated legions were never used again. The slaughter was a turning point in Augustus' unexpectedly long reign.[2]

This, one of the greatest ambushes of all time, was masterminded by Arminius,[3] a prominent member of the German Cherusci. With his brother Flavus, he was serving as an officer in the auxiliary forces of the Roman army, alongside other provincial and barbarian aristocrats. However, his main secret ambitions lay among his fellow Germans, leading to a spectacular act of treachery. The *clades Variana* (Varus disaster) was a catastrophe comparable to Cannae in scale, and in the long term worse for Roman ambitions.

Arminius was able to inflict such a terrible blow on Rome for two reasons: he exhibited outstanding personal political skills in persuading normally independent Germanic groups to collaborate in attacking the Romans; and as an insider he was able to find and successfully exploit Roman vulnerabilities. Germans had been serving Rome since Caesar's advance into Gaul, and had learned Roman ways through enlisting with the invaders. Arminius himself was not only an officer of auxiliaries, but reputedly had been made a Roman citizen, even achieving equestrian status. His military triumph over Varus, however, was not followed by the personal political power in Germany he hoped for: he was soon assassinated. In some respects, Arminius was more Roman renegade than wild barbarian. In his treachery he was also highly unusual: his brother Flavus, who stayed loyal to Rome, was much more typical, and perhaps ultimately, personally more successful in making a life for himself.

39. Germany in the early imperial era, showing the peoples, regions and places mentioned in the text.

Loss of the legions broke the will of the ageing first emperor. He lived to see Roman armies devastate Germany in major reprisals, but before dying in AD 14 he exhorted his successor, Tiberius, to keep the frontiers where they were, on the Rhine and Danube. Later, the re-entrant between the upper reaches of the two rivers would be annexed, but there would be no further attempt to absorb Germania as a whole.

The *clades Variana* was unexpected and deeply shocking, indeed almost unimaginable, to Romans of the era. Virtually an entire field army was annihilated by barbarians who were deemed in popular opinion even more primitive than the Gauls. Further, the defeat occurred at a time when, despite the difficulties to be expected in imperial wars (there had just been a major revolt in the recently conquered Balkans), in general it seemed that the Roman empire had weathered the fratricidal storms of the previous century and found renewed self-confidence. This new era had opened with seizure of the fabulous wealth of Egypt, greatest of all imperial prizes. Subjugation of Hispania was at last complete, and Rome's soldiers had advanced to the Danube. Encouraged by the new imperial regime, Romans were inclined more than ever to think that ultimate global dominion was their divinely ordained destiny. The *clades Variana* just didn't fit.

†

> Strife has been banished from the forum…justice, equity, and industry…have been restored to the state; the magistrates have regained their authority, the senate its majesty. …The *pax augusta*, which has spread to the regions of the east and of the west and to the bounds of the north and of the south, preserves every corner of the world safe from the fear of brigandage…
>
> VELLEIUS PATERCULUS, *HISTORY OF ROME*, 2.126.1–3[4]

The reign of Augustus has long been thought a golden age for Rome, partly owing to sincere feelings of relief, gratitude, optimism and renewed self-confidence expressed by contemporaries at his ending of domestic political violence and civil war, and partly to the new regime's skilful 'spin'. Presenting himself as restorer of the republic, Augustus actually conducted a successful revolution, establishing monarchy in all but name (avoiding Caesar's error of open autocracy), and carefully veiling the reality that power, in Rome as well as in the provinces, now depended on the soldiers (Fig. 40).

Augustus' power was won, guaranteed, and expanded by the sword. It had started in illegality and political murder. From the moment young Octavian learned that he was the slain Caesar's heir, he displayed the ruthlessness he would need merely to survive the snake-pit of political violence, let alone claim his inheritance. At nineteen he literally used the sword to force the government to make him consul, sending soldiers into the senate house. Cornelius, the centurion leading the 'deputation', opened his military cloak to reveal his sword-hilt and said: 'if you don't make him consul, this will!'[5] Subsequently, Octavian's dealings with Caesar's hard-bitten lieutenant Mark Antony and others saw him sign up to political murders, partly to secure lands for their all-important veterans.

Even when, with the death of Antony, Octavian became last warlord standing, it looked likely that he, too, would soon perish like all the others, from natural causes (he was sickly in youth) or at the hands of some new rival. None could have predicted that this bloodstained young man would rule for over forty years, and that he would prove a consummate politician who ended the cycle of domestic violence and created a new, more stable system of government. That Roman power did not permanently fragment in the last century BC, but found long-term internal stability, was in large measure due to his personal genius in effectively neutralizing the causes of internal conflict – not least, the symbiosis of soldiers and rival warlords.

40. Augustus idealized as a victorious general, in a statue from his wife Livia's villa at Prima Porta near Rome (now in the Vatican). On his breastplate he chose to emphasize his bloodless 'triumph' over the Parthians (see Fig. 41).

During the 20s BC he consolidated his grip on power, by a judicious combination of the open hand and the sword. Octavian's genius was characteristically Roman; ostensibly deeply conservative, he was actually reforming and innovatory to a revolutionary degree. Greco-Roman mindsets did not think in terms of 'progress': changes and innovations were made less threatening by presenting them as somehow returning to the ways of the revered past.[6] This was truer of Romans than of Greeks, and among Romans, Octavian proved matchless. He successfully transformed himself from a warlord to a venerated pillar of the constitution, presiding over an ostentatious but largely cosmetic 'restoration of the republic', publicly handing back illegally held authority (justified by the exigencies of civil emergency) to the senate, thereby restoring its dignity. However, that body, packed with his supporters and knowing what was good for it, implored him to accept a special 'super-promagistracy' on behalf of the state, taking on the onerous task of governing through his own legates all the militarily active provinces. He 'reluctantly' accepted; thereafter, almost all the soldiers in the empire legitimately swore personal allegiance to him as their constitutional commander.

Octavian accumulated other powers that formed the basis of a new supreme office, eclipsing the consulship. Ostensibly just the most eminent senator, or *princeps* (from which the new order is known as the Principate), in 27 BC he took the new name Augustus, which along with his inherited family name of Caesar would later become one of the titles of the evolving office we call emperor. This word derives from *imperator*, the old honorific with which, since Scipio, soldiers had acclaimed victorious generals, and which Augustus also prominently employed. Subsequent rulers would still have to demonstrate to the *milites* and wider political opinion their fitness for power by displaying *virtus* in war, and earning acclamations as *imperator*. Even as the word also gradually morphed into another principal imperial title, it still underlined the fact that the emperorship ultimately relied on the soldiers.

Augustus treated the senate with public honour, and sought to heal wounds by trying to mitigate the impact of his early veteran settlements on lands seized in Italy, establishing many veteran colonies in the provinces. He also gave powerful groups such as equestrians, and even prominent freedmen, stakes in the new imperial regime. Roman citizenship spread ever further among provincial aristocracies, bringing Greeks and Gauls into the equestrian order and ultimately even into the senate. Over following generations, citizenship spread into the populations of provinces, which, if they lacked them before, were soon dotted with Classical-style cities. The new Augustan vision of Rome was not narrowly Italian, but global, in a profound ideological shift; Rome was no longer just a city, it was a universal empire.[7] Augustus' will was ultimately backed by the soldiers, whom he also unleashed on further wars of conquest for the glory of Rome and to display his own *virtus*.

The Augustan age saw great optimism among those who supported the regime, or made their peace with it. If there was relief and joy at the end of civil conflicts and general peace within the empire, aggressive wars still raged on the frontiers. Pursuit of glory and the cult of Victory remained Roman obsessions. In 31 BC, to commemorate the defeat of Mark Antony and Cleopatra at Actium, the future Augustus set up an altar to Victory, decorated with a statue of the goddess captured long before from Tarentum, in the senate house, where it remained for four centuries.[8] His subsequent reign as Augustus saw one of the most aggressive of all periods of military expansionism, beginning with the annexation of Egypt, which was not only the greatest single prize Rome had ever taken, but also secured the City of Rome's grain supplies. He completed the 200-year conquest of Hispania. He erased the humiliation of Crassus' defeat at Carrhae not by war, but by a diplomatic deal with the Parthians, which secured the return of the lost legionary eagles – and which was presented as a bloodless Roman triumph (Fig. 41). Augustus launched massive wars of conquest in the Balkans, and sought to imitate and outdo his adoptive father's annexation of Gaul by conquering Germany, at least to the Elbe. This proved difficult but, until AD 9, seemed to be succeeding. In the optimistic Augustan age, Romans again believed they could achieve anything. For most of his long reign Augustus seemed to be smiled on by the gods – as a Julian, he claimed direct descent from the Trojan hero Aeneas and his mother, Venus, a lineage immortalized in Virgil's *Aeneid*. It was an era of internal peace and harmony, with victories, glory and booty from the foreign wars that Romans believed were necessary to sustain *virtus* and keep the state strong. However, less welcome forms of violence still threatened.

41. Detail of Augustus' breastplate on the Prima Porta statue (Fig. 40), showing the Parthian king returning Crassus' lost legionary eagles in 20 BC. The identity of the Roman figure is uncertain.

In a slave-owning empire, strongly hierarchical and becoming ever more so, permanent underlying tensions remained. At the top, friction between senators and the imperial house was endemic, even though emperors would long come from senatorial families. Augustus and his successors still placed senators in command of legions and used them as provincial governors-cum-army commanders, but now they were strictly subordinates, often silently resentful at their lack of real power. The old system of senatorial competition was emasculated, consuls lost most of their practical powers, and only the ruler or his kin could hold triumphs. The emperor gave the orders and took the glory, causing generals such as Corbulo to sigh wistfully for the autonomy of their forerunners. The reality behind the elaborate façade of the Augustan constitution was a great warlord pulling the strings of the state, backed by the swords of his soldiers. Over the next two centuries, this reality became increasingly obvious to all – not least the *milites* themselves.

Since Augustus inherited the disaffected remains of several civil war armies, he especially needed to reform the military. His long reign gave him, his generals, unit commanders and centurions time to complete the most important and fundamental changes in its history. Augustan reforms of recruitment and conditions of service for Rome's soldiers had unpredicted and unintended consequences as profound as his planned civil policies towards the Roman orders, freedmen and the development of the provinces. The changes in his reformed armies were apparent in all senses: in their composition, their organization, and literally, in the appearance of soldiers and their equipment.

Appropriately in an age of revolution, under Augustus the design of Roman swords changed markedly. The 'Delos' type, believed to be the later republican *gladius Hispaniensis* (p. 80), developed into a new form, today known as the

Mainz type.[9] This, or the Pompeii type that succeeded it during the mid-first century AD, is the weapon often stereotyped as 'the Roman short stabbing sword', although both retained two good cutting edges as well.

The Mainz type (perhaps better, family of swords: Christian Miks identifies six or seven variant shapes) retained a long point for thrusting (up to 200 mm or 8 in).[10] Its blade was substantially shorter than the republican weapon, usually about 500 mm (20 in) long. Some were shorter still (as little as 344 mm, under 14 in), others remained longer (up to 590 mm, almost 24 in).[11] Early forms remained relatively slender, while later examples were much broader than before, up to 75 mm (3 in) wide at the shoulder. While the tip tapered in plan, it did not in thickness, and so near the point was squarish, bodkin-like in section. Some blades are slightly waisted, but others are actually parallel-edged, the triangular point and flared shoulders giving an illusion of waisting.[12] Such geometry is seen on a fine Mainz sword, complete with hilt, from Rheingönheim (Fig. 42). Hilts comprised three components: a pommel, guard, and grip usually of octagonal section. These could be wood, bone, ivory or plated, as on the Rheingönheim example, which is covered in silver, and which also originally possessed a wrist-chain to prevent loss in combat.[13] Scabbards were still suspended by rings on each side, attached to the sword by metal bands. They had a metal chape (scabbard end) and other decorative plates, some with openwork decoration, perhaps betraying Gallic influence.

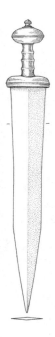

Slightly later blades from the early first century AD tend to be wider and have more elaborate repoussé-decorated scabbard plates, and the edge-channelling seen on the *gladius Hispaniensis* and its Iberian precursors, making a 'frame scabbard'. One of the most famous Roman swords is of this type, the so-called 'Sword of Tiberius', from the Rhine at Mainz (see Plate III). The blade is almost complete, although tang and hilt are lost. Its spectacular and substantially complete plated scabbard, sporting elegant reliefs of imperial figures that date it to the reign of the second emperor (AD 14–37), has resulted in its treatment primarily as an *objet d'art*, rather than an ostentatious symbol of martial masculinity, let alone an instrument of death.[14] Perhaps a presentation piece, it is unlikely to have belonged to anyone very exalted; scientific analysis has shown that it is not, as long thought, silvered, but tinned.[15] Rather, it indicates how showy much Roman equipment was becoming, a trend also seen in elaborately decorated daggers and cavalry

42. Restoration of the near-perfectly preserved Mainz-type sword from Rheingönheim, Germany, with silver-plated hilt. It originally also had a wrist-chain. (Scale 1:8)

helmets. This trend perhaps began with Caesar, who encouraged bullion decoration on arms to further motivate soldiers to look after them.[16] The Mainz-type sword was still in use when the Romans invaded Britain in AD 43, but by the 70s it was replaced by the Pompeii type (p. 150).[17]

The Mainz family seem not to have been the only kind of Roman sword during the era. From at least the mid-first century BC two longer sword varieties are known, some with distinctly Roman-looking hilt fittings and ring-mounted frame-scabbards. These are the 'Nauportus' type (used until *c.* AD 25) and the 'Fontillet' type (which survived until *c.* AD 50 or later) (Fig. 43).[18] In form both seem, like the shorter Mainz type, to derive at least in part from the later republican sword. However, they also bear resemblances to Gallic weapons, and indeed dated examples are largely Roman-period grave finds from Gaul to the Danube lands. These may, then, be Roman-looking hybrids deriving from both republican Delos-type swords and Late Iron Age Gaulish weapons. This would make sense given the historical context of progressive integration of Gaulish and other northern auxiliaries, infantry and cavalry, into the Roman military, formalized by Augustus. Such auxiliaries were originally recruited with their native arms, but their equipment soon converged on Roman designs, as they adopted face-mask cavalry helmets of Greco-Roman origin (Plate 1), while Gallic armourers turned their skills to equipping both auxiliaries and legionaries, a trend especially clear in iron 'Imperial Gallic' legionary helmets.[19] With more and more auxiliary formations constantly being raised during the period from peoples accustomed to using flat shields smaller than the Roman body shield with spear or long sword, it is no surprise to encounter a range of longer sword types in use into the first century AD, from very 'Roman'-looking to very 'Celtic', some finding their way into the graves of former Roman auxiliaries.[20]

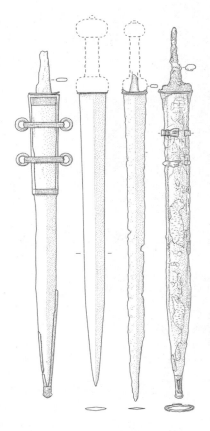

43. Reconstructions of the long sword from Fontillet, France (left), and a Nauportus-type weapon, based on examples from Boyer, France, and Giubiasco, Switzerland. (Scale 1:8)

Most Nauportus and Fontillet blades were comparable in length to later republican *gladii Hispanienses*, i.e. 600–700 mm (24–28 in), although some reach 770 mm (30 in).[21] Even though many Gallic auxiliaries were cavalry, others were infantry, and so it would be simplistic to call all Nauportus and Fontillet types

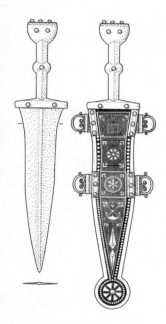

cavalry swords, let alone to label such weapons 'spathae'. However, they probably formed one source, at least, for the origin of the longer swords dominating middle imperial times.

Roman swords still normally hung from a waist-belt. Many first-century infantrymen sported a pair of belts, worn parallel, or crossed, hooked over each hip, with an often elaborately decorated Spanish-style dagger (*pugio*) hung from the second (Fig. 44). (Cavalry belts may have been different.)[22] There was a gradual shift to a single waist-belt during the first century AD, although sometimes the sword was carried on a separate narrow over-the-shoulder baldric. Waist belts had additional practical functions, not least helping relieve the weight of mail shirts on the shoulders by transmitting part of the load to the hips. Belts also carried a soldier's purse, and provided somewhere to tuck writing tablets. Waist belts were elaborately decorated, increasingly becoming a marker of military status, perhaps especially due to their association with the sword.[23] Decorative (and stiffening) belt-plates that could display, even store, wealth were extensively used. Pliny notes first-century soldiers' habit of silvering scabbards and belt-plates,[24] continuity of the kind of embellishment encouraged by Caesar. However, silver was also widely simulated using cheaper tin. 'Aprons' of studded pendant strips hanging from the front of the belt, apparently elaborations of belt-strap terminals like those on the Pula relief (Fig. 101), probably had little to do with protecting the lower abdomen or genitalia, as commonly thought.[25] They present no real obstacle to thrusts, and experience with replicas suggests that they also inflict bruising when running. More likely they emphasized the belt visually and aurally (by jangling as the wearer walked).[26]

The reign of Augustus was a time of rapid, far-reaching innovation in other equipment as well, seen in material recovered from the Varus battlefield at Kalkriese. Like swords, armour also exhibits an Augustan blend of tradition and continuity, evolution and innovation amounting to revolution. *Milites* still wore iron mail, for example, but at Kalkriese some were already wearing the famous laminated iron body armour we call *lorica segmentata* (its Roman name is unknown). It was probably an adaptation of Hellenistic cavalry limb armour, although mail and scale armour were widely used as well.[27] New Gallic iron helmet types were also being introduced. Another striking Kalkriese find was a face-mask from a cavalry helmet (see Plate I), reflecting further Hellenistic ideas feeding into the new armies.[28]

44. An early imperial *pugio* from Velsen, Netherlands, with niello decoration preserving Spanish tradition. (Scale 1:5)

Why did these changes take place? Not least, why the new shorter sword, if for any practical rather than aesthetic reason? Roughly simultaneous developments in other parts of the panoply offer clues. In particular, infantry soldiers fought with sword and shield together, and their shields, too, changed shape around this time. The long oval republican *scutum* gave way to the familiar curved-rectangle form, optimized to lock closely with others over the soldiers' heads in the *testudo* formation.[29] Together, roughly simultaneous changes in sword and shield may reflect shifting fencing methods too. Shortening of the sword may suggest even greater emphasis, in training and indoctrination, on getting ever closer to the foe in combat, especially since in this period soldiers were dealing primarily with unarmoured Germans and similar 'barbarians'. Barging in with the shield denied the foe room to wield spear or longsword, and favoured a short thrusting weapon – now so short it could readily be entirely concealed behind the shield, making its strike even harder to anticipate. Are we seeing here a modified 'tactical package' of infantry arms and techniques? Perhaps, although the new weapon was also adopted by non-legionary infantry, with their flat shields.

### 'New model armies'

The new arms reflect Augustus' 'new model armies', which bore them. Indeed, his organizational reforms were even more revolutionary. Abandoning the centuries-old Roman tradition that the military was a citizen militia, Augustus formalized what had become the unacknowledged reality during the last century BC: Roman *milites* had become, and needed to be, specialist professionals. He established a permanent standing military of long-service career soldiers, largely volunteers (although conscription remained important), organized into permanent regiments.

Augustus created new Praetorian cohorts, a development of republican commanders' bodyguards. These well-paid, Italian-recruited *milites* were no fighting elite, but political troops protecting the new regime, analogous to the KGB divisions around Soviet Moscow. (Although the emperor's horse-guards of the following two centuries, the *equites singulares Augusti*, can plausibly be argued to have been a fighting elite as well.)[30] Augustus made some attempt to keep most of his Praetorians out of immediate sight, but his successor Tiberius concentrated them at Rome, established in a permanent camp. It lay beyond the *pomerium*, but that was now an empty symbol; Praetorians, other guard units and paramilitary police cohorts were now routinely on the streets of the city. Rome itself became, in effect, a city garrisoned by men loyal to the emperor first. Two new major permanent fleets, established at Misenum near Naples and Ravenna on the Adriatic, were also primarily concerned with internal security, keeping the sea-lanes free of pirates, their marines also providing reserve forces in case of trouble in Italy.

The core of Rome's armed forces continued to comprise legions (roughly thirty for the next two centuries). Henceforth these were permanent formations, some destined to last for 500 years. Each now comprised roughly 5,000 heavy infantry, overtly professional long-service soldiers.

The transition from a residual chaos of civil war legions, many raised by now-dead warlords, to a loyal standing military was not entirely smooth. Tens of thousands of veterans had to be settled, many in new or refounded cities in the provinces, from Beirut to Spain; sometimes entire discharged legions were settled as nascent functioning city communities. There were also serious financial stresses. In the first century AD the costs of maintaining the soldiers comprised the largest single item, perhaps the majority, of state expenditure. This just covered soldiers' pay and veterans' discharge bonuses, not including irregular cash donatives (gifts of money to the soldiers, made on occasions such as imperial accessions, when they could be hard to distinguish from bribes to ensure loyalty), or any other visible costs.[31] To establish a sustainable system, Augustus had to increase the term of service from sixteen to effectively twenty-five years. Resentment at delayed discharge and poor conditions led to major mutinies on his death in AD 14.

One or more legions formed the mainstay of each provincial standing army (*exercitus*). The armies were commanded by imperially appointed provincial governors or sometimes, for really major wars, by members of the imperial family and later by some emperors themselves. All wars, whoever led in the field, were nominally conducted by the emperor, who took the credit – or the blame.

Not the least revolutionary step taken by Augustus was the creation of permanent formations of *auxilia*. Their name indicates that, like allied contingents hitherto and hereafter, they were initially conceived of as support troops to the legions.[32] They provided specialists such as archers, cavalry for reconnaissance and pursuit, and infantry more mobile than the close-order legionaries.[33] However, unlike allied troops (in wartime also still levied from client states), the new auxiliaries were now an integral part of the Roman military. Even though most were not Roman citizens, like legionaries they were now long-service professional soldiers under oath to the emperor, and directly paid by him. This was itself another profound innovation.

The new imperial auxiliaries were primarily recruited from provincials, and even 'barbarians', with martial traditions and useful military skills. By the mid-first century AD auxiliary units were raised from Thracians,[34] Pannonians, Spaniards, Rhine Germans, Gauls – men such as the Treveran cavalryman Insus, whose magnificent tombstone was recently discovered in Lancaster (Plate IV) – and others including Arabs and Parthians. This marked a radical extension of the status of Roman *miles* to subject peoples and foreigners, who hitherto had provided levies for *ad hoc* service as a form of tax, or had been hired as mercenaries.

The *auxilia* comprised cohorts of infantry, *alae* ('wings') of cavalry and (increasingly employed after Augustus) *cohortes equitatae* of horse and foot combined. Initially around 500 strong ('quingenary'), some were later 800–1,000 men ('milliary'). In the first century AD specific groups of auxiliary units seem to have been attached to specific legions (such as the eight Batavian cohorts attached to *legio* XIV in AD 69),[35] but such ties loosened later.

Although often equipped with Roman arms, the new auxiliary *milites* initially retained many aspects of their native martial cultures, including weapons, tactics and terminology. Some of these, following established tradition, became accepted as Roman over succeeding generations. If only among the auxiliaries, this even included the Gallic taste for taking heads as trophies (Plate IV, Figs 45 and 100).

Augustus' ethnically diverse standing armies were revolutionary in Roman terms, but not unprecedented. They resembled the similarly complex armies of Hannibal and of the Hellenistic states, and so were in line with the wider Greek influence on Augustus seen in his portraits. He was also, however, anxious to be seen as a stern Roman traditionalist, especially prone to moralizing reforms relating to family life, and is usually credited with banning marriage in service for all soldiers below the rank of centurion. In practice, this was not aimed at keeping soldiers' minds focused on war alone. Augustus knew he could not turn *milites* into fighting monks; they would form unofficial liaisons anyway. Rather it was a practical way to avoid the new long-service regiments becoming encumbered with responsibility for crowds of dependants, losing mobility and on campaign starting to resemble migrating Gauls. This measure would have profound unforeseen consequences for soldiers and the empire.

45. Scenes from Trajan's Column showing Roman auxiliaries taking heads in battle (top left), even fighting with them swinging by the hair from their teeth (top right), and presenting these trophies to the emperor (bottom).

Many auxiliaries and some legionaries were conscripts, but military service also attracted volunteers.[36] Military service had an ambiguous social standing, as a form of servitude (especially for involuntary conscripts), but with honourable status offering glittering prospects to the able. Despite the constraints of a virtual lifetime's commitment and the marriage ban, service provided opportunities no longer available at home for young and warlike provincial males to prove their mettle with the sword, and to receive regular pay for it. Military service was an increasingly important route to social mobility; it soon also became the norm for service in the ranks of the *auxilia* to be rewarded with full Roman citizenship after twenty-five years' service, which in practice about 50 per cent of recruits could hope to complete.[37]

From the beginning, Augustus had extended traditional Roman openness to provincial aristocrats, and even friendly foreign princes growing up in Rome as political hostages, serving with the armies as officers of *auxilia*. Such men were enfranchised, and if already rich enough, might rapidly enter the equestrian order. This continuation of republican inclusiveness to friendly foreign aristocrats, not least as a reward for military service, generally worked very well as a means of integrating provincial ruling classes into imperial politics, and encouraging the spread of Roman culture and values. However, on occasion teaching barbarians the Roman art of war could backfire spectacularly, as it did in the case of Arminius.

Until Augustus, Rome did not have a military as either a formally separate standing institution or a community of soldiers. Armies had remained, in theory, the male citizenry temporarily under arms. Although his creation of both standing imperial military organization and professional soldiery can be seen as formalizing trends in these directions visible during the preceding century, the way Augustus accomplished this – in particular, his reform of soldiering – had the most profound consequences for the history of the Roman world, some of which he did not foresee and certainly did not intend.

Already declining in the first century BC, *de facto* military service ceased to be part of the typical life experience of the average Roman male citizen in Italy. While conscription still occurred, service in the legions now normally became the professional preserve of a shrinking minority within a rapidly expanding citizenry.

As Augustus effectively shrank the boundary of who was a Roman *miles* to exclude most Roman citizens, he was simultaneously extending it beyond the boundary of the citizen body to embrace suitable provincials and barbarians at best deemed to be in the process of *becoming* Romans through military service. This effectively formalized the *de facto* recruitment practice of the civil war era. Most famously, Caesar's *legio* V *Alaudae* was raised from 'men of Transalpine

Gaul', provincials of modern Provence and Languedoc whom Caesar subsequently enfranchised. He also probably quietly enrolled suitable non-citizens in other legions, such as that recruited 'north of the Po' during the Gallic War.[38] Augustus himself turned Roman-style Galatian allied units directly into an imperial legion, XXII *Deiotariana*.[39] Recruitment of non-citizen auxiliaries as formally Roman soldiers, rather than allies or mercenaries, redefined the very nature and boundaries of Roman military service in a truly revolutionary way.

The impact of this radical shift in the basis of Roman soldiering was amplified by a further profound change during the period. Under the late republic, wherever they may have been sent to serve, most Roman soldiers and armies had been raised in Italy and survivors had ultimately returned there. Henceforth, except for those in Guards units, the new minority of professional citizen-soldiers followed their very long careers unseen, in distant lands where their legions were permanently based, and few would ever return. Imperial legionaries became largely expatriates, who like many of their kind remained fiercely attached to their cultural roots, yet whose outlook and experiences would inevitably diverge from those of Italians, becoming increasingly 'provincialized'. This was further encouraged by Augustus' marriage ban, an unintended consequence of which was that Italian-born legionaries increasingly established 'unofficial' families among provincial communities, and henceforth many veterans stayed near the frontiers on retirement, rather than returning to Italy. Though the Praetorian Guard and occasional new legions were raised in Italy, Italian recruitment to established legions rapidly declined during the first century AD. Legionaries were increasingly drawn from citizens born in the provinces, especially locally born sons of legionaries or enfranchised auxiliary veterans.[40]

46. Detail of the tombstone, found at Philippi in Greece, of the military hero Tiberius Claudius Maximus. He was a legionary, junior officer of auxiliary cavalry, and captor of the Dacian king Decebalus. Beneath the scene depicting this famous feat are some of his military decorations, torques.

Further, early imperial citizen legionaries now shared their identity as Roman *milites* with the overwhelmingly non-citizen, provincial and barbarian auxiliaries alongside whom they lived and fought. While there was demonstrably rivalry, friction and even sometimes lethal violence between the two halves of the imperial armies (p. 156), legionaries came to have more in common with their auxiliary *commilitones* than with their fellow Roman citizens in Italy, which fewer and fewer of them had ever seen. Intertwining of auxilia and legions is exemplified in the career of the much-decorated Tiberius Claudius Maximus (Fig. 46).[41] Probably born near the Roman colony of Philippi in Macedonia, he was a Roman citizen, but his names indicate that this was a grant from Tiberius or Claudius to a recent ancestor of provincial origin, probably for auxiliary service. Maximus served as a *miles* of *legio* VII *Claudia pia fidelis* based at Viminacium in Upper Moesia, east of Belgrade. He became a legionary cavalry standard-bearer before transferring to the auxiliary cavalry as a decurion of *ala* II *Pannoniorum* in the same province. During Trajan's Dacian War (p. 159) he achieved fame as the captor of the dying king Decebalus. He took the Dacian king's head to the emperor, as proof Trajan's foe was dead – and probably, despite Maximus' citizenship and legionary service, as a barbarian-style trophy of war, according to increasingly naturalized Roman military custom.

With the emperors, then, a distinctive new Roman identity began to develop, a specifically military 'Roman-ness', one rooted equally in the traditions of the republican legions and of the peoples of the provinces and frontiers, geographically and culturally distinct from that of the civil core of the Roman world, which was undergoing equally profound but very different changes of its own. For in Italy especially, over subsequent generations, Augustus' reforms had another unintended, and (from the viewpoint of emperor and senate) certainly undesired outcome.

Effective ending of universal liability to military service for Roman citizens led *de facto* to the creation of the Roman civilian, and the progressive demilitarization (although not disarming) of Italy. Military training of youths continued, and gladiatorial games were valued for keeping Romans familiar with violent death, but most Italian males no longer served as *milites*. Manhood was increasingly redefined in Italy, with emphasis no longer placed on personal participation in warfare. While the unpropertied might still see enlistment as a step up, and the adventurous seek a place in the Praetorian Guard, the better off increasingly bribed their way out of episodic conscriptions.[42]

Already in the later republic, distinctions had begun to open up between the nascent, quasi-professional soldiery and Roman society at large. From the reign of Augustus onwards, the gap between soldier and civilian widened into a chasm, as the events of AD 69 would reveal (p. 155). Thereafter, emergent martial and civil versions of 'Romanness' would diverge ever further.

### No bounds of empire

*His ego nec metas rerum nec tempora pono;*
*imperium sine fine dedi.*
To them no bounds of empire I assign,
Nor term of years to their immortal line.
JUPITER DECREES FUTURE INFINITE AND IMMORTAL POWER FOR ROME:
VIRGIL, *AENEID* 1.278–9[43]

Augustus' new armies probably totalled around 300,000 men, not an excessive number to dominate the entire Mediterranean world and western Europe, perhaps, but by ancient standards representing enormous armed might, backed by the almost limitless resources of the provinces and the pick of the manpower of innumerable peoples. The civil wars over, Rome's apparently unstoppable advance continued. Augustus' reign may have been remembered as internally tranquil, yet he ordered aggressive expansion as great as ever. Augustan propaganda, above all the *Aeneid*, portrayed Rome advancing towards ultimate divinely sanctioned rule of the whole world: *imperium sine fine*, 'empire without limit'.

She already controlled the whole of the Mediterranean basin, as directly ruled provinces or through approved client rulers. After 200 years of intermittent warfare, Augustus completed the conquest of the Iberian peninsula and annexed the Alps, achieving the subjection of all Continental Europe west of the Rhine and south of the Danube. Beyond this northern perimeter Rome also supported 'friendly kings' among neighbouring barbarians, from the shores of the Black Sea to southern Britain, where Caesar had ventured. Where would the legions go next?

Roman arms were already reaching the limits of the habitable world on the shores of the Atlantic west and amidst the sands of the Sahara. However, the north and east still beckoned. The latter offered more obviously glittering prizes than the cold barbarian north. The fabled footsteps of Alexander led towards Parthia, with prospects of fabulous booty from the great cities of Mesopotamia, of overrunning Iran and invading India. What was to stop Rome's legions one day even outdoing Alexander's Macedonians, and penetrating Central Asia to crash through the Great Wall into Han China?[44] How far might Roman arms one day be carried?

The answer would prove to be: not much further than they had already reached. Many of the provinces created by Augustus and his successors would mark annexation of territories over which the Romans already had hegemonic control: existing client states. The pace of military expansion ground towards a general halt after Augustus, albeit punctuated by frequent attempts by later emperors at new conquests, modest or major, some of which succeeded, some of which failed.

The reasons why military advance became hesitant were partly domestic. Expansionism had been driven largely by internal dynamics: state ideology of conquest and victory, martial masculinity firing Rome's soldiers and fierce competition between her leading aristocrats, all played a role in driving the sometimes frantic pace of wars and conquests. The result, as rivals rotated in and out of political office and military commanders seized whatever chances for glory came their way, had been chaotic, fitful, opportunistic, *ad hoc* expansion, with competitors seeking to outdo each other in audacious conquests. This succeeded spectacularly in Gaul, but led to catastrophe against Parthia. No clear, sustained 'grand strategy' was possible under such a system; at most there were shared ideological beliefs in Rome's global destiny. In principle, all this changed with the rise of Augustus, who eliminated the deadly spiral of senatorial competition that had led to civil war. Now, with a single hand at the helm, a quasi-monarch who brooked no competitor, policy could be more consistent. But in practice Rome developed nothing resembling a modern foreign ministry, providing longer-term continuity while administrations came and went. Policy remained determined by the personal idiosyncrasies of the powerful, now the emperor and his personal advisors. A consistent line might be followed for a time, but only until a new emperor succeeded, with his own anxieties and ambitions.[45]

It is significant that the decision to abandon provincialization of Germany was made soon after the end of the murderously competitive later republic, at a time when the rules had changed at Rome. Pressures to engage in expansionist aggression remained, but were less intense. Public thirst for victories continued, and emperors still needed to demonstrate to senators and especially their soldiers that they were good Romans possessing martial *virtus*, worthy of their forerunners – but they were no longer competing directly with rivals. Now there was only one warlord: the emperor himself. No hint of competitive ambition from senatorial generals outside the imperial family was tolerated: Nero recalled the too-successful Corbulo from Armenia, and ordered his death; he opted for suicide by sword.[46] Some emperors, once they had achieved the necessary formality of a victory and their soldiers had proclaimed them *imperator* – for example Claudius after his initial triumph in Britain in AD 43 – thereafter took much less interest in aggressive wars than had their ancestors a century before.

On the other hand, if emperors were under less acute pressure to achieve repeated victories than their senatorial ancestors, only someone with the unassailable prestige of Augustus could have taken the domestic political risk of being seen to accept defeat in Germany. No republican figure could have done so. Had the republic still been in place, Germany might have become a new Hispania, with the Romans persisting in wars for centuries, with no one willing or able to admit defeat, and successive generals keen to seek glory. In the Iberian peninsula the Romans were eventually successful. They might eventually have succeeded in consolidating to the Elbe if, as in Hispania, they took little heed of the costs – although Iberia was at least delimited by oceans, whereas beyond Germania lay…what?

Even before AD 9, there may already have been nagging general unease at the imperial court, which prepared the ground for the Augustan U-turn on Germany. As we have seen, the *clades Variana* caused such shock to Rome because it seemed so out of tune with this picture of unstoppable global expansionism. Another possible reason contributing to Augustus' decision may have been developing private awareness at the top that, even as Virgil span divine promises of global rule in the *Aeneid*, an awkward gap was opening up between the assertions of imperial ideology, and hard geographic and political realities.[47]

I. Iron mask, originally covered in silver, from a Roman auxiliary cavalry helmet, recovered from the site of the Varus disaster of AD 9 at Kalkriese, Germany. This artefact has become an icon of the battle, and of thwarted Roman ambitions east of the Rhine.

II. Roman helmet, *c.* second century AD, found at Crosby Garrett, Cumbria, northern England in 2010. Probably for so-called cavalry sports, its 'Phrygian cap' shape suggests it represents a Trojan, for mock battles with others representing Greeks. The face-mask is strongly Classicizing, reflecting the contemporary fashion for Greek culture.

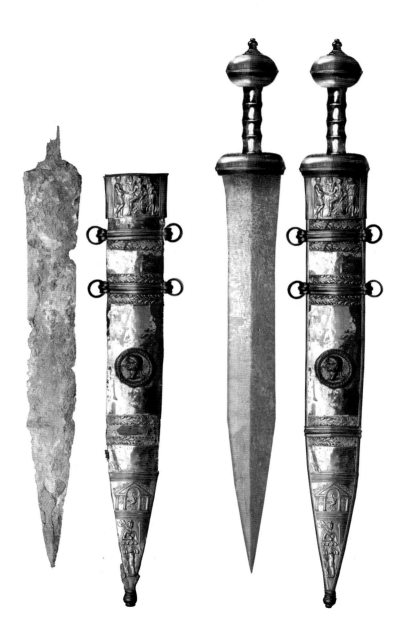

III. The so-called Sword of Tiberius from the Rhine at Mainz, now in the British Museum. Left, the sword as it looks today. Right, a reconstruction of its possible original appearance. This showy weapon was perhaps a presentation piece: its 'silver' scabbard is actually tinned bronze. The blade is *c.* 533 mm long.

iv. *Right.* Digital restoration of the tombstone of Insus, son of Vodullus, auxiliary cavalryman, recruited from the Treveri of eastern Gaul, found at Lancaster, northern England in 2005. (See p. 2 for the tombstone as found.) The severed head of a barbarian hangs from Insus' sword-hand. The sword, like his horse and shield, was 'shrunk' to fit the dramatic composition. The tombstone would have been brightly painted, but the colours shown are speculative.

v. *Below.*Wall painting of *cohors xx Palmyrenorum* at 'church parade', Dura-Europos, Syria, AD 230s. The tribune Terentius sacrifices to the regimental standard, the Fortunes of Dura and Palmyra, and gods of the regiment's mother city.

VI. The only complete example of the rectangular imperial legionary shield. Found at Dura-Europos, Syria, minus its boss, but still with brilliant coloured wax painting showing an imperial eagle and lion (deposited *c.* AD 256).

VII. A perfectly preserved middle-imperial Roman sword, complete with wooden hilt, at the moment of discovery in the Illerup bog deposit, Denmark. These offerings in waterlogged places have yielded many of the finest surviving specimens of the Roman sword-maker's art.

VIII. *Right.* Another splendid Roman sword from the Illerup deposit, with an ivory hilt, further embellished to suit Germanic taste with a silver-gilt grip.

IX. *Below.* Detail of a Roman sword from Illerup, the pattern-welding visible in the blade, which also bears an inlaid figure of Mars. The tang has been repaired.

x. *Below left.* A replica *spatha* of *c.* AD 200, with Greek-style 'pelta'-shaped scabbard chape, Asiatic-inspired slide and baldric. The baldric sports openwork fittings, featuring Jupiter's eagle and a collective prayer. To the left is an original eagle mount from such a set, from Illerup.

xi. *Below right.* A spectacular late Roman helmet, of iron covered in gilded silver plate and encrusted with glass 'jewels', buried with a second, plainer helmet of similar form at Berkasovo, Serbia, in the early fourth century.

XII. Reconstruction of a late Roman shield, based on a gilded, glass-'jewelled' boss from Vermand, France, and painted design from a fragmentary shield board found in Egypt (now in Cologne).

xiii. A swordsmith at work. *Centre, above.* Paul Binns hammer-welds metal strips destined to form a pattern-welded blade. *Left.* Welded and twisted rods ready to be forged into a replica of a Roman pattern-welded longsword blade like that seen cooling (*centre, below*) and after finishing (*right*, with a detail of the fuller and surface patterning).

Even before the Varus disaster, Roman leaders were beginning to realize that the world was far bigger than they had assumed, and that much of it was unattractive and going to be downright intractable to conquer. During Augustus' reign, Romans had explored the northern coasts and the overland amber route to the Baltic, were present in the Black Sea region and the Caucasus, and later legionaries would reach the Caspian.[48] Augustus had sent reconnaissance expeditions up the Nile and down the Red Sea towards Yemen. Via the new monsoon-driven shipping trade from the Red Sea, Romans were becoming more aware of the existence of – and their distance from – India. They knew vaguely of China via the Silk Route, which spanned the intervening vastness of Central Asia and ran through the Parthian empire, which the Romans had also recently discovered was formidable as well as huge. The implication, perhaps most obviously in the cold, 'barbaric' and relatively poor north, was that global annexation, even if possible, would largely prove very tough and/or unrewarding; yet thoughts of stopping contradicted Romans' now deeply ingrained self-image as conquerors divinely destined for global rule.

If India and China now looked soberingly remote, the fame of Alexander's conquest of Persia still burned brightly. More than one emperor would dream of emulating him by conquering wealthy Arsacid Parthia, the last, vast empire immediately abutting Roman territory, spanning Mesopotamia and Iran (Fig 54, inset). More immediate than dreams of distant glory, Augustus also had practical reasons, almost a political obligation, to consider invading Parthia. In the longer term, if the Romans knew little of Iran beyond it, then Mesopotamia – rich, productive and extensively urbanized for millennia – looked as suitable for imperial integration as many other already-incorporated regions such as neighbouring Syria, one of Rome's richest provinces. More pressing were recent military events in the region. For even before the Varus disaster, Roman expansion beyond the Euphrates had already been checked for decades. It had been stopped by another military catastrophe even greater than the *clades Variana*.

Although the Romans considered the Parthians effeminate oriental barbarians (males wore trousers, female apparel in contemporary Roman eyes), they had proved unexpectedly tough on the battlefield, despite the 'feudal' organization of the Parthian empire, which relied on levies in time of war, lacking a standing army anything like that which the Romans were in the process of developing. When Octavian was a child, military disaster had struck Crassus at Carrhae (p. 113). His soldiers came up against something for which they had no answer, a very different military technology and system of martial values: a powerful bow used from horseback, and lance-armed heavy cavalry, a hybrid of Central Asiatic and Hellenistic warfare. Caught on open steppe ideal for Parthian cavalry, Crassus' legionaries could not bring the enemy to close quarters for Roman physical valour to tell. Shields were not enough: they were slaughtered under a relentless arrow-storm. Caesar was about to seek vengeance for Carrhae when he was assassinated. Mark Antony was also lucky to escape death at Parthian hands, losing over 30,000 men.[49] These were humiliating blows to Roman arms and prestige in the region, dangerous to leave unavenged. However, given the military realities, Augustus, who loved glory but valued caution, decided not to seek vengeance for Crassus by the sword. Instead of pursuing this unfinished piece of family business (Caesar's projected Parthian invasion), Augustus would instead emulate and strive to outdo his adoptive father in the theatre of his greatest glory: the north. In the east he would restore Roman face as best he could by other means. Through diplomacy he recovered Crassus' lost eagles, an event his propaganda presented as a bloodless triumph over the barbarians. Augustus left Parthia alone – for the foreseeable future. The border between the two empires would remain on the upper Euphrates for generations. Fortunately for Rome, Parthia lacked an aggressive expansionist state ideology, and its kings were often preoccupied with other frontiers or internal dynastic strife, so it did not normally pose a major direct threat to the provinces. Generally, the early emperors lived with the Parthians, sometimes even diplomatically accepting their kings as equals. Unfortunately for Parthia, however, Romans never relinquished their dream of *imperium sine fine*, and never forgot Alexander. They continued to believe that they might, eventually, conquer Mesopotamia and beyond. It might take time – hadn't the struggles with the Samnites and Carthage spanned generations? – but it remained an ambition. For now, the contest between the empires was especially focused on competing for control of the mountainous buffer state of Armenia, mostly through cold war. There was fighting as well, during which Roman commanders and soldiers gradually learned how to take on and defeat Parthian horse-archers and armoured lancers. Eventually they would work out how to wage successful war on the dry steppe of Mesopotamia. However, holding territory there would prove more difficult. In the east, history would show that the Romans had, after all, already almost reached the limit of their grasp, for reasons they did not comprehend (p. 204). In the north, they would more rapidly run into the buffers, and here Augustus would recognize reality.

On the northern frontiers, since the lands up to the middle and lower Danube were still being pacified, Augustus chose as his next major target the Germans bordering consolidated Roman Gaul. From 12 BC his armies, led by members of the imperial family, ranged through Germania to the Elbe which, as the last major river debouching into the North Sea rather than the Baltic, formed the next obvious temporary halt-line and supply route for Roman arms. Fighting was hard, and the terrain difficult, but a number of major bases had been established far up the Rhine's eastern tributaries and in the Weser basin, while archaeology has proved that there was more than hyperbole to literary claims that the Romans felt sufficiently confident of their hold on the territory that they were starting to establish proto-towns.[50] Then Arminius sprang his trap.

While the elusive prospect of future expansion in the east continued to beckon enticingly, the *clades Variana* had a profoundly different effect on imperial thinking about Germania. It directly precipitated complete reversal of Augustus' policy and thinking, a realization – or moral decision – that the Romans could not, after all, annexe Free Germany. To be sure, Roman armies returned to rampage through Germany. Through high-profile punitive expeditions, vengeance was sought for the military losses and retribution inflicted for the political humiliation. However, the loss of Varus' legions made Augustus abandon his long-cherished plans to create a province east of the Rhine, writing off the massive investment in men and gold he had already made. He did something Romans, acutely aware that peoples are beaten only when they think they are beaten, prided themselves on not doing: he tacitly accepted strategic defeat. In this very Roman sense, Arminius' victory may indeed be considered a 'decisive battle'. It had profound consequences for the history of Europe, as the archaeologist Peter Wells has recently reemphasized.[51] At its most basic, it is why to this day Latin-based languages dominate Europe west of the Rhine, and Germanic languages to its east.

Germany provides an instructive case of the dynamics and limitations of Roman imperialism, especially when compared with Gaul. During the last century BC, the Romans were experimenting with how far they could extend the open hand to barbarians. In Gaul, they would succeed. In Germany, Rome failed comprehensively. The *clades Variana* convinced them that most Germans were too difficult, if not impossible, to bring into the fold. They seemed to live down to their stereotype of being changeless, indeed unchangeable, primitives.

In Germany the Romans found the sword could only succeed up to a point – their soldiers could rampage almost at will, but could barely support themselves from limited local agricultural output, and encountered difficulties convincing the Germans that they were conquered – because the open hand really found no one to grasp. The reality was that, while they had some powerful 'tribal confederations' like the Chatti, these were relatively loose. The fiercely independent German peoples were not then amenable to larger-scale, more centralizing political federation, under Rome or indeed Arminius. Archaeology confirms that, by comparison with Gaul before the conquest, population densities were relatively low, with agricultural regimes producing limited surpluses, which could not support an occupying army. Further, while there were some prominent and relatively wealthy individuals, German societies generally lacked the kind of well-defined ruling classes that the Romans had threatened or seduced in Italy and later in Gaul, facilitating arrangements in which annexed peoples largely governed themselves. Consequently, the Romans could not get a political grip on the Germans. Both Rome and Arminius profoundly miscalculated their prospects of establishing power east of the Rhine. It cost Augustus three legions, and Arminius his life.[52]

First-century Germany underlines the general principle that successful application of the sword and open hand required that the targeted peoples should possess certain characteristics and vulnerabilities: infrastructure and resources to threaten, and powerful elites to seduce. In Europe, as they reached the Rhine and Danube, and crossed the English Channel, the Romans were running out of societies populous, productive and stratified enough to be both vulnerable to conquest, and amenable to incorporation.

Take, for example, the British Isles, last unconquered territory west of the Rhine. It is now apparent that Claudius' 'conquest' of southern Britain from AD 43 was really more a rapid annexation of extant client kingdoms established after Caesar's brief forays in 55–54 BC, involving limited resistance (the open hand alongside the sword again).[53] However, once they got beyond this already partly integrated zone, it took the Romans a generation of fighting to conquer the rest of what is now England and Wales. They several times invaded northern Scotland but failed to hold it; Rome's ability to consolidate control ran out little more than halfway up the island, resulting in a permanent internal frontier zone in which Hadrian's Wall was built. And they never got to Ireland at all. Had they conquered and pacified the whole archipelago, as they did in Hispania, they would eventually have been able to withdraw most of the soldiers for service elsewhere. However, they failed, and found themselves having to maintain a very large garrison (in the second century, about an eighth of the entire armed strength of the empire) in a peripheral island. Fundamentally this was because, while southern Britain comprised Gallic-like kingdoms, which the Romans knew how to deal with, upland Britain and Ireland were home to less centralized societies which, like contemporary Germania, were vulnerable to attack but not amenable to military occupation or Roman-style negotiation. Just as Rome's rise was a result of interaction of her own political and military characteristics with those of her foes and victims, so too was the end of her expansion. The power of the sword was finite, not least because of its inseparable link to the open hand; the former could not reach far beyond where the other could get a grip.

Romans, still hankering for victories and endless expansion, found it hard to deal with this situation. After Augustus they seized opportunities for new conquests where they presented, or in order to fulfil limited strategic objectives, for example to control the deep re-entrant between the upper reaches of the Rhine and Danube (the Agri Decumates). That the Rhine and Danube came to mark the frontier line was not because they (yet) marked any major cultural or political boundary. For most of their combined length, the peoples on each bank were quite similar. To be sure, the rivers could function as a moat, or at least trip-wire, although Romans were not yet thinking in terms of defence. Rather, in lands without pre-existing cities or roads, they provided vital arteries for communication and logistics, for the vast quantities of supplies needed by tens of thousands of soldiers and horses. Hence, largely for logistical reasons, the winter quarters of many northern legions came to be built on their banks, which only later came to be seen as a boundary; the armies expected to operate, and eventually advance, beyond them.

The logistic convenience of advancing to the banks of the great rivers meant that Rome incorporated a number of peoples who, like the Germans, would not prove very amenable to the preferred method of incorporation into the empire. They lacked well-established aristocracies, which could be encouraged to join the burgeoning imperial ruling classes, developing Greco-Roman towns and civil lifestyles, while exporting their warriors to where their talents could be usefully employed. In such regions, the Romans developed an alternative way of incorporating recalcitrant barbarians, especially the most warlike. Instead of seeking to draw off the warriors to facilitate demilitarizing civil development, native martial traditions were encouraged – provided their outlet was in Roman service. They might never come to boast fine cities comparable with those of Italy, Syria, or southern Gaul, but areas such as remote northwestern upland Hispania,[54] and especially the lands south of the Danube, would find their place in the imperial order by providing many of Rome's best soldiers. This was another form of integration, very different from canonical 'civil Romanization'. That this martial model of integration could be applied to some Germans, too, was seen in the case of the Batavians.

Of all these peoples those with the greatest *virtus* are the Batavi…once a tribe of the [Germanic federation of the] Chatti. …Their distinction persists as the emblem of their ancient alliance with us: they are not insulted, that is, with the exaction of tribute…immune from burdens and contributions, and set apart for fighting purposes only, they are reserved for war, to be, as it were, our weapons and armour (*tela atque arma*).
TACITUS, GERMANIA 29[55]

After AD 9 Rome might no longer have sought direct rule east of the Rhine, but she saw it as her sphere of influence, and continued to interfere. The suffering and destruction of Caesar's bloody advance to the English Channel and the terrible German wars were exacerbated by massive social engineering in the Rhine basin.

Having destroyed some groups such as the Eburones, the Romans recast the frontier zone, moving entire peoples, Stalin-style, to new lands to suit imperial interests. Doubtless this led to massive suffering, although there were also winners. Rome established especially mutually profitable relations with the Germanic Batavi, who were settled on the Roman side of the Rhine close to its mouth. Here, during the first century AD, the Batavians prospered, growing crops and raising cattle, horses, and above all soldiers for Rome's armies.[56]

47. Tombstone of the Batavian cavalryman Imerix, who served in the *ala Hispanorum*, and was buried in Croatia. Unlike other 'ethnic' cavalry, Batavians did not take up the Thracian tradition of rider-tombstones, but Imerix died while serving in a non-Batavian unit.

Batavian soldiers, their cavalry able to swim rivers fully armed, provided some of the finest early auxiliary regiments. Considering their numbers and territory, the Batavi contributed an exceptional number of known regiments – nine quingenary cohorts especially prominent in the conquest of Britain, apparently later reorganized into four milliary regiments, plus an *ala*.[57] One of these units, *cohors* IX *Batavorum*, is one of the two best-documented of all Roman regiments,[58] its structure and routines recorded in remarkable detail in the late first-century wooden writing tablets from Vindolanda near Hadrian's Wall. These attest the soldiers' preference for beer (fitting for proto-Dutchmen!), and the comfortable lifestyle of their equestrian commander, Flavius Cerealis (himself a Batavian) and his family.[59] Batavians also served in non-Batavian units (Fig. 47), and were so prominent in the emperor's horse guards of the first two centuries AD that these became collectively nicknamed 'the *Batavi*'.[60]

The special status of the Batavi recorded by Tacitus (above) actively deepened their indigenous martial ethos. They are sometimes described as the 'Gurkhas of the Roman empire', drawing a direct parallel between Roman policy on the lower Rhine and the ways in which the British in India designated certain peoples (Gurkhas, Sikhs, Rajputs) as 'martial races', turning potential 'troublemakers' into mutually beneficial assets by harnessing their pre-existing warrior value-systems and energies to fight the empire's wars. The British had already applied this strategy to the Scottish Highlanders in the eighteenth century, and the Russians long employed Cossacks in similar ways.[61]

Despite the extreme asymmetries of power, such groups could be willing participants, standing to gain from their pacts with imperial authorities in their own terms – opportunities to display martial prowess and to bring home wealth – while maybe drawing on wider imperial culture in other ways. Archaeologist Carol Van Driel-Murray sees the Batavians as a society in a unique symbiosis with Rome, in which military service was a key element in the development of a polity that flourished primarily through exporting extraordinary numbers of soldiers, benefiting from their pay and booty, while settlement and agriculture in the homeland was, perhaps, primarily in the hands of women.[62] Batavian territory for the most part developed along lines very different from some neighbouring groups; its byre-house settlements largely retained an Iron Age aspect, and there was little urbanization, in contrast to the flourishing cities, such as Cologne, developing among the peoples upstream. This underlines the depth of regional differences across the empire, and along the frontiers: the Batavians partook of

Roman culture, but not by building villas and towns; rather, they helped build a new military-based Roman culture of the imperial frontiers (p. 191).

However, Rome's relations with the Batavians became more cautious as a result of a terrible shock she suffered when in 69 the Batavian leader Civilis rebelled. In a waking nightmare, the legions now had to fight their own auxiliaries. Worse, they had also been fighting each other once more, in renewed civil wars over who should sit on the imperial throne. It is probably no accident that these wars and rebellions, in which legionaries and auxiliaries were suddenly pitched against each other, coincided with significant changes in Roman arms, not least swords themselves.

## Weapons, wars and regime change

One of the best-explored aspects both of Roman-era ironworking and weapon manufacture is the sword blade, perhaps the most challenging item an armourer had to make. Modern metallographic analyses of archaeological finds (so far, mostly Roman, Gallic and British examples) reveal much that no ancient writer recorded – and which no ancient smith fully understood.

Roman-era smiths made swords by hammering heated iron to shape, judging desired temperature by the colour of the glowing metal. Blades were commonly made from a number of different pieces, often deliberately selected alloys with varied physical properties or visual appearance. These were pre-shaped into strips or bars, heated and hammer-welded together to form the core of the blade and tang. It was this central process of metal selection and assembly of core components which would undergo the most significant developments during the middle imperial period (p. 184).

In a 1988 study of early imperial blades, three Mainz types were examined, one from Chichester, another from the Thames at Fulham and the Sword of Tiberius from Mainz itself, along with three Pompeii types. These were commonly hammer-welded sandwiches made from strips of varying composition. The 'Sword of Tiberius' comprised softer, low-carbon iron and carburized iron (steel) strips; others exhibited less sophisticated or controlled carbon content.[63]

Quenching – plunging the hot blade into water – was often used to harden the metal.[64] However, this also makes iron brittle, something that can be ameliorated by tempering (limited reheating). Roman smiths appear to have had some idea of tempering, although it was not yet well understood as a separate process. It may have happened near-accidentally, when blades were quenched but removed before the core cooled ('slack-quenching'); during subsequent slow air-cooling, convection of heat from the core reheated the outer layers of the blade just enough to temper them.[65] The sword's cutting edges were formed either by hammering to shape, or by grinding on a wheel.[66]

The 1988 study concluded that early imperial swordsmiths could make good metal with few inclusions; carburize it to make steel; select suitable materials and hammer-weld them; shape blades by hammering hot metal and grinding it cold; quench heated blades to harden them and possibly temper them for strength.[67] However, practice was inconsistent, sometimes losing carburization or even grinding away the steel edge, as happened with the Sword of Tiberius.[68] Besides limited understanding of the composition of materials, this was probably a consequence of lack of means for analysing others' work; in a world of independent and rival craftsmen, new discoveries and techniques were doubtless jealously guarded as secrets to be passed on only to select apprentices. Transmission of expertise was haphazard.

†

Roman swords, and other items of ancient military equipment, correspond to a limited range of shapes and sizes, and most cluster into distinct recognizable types. An intriguing question is, what regulated this? Modern armies have detailed written specifications and regulations controlling what is made for and used by soldiers, obviously necessary to minimize the range of spare parts and ammunition types required. However, in a world lacking mass production of precisely identical artefacts, and among societies (including Rome until the later republic) where fighting men procured their arms on an individual basis, these concerns applied little if at all. How did even the vast Roman imperial military regulate equipment? Items such as swords show considerable variation in dimensions, and at any one time a variety of types existed. Embellishment could also be highly individualistic. Yet there are also always fairly clearly defined dominant types of blades (and indeed hilt-, scabbard- and sword-belt-fittings), within a limited range of variability.

There was sometimes supervision at the manufacturing stage. Josephus reports that the Jews were able to make and stockpile swords by deliberately making them to standards rejected by the Romans who were demanding their production.[69] The only other piece of evidence known to me suggesting any kind of formal regulation comes from a late first-century writing tablet from Carlisle, which, evidently a report on a check that some cavalrymen have the correct complement of weapons, also apparently mentions *gladia instituta*, translated as 'regulation swords'.[70] What actually were the standards applied? By modern defence procurement standards, they were probably pretty subjective, involving no more than handling, visual inspection, and perhaps a standard measuring-stick. 'Not too long or short, about the right shape and weight, metal looks adequate, when I stuck it in the straw dummy it didn't bend and the pommel didn't feel loose: acceptable.' Provided a sword met such basic criteria, it may well have been that matters such as the exact size and weight of the blade, and whether it had a rock-crystal sword pommel or silvered scabbard fittings, were at the discretion (and expense) of the user. Here there was scope for personal expression and evolving fashion. We may conclude that equipment standards were regulated primarily by custom and convention within units and arms of service, notions of what was acceptable being transmitted and policed by commanders, centurions and each unit's *custos armorum*, 'keeper of arms'.

Where did military equipment come from? Under the earlier empire, it seems that normally much was still commissioned and purchased from private sources, men such as L. Acilius, a *gladiarius* (sword dealer and/or maker) commemorated at Clusium, or the ex-slave M. Caedicius Felix, another *gladiarius* attested at Rome, where two *spat(h)arii* (*spatha* makers and/or dealers) are also recorded.[71] Roman regiments produced some of their own equipment as well, notably in the *fabricae* of legionary bases, especially on the un-urbanized northern frontiers, but also even where the armies were based in urbanized regions such as the east.[72] These facilities could operate on a substantial scale. A middle-imperial papyrus from Egypt records two days' production in a legionary *fabrica*, presumably at Nicopolis, and lists legionaries, apparently auxiliaries, '*galliarii*' (military servants) and others working there. On the first day ten swords were completed ('*spat[h]arum fabricatae x*'). On the second day some bows, artillery frames and shields of two different types were completed.[73] Legionary *immunes* (skilled soldiers excused menial fatigues)[74] included arms specialists, such as *sagittarii* and *arcuarii* (makers of arrows and bows), as well as *gladiatores*, either 'sword cutlers' or actual swordsmiths.[75] Third-century military facilities for manufacture and repair of military equipment have also been excavated at Corbridge, near Hadrian's Wall.[76] The arms trade was also an obvious business for veterans, some of whom will have been experienced armourers.[77] C. Gentilius Victor, commemorated at Mainz, was a veteran of *legio xxii Primigenia* turned sword dealer, *negotiator gladiarius*.[78]

A substantial proportion of arms production capacity was, then, in military installations. However, there are also indications of specialized production traditions in the provinces, notably central Gaul. An inscription of earlier imperial times records one Avitus, a seconded centurion, overseeing production of body armour in the territory of the Gallic Aedui.[79] It seems likely that an arms manufacturing tradition in this region existed unbroken from pre-Roman times. The region was producing large quantities of weapons by AD 21, including legionary kit and heavy gladiator armour, used in the abortive revolt of the Aedui under Sacrovir in AD 21.[80] Continuity of this industry would explain the subsequent location of two late Roman state arms factories at the Aeduan city of Augustodunum (Autun), including one of the most specialized, which equipped armoured lancers and built artillery.[81] Further, two of only three dedicated sword factories (*spatharia*) were in Gaul, although swords were undoubtedly made in

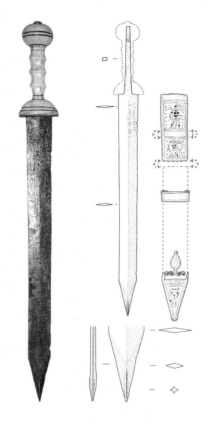

other centres.[82] During the AD 60s,[83] a new weapon started to replace the long-pointed Mainz sword: the Pompeii type. This is so called because several were buried there in AD 79 when Vesuvius erupted, and another was recently found on the 'marine' who died on Herculaneum beach during the same catastrophe.[84] The Pompeii type was on average even shorter than the Mainz types: known blades, excluding hilts, range from 377 to 550 mm (15–22 in), although most are between 400 and 500 mm (16–20 in).[85] However, the blade shape was notably different from most of its forerunners: narrower (42–55 mm: 1¾–2¼ in), parallel-edged and usually with a shorter triangular point, it evolved from the late 'Wederath' variant of the Mainz sword.[86] The hilt was also modified, with a generally deeper guard and 'flattened-onion' pommel. Pompeii-type scabbards, still suspended on four rings, are also different from those of later Mainz swords, which often have elaborate repoussé decoration like that on the Sword of Tiberius. Pompeii scabbards tend to sport simpler, less varied, flat decorative plates, with figures of Mars etc. picked out in openwork and engraving. An especially finely preserved blade, lacking its hilt assembly but still with much of its scabbard, is now in the Royal Armouries at Leeds, UK; rather confusingly, this Pompeii-type weapon was found at Mainz (Figs 48, 49).[87]

Changeover to the new form seems to have been fairly rapid, perhaps hastened by high rates of attrition and replacement during a burst of especially intensive warfare. Its dimensions indicate that the aggressive Roman preference for getting extremely close to the foe in foot combat, denying him room to wield longer weapons, remained as strong as ever (Fig. 50). The Pompeii type subsequently remained standard until well into the second century. The Mainz and Pompeii forms each lasted roughly a human lifetime, that is, about three generations of serving soldiers.

48. *Above left.* The Pompeii-type sword: a composite photo of a weapon from the Rhine now in the Royal Armouries, Leeds, northern Britain, with a (plausible, but speculative) reconstructed hilt.

49. *Above right.* The Royal Armouries Pompeii-type sword, which has several owner's inscriptions punched into the blade, with decorative components from its scabbard. (Scale 1:8)

The middle decades of the first century AD are the historical context for the earliest surviving reference to the auxiliary *spatha*, a term that was later certainly used for longer weapons (p. 29). First-century tombstones suggest that auxiliary infantry generally used the shorter Mainz and Pompeii types; cavalry monuments are more ambiguous, but some clearly show longer weapons. Auxiliary cavalry tombstones show swords, but most of these depictions are of little assistance, because relative sizes of items of equipment are among their least reliable features, being often distorted to fit the composition of the scene. (For example, Insus' horse is clearly scaled down to fit its frame, his sword surely likewise: Plate IV). However, some, like the stone of C. Romanius, cavalryman of the *ala Noricorum* found at Mainz (*c.* AD 60s), do seem to show long slender blades in frame scabbards (Fig. 51).[88]

Archaeological finds suggest the relatively long Fontillet type (p. 123) continued in use into this period, but stopped perhaps around the time the Mainz sword gives way to the Pompeii type. It seems that longer swords underwent simultaneous redesign. Certainly by the end of the first century a new form of longsword was current. An example from Rottweil in Germany may date to the 70s, but could be later.[89] Similar blades securely dating to AD 80–100 were found at Newstead in Scotland. One is complete, with a blade about 624 mm (25 in) long, a second essentially complete but broken in two; originally its blade was just over 630 mm.[90] They are 30–35 mm (1¼–1½ in) wide, diamond section with parallel edges, and 'gothic arch' points (Fig. 52). Three other incomplete blades from the site may be from similar weapons.[91] These swords look rather like narrowed, elongated versions of the Pompeii types, of which variants with curve-sided rather than triangular points appeared around this date.

Newstead-type swords are often considered to be the earliest reliably identified and provenanced

50. Early imperial sword-fighting stance: still a semi-crouch, the shield held forward by its single, central grip behind a projecting boss, with short Pompeii-type sword levelled ready to thrust. A legionary on a relief of *c.* AD 70 from the *principia* (military headquarters building) at Mainz, Germany.

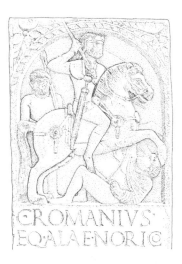

51. Tombstone of the cavalryman C. Romanius of the *ala Noricorum*, buried at Mainz in the first century AD. He sports a narrow-bladed long sword. Note the saddle horns, and the servant carrying his spears.

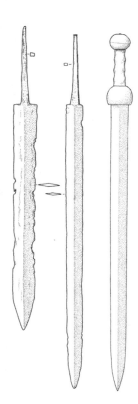

candidates to be Tacitus' *spathae*, and the forerunners of later Roman longswords. They are also usually thought to be cavalry weapons, and indeed doubtless were used by horsemen who appreciated the greater reach. However, it is not certain that they were exclusively cavalry arms, or indeed that Pompeii types were exclusively infantry weapons. Newstead blades are actually similar to late republican Delos-type *gladii Hispanienses* in length, and are on the short side compared with many third-century weapons used by horse and foot.

While the early history of the Roman longsword remains relatively unclear, the better-understood Pompeii type represents the kind of limited redesign seen in other items of kit during these decades, for example refinement of the construction of the '*lorica segmentata*'. Helmet forms saw increasing elaboration, with lowering of neckguards – perhaps suggesting a less crouching stance in sword fighting – and additional protection to the crown.[92] Some changes are clearly tactical, such as use of *manicae* – articulated arm defences – against the two-handed Dacian *falx*, which combined a long blade with a curved point that threatened lopped limbs and pierced skulls (Fig. 53). But why the wholesale change to the new sword type? Was it any more than fashion? There is no evidence (yet) that it was marked by any major technological developments in construction. However, at least a couple of known examples exhibit a real innovation: a cruciform-section point, which resembles the tips of some medieval and later weapons designed to pierce armour (Fig. 49).[93] Was the new shorter point, with or without this 'mail-opener', better for dealing with armoured foes, being less likely to break on impact? If so, which armoured men constituted this enemy? Some of the toughest hand-to-hand fighting faced by legionaries in this period was not against foreign enemies; it was against each other, and their own heavily armed auxiliaries.

In the early empire, emperors took care to ensure that *in extremis*, the legions could outmatch any rebellion by provincials or auxiliaries, in terms of numbers; it is likely that this consideration also extended to equipment, especially given the upheavals surrounding the death of Nero in AD 68 (see below, p. 154). During the Aeduan revolt of AD 21 legionaries had been reduced to battering heavily armoured gladiators with pickaxes.[94] They needed swords more capable of dealing with armoured foes.

52. Late first-century swords from Newstead, Scotland: a Pompeii-type weapon, and one of several longer blades identified as early *spathae*, reconstructed on the right with hilt components also from Newstead. (Scale 1:8)

†

The Pompeii sword came into widespread use during a decade marked by some of the most dramatic internal wars the empire had faced. First, during the reign of Augustus' last surviving blood-descendant, Nero, two unusually grave provincial revolts flared, in Britain and Judea.

The revolt in Britain under Boudica, queen of the Iceni, in AD 60–61 was triggered by a combination of maladministration – brutal even by Roman standards – and abuse of provincials by ill-disciplined soldiers and veterans settled in the new military colony of Camulodunum (Colchester). The native backlash was so massive that Nero allegedly considered abandoning the island. The ensuing slaughter, by rampaging rebels and Roman troops crushing them with extreme force, exacerbated by an ensuing famine, left hundreds of thousands dead.

At the other end of the empire, the even more catastrophic Jewish Revolt (AD 66–70) was also in part triggered by imperial insensitivity to the provincials. The long build-up to revolt included provocations surrounding the great focus of Jewish identity, the Temple at Jerusalem. These came from emperors (for example Caligula's plan to set up a statue of himself in the Holy of Holies), officials and private soldiers, such as the *miles* who exposed himself to worshippers during a festival, provoking a riot and mass casualties.[95] However, such sparks simply risked igniting the tinder of existing regional tensions between Jews and gentiles, which finally erupted in 66.

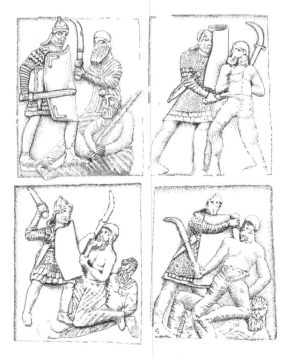

53. The *metopes* of the Adamklissi monument in Romania give an impression of Trajan's Dacian wars different from the familiar scenes on Trajan's Column. They detail *milites'* armour and sword techniques, used against Dacians often equipped with the fearsome hooked *falx*.

The Roman response has become a by-word for the brutality of Roman forces – and their allies – against civil populations. After a serious defeat of the initial expedition sent to put down the revolt, Nero appointed the proven general T. Flavius Vespasianus to annihilate opposition. Assisted by his son Titus, Vespasian began reducing Jewish strongholds by siege, closing in on Jerusalem. At Jotapata, the Romans captured its garrison commander, Josephus, who changed sides and survived to write the history of the war.

While the Jewish revolt raged, discontent simmered among Roman senators and soldiers at the erratic and 'unmanly' antics of Nero. Abortive revolts and defection of the Praetorians in 68 forced him into suicide. With the help of a freedman, Nero stabbed himself in the throat, at least meeting an honourable death.[96] He left no heir: Augustus' dynasty was extinct. A century after Actium, the consequent power vacuum triggered new civil wars.

Neither Augustus nor his successors ever resolved how to ensure peaceful imperial succession. Various methods were later tried, including senatorial selection, and adoption of adult heirs of proven ability, but the two most common routes proved to be by simple dynastic succession, or via the sword itself. In both of these the soldiers had their say, through attachment to established imperial families, or supporting favoured candidates in civil war. However, demonstrating *virtus*, fitness to command them, remained essential to winning and keeping the all-important support of the *milites*.

In 69 a violent scramble for the throne between rival provincial governors saw Roman armies clash twice at Cremona. This 'Year of the Four Emperors' had serious aftershocks: further revolts among the Gauls, and the powerful Batavians, before order was restored under Vespasian, first emperor of the new Flavian dynasty.

Meanwhile, the war in Judea was approaching its climax: the siege of Jerusalem, entrusted to Vespasian's son Titus. The relentless reduction of the city was a political as much as a military act, intended to maintain Rome's moral ascendancy over her subjects, and her self-image of ultimate invincibility. Resistance had to be seen to be crushed. If Rome's subjects could be made to believe that retribution would be certain and terrible, regardless of the cost or how long it took, they were less likely to risk imperial wrath. To achieve both impression and effect, as the historian Adrian Goldsworthy has emphasized, Roman doctrine was to attack any perceived threat to their power as soon as possible, with immediately available forces – even risking initial setbacks in an attempt to prevent trouble spreading. This explains why, when the Jewish Revolt broke out, the governor of Syria immediately invaded with the troops available to him – and met defeat.[97] Rome's lost opening gamble raised the stakes, making massive and high-profile imperial retaliation inevitable, to punish the rebels and warn off potential imitators. Hence a more powerful army under an experienced general was despatched. This background explains much of the savagery of the subsequent fighting, and the terrible siege of Jerusalem, which fell with enormous slaughter in 70. It also explains why, after the rest of the revolt had been suppressed, the Romans undertook the famous siege of Masada. A surviving group of Zealots held out in Herod's fortified desert mountaintop retreat near the Dead Sea. This remnant constituted minimal practical threat to the Romans, yet, despite the strength of the place, the heat and the logistical difficulties – even water had to be brought 15 km (9 miles) from en-Gedi – in 72 *legio x Fretensis* surrounded Masada and prepared to take it by direct assault. They raised a huge siege-ramp and attacked, only to find the defenders had chosen suicide. This event, remembered as heroic in modern Israel, nonetheless served its purpose for Rome. Masada warned provincials that Rome's soldiers would pursue rebels to the ends of the earth if necessary.[98]

Was the fate of Judea down to racism?[99] Although much of the time Romano-Jewish dealings were fairly peaceful, Romans themselves, usually tolerant of other religions in a polytheistic world, had limited sympathy with Jews, finding the exclusiveness of the Jewish god alien and unattractive, while murderous Jewish in-fighting (partly triggered by proximity to Rome) constituted a problem for imperial authority. Ethnic and religious hatreds certainly played a role in the horrors of the revolt, especially in motivating Rome's local allied contingents. Little love was lost between Jews and many of their neighbours, and Syrian auxiliaries especially committed atrocities on Jewish prisoners.[100] In part, however, the fate of Judea, like that of Gaul in Caesar's time, was driven by internal Roman power politics. Titus acted to extract maximum political and economic capital from the war for his father's new regime. The fall of Jerusalem resulted in a famous triumph through Rome,[101] and much-needed loot: Vespasian found the state coffers empty. The spoils of Jerusalem funded a new Temple of Peace and the Colosseum, both monuments built by Jewish prisoners.

The fall of Jerusalem was horrendously brutal, but the evidence, perhaps even more horrifyingly, is that the human suffering inflicted by Rome's soldiers in Judea was exceptional only in scale. In kind it was little distinguishable from the horrors other Roman soldiers had just inflicted on fellow Romans, at Cremona in the Po valley.

By this period, even for most citizen legionaries of Rome's northern or eastern armies (let alone auxiliaries), Rome was an abstraction, somewhere they had never seen, and Italy a foreign land. Of course they thought of themselves as Romans as good as any Italian, but their 'expatriate Romanness' was already significantly diverging from that of the old imperial heartlands, and was incorporating traits from the cultures of its provincial deployments. This divergence between the soldiers of the frontier provinces and metropolitan civilians had already been starkly illustrated earlier in 69 when, on their arrival in the capital, the men of Vitellius' northern army seemed to the people of the city to be shaggy aliens, and mutual misunderstandings and antagonism led to bloodshed.[102]

Besides unleashing rivalries among senators, violent contest for the throne laid bare underlying tensions among the soldiers, between and even within the warring provincial armies. In 69, Vitellius' northerners were notably prone to internecine strife. When an auxiliary cavalryman wrestled a *miles* of *legio v*, Gallic jeering provoked the legionaries to massacre two cohorts.[103] More generally, the pride of Vitellius' Batavian units was so overweening that they kept fighting the legionaries and they eventually had to be sent home, presaging worse trouble.[104]

If they despised each other, Vitellius' men held even harsher views of other Roman armies:

> All the eastern forces had been fired with rage over the arrogance of the soldiers of Vitellius who came to them, because though savage in appearance and barbarous in speech, they constantly mocked at all the others as their inferiors.
> TACITUS, *HISTORIES* 2.74.[105]

This reflected divergent regionalization and provincialization of the culture of Roman soldiers, which was just as strong in the east. Some months later, soldiers of the Rhine and Britain loyal to Vitellius, and Danubian and eastern *milites* loyal to Vespasian, clashed in the decisive second battle fought at Cremona. During the fighting the Flavian *legio iii* turned to hail the rising sun, a Syrian custom.[106]

To such men in this civil war, Vitellian-held Cremona was enemy territory, as foreign as Jerusalem. The city's civil population paid the terrible price, and in a four-day sack by victorious Vespasianic troops (and their camp servants) were subjected to rape, torture and the full horrors of any foreign city falling to Roman arms.[107] How far they were simply out of control, and how far their officers tacitly approved, is unclear. Satiated, the victorious army began to advance on the capital where, in anarchic chaos, Vitellius was killed. Vespasian was now undisputed emperor, but the wars were not over; Titus was still putting down the Jewish revolt, while the new regime faced further serious trouble in the north, partly of its own making. Vespasian's partisans had sought to undermine Vitellius by fostering sedition in his provincial power-base. In 70, this flared into a dangerous rebellion among leading Gauls and the Batavians under their ambitious leader Civilis. However, with the rapid suppression of these northern rebels and the fall of Jerusalem, the power of Vespasian's new Flavian dynasty was consolidated.

A decade of internal wars traumatized provincials and Romans alike. Towards its climax, the sack of Cremona had been followed by an even greater shock to the Roman psyche. While the Flavian army advanced on the capital, confused fighting broke out there between Vespasian's supporters and soldiers of the now-doomed Vitellius. This resulted in the burning of the ancient Temple of Capitoline Jupiter himself, an event that Tacitus in his *Histories* bewailed as 'the saddest and most shameful crime that the Roman state had ever suffered since its foundation'.[108]

Just a year before they sacked the Second Temple in Jerusalem, then, as a consequence of turning their swords on each other, Romans had sacked one of their own major cities, and encompassed the destruction of the holiest shrine in their own capital. The potential brutality of the *milites*, whether under orders, with the connivance of officers, or simply out of control, was inflicted with relative impartiality. Britons, Jews, fellow Romans, even the house of the king of their own gods, nothing and no one was safe from the teeth of the wolves.

## The 'Roman peace'

> To robbery, slaughter, plunder, they give the lying name of empire;
> they create desolation, and call it peace.
> TACITUS, *AGRICOLA* 30[109]

These famous lines were put into the mouth of the Caledonian war-leader Calgacus by Tacitus, in his account of his father-in-law Agricola's invasion of future-Scotland during the early 80s. If fictional, these words certainly reflected the real views of many of Rome's victims during this period, including the thousands of Jewish war slaves worked to death building the new Flavian amphitheatre, or Colosseum, in Rome. Within the empire, the years following Vespasian's victory in the civil wars were a time of renewed optimism. However, the destruction of Pompeii and Herculaneum by Vesuvius in 79 during the brief reign of Titus seemed to hint divine displeasure, and the rule of Titus' younger and less stable brother Domitian was remembered as a darker time, at least by senators like Tacitus who lived through it, and ended with Domitian's murder in 96. New civil wars were averted by the senate's appointment of the elderly Nerva as 'caretaker' emperor. He adopted as his heir another senator of proven ability: Trajan.

Trajan (r. 98–117) was hailed as best of emperors by senators, whose sycophancy mixed with sincerity when comparing his actions with Domitian's. Trajan followed Nerva's precedent, adopting as heir his adult kinsman Hadrian (r. 117–38), who in turn arranged for the succession of Antoninus Pius (r. 138–61) and the philosopher-emperor Marcus Aurelius (r. 161–80). This adoptive system produced the series of 'good emperors' of the 'Antonine Age', long seen as presiding over the zenith of the *pax Romana* and of Roman imperialism. However, it relied on *Augusti* not producing legitimate natural sons: Marcus Aurelius returned to dynastic succession with his son Commodus (r. 180–92).

This was the period when the cities of the Roman provinces approached the height of their grandeur, and the villas of the wealthy were coming to dominate many landscapes. Roman consumer goods – factory-made ceramics, glassware, jewelry – were widely available through the trade routes watched over by the imperial fleets and soldiers, a network which also facilitated the peaceful movement of people and ideas; Christianity would spread this way. Also, Roman citizenship was spreading through the provincial populations.

It is easy now to construe these decades as a golden age, especially compared with preceding wars of conquest, and later 'decline and fall'. Certainly, some contemporaries saw their times as especially blessed, in panegyrics praising the sagacity of the emperors and the bravery of the soldiers standing sentinel on the distant frontiers. Hence Epictetus enthused at the cessation of wars, of brigandage (well, 'on any large scale', anyway) and piracy, so that people could travel by land or sea from the rising to the setting sun whenever they wished.[110] The rich Greek orator Dio of Prusa presented Roman soldiers as shepherds who, alongside the emperor, guarded the imperial 'flock'.[111]

Doubtless panegyricists were often sincere in their propagandizing for the imperial order, for some did very well out of it, and more hoped to join them. As the historian Peter Heather has noted, while law enforcement was sporadic and corruption endemic, Roman hegemony brought 'a massive peace dividend in its wake, creating regional interconnections that provided many new economic opportunities.'[112] Perhaps, but for whom? Was the 'zenith of the empire' really so rosy for everyone, or even for a majority? Just how peaceful was the 'Roman peace'? Today, surviving frontier installations of the era foster an impression of watchful calm. In fact, the era saw some of Rome's bloodiest foreign wars, and further near-genocidal internal violence.

The 'zenith of empire' coincided with development of elaborate fixed frontier systems, notably on the Rhine and Danube. These comprised zones or lines of now-permanent unit bases, and lesser facilities such as chains of watch-towers linked by patrol roads. Such a track was called a *limes* (plural *limites*), a term which subsequently came to designate the frontier as a whole. Many such systems also incorporated demarcation lines or barriers, whether great rivers, or artificial structures such as ditches and banks, wooden palisades or, most elaborate of all, the famous stone wall built from sea to sea across Britain in the 120s at Hadrian's orders.

Hadrian's Wall looks like a fortification, and might appear to corroborate an impression that the Roman military in the early second century had definitively turned from aggressive warfare to defence, protecting the provinces from barbarian attacks. However, this is false.[113] Linear frontier systems were policed lines, primarily intended for surveillance and control of movements of people and goods, to prevent smuggling, small-scale raiding, and so on. Roman armies expected to detect and anticipate larger-scale trouble beyond the frontiers through intelligence gathering, and to send forces to crush it before it reached Roman soil. This applied even to Hadrian's Wall, crowded with auxiliary bases ready to project Roman power northwards when needed. Its exceptional elaboration probably had less to do with defensive necessity, and more to do with the expression of imperial power (Hadrian was an obsessive builder) and keeping an unruly provincial army busy for an extended period.[114] Indeed, the wider history of the period proves that the Roman military had not gone onto the defensive, either in doctrine or practice.

## Savage wars of peace[115]

Like Augustus, Trajan, 'best of emperors', enjoyed a reputation for peace and justice at home, yet elsewhere was a brutal aggressor – to the delight of his *milites*. One of the last of the great expansionist emperors who brought glory and booty to his men, he waged two major wars, one across the Danube to conquer Dacia, the last major free 'barbarian' kingdom in Europe, the other against Parthia (Fig. 54). Rome still lacked any consistent 'grand strategy' or 'rational' frontier policy: emperors still made war largely for personal glory.[116]

Trajan's conquest of Dacia, roughly modern Romania, was celebrated on the famous column in Rome, which has given us our canonical visual impression of Roman soldiers at war. He aimed at conquest of the eastern Carpathian basin and its settled peoples, who were similar to those on the south bank of the Danube. By the time of Trajan's invasion, in part due to interactions (often violent) with Rome, Dacia had become a well-defined kingdom. Its conquest required a series of campaigns by massive armies involving up to twelve legions, from 101 until the new Roman province was established in 107. Celebrated in the famous spiral relief on Trajan's column (Fig. 45), and the less well-known but in many ways more interesting monument at Adamklissi in Dacia itself (Fig. 53), these operations brought one of the last vast hauls of booty from Roman expansionist warfare, reputedly half a million Roman pounds weight of gold and a million of silver. However, resistance to this final great Roman lurch forward in Europe was so bitter that it resulted less in another example of sword and open hand, than in a military beheading of an indigenous society, with general replacement of native leaders, and perhaps much of the indigenous population, by soldiers and other incomers.[117] In contrast to regions like Gaul, the subsequently developing provincial cities did not evolve from indigenous tribal units, and were not controlled by descendants of native leaders-become-Romans. They were colonial implantations. It is unclear whether Trajan simply couldn't find amenable Dacian leaders to negotiate with, or simply opted for destruction of

54. The early Roman empire, showing the provincial boundaries as they were in *c.* AD 100, with other states, peoples and places mentioned in the text. Inset: a comparison of the territorial extent of the Roman and Parthian empires at the time.

'OUR WEAPONS AND ARMOUR'

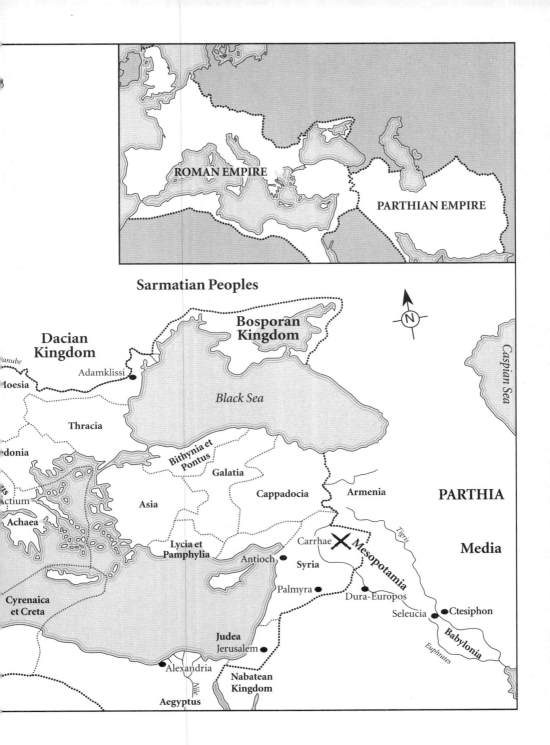

ROMAN EMPIRE

PARTHIAN EMPIRE

Sarmatian Peoples

Dacian
Kingdom

Bosporan
Kingdom

Caspian Sea

Danube

Adamklissi

Moesia

Black Sea

Thracia

Bithynia et
Pontus

donia

Galatia

Cappadocia

Armenia

PARTHIA

Asia

Actium

Achaea

Media

Tigris

Lycia et
Pamphylia

Carrhae

Mesopotamia

Antioch

Syria

Palmyra

Cyrenaica
et Creta

Dura-Europos

Seleucia

Ctesiphon

Babylonia

Euphrates

Judea

Jerusalem

Nabatean
Kingdom

Alexandria

Nile

Aegyptus

indigenous society as punishment for its sustained resistance. In Dacia the Romans were perhaps beyond the boundaries of societies that could be incorporated through 'traditional' means, and, as with the Eburones of northern Gaul (p. 105), had to resort to virtual 'ethnocide' to establish their rule. Still less were they able to absorb the semi-nomadic Sarmatian horse-peoples of the plains around Dacia, which remained a potentially vulnerable salient north of the Danube.

Not satiated by conquering Dacia, Trajan also acted aggressively on the Euphrates. On the pretext of Parthian plotting over the throne of Armenia, he reduced that kingdom to a province in 114, conquered northern Mesopotamia, and besieged the Parthian winter capital of Ctesiphon near modern Baghdad (seizing the royal throne as part of the booty), before advancing to the Persian Gulf. He probably dreamed of annexing Iran too. Yet his success was short-lived. Revolts broke out across Mesopotamia, while Parthian armies threatened from Iran. Roman commanders and soldiers had now developed the skills to take on the Parthians on the battlefield, but were unable to sustain their conquests. Trajan was forced to retreat, dying on the road in 117. His successor Hadrian abandoned Mesopotamia.

Trajan's aggression against Parthia set a pattern repeated several times over the following century. Further invasions of Mesopotamia would demonstrate that the Roman military had adapted well enough to warfare on the dry steppe and could defeat Parthian armies of horse archers and cataphracts, allowing it to reach and besiege the great cities of Babylonia. Yet it proved unable to hold southern Mesopotamia, let alone advance into the eastern Parthian empire, roughly modern Iran. Rome repeatedly failed to conquer Parthia, the same lands which Alexander had so quickly conquered from the Achaemenid Persians. Why? The likely reasons are discussed below (p. 204).

Resistance to Trajan in Mesopotamia was especially strong amongst the large Jewish population of Babylonia, and violence blew back into the empire through the *diaspora*. Massacres and counter-massacres perpetrated by both Jews and Greeks in Cyrenaica, Cyprus and Egypt reportedly left hundreds of thousands dead.[118] The major long-established Jewish community in Alexandria already had a long history of ethnic violence with the Greek majority in the city. Risings here and among other Jewish communities in Egypt during 116–17 led to enormous slaughter, and effective destruction of most of Egyptian Jewry. However, these revolts helped keep Babylonian Jewry free of Roman power, with profound consequences for Jewish culture; it shifted the centre of cultural gravity east-wards, towards the communities that would produce that vast corpus of rabbinic writings, the Babylonian *Talmud*. The Trajanic risings were followed some years later by renewed Jewish revolt with equally profound consequences, this time once more in Judea itself.

Hadrian, like Trajan, is widely considered a cultivated and benign ruler who, already a proven soldier when adopted by Trajan as his heir, felt no need to estab-lish his *virtus* by conquest, but kept the *milites* on their toes by prolonged tours of frontier inspection, most famously resulting in building the wall across Britain. However, the philhellene Hadrian disliked many Jewish practices, espe-cially circumcision, which Greeks regarded as barbaric mutilation. In a series of provocations, Hadrian decided to build a pagan sanctuary on the site of Herod's temple, and banned circumcision. This triggered another massive revolt, led by Simon Bar Kochba. Suppression of the Second Jewish (or 'Bar Kochba') Revolt of 132–36 approached genocide, involving vicious guerrilla warfare and fighting between Roman soldiers and Jewish fighters in tunnels and caves. Those directly killed totalled at least 580,000, while the numbers who died of privation were beyond counting.[119] Desolated Judea was renamed Palestine.[120]

### Violence and soldiers in civil society

The second-century Jewish revolts were catastrophic instances of mass violence inside the empire, but they were also exceptional in scale for the period. The 'peace' of the early empire generally did mean that wars within its territories were far fewer than they had been before they were conquered. Yet even at the height of the Roman peace, everyone in the Roman world could expect to endure physical violence, at least in youth – including future emperors flogged by their tutors – and many faced crippling injury or violent death. Violence remained structural in Roman society, generally against subordinates and especially against the servile and the criminalized. This is clear in the literature of the era, for example in Petronius' novel *Satyricon*, or Juvenal's *Satires* (p. 165).

Practices like raiding, in many provinces recently a glorious part of a warrior's life, were redefined as brigandage and attempts made to suppress them. As we shall see, these were not very successful, and throughout the empire banditry remained endemic, sometimes a plague. Galen advised fellow-doctors seeking bodies to dissect to go to the mountains to collect unburied bandits.[121] Even in the capital, violent criminality remained a problem.

In fact, while Rome sought to control illicit mayhem, she was equally con-cerned to maintain the martial spirit of her peoples, and actively exported new forms of armed violence to the provinces by spreading the taste for gladiatorial combat. The Gauls took to the idea with relish, Aeduans training gladiators in the early first century AD.[122] However, so did many Greeks (who also had their own long traditions of violent, if nominally sub-lethal, games). Galen was doctor to the gladiators of Pergamon, while Ephesus has produced a gladiator cemetery.[123] Amphitheatres are known from Scotland to the Euphrates. Gladiatorial combats became popular motifs of provincial art.

At Rome, ritualized violence in the Colosseum acted as a political safety-valve. The masses largely acquiesced to loss of political rights, in return for subsidized food and imperially sponsored spectacles such as chariot races and gladiatorial games, which allowed them to experience viscerally their superiority as Romans over the non-Roman world. Violence rarely spilled out of this carefully orchestrated theatre of death, although crowd trouble associated with partisans of chariot racing teams grew over time, culminating in the sixth-century 'Nika rebellion', which would almost topple the Byzantine emperor Justinian. Within the city of Rome itself, Praetorians and urban cohorts usually kept a lid on mass rioting, but even in Italy, there were some serious breaches of the peace during the early empire. In AD 59 during gladiatorial games in Pompeii there had been an armed ambush of visiting 'fans' from nearby Nuceria, in which a number of people were killed.[124] Nero had closed Pompeii's amphitheatre for ten years as an exemplary collective punishment for the riot. However, juridical responses to criminal violence were more often themselves very brutal, and carried out in the arena. Like that of eighteenth-century European societies, Roman judicial savagery was largely an attempt to deter through terror, because authorities lacked the means or manpower to prevent crime, or even to reliably apprehend perpetrators. Local governments had few officials resembling modern civil police.[125] If the civil judiciary could not keep trouble in check, then recourse was had to the swords of the soldiers.

Soldiers backed up the civil power throughout the empire, whether this comprised Roman governors, imperially sanctioned local magistrates, client rulers or others such as, until the great revolt, the Jewish temple authorities in Jerusalem. *Milites* acted as juridical agents, for example during the interrogation, execution and burial of Jesus.[126] Some undertook what we would regard as normal policing duties, for example in Egypt, where they also served as riot police, notably in violence-prone Alexandria.[127] Praetorians were on occasion unleashed to quell unrest in Italian cities.[128]

However, the main motive for keeping the peace, as the biased structure and enforcement of the law made clear, was not protection of the empire's peoples at large, Roman or provincial, but ensuring the functioning of the structures of domination. Soldiers under orders acted on behalf of the emperor, and therefore (normally) in the interests of the landed elites who dominated provincial societies and collected the taxes that bankrolled the emperor and his soldiers.

Consequently, emperors were much more anxious about sedition than mere criminality, keeping watch on civil organizations like burial clubs and even municipal fire brigades, and sometimes banning them. Soldiers were widely employed on such internal surveillance, social control and repression, from patrols in the hills of Judea to Praetorians on the streets of Rome itself.

Such an inherently abusive system also invited even greater abuse of the vulnerable at the behest of influential people. An inscription from Africa records soldiers used by imperial procurators to illegally beat up citizens and torture tenants on an imperial estate.[129]

Unsurprisingly, then, to most inhabitants of the empire, including those in the capital, *milites*, even when under legal orders, were not 'our boys' or friendly defenders, but agents of control and oppression. At the height of the *pax Romana*, in some regions, notably Judea, they simply remained foreign military occupiers.[130] And too often, soldiers exceeded their orders, or even broke free of military discipline entirely.

> And the soldiers likewise demanded of him, saying, And what shall we do? And he said unto them, do violence to no man, neither accuse any falsely; and be content with your wages.
> LUKE, 3.14

Against slaves, provincials and even poorer Roman citizens without influential friends, soldiers were very often tempted to use threats and violence on their own private behalf, to extort goods and services or simply to enjoy their power. This is the period of Juvenal's *Satire* on avoiding trouble with *milites* in Rome itself.[131] If you get beaten up by soldiers, he advises, just keep quiet, since if you complain, the hearing will be held by his comrades, and you can be sure of a worse beating afterwards for your temerity.

Juvenal did not exaggerate. Such soldierly brutality and rapacity were empire-wide. The Vindolanda tablets preserve a draft of a letter of complaint from someone, probably a Gaulish trader, who in *c.* 100 fell foul of a centurion and was, in his view entirely unjustly, 'beaten with rods'.[132] Having failed to get redress from other officers locally, he is complaining to higher authority, probably the governor. Around the middle of the second century, Apuleius' novel *The Golden Ass*, set in Greece, is also peppered with violence, some of it committed by soldiers. For example, a *miles* tries to 'requisition' (actually, steal for himself) a donkey from a vegetable-seller who resists. The soldier beats him with his *vitis* (vine-staff, so perhaps a centurion), then reverses it to hit him again with the knobbed end (*nodulus*). The civilian fights back successfully, but the soldier has the last laugh: with his cronies he catches up with the vegetable-seller, gets him dragged before the magistrates, facing almost certain death on trumped-up charges – and gets hold of the donkey.[133] That this satire at most exaggerated reality is confirmed by the first-century philosopher Epictetus, who advises mule-owners not to resist military requisitions, 'for if you do, you will get a beating and lose your mule all the same'.[134] Another favourite practice among soldiers on the road was illegally demanding accommodation and entertainment from villagers, as condemned in a letter from the governor of Syria of 185–86.[135] For *milites* deployed across the provinces on policing, surveillance, tax-gathering or supply duties, there were easy opportunities for systematic extortion from the locals. Mid-second-century Egyptian papyri detail regular payments of 'protection money' to soldiers stationed nearby.[136] Perhaps the murdered soldiers secretly buried in Canterbury later in the century (Fig. 55) attest provincials avenging themselves on rapacious *milites*.[137]

It was not, then, only during revolts or civil wars that everyone faced danger from the soldiers, from the lowest British slave or Jewish peasant to the *milites'* own employer, the emperor himself.

## The emperor and his soldiers

Imperial soldiers, like their later-republican forerunners, were not entirely unthinking, although possessing only limited education or political knowledge, and with little clear agenda apart from honour, glory and money.[138] Far into the imperial period legionaries preserved the traditions of independence of mind of the free, propertied citizen militia and Italian warriors of the republican era. Continued unruliness marked the persistence of this traditional Roman soldierly liberty. This spirit doubtless chimed with the new auxiliaries, recruited from warrior groups characterized by outspokenness and touchy pride. Collectively liable to emotional tides of sentimentality, enthusiasm, dismay, surly disgruntlement or fury, *milites* remained prone to violent mutiny triggered by their own grievances, such as Tiberius faced in AD 14. On Augustus' death a number of legions mutinied over conditions and the delayed discharge of veterans. Tiberius' nephew Germanicus, seeking to quell the mutiny, at one stage theatrically drew his sword and threatened suicide – at which a soldier called Calusidius offered him his own sword, saying that it was sharper, an astonishing instance of sarcastic soldierly insolence.[139] The rising was finally put down, partly by negotiation, partly by the power of shame; Germanicus decided his wife and his little son Gaius would be safer among the Gallic provincials than in a mutinous camp. Gaius had become the darling of the sentimental soldiers (who nicknamed him 'Caligula' after the *caligae*, or miniature military boots, that he wore). When the soldiers saw that Germanicus was entrusting the boy's safety to the Gauls due to their behaviour, it helped shame them into submission – as Germanicus doubtless intended.[140]

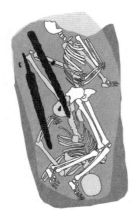

55. In the late second century two bodies were crammed facedown into a pit, inside the walls of Canterbury, southern Britain. This illegal burial looks to be the clandestine disposal of murder victims – soldiers, judging by the dress items and swords buried with them (see also Fig. 63).

Even more serious than disorder originating in the ranks was manipulation of *milites* by their own generals, unit commanders, centurions and other influential office-holders such as standard-bearers. Soldiers were always potentially swords in the hands of others, something emperors never ceased to fear. Early in the reign of Claudius the governor of Dalmatia, Camillus Scribonianus (who had been mooted as a possible rival claimant to the succession) attempted to lead his legions in revolt. He was thwarted when, reportedly, the legionary eagles 'refused to be removed from the ground'. This dire omen was surely orchestrated by the standard-bearers, at the behest of officers who had decided to remain loyal to Claudius, or because the soldiers had no stomach for a civil war.[141]

Over time, *milites* became increasingly aware of their own potential power as makers and breakers of emperors. A perennial anxiety for all emperors was, then, how to keep these ultimate guardians of the regime under discipline, fit for service and, not least, loyal. Maintaining the soldiers' loyalty would help ensure continued acquiescence of the aristocracy to the emperor, but all who occupied the throne remained fearful of military revolts fomented by senatorial rivals.

Yet, although the senate as a body had no contact with most armies, which were the emperor's special province (in its original sense of 'area of authority', not necessarily simply geographical),[142] the emperor commanded most of his soldiers through senatorial legates, governors-cum-army commanders of individual territorial provinces. Augustus' granting of military commands to senators was a means of allowing them, as far as possible, to pursue traditional mixed military/civil careers, necessary to their tacit acquiescence to his 'restoration of the republic'. It was also public recognition that only senators possessed the experience, connections and leadership skills required for provincial government and to command troops. However, while sincerely attached to many such hallowed traditions, Augustus applied special rules to strategically sensitive Egypt. Determined no new Mark Antony should seize the wealthiest province, the emperor forbade senators to go there without his permission. Egypt was governed, and its legions led, by equestrian prefects. With the emperors, the equestrian order (the wealthy class below the senatorial order) 'arrived' through commands of auxiliary regiments and a range of higher appointments in the imperial service, of which the prefectures of Egypt and the Praetorian Guard became ultimate prizes.

All of Tiberius' wolves (p. 26) – senators and soldiers – had to be watched. The emperor sought to minimize potential for subversion by having each provincial legate report directly to himself personally, and by having these men watched by equestrian finance officials in their provinces. But how to watch the soldiers? Most of the time, senatorial governors and legionary commanders, and equestrian commanders of auxiliary units, shared a common interest with the emperor in keeping their men contented and under control.

&#10013;

*Quis custodiet ipsos custodes?* 'Who will guard the guards themselves?'
JUVENAL, *SATIRES* 6.347–8

Emperors and their appointed commanders sought to control their soldiers through a traditional mix of means: fear and flattery, indoctrination and indulgence, reward and punishment. Not least, they sought to watch the *milites* closely, and to head off impending trouble.

Traditional means still emphasized metaphorical carrot and literal stick. Powerful emphasis remained on traditional Roman discipline, enforced by corporal punishment: centurions still used their vine-staffs on recalcitrant soldiers' backs. Some brutal punishments remained quasi-democratic, for example collective stoning of negligent sentries who put all at risk. There were also occasional revivals of old-style severe discipline, and brutal training regimes (for example Corbulo's 'restoring' of the Syrian legions in Armenia).[143]

The baseline tangible benefits of military service were relatively generous pay, and periodic bonuses, donatives from the emperor. Less tangible, but also valued, were legal perks of military service (for example, privilege of trial in military courts and special rights over property and wills) and the significant social status that bearing arms for the emperor brought; civilians may have despised soldiers, but they feared them. Soldiers were among the 'haves' in the tall, stratified imperial social pyramid, their right to carry swords also bringing opportunities for illegal exploitation of their position outside camp, as we have seen. This could be tacitly tolerated or connived at by superiors too fearful or venal to suppress it.

One especially desired compensation for tolerating the rigours of service and discipline in camp was the chance for soldiers to fulfil their dreams of glory and plunder on campaign. Military decorations remained hugely prized as tangible evidence of personal courage and its recognition by the emperor, bringing prestige both among *commilitones* (fellow-soldiers), and in civic society. However, with the slowing of imperial expansion, opportunities to gain honour and wealth in war became fewer. Rome faced diminishing capacity for projecting violence profitably, in terms either of glory or, especially, of maintaining the flow of war-booty that had long subsidized the state. Certainly, internal pressures for booty had reduced, as expansion of the imperial economy led to internal generation of most of the empire's wealth. It also brought about demilitarization of Italy, and other provinces of the imperial core. In these regions wars were still celebrated, but among civilian Roman citizens masculinity was redefined: for them, *virtus* no longer required personally going to war (although it still required that the *vir* remained a dominant figure in society, able to inflict violence while not tolerating personal injury). What of the professional soldiery, now the main custodians of traditional martial *virtus*? How, if the empire was not expanding, to manage *milites'* yearning for battle and booty, glory and victory?

Roman martial *virtus* was supposed to be characterized by self-controlled bellicosity. Emperors and commanders employed methods aiming to maintain both *virtus* and *disciplina*, to achieve the fine balance between potentially contradictory aims, of keeping the wolves fierce and hungry, but also caged and obedient until the need to unleash them arose.

In part this was achieved by modifications to military conceptions of *virtus* as well as civilian. Since the republic, because soldiering involved so much heaving of heavy equipment and – that Roman speciality – entrenching, it had always been accepted that *militia* involved forms of *labor* (toil) and *sudor* (sweat), made honourable rather than demeaning because integral to military service for the state. This tradition formed the basis for the early imperial idea that *virtus* was demonstrable through training and building work, as well as on campaign.[144] Hadrian's addresses to African troops at Lambaesis, subsequently recorded on inscriptions set up at the military exercise ground, illustrate the point. After watching a training display by the horsemen of *cohors* VI *Commagenorum equitata*, a mixed infantry and cavalry unit enjoying less pay and prestige than a cavalry *ala*, he said:

> It is hard for horsemen of a cohort to please…[especially]…after a show by horsemen of an *ala*. …But you have banished weariness by your eagerness…everywhere you jumped nimbly onto your horses. The outstanding *virtus* of noble Catullinus, my legate, shows itself in that under this *vir* you are such *viri*.[145]

Indoctrination, backed up by religion, remained vital. *Milites* were inculcated with the new ideology of universal, eternal Rome and the imperial cult developed by Augustus. Official sacrifices and regularly renewed oaths of loyalty to the emperor constantly reminded *milites* who was their commander-in-chief, patron and benefactor, and made revolt a sacrilege. The second century AD saw development of the cult of *Disciplina* as a goddess. Most Romans were pious and superstitious, and such measures had real impact, but were far from infallible. As effective might be direct appeal through the soldiers' purses. Imperial portraits and messages on the newly minted coins in their pay reinforced the message. Pay and donatives – monetary gifts that, especially when made at a questionable imperial accession, were barely distinguishable from bribes – provided the most tangible motivation for soldiers' obedience.

Another vital incentive to loyalty to superiors within the military, as in wider Roman society, was patronage. The favour of centurions, commanders and ultimately the emperor was the route to advancement for the individual *miles*. Soldiers' yearning for favours, recommendations and advancement is a striking theme of the Vindolanda tablets,[146] and it has been plausibly suggested that the reason the army and province of Britain proved chronically rebellious was that, being literally isolated, soldiers, officers and provincial aristocrats felt they were missing out on their proper share of imperial favour.

The soldiers' loyalty had to be earned as well as demanded and purchased. The occupant of the throne had to fulfil their expectations as Romans, proving himself worthy of the title of *imperator* by displaying martial *virtus*. In AD 41, when Tiberius' successor Caligula was assassinated, his obscure uncle Claudius was made emperor, to his own shock, by the Praetorians. He had had no prior public career; he had to bribe the *milites* and also quickly prove his *virtus*, or he would soon himself die by soldiers' swords or senatorial daggers. Facing a literal choice of death or glory, Claudius ordered and nominally led the invasion of Britain in AD 43 (p. 132). Victory secured his survival. The attractions of glory, and the perceived need to demonstrate *virtus* by successful war, were bowed to even by that exceptionally peaceful emperor Antoninus Pius, who outdid his adoptive father Hadrian by both advancing back into Scotland and building a new wall across Britain. Marcus Aurelius had war forced upon him, and rose to the challenge; Commodus was thought weak, and it helped kill him.

Once established as first emperor, Augustus sought to distance himself from the soldiers who had raised and still ultimately sustained him, ceasing to call them *commilitones* ('fellow-soldiers'), but *milites* instead.[147] Later emperors felt it undesirable or simply unrealistic to maintain this degree of aloofness from their troops. They were increasingly obliged to pander to the demotic ideology of the soldiers, continuing the Roman tradition of commanders exhorting their men as much as commanding them on pain of death. Some ostentatiously acted as *commilitones*, being seen to dress, eat and live like the men on campaign, and to make theatrical gestures, such as that soldiers' soldier Trajan tearing strips from his own clothes to bind his soldiers' wounds.[148] *Milites* increasingly expected this of their commander-in-chief – up to a point. While appreciating such material demonstrations that their leaders did not despise them, soldiers still expected officers to retain their dignity.[149] Overdoing it, as Caracalla did, could lead to loss of respect, with deadly consequences.

Control of the soldiers was a constant preoccupation of Roman commanders. If there was no active campaigning to absorb their energies, other activities were devised to keep them busy, such as training and exercises, or what is now known as 'military bullshit'. For example, Frontinus, former governor of Britain and commander of its large army, which had a reputation for mutinousness, suggests in his *Stratagems* that idle soldiers could be set to building unnecessary ships.[150] This is why I believe that, whatever Hadrian's primary reasons for ordering construction of a wall across the island in the 120s, he also had in mind the valuable side benefit that it would long keep the unruly *milites* of Britain too busy to make trouble.

It was vital to authority to keep soldiers under surveillance, and to prevent potentially dangerous unsupervised 'networking'. Hence officers were concerned to prevent large, unauthorized assemblies of soldiers, and to watch smaller, authorized gatherings. This is seen from the time of Severus in control and close supervision of military *scholae* – permitted associations of military peer-groups such as standard bearers and musicians – within units. As units increasingly spent not just winters but also many peacetime campaigning seasons in and around fixed bases, the nature of these installations became a central factor in surveillance and control of the *milites*.

Soldiers' special pride is in their *castra*; that is their *patria*, that is their *Penates*.
TACITUS, *HISTORIES* 3.84

The appearance of longer-lived military bases during the early empire was a major development in the 'material culture' of Roman soldiers. With Augustus, regiments had become permanent entities, institutions with continuous histories and evolving traditions. If the primary material culture of soldiers comprised their arms and dress, that of their units comprised their standards, 'paper' records and, increasingly, the facilities in which they were housed. Tacitus, in the quotation above, uses heavily laden terms indicating how *milites* came to see such places. *Patria* means 'fatherland', 'native country', 'dwelling-place' or 'home'; *Penates*, literally deities of the household, was also figurative for home and hearth, and for households collectively constituting the state. Both terms also perhaps imply a city.

During the republic, Roman soldiers generally wintered at home or in friendly cities, and, until they began to operate long-term in little-urbanized regions such as upland Hispania, had little need for dedicated military installations beyond marching-camps or the elaborated versions used in sieges.[151] In Europe, the permanent advance to the Rhine and Danube, where there were no cities in which to base garrisons, led to the development of marching camps into more substantial single-winter camps, and then military supply and operating bases with ever-increasing life-spans. This was the genesis of the familiar 'Roman fort'. For such stations Romans of the time used terms such as *praesidium*, 'garrison', or for the built base *hiberna* ('winter quarters'), *castra* (plural of *castrum*, a fortified post, so perhaps 'the fortifications') or sometimes the diminutive *castellum*.[152] The last is the root of the English word 'castle', apparently validating modern terms for these installations such as 'auxiliary fort' and 'legionary fortress'. However, these are misleading translations, since 'fortress' especially, like 'castle', connotes to English-speakers a primarily defensive stronghold. To be sure, such establishments were provided with wall-circuits, and on occasion were besieged, but their purpose was not 'point defence' at all. In doctrine, tactics and strategy, they were bases for soldiers undertaking active surveillance of territory, subjects and foes, and for offensive operations. As noted earlier in this chapter, Romans expected to anticipate danger through intelligence gathering (spies, informants, cavalry reconnaissance), to attack first, and to deal with enemies in the open. Soldiering remained something to be conducted in the field, not from behind walls (implicit in terms like *hiberna*). If such bases were besieged, a major failure had already occurred elsewhere. Hence 'military base' is more appropriate than 'fort' or 'fortress'.

Through the first century AD, at least in Europe, bases were still constructed from timber and earth or turf, their ramparts having rounded corners for stability (resulting in the familiar 'playing-card' shape) and they were thought of as temporary. Units could expect to move within a few years, and build new ones. However, by AD 100, tacitly accepting that most armies were not going anywhere soon, units started rebuilding in stone.

The base, then, with its central shrine of the standards and the imperial cult, and its elaborate routines, festivals and ceremonial, was the physical manifestation of Rome and the emperor, and of the regiment as an entity, just as the sword itself physically embodied the soldier.[153] They comprised rest, recuperation and training centres, foci of logistical networks (navigable rivers as much as roads), and 'jumping-off points' for military operations.

During this period there were various types and sizes of bases, especially in the first century AD, which saw bases designed for pairs of legions (for example Xanten, Germany), or for 'battle-groups' of legionary detachments (vexillations) and *auxilia*. However, increasingly they were designed nominally to hold a single auxiliary unit or legion, although in practice there remained considerable fragmentation and brigading of contingents (Figs 56, 57).

Such bases, all laid out in much the same way, give a striking impression of that regularity and order which had long impressed foes, and which was also to be impressed on the soldiers within. It is instructive to compare Roman military bases with more recent ones, which routinely incorporate large internal open areas for parade and exercise. There are no such spaces inside relatively crowded Roman bases, except the great junction immediately in front of the *principia* (headquarters building). Rather, the layout reflects the concern – anxiety – of commanders to ensure surveillance and control of their men. The *principia* dominates the main axes and gates while (especially clear in legionary base layouts), each barrack block usually has the centurion's accommodation nearest the perimeter. This was convenient for forming up cohorts to march out via the perimeter road, but also meant that the soldiers in barracks were ringed by their centurions. Similarly, even when later rebuilt in stone rather than friable timber and turf, perimeter watchtowers were not projected outwards towards potential external danger, where they could be most effective if the base was attacked; they still straddled the walls. Like razor-wire perimeters of modern military bases, these defensive circuits were designed against surprise attacks and

56. Inchtuthil, Scotland, northernmost legionary base of the empire. Built during the 80s, it was never completed: only a temporary headquarters (*principia*) was erected, and the legate's house (*praetorium*) not started.

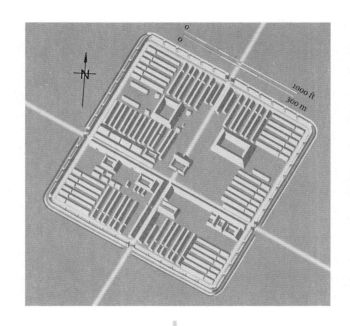

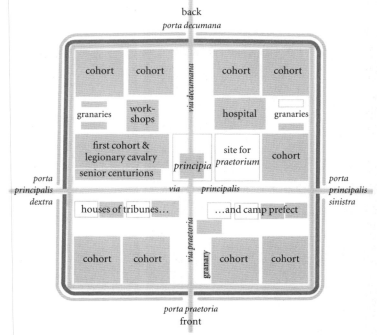

back
*porta decumana*

| cohort | cohort | | cohort | cohort |

granaries — work-shops — hospital — granaries

first cohort & legionary cavalry

senior centurions — *principia* — site for *praetorium* — cohort

*porta principalis dextra*

*via*    *principalis*    *porta principalis sinistra*

houses of tribunes… …and camp prefect

cohort — cohort — granary — cohort — cohort

*via decumana*

*via praetoria*

*porta praetoria*
front

infiltration, but sentries were likely more concerned with illicit movements of soldiers around or out of the camp. Criminality, desertion or, worse, mutiny and sedition were eternal anxieties of commanders.[154] Bases were social pressure-cookers, the 'inveterate venality' of camp communities shocking recruits and even some generals.[155] If they were located with an eye to controlling provincials or threatening foreign foes, internally Roman military bases were designed for surveillance and control of concentrations of potentially dangerous men. Not castles, but wolf-cages.

Bases such as those described above dotted the European and North African provinces. However, little is yet known about early imperial bases from the Black Sea to Egypt. Some 'playing card' sites are known, but most units were stationed in or adjacent to the major cities of the long-urbanized east. How far such urban bases corresponded to the marked, almost obsessive regularity of western 'playing-card' bases remains unclear, as most are inaccessible under later occupation. Yet perceived differences, especially greater irregularity of layout perhaps forced by squeezing them into already-built-up landscapes as seen later at Dura-Europos (p. 194) – not a problem with 'green-field' sites in Europe – may well have contributed to western Roman prejudices about the lack of discipline of eastern soldiers.

In the aftermath of the civil wars of 68–70, additional measures were taken to maintain control of the soldiers. To make it harder to subvert more than one legion at a time, double legionary bases like that at Vetera (Xanten, Germany) were abolished. Yet fear of military rebellion persisted. Renewed civil wars at the end of the second century resulted in all provinces with large garrisons, such as Britain, Pannonia and Syria, being split into two commands, further reflecting how internal security concerns could take priority in military deployment and command structures.

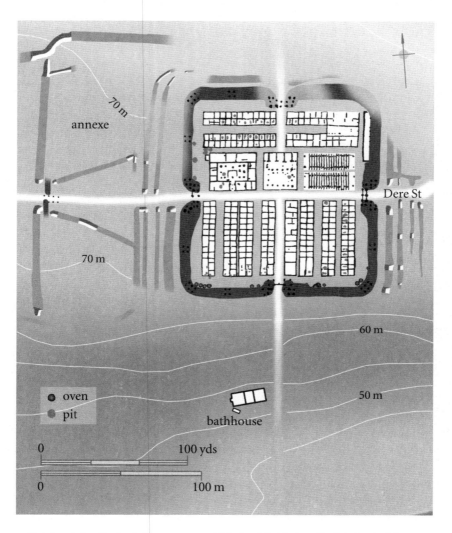

Within the map:

annexe

70 m

70 m

Dere St

60 m

50 m

oven
pit

bathhouse

0            100 yds

0            100 m

57. Elginhaugh fort, Scotland. Contemporary with Inchtuthil, this short-lived timber-built base for auxiliary soldiers is one of the few Roman military sites to have undergone virtually complete excavation.

# Deadly Embraces
## The Middle Empire 167–269

### From 'golden age' to military anarchy

The reigns of Hadrian (r. 117–38) and Antoninus Pius (r. 138–61) had, with bloody exceptions, seen an era of general peace. Marcus Aurelius, Rome's 'philosopher-king' (r. 161–80), humane, stoic, last of the second-century 'good emperors', was fated to spend most of his reign at war.

In AD 161 the Parthians installed their own nominee on the throne of Armenia, and defeated Rome's eastern armies. In the ensuing war Rome opportunistically expanded her frontiers across and down the Euphrates at Parthian expense, once again sacked Ctesiphon and in 166 raided into Media, further east than Roman arms had ever penetrated. However, triumph was marred by a major plague outbreak, brought back by returning soldiers. It was also rapidly overshadowed by disaster on the Danube.

In 167, seizing the opportunity presented by depletion of Roman garrisons for the Parthian war, German Marcomanni and Quadi crossed the Middle Danube, while the Sarmatian Iazyges of the adjacent Hungarian plain, westernmost of the Iranian-speaking horse peoples who dominated the Asiatic steppes, attacked Dacia. It is unclear what dynamics in Barbaricum (barbarian territory) lay behind these events, although it was a period of internal social upheaval and migration as far as the Baltic, from where the ancestors of the Goths were already migrating towards the Black Sea. The savage ensuing Marcomannic Wars, breaking out in 168 with fighting on the Danube frontier lasting until 180, saw the first barbarian incursions into the Po plain for generations, and were depicted with unusually brutal realism on a new column raised in Rome (Figs 58–60).[1]

The grim fightback by Marcus' soldiers was interrupted by military rebellion in the east, led by the architect of Rome's recent victories there, the Syrian general Avidius Cassius, and precipitated by erroneous reports of Marcus' death. Cassius was soon eliminated, and Marcus, eventually victorious on the Danube, was planning to create new provinces of Marcomannia and Sarmatia north of the river when he died. His son and heir Commodus (r. 180–92) abandoned these plans, although the defeated barbarians were required to provide men for Rome's armies. These events prefigured the future: simultaneous foreign wars in both

58. Scenes from the Marcomannic Wars, from the Column of Marcus Aurelius at Rome. They show marching and battle scenes, but also graphically depict the wider horrors of war. Here *milites* and (centre left) their German allies slaughter unarmed prisoners, including women, with swords (using cuts and reverse-handed downward thrusts) and spears.

north and east, military revolts and civil war became Rome's living nightmare for the following century.

Commodus was assassinated in 192, triggering a new round of devastating civil wars on the scale of AD 69, revealing afresh, and even more starkly, the role of the soldiers as arbiters of empire. From the walls of their camp, the Praetorians actually auctioned the throne to the highest bidder.[2] The fighting ended in Gaul in 196, with a major battle at Lugdunum (Lyons), in which thousands of Roman troops were killed. The winner, Septimius Severus (r. 193–211), had been governor of Pannonia, strategically central and garrisoned by especially tough soldiers. He set about ensuring that no one should be able to imitate his rise, by dividing the biggest provinces and their garrisons.

Severus and his dynasty epitomize the transformation of the Roman world by the second century AD, which saw 'Romanization' of the provinces – and 'provincialization' of Rome. A senator of North African origin who (reportedly) spoke Latin with a Punic accent, Severus married a Syrian aristocrat, Julia Domna. His son and successor Caracalla (r. 211–17) was thus half-African, half-Syrian, while later emperors of the dynasty were wholly Syrian. This process marks the culmination of the long Roman tradition of offering the open hand to amenable foreigners, especially aristocrats, leading to deep integration of ruling classes across the whole empire. At the same time, Roman citizenship had

59. The Marcomannic Wars on the Column of Marcus Aurelius: rare depictions of Roman soldiers spreading terror among civilians, plundering and burning German farms, raping and killing at will, and enslaving the survivors.

60. The Marcomannic Wars on the Column of Marcus Aurelius: spoils of war. Livestock is driven away (bottom left), while captured German families are led into slavery. Children are dragged from their mothers (bottom right), men and boys separated from women. Younger females (top left) were especially prized.

long been spreading through the wider provincial populations (as in the case of that Greek-speaking Jew from Tarsus in Turkey, St Paul). Caracalla famously extended it to virtually the entire free population of the empire, effectively erasing the distinction between 'Roman' and 'provincial'.

Yet on the other hand, the civil constitutional façade of imperial rule was rapidly crumbling. In stark contrast to Augustus' self-transformation from warlord to constitutional ruler, Severus had no time for such niceties and remained a military autocrat, setting the pattern for succeeding generations. He advised his sons to look after the soldiers and ignore everyone else, raising military pay so far that the coinage had to be debased. In pursuit of glory, and to indulge and toughen the soldiers – and his own sons – Severus engaged in aggressive wars, attempting renewed expansion. From increasingly enfeebled Parthia he seized new provinces beyond the Euphrates, and once again sacked Ctesiphon – although, like Trajan, Severus found he could not hold southern Mesopotamia. He also waged a major war in Britain, but failed finally to annexe Scotland, dying during the attempt. His son Caracalla again attacked Parthia, but was assassinated there.

During this era, portentous changes overtook the battered Parthian world. In 224 the last Arsacid king was defeated by one of his Iranian vassals, Ardashir, who took over the Parthian empire in Iran and Mesopotamia, establishing a new dynasty: the Sasanids. Sasanian Iran ('Persia' to the Romans) was to prove a much more formidable and aggressive military power than Parthia had been. Suddenly, in the east, Rome was thrown onto the defensive.

In the 250s, disaster struck Rome in both east and north (Fig. 61). After a series of damaging incursions into Roman Syria, in 260 the Sasanian king Shapur I 'the Great' destroyed a major Roman expeditionary army near Edessa and captured the emperor Valerian, exacerbating massive military defeat with unprecedented political humiliation. At the same time, powerful new Germanic confederations were smashing through the western frontiers and devastating the western provinces. Rome faced simultaneous catastrophe on two fronts. The result was internal military and political chaos, with a string of emperors or usurpers appearing, most soon overthrown by assassination or war between their soldiers. Roman power collapsed in the east, lasting Sasanian conquest of Roman Asia and Egypt being prevented only by the audacity of Rome's ally, Syrian Palmyra, which briefly established control over several Roman provinces, initially on behalf of the emperor, but then as a breakaway empire of its own.[3] In the west, from Spain to Britain, as the central state lost power and credibility, military officers and provincial magnates set up a breakaway 'Gallic empire' to safeguard their own interests. The Roman empire appeared finally to be fragmenting into successor states, as Alexander's had done.

In the mid-third century Rome's soldiers failed her. In contrast to the glory days of the republic and early empire, during this period they proved unable to

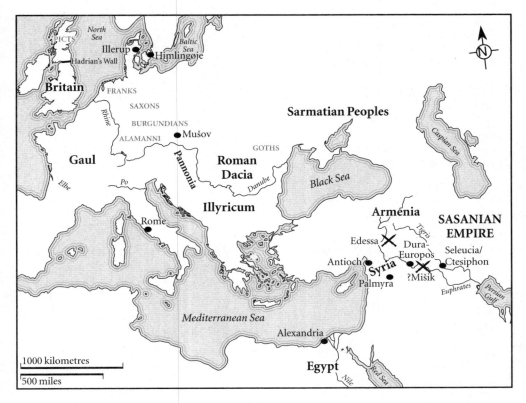

61. The Roman empire, its neighbours and enemies in the third century AD, showing the regions, states, peoples and places mentioned in the text.

contain, let alone conquer, Rome's foreign enemies. They came to spend as much energy fighting each other, at the expense of the provincials and the state, as foreign foes. How did this situation arise? Was it due to a decline in the quality or commitment of the soldiers, their morale, training, or arms? Was it failure of leadership? Or was it down to external factors?[4]

Certainly, Rome's military did not stand still during the second and earlier third centuries. New legions were raised, in Italy as tradition demanded, under Marcus and Severus, but established legions, as well as auxiliary formations, now tended to recruit in what had become their home provinces. Additional *alae* and cohorts continued to be raised, and entirely novel formations, simply called *numeri* ('regiments'), also appeared. These were smaller regiments drawn from 'wilder' peoples such as northern Britons, as long-established auxiliary formations became ever less distinguishable from the legions in recruitment, culture, ethos and arms. From early in the third century, auxiliaries as well as legionaries were normally Roman citizens.

Overall the military grew significantly larger, with an establishment of perhaps 450,000 men, as much as 50 per cent more soldiers than under Augustus – if units were kept up to strength. The total number of legions only rose to thirty-three (almost as many old legions had been destroyed or cashiered as new ones created), but many more auxiliary formations were raised, and so the proportion of auxiliaries increased significantly, to about 60 per cent of military manpower. Regiments were still grouped into provincial armies, mostly commanded by senatorial governors. The number of armies had grown since Augustus with the number of frontier provinces, as client kingdoms were annexed, new lands conquered and, especially from the reign of Severus, existing provinces were divided.

Middle imperial units were also increasingly fragmented, more of the time. On campaign, temporary detachments (vexillations) had long routinely served in *ad hoc* brigades of legionaries and/or auxiliaries, but in the middle empire, longer-term outposting of contingents from regimental bases became the norm. At the same time, as bases became fixed for generations, with soldiers putting down local roots, so it became harder – certainly, less normal – to uproot entire units for campaigns on, and possible permanent transfer to, other fronts. Major wars on the Rhine, Danube or Euphrates would see campaign armies assembled from many provinces, composed of some whole units but especially of vexillations, leaving the bulk of most units on their home beats – which may indeed have involved increasing levels of police work.

In summary, the period saw a continuation of the characteristic Roman mix of continuity and pragmatic change, which over a few generations also altered the equipment and visual appearance of Rome's soldiers beyond recognition.

### The 'Antonine revolution' in arms

The 'Antonine revolution' is the name archaeologists give to a profound change in Roman arms and military dress completed, roughly, during the second half of the second century AD, establishing a repertoire which then remained relatively stable into the early fourth century.[5]

Roman arms never stopped evolving, and Trajan's reign saw important innovations in artillery, with a new type of catapult frame for short bolts. Stirrings of the forthcoming wider changes can also be seen quite early in the second century, with the first depictions of scabbard-slides and ring-pommel swords (p. 186) in Roman use, but these gathered pace during the next two generations, resulting in reconfigurations of Roman military 'material culture' even more profound than those of the Augustan period. Trajan's troops would have had difficulty recognizing their great-grandsons of AD 200 as Romans.

At first glance, much middle imperial equipment looks inferior in quality by comparison with that of the first century, especially in terms of finish and décor. For example, belt and harness fittings, mostly of wholly new designs,[6]

look cruder than before. However, this is misleading. Such fittings may be simpler and
stronger. Generally speaking, middle imperial
equipment was no less serviceable, and some
items were technologically superior. Use of '*lorica
segmentata*' declined, although it still appeared
into the third century.[7] Mail shirts were simplified, into 'T-shirt' form. There were improved
types of scale armour, 'semi-rigid', stapled vertically as well as horizontally.[8] Some mail and many
scale shirts were provided with paired upper-chest
plates, which provided better protection and
allowed easy opening for donning. Rectangular

62. Bronze head of a *draco* standard from
Niederbieber, Germany. Mounted on a pole
with a silk windsock attached to the rear
collar, in the wind or at speed on horseback
this resembled a hissing, gyrating snake.

legionary shields continued in use past the mid-third century (Plate VI), but by
AD 200 were increasingly being replaced by a broad, dished oval form that
became the standard Roman design into the fifth century (Plate XII). Metal shield
edging declined in use, but this need not have meant a decline in effectiveness;
stitched rawhide was lighter and, experiment suggests, impressively resistant to
blows.[9] Infantry and cavalry also generally adopted common helmet types.
Taken as a whole, Roman legionaries increasingly adopted equipment hitherto
used by auxiliaries.

There were also innovations in Roman service, including new dragon-
headed windsock standards (Fig. 62), increasing use of long cavalry lances, and
scale armour for some horses.[10] However, some of the most important innovations of the 'Antonine revolution' were in swords.

†

We actually have more archaeological information about Roman swords of this
period than any earlier time, owing to the recovery of scores of blades, many
complete and almost perfectly preserved. Most come not from the Roman
empire, but from areas of Free Germany, deposited in peat bogs or graves.

During the mid- to late second century AD – the exact chronology is unclear
– Roman swords underwent dramatic changes, both in general design and in
methods of manufacture. In Trajan's time early in the century, the Pompeii type
had, in Christian Miks' view, spawned several variants. Besides the 'classic' tri-
angular-pointed form, variants had appeared with 'gothic-arch' points, some
very broad and looking ill-suited to anything but cutting.[11] There were also other
swords of similar limited length (*c.* 500 mm/20 in), and with similar 'gothic-arch'
points, but otherwise with a distinctly different geometry, slenderer than
Pompeii variants, edges converging noticeably towards the tip.[12] An even slenderer tapering type flourished sometime during the second century.[13] The

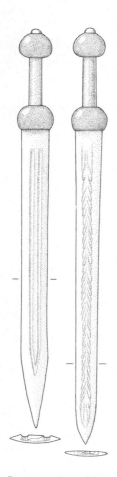

63. Reconstructions of the two swords from the Canterbury burial (Fig. 55), forged during the development of pattern-welding techniques, with enlarged cross-sections beneath. The exact forms of the hilts are conjectural. (Scale 1:8)

inspiration for these tapering outlines is unclear, but they were to become important. Alongside these short weapons continued the longer Newstead type swords, presumed to be the 'spathae' of Tacitus. Although more parallel-edged, these bigger weapons somewhat resemble in their slender proportions and tip-form the small tapering blades just described.

It is clear that there was a great deal of experimentation going on in blade manufacture during the second century, in length and width, parallel versus converging edges, in point form, cross-section (fullered and polygonal sections begin to appear alongside the established rhomboid and lens-like forms) and not least construction technique. Middle imperial blades reveal a major innovation in Roman sword technology.

During the second century AD, Roman sword manufacture became markedly more sophisticated, and apparently more consistent. This seems to have been the result of further development of late Iron Age 'barbarian' sword-making techniques. Polybius recorded the mastery of Spanish swordsmiths around 200 BC (p. 82). Some late Gaulish blades were 'piled', made with a core of strips of different alloys selected for their varied properties, placed side by side rather than in a flat sandwich, with separate cutting edges, hammer-welded together.[14] A key, subsequent refinement of this, probably developed by armourers in the northern provinces during the second century,[15] was to twist the core strips together before hammer-welding them. During the later second century, increasingly elaborate combinations of alloy strips and patterns of twisting evolved into fully fledged 'pattern-welding'. Two blades buried with murdered soldiers in Canterbury may capture the development of the new technique underway (Fig. 63).[16] Full pattern-welding was commonplace in third-century and later swords.[17]

Pattern-welding imparted better strength and resilience than earlier methods to weapons made mostly from softer iron alloys with only limited proportions of harder-to-produce steel.[18] It also offered additional aesthetic attractions, which remained a significant element of sword manufacture thereafter (Plate XIII). For the different alloys twisted into the blade also possessed differing visual properties, forming complex surface patterns, which could be enhanced by polishing or etching. Bog-preserved blades show an astonishing range of welding patterns, some of which even seem to prioritize aesthetic effects over mechanical properties. This may mark flaunting of virtuosity by sword-smiths exploring the techniques they were pioneering, or production of showy pieces specifically aimed at the 'export market' (comparable to the gold-plated Kalashnikovs reportedly favoured by Saddam Hussein's sons). The apparently greater consistency of manufacture of pattern-welded swords may hint something about the developing organization and quality control of Roman arms production, as may makers' marks and other stamps on blades.[19] Some were further embellished close to the hilt with inlaid brass eagles and standards, victories or gods, orientated with the sword point upwards.

This advance in manufacturing technique facilitated the other major detectable trend over the period: a marked increase in average blade length (see Fig. 8). In the first half of the century, most known blades are in the vicinity of 500 mm (c. 20 in) long: only 20 per cent are over 600 mm (2 ft), and a handful over 700 mm (c. 2 ft 4 in). In the second half of the century, the balance was tipping: slightly more than 50 per cent of known examples were now over 600 mm, and 14 per cent over 700 mm. Between 201 and 250 the shift to long blades was decisive, and the trend to greater length continued: over 93 per cent of known blades are over 600 mm, and half are 701–800 mm (c. 2 ft 4 in–2 ft 7½ in). The trend continued during the later third century, by which time the half-metre swords of early imperial times were extinct.[20] Henceforth, Roman weapons were longswords, usually known as *spathae*, but also still generically as *gladii*. It is unknown whether longer swords resulted from the technical innovations, or whether pattern-welding was developed in response to demands for longer, but still strong, blades (although they could still bend or break in use).

While shorter weapons vanished from the scene, the generally lengthening blades continued to exhibit considerable variety, both in sizes within the 600–800 mm range, and in shape. Some, with parallel edges and triangular points, such as one of the Canterbury examples (Fig. 63, left), simply look like scaled-up 'classic' Pompeii swords.[21] However, such weapons disappear in the earlier third century. Much more enduring were forms (such as Fig. 63, right) which seem to derive from other shorter swords of the early second century, with perhaps influence from the longer Newstead type. Third-century weapons tend to cluster around two main shapes, although there is extensive variation on these themes, and some transitional forms exist.[22]

The first common shape tends to be broad with parallel or near-parallel edges and a 'gothic-arch' tip, probably derived primarily from second-century Pompeii-type variants with similar geometry. Such 'broadsword-like' weapons (with length:width ratios around 8–12:1) are known as the 'Lauriacum-Hromókowa' type (Fig. 64, left). These appeared around the middle of the second century AD, and continued through the third.[23] The second shape, with its continuously tapering outline and often more elongated arched point, looks like a

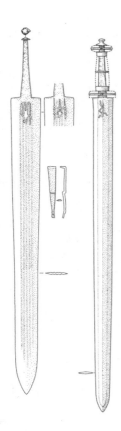

derivative of the small weapons of similar outline of the early second century. Examples tend to be slenderer than Lauriacum-Hromókowa swords (with blade length:width ratios around 15–17:1), some markedly so, and also longer, looking almost 'rapier'-like. This second family of blades is known as the 'Straubing-Nydam' type (see Fig. 64, right), some variants of which appeared in the later second century, while others continued into the fourth.[24]

The hilts of most middle imperial swords show continuity from earlier Roman weapons, being of traditional three-part design, usually in wood or bone. However, early in the second century a radically different all-iron hilt assembly was also introduced, comprising a squared guard, and a large loop-shaped pommel, the latter usually riveted to the tang, and often inlaid with contrasting metals. A weapon so furnished is commonly called a 'ring-pommel sword' (*Ringknaufschwert*), although such hilts do not appear exclusively associated with a particular type of blade.[25] Ring pommels were widely used during the later second century (examples are known from Britain to Syria), although they apparently vanished soon after *c.* AD 200 (Fig. 65).[26]

64. Third-century Roman sword designs. Left, restoration of the broad Lauriacum-Hromókowa type, based on the folded example from Hromókowa in the Ukraine, found with its scabbard slide. Right, restoration of the slenderer Straubing-Nydam type, based on a sword from the Illerup bog deposit, with a locally embellished hilt. Both weapons have brass inlays at the root of the blade, the Hromókowa weapon representing Mars on one face and a legionary eagle flanked by other standards on the reverse; the Illerup sword sports a simplified winged Victory.

✝

So many simultaneous changes in swords and other arms did not just happen. Cultural reasons behind these developments will be discussed later, but the practical reality was that helmets, armour, swords and shields all had to work together. Changes in swords and body shields in particular will have been coordinated to ensure that fighting techniques remained effective. The changes imply shifts in individual fighting methods and probably unit tactics. Some reflect introduction or wider dissemination of new 'tactical packages' of weapons and techniques.

Cavalry was of growing importance generally, and horse archers already in Roman service (Fig. 74) probably increased in numbers. The second century also saw greater use of horsemen armed with long, two-handed lances,[27] and the introduction of units with armoured horses too (cataphracts). However, more significant were developments affecting the still-dominant infantry.

During the later second century both horse and foot began largely to replace their earlier shield types, including the familiar curved-rectangular legionary form, with a new, large, dished broad oval shield (still with central boss: see Plate XII).[28] This was broadly contemporaneous with the general trend to longer swords, which by the third century if not earlier were certainly used by infantry, including legionaries. As we have seen, Roman hand-to-hand combat involved combined use of sword and shield, and so the coincidence of changes in both during the same period is likely to relate to changing infantry fighting methods. Decline in the use of the rectangular shield is comprehensible in the light of lengthening infantry swords; its back-projecting square corners are likely to have been cumbersome with longer blades, especially when trying to cut. The new broad oval shield made a better combination with a longer sword, and as noted above is perhaps best seen as a 'tactical package', new to legionaries at least. Simultaneous changes in infantry helmet design also point to shifts in fighting technique.

The high infantry helmet neckguards of Caesar's time, facilitating the kind of half-crouching stance implied in Augustan descriptions of hand-to-hand combat (p. 35; Figs 10, 50). were progressively lowered during the first century AD. Early cavalry helmets already had low neckguards, reflecting the rider's upright posture. By the end of the second century AD, both cavalry and, apparently, most infantry, including legionaries, wore helmets with low neckguards (see Fig. 66.2), implying a shift to a more upright stance for foot combat as well.

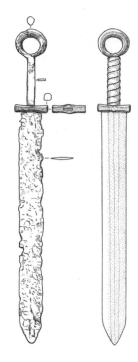

65. Current state and reconstruction of the *Ringknaufschwert* from Pevensey, southern Britain (late second century, now in the British Museum). The ring-topped hilt was a Sarmatian-inspired fashion of the time, here coupled with a short Pompeii-like blade. (Scale 1:8)

Exactly what the changes in fighting technique comprised is hard to discern. Even if some of the new sword types, especially many of the new Lauriacum-Hromówka 'broadsword-like' weapons, look especially suited to cutting, they do retain effective points, while the more 'rapier-like' Straubing-Nydam variants have two long edges and would have been effective for cutting. Texts of earlier and later date describe Roman troops using both modes in battle. It is not clear that one blade form was an infantry arm, the other for horsemen; lengths overlap across both families, and both provide improved reach. For infantry, such weapons probably required more space to wield in either manner, and would have been hard to wield crouching. In this period, choice of sword may have been more a matter of individual stature, strength, talent and taste. While we can glimpse the nature of a shift in Roman infantry combat, explaining why it happened is another matter. The change may have been in part practical; Roman troops, substantially recruited from northern provincials and barbarians rather than Italians, may have been of increasing average stature. More likely the major reason was the shift in the nature of Rome's foes during the middle empire; increasingly, her most dangerous antagonists were now Sarmatian, Parthian and later Gothic and Sasanian cavalry forces, against which the weapons and very close combat traditions of the past were of little use.

†

Alongside developments in weapons and armour, there were equally substantial changes in how weapons – notably, swords – were worn and, more generally, in basic military dress.

By AD 200 swords were usually worn on the left rather than right, and hung from broad baldrics rather than waist belts. The scabbard also now had an entirely new suspension system. Side-rings were gone, replaced by a single suspension-point, usually metal, bone or ivory and known as a slide or runner, on the front of the scabbard. Usually wood often covered with leather, the sheath terminated in a metal or bone chape in a variety of new forms (Fig. 66, Plate x).

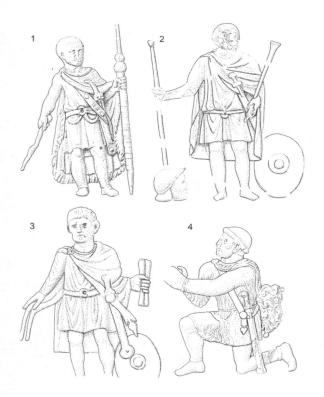

66. Mid-imperial military dress featured a waist-belt, often with swagged strap ends, and a baldric from which the sword was suspended via a slide. 1: tombstone of M. Aurelius Lucianus, Rome; 2: tombstone of Aurelius Surus, trumpeter of *legio* I *Adiutrix*, (Istanbul Museum); 3: unnamed soldier holding the bifurcated end of his belt-strap ('look, I am a soldier': Istanbul Museum); 4: the emperor Philip on a relief of Shapur I at Bishapur, Iran.

The baldric strap passed over the right shoulder and across the back, its narrowing tail end passed through the scabbard slide, to be attached behind a metal fastening plate attached to the baldric over the lower chest. Below this hung the broad end of the strap, often sporting a metal terminal, swinging free. Fastener and strap-end created new fields for embellishment, and were sometimes elaborately decorated (see Fig. 66; Plate x).

This package of changes – scabbard slide and baldric – was an integral part of the 'Antonine revolution'. A slide is depicted on a Roman tombstone of the earlier second century, but on a waist belt.[29] The general shift to scabbard slide and baldric occurred during the middle decades of the second century. Universal adoption of baldrics had a practical aspect; with swords getting longer and still worn vertically, it seems it was deemed necessary, especially for infantry (although cavalrymen also followed suit), to wear them rather higher – with the hilt around armpit level – than was possible with a waist belt.

Military daggers are no longer seen on tomb representations, but textual references and archaeological finds confirm they were still carried.[30] Archaeological examples are often larger than earlier ones.[31] In contrast to swords, they retained frame scabbards and ring suspension into the third century. Presumably they are unseen on tombs because they were still worn on the left hip attached to the waist belt, but were now obscured by the sword.

If Roman arms and equipment had changed radically during the second century, then in terms of basic dress the appearance of *milites* of Severus was even more radically altered compared with those of Trajan. We know a great deal about the new dress from tombstones, paintings and archaeological finds, and can decode its symbolic meanings in some detail.

Trajan's soldiers still wore the traditional Italian baggy short-sleeved tunic, with a poncho-like cloak or the *sagum*, the rectangular cloak-cum-sleeping-blanket fixed with a brooch, a garment of barbarian origin but already long in Roman use (Fig. 37). Short breeches had been introduced as a partial concession to the permanent move from Mediterranean to more extreme climates, but, with open sandal-boots, the ensemble remained recognizably Italian. All this changed profoundly by AD 200, when Roman soldiers generally were wearing the *sagum* over a tunic with long, fairly close-fitting sleeves, and hose – full-length trousers with sewn-in sock-feet. Footwear, still hob-nailed, now comprised closed types more like modern boots. The material change in clothing of soldiers, in appearance, 'feel' and physical properties, was dramatic (Fig. 66, Plate v).

Soldiers' grooming styles changed equally radically. Short hair and shaven chins had marked Roman males for centuries, but in the second century soldiers, emperors and other prominent Romans alike began sporting beards and longer hair, becoming very shaggy by AD 200 (see Figs 58–60, 70). Imperial and military styles continued to track each other thereafter, with shorter styles (Fig. 66) – eventually crew-cuts and 'designer stubble' (see Fig. 82) – prevailing until the early fourth century.

This was, though, a typically Roman revolution; important details of dress clearly reflect continuities in expression of soldierly masculinity. *Milites* still regarded themselves as proud Roman males with values and traditions to uphold. Trousers were drab, usually greyish, while cloaks were normally yellow-brownish, suitably subdued and practical colours for men whose ideology emphasized traditional Roman plainness and the sweat, dust and toil of service, contrasting appropriately with the gaudy colours and elaboration of the dress of barbarians and women. However, officers' cloaks, and all ranks' tunics (at least for so-called 'camp dress'), were white with purple details (Plate v). This expressed the status of soldiers as free and privileged males, for purple-detailed white tunics were the dark business suit and necktie of the era, worn by all respectable male Italians, Greeks, Jews and others. Alongside such visual symbolism, the crunch of his hob-nailed boots and his jangling belt-terminals (see below) helped to create and advertise the persona of the soldier, perhaps supplemented by characteristic smells, of unbleached wool from his cloak, and often the odour of horses, animals associated with privilege and war.

Of course, their specific status as men licensed to kill for the state continued to be manifested physically and visually by wearing the sword itself, prominently, on a showy baldric.

By 200, Roman military dress was typified by two belts: the sword-baldric and the waist belt. Representations suggest that the free-hanging end of the baldric, and the front part of the belt, were normally visible beneath the folded-back cloak, and were used extensively for visual display (Fig. 66, Plate v).

The soldier's waist belt, hitherto called the *balteus*,[32] ceased to be the sword-belt; as described above, this function now passed to a separate baldric, which also took over the name. The waist belt therefore needed a new name, during the third century AD becoming commonly known as the *cingulum militare* (or *militiae*).[33] Despite losing the sword, the waist belt actually gained in symbolic significance during this period.

Alongside new opportunities for display provided by the broad baldric, the waist belt continued often to be elaborately decorated with showy fittings. These were evidently deemed not to compromise 'soldierly plainness' because, technically, they related to arms rather than clothing (the waist belt still held the dagger). Both belts were embellished with fittings of metal (sometimes silver, more often bronze, frequently tinned), bone or ivory. These provided scope for visual expressions of the wearer's beliefs, personal prowess and pride: writing messages on the body, sometimes literally.

Some belts bore letter-shaped plates spelling *FELIX VTERE*, 'use with good fortune', implying presentation pieces awarded for merit by a superior – sometimes by the emperor himself. In the *Augustan Histories*, Severus is recorded to have staged military games on the birthday of his younger son Geta, awarding prizes of military accoutrements made from, or decorated with, silver, including *armillae* (arm-rings), *torques* (neck-rings) and *baltei* (belts or baldrics).[34]

Some openwork baldric fittings depicted Hercules or various gods, and especially Jupiter's eagle (Plate x). Eagle mounts were part of a set of baldric fittings, incorporating the text of a prayer for the well-being of the soldier's unit.[35] Belt fittings thus reflect both individual and collective aspects of a soldier's motivation, his concern for personal status among his peers, and his advancement within the military hierarchy. They also advertised his connectedness with his *commilitones*, his unit, and beyond: some baldric fasteners just bear the motto *ROMA*.[36]

These fittings reflect the heightened symbolism of military belts, which materially expressed the soldier's taste, wealth and special social status. The *cingulum militare* became a key marker of soldierly identity. From the third century, 'wearing the *cingulum*' became a figurative expression for military service. When Severus cashiered the Praetorians (p. 199), he took their belts, as well as their weapons.[37] Some soldiers, on becoming Christian, symbolically rejected military service by throwing off their *cingula*, an act inviting capital punishment.[38]

### Milites and empire

The new Antonine military dress and equipment exhibit striking (albeit not total) uniformity from Britain to Syria, in functional design and even in details of decoration, sharing a repertoire of motifs, styles and patterns. This was achieved in a world without mass production, and governed by custom and tradition rather than modern-style dress regulations or equipment specifications. Although rankers rarely transferred between regiments, styles and motifs were disseminated between units and armies by frequent moves between provinces of centurions (those living repositories of military traditions, standards and practices). They were also carried across the empire literally on the backs of the soldiers, during mass movements of troops between frontiers in military campaigns, and bought, stolen and copied locally. This resulted in styles spreading throughout the armies, converging to create an evolving, universally recognizable repertoire of soldierly dress. Fashions were taken up for a variety of reasons, relating to practicality and 'military cool'. There were, however, also darker motivations for maintenance of virtually uniform soldierly appearance. Overtly, it clearly marked membership of the 'imagined community' of *milites*, distinguishing this powerful professional group from oft-despised civilians. It also visibly expressed solidarity of the military brotherhood – which political events showed was riven with potentially lethal internal tensions (p. 201).

In daily practice, most soldiers' experience was of a tiny subsection of the imagined community of *milites*, in one of hundreds of local military communities scattered across the empire: in a legion or auxiliary regiment, vexillation or small outpost contingent, warship crew, or governor's *officium* (staff) and bodyguard. However, everywhere these actual military communities had long comprised many more people than the soldiers alone.

†

All contingents of soldiers were routinely accompanied by a very substantial (but now unquantifiable) proportion of officially recognized dependants. These 'non-combatant tails' comprised military servants of various kinds: *calones*, *galearii* and *lixae*.[39] These were largely, but probably not entirely, of slave or freedman status.[40] It is hard to decide, as the terms for them were used inconsistently in surviving texts: the term *lixae*, for example, is sometimes qualified as describing 'valorous' male servants, on other occasions to include a motley crew of entertainers, seers and whores.[41] These groups looked after the baggage train when in transit, and performed a host of menial tasks in camp, not least looking after horses and pack animals. Many were perhaps owned or employed corporately by the unit, others privately by individual soldiers, especially the grooms retained by cavalrymen. A servant is often shown on auxiliary tombstones, leading the dead cavalryman's horse and, like a medieval page, sometimes holding his spears while (as the easiest way to carry it) wearing his helmet. This is, presumably, a *galearius* or 'helmet-man' (Fig. 67) Some were likely sons of soldiers and other 'wannabe' warriors not yet old enough to enlist.

Many such soldiers' servants were effectively paramilitaries themselves. They received elements of military training to enable them to keep up with the soldiers, and were used to handling weapons. They were tough, sometimes getting caught up in the fighting, defending baggage train or camp.[42] On occasion muleteers were drawn up as decoy 'cavalry' to inflate the apparent strength of an army.[43] On the march they and their charges – animals, wagons – could form up under their own 'standards'; this made practical sense as a measure to maintain order in the column, but also helped foster a sense of corporate identity among these men as an affiliate branch of the military, from which they took their status. Like so many social groups in the Roman world, they seem to have developed their own *esprit de corps*. Far from being downtrodden, they took license from the soldiers, and could behave arrogantly, expecting to be protected by their units. Tacitus recorded how in 69 Vitellius' ill-disciplined soldiers were outnumbered by their even more unruly servants.[44]

†

67. First-century tombstone of Longinus, cavalryman of an *ala*, dining Roman-style (top), while his horse and equipment are tended by his *galearius* (bottom). From Cologne, Germany.

There was point in the old regulation which prohibited the dragging of women to the provinces or foreign countries: in a retinue of ladies there were elements apt, by luxury or timidity, to retard the business of peace or war and to transmute a Roman march into something resembling an Eastern procession. Weakness and a lack of endurance were not the only failings of the sex: give them scope, and they turned hard, intriguing, ambitious. They paraded among the soldiers; they had the centurions at beck and call...

TACITUS, *ANNALS* 3.33.[45]

Despite such traditionalist strictures from Tacitus and other writers, early imperial units came to be accompanied by substantial numbers of women and children, alongside male servants performing necessary military tasks. Some were officially recognized. Centurions were allowed to marry in service, and the Vindolanda tablets show that, already in the first century AD, equestrian unit commanders were also regularly accompanied by their families.

Despite the formal ban on marriage during service, many older soldiers also kept 'unofficial' wives (whether wooed or initially purchased as servants/concubines) and raised families.[46] Even in Tacitus' time, this had probably long been *de facto* reality in many units, as the women's and children's shoes from barrack rooms of *c.* AD 100 at Vindolanda suggest.[47] They also often retained links with, and responsibility for, blood relations, especially as heads of family on their fathers' deaths. Under Severus, the official marriage ban was dropped, and soldiers were permitted to cohabit with now-recognized wives.[48] Families now became officially visible, openly part of the broader community of those dependent on the soldiers for their subsistence and identity in the wider world: soldiers' wives, but also widowed mothers, sisters, daughters – and sons, many destined to follow their fathers behind the eagles. Veterans too often remained part of military communities, settling in the vicinity of their regiments.

Even this long list of those with direct ties to soldiers or regiments still excludes people traditionally referred to as 'camp followers', usually envisaged as hangers-on such as independent traders and prostitutes seeking to earn a living by providing 'essential' services to garrisons. However, even some of these may have been more closely integrated into the armies than is commonly thought; a troupe of entertainers and prostitutes catering to the needs of the soldiers at Dura-Europos in Syria may actually have been owned and managed by the military.[49]

By AD 200, such accretions of dependants around military units had been a progressively developing reality in many frontier zones during the course of preceding generations, as military bases became permanent.

In the east, major bases were still typically located in or near cities, but remain little known archaeologically, except for the middle imperial example at Dura-Europos on the Euphrates. This nominally Greek city had been seized from Parthian rule in the 160s. By the 210s, its northern quarter had been taken over by the *exercitus* of Syria Coele, to accommodate vexillations of the province's two legions based far up the Euphrates, and the headquarters of the large *cohors xx Palmyrenorum equitata*, several brigaded contingents each with its dependants. Existing houses were converted to barracks, and new administrative buildings, military baths and an amphitheatre constructed. The city walls thus enclosed two distinct communities, an incoming provincial military one and the civil Durene population, itself comprising old Macedonian families, local Mesopotamians, Palmyrenes, Jews, Christians and others (Fig. 68).[50]

Most military cantonments in Europe remained the familiar custom-built 'Roman forts', which by the second century usually also possessed built-up areas immediately beyond the walls, so-called *vici* (outside auxiliary bases) and *canabae* (at legionary bases). These secondary developments were not, as usually imagined, simple shanty-towns full of civilian hangers-on. Often including important official facilities as well as accommodation for the extended military community, they were extensions of, and one with, the walled base, usually under direct control of the unit.[51]

At some distance from major military complexes such as legionary bases, perhaps sited just beyond the boundary of directly controlled military land, there might be another, more obviously 'civil' settlement, living off the commercial opportunities presented by the long-term presence of a major organization consuming vast quantities of goods and materials, with its captive market of soldiers carrying coins in their purses. Some *canabae* and satellite settlements rapidly developed into towns, and even major cities. Eboracum (York) and Aquincum (Budapest) started from such roots.

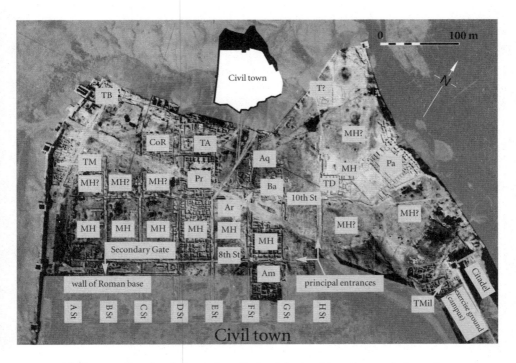

68. The Roman military base in the northern district of the city of Dura-Europos, Syria, a unique example of an eastern, urban cantonment, which has been extensively excavated.

**Key**

Am = amphitheatre
Ar = arch
Aq = aqueduct
Ba = baths
CoR = probable commander's
    residence
MH = military housing
    (converted civil dwellings)

Pa = 'palace of the *dux ripae*'
    (thought to be a regional
    commander)
Pr = *principia* (HQ)
TA = temple of Azzanathkona
TB = temple of Bel
TD = temple of Jupiter
    Dolichenus

TM = temple of Mithras
TMil = 'military temple'
T? = temple to unidentified
    deity

Cases such as York and Budapest, to which might be added many other examples of military-derived Roman cities and veteran colonies of the frontier provinces such as Vindobona (Vienna), Moguntiacum (Mainz), Colonia Claudia Ara Agrippinensis (Cologne) or Lindum Colonia (Lincoln), give us pause to consider the implications of the sheer aggregate size and impact of the 'community of soldiers' including their dependants. Its scale was staggering. The military establishment in AD 200 was well over 400,000 soldiers (even if it was doubtless usually somewhat under strength, owing to desertions, discharges and deaths).[52] Including 'support personnel' such as *lixae*, soldiers' private dependants – all who relied on *milites* for subsistence, identity or affiliation – and military veterans and their households, what we might term the 'extended imperial military community' would have totalled well over a million. This was as big as the city of Rome itself, and by 200 had eclipsed it in practical significance, if not in prestige. Here was a special imperial community, in its own way as intensely Roman as the population of the City, or the convergent Romanizing civil aristocracies of the 'core' provinces. Yet it was largely distinct from either.

Beyond the City of Rome itself, with its glorious monuments, history and vast population, Augustus had created a new 'global' imperial ideology to integrate the empire. This was a universalized idea of 'eternal Rome', expressed through the gods and the person of the emperor, and shared bodies of myth and historical tales. Within this framework, common Greco-Roman aristocratic values and culture (manifested in trappings of elite life such as villas, and practices such as ostentatious funding of public buildings in one's home town) served to unite, and promote the interests of, the landed aristocracies ruling and developing the civil provinces at the local level. These aristocracies became an empire-wide stratum from which senators, imperial administrators, officers and eventually emperors themselves were drawn. However, Greco-Roman culture did not simply spread through the civil provinces. Rather, it was transformed, incorporating traits from Levantine, Egyptian, Gaulish and many other subject societies, which became relabelled as 'Roman', generating the regionally nuanced, hybrid culture of a world empire. This cultural revolution, initially driven by wealthy provincials' aspirations to 'become Roman', affected provincial societies from top to bottom. To varying degrees subordinate classes also aspired to Greco-Roman civil culture, and more practically to Roman citizenship, which became effectively universal in 212.

However, alongside his deliberate creation of this second, civil, 'universal Rome', Augustus also unwittingly triggered the genesis of what we might think of as a third, 'military Rome'. Its rise was a process paralleling and related to that taking place in the civil core of the empire. Certainly, the soldiers shared many aspects of universal Roman culture, most obviously imperial cult and state religion. *Milites* also imbibed myth and history: Virgil was read at Vindolanda.[53] But they had their own characteristic preoccupations.

Although many senators and equestrians continued to fill military commands, for most males in the empire, rich or poor, war was increasingly a matter for the emperor and his distant soldiers. While still hailing military glory and victory over foreign foes, the culture of Italy and the civil provinces generally placed decreasing emphasis on personal involvement in war: masculinity was redefined in other ways (p. 168). In contrast, the *milites* themselves, exposed to the same propaganda of eternal Rome as the rest of the empire, more than ever placed martial valour at the centre of their sense of masculinity, of professional identity, and of their place in the imperial cosmic order. The festivals of the military calendar celebrated not only the traditional gods but also the birthdays of great soldier-emperors.[54] *Milites* embellished their arms with representations and symbols of Jupiter, Mars, Hercules and the *Dioscuri*, the divine twins who, according to popular legend, had come to Rome's aid at the ancient battle of Lake Regillus.[55] Their lengthening regimental traditions will have recalled the collective battle-honours and individual deeds of their predecessors in the ranks – often their own fathers and grandfathers. There were now two divergent masculinities, civil and military, each thinking itself truly Roman. As males set the agenda for ancient societies, the identity-group of soldiers led the wider imperial military community in developing a 'military Rome', distinct in ethos and, especially in Europe, also geographically quite separate.

As we saw, imperial *milites*, including legionaries, were mostly stationed near the frontiers, and recruits were soon overwhelmingly of provincial birth. Few having ever seen Italy or the City, their notions of what constituted Roman life, values and material culture were doubtless influenced by imperial propaganda and the lifestyles of officers drawn from the cosmopolitan elite. However, they were largely inherited from those of the legionaries Augustus had stationed on the frontiers, and from interpretations of Roman culture made by the frontier peoples amongst whom they dwelt and who provided the majority of recruits. The culture of the *milites* became, as we saw, a distinctive 'expatriate Romanness' increasingly independent of those of the City and Italy.

Like the new universal civilization of the civil provinces, military 'Romanness' was also an evolving hybridization of Greco-Roman and other cultures, substantially driven by men aspiring to 'become Romans'. Shared identity as soldiers of the emperor, incorporating both Romans and soon-to-be Romans loyal to the same leader and paymaster, provided a social glue analogous to the rapprochement between landowning elites and the state in the civil provinces. However, focused less on aristocrats than on humbler provincials seeking citizenship through military service, the process was more demotic. Also, whereas Roman civilization in the civil core mainly drew its multi-cultural influences from the lands bordering the Mediterranean, evolving military Roman culture drew on a quite different range of societies on and beyond the frontiers, incorporating Saharan and Iberian, British and Gaulish, Rhine-German and

Pannonian, Thracian, Dacian and Sarmatian, Syrian and Partho-Sasanian cultural traits.

Although civil and military-centred populations exhibited parallel processes of cultural evolution, these differing patterns of interaction resulted in visible divergence of frontier 'Romanness' from that of the civil core. By AD 69, to civilians, soldiers seemed uncouth semi-barbarian frontiersmen; yet *milites* believed that, as much as cosmopolitan grandees or Italian peasants, they *were* 'Rome'. And they were right; this was part of a wider truth. After centuries of common borders, and with effective abolition of distinctions between citizen and non-citizen in 212, what constituted 'Roman' in political or cultural terms was now decided in the provinces – in Spain or Gaul, North Africa, Pannonia or Syria – as much as in Italy. Indeed, more so: by this time emperors, still senators but now rarely of Italian birth, were also increasingly to be found close to the frontiers rather than in the capital, leading their soldiers in foreign wars, or simply keeping a wary eye on them.

'Military Rome' was of great political, social and economic importance across the empire, manifested in different ways in different regions. The lion's share of early imperial tax revenues was spent on the armies, driving development of provincial cities and economies in the hitherto little-urbanized northern frontier regions. In northern Britannia, military bases and their regimental communities occupied the niches taken by civil towns in the south of the island. Batavia provides an extreme example of peculiarly military 'Romanness' (p. 145), while the Danubian lands were also notably martial in their cultural trajectories, towns remaining relatively few, small, and mostly satellites to military bases. Even in the populous, already-urbanized east, the aggregate socio-economic impact of the armies, and of the soldiers and veterans as politically privileged males with economic clout, was significant.

'Military Rome' was a prominent outcome of the impact of Roman imperialism, one of the greatest illustrations of how the sword could have constructive as well as destructive consequences. Yet it remained double-edged. The arrogance of the soldiers grew as they became ever more aware of their own potential as a distinct power-base within the empire, a special Rome within Rome. However, fragmentation and dispersal of the community of the soldiers across thousands of miles of frontier fostered divisions and tensions between provincial armies, which their regional cultural distinctions exacerbated. Distrust also deepened between *milites* and the civil populations, partly simply on grounds of mutual incomprehension, but also because soldiers were an increasing source of fear.

### Soldiers and internal control under the middle empire

The middle imperial period saw not only more frequent and serious foreign and civil wars, but also – probably related – greater internal disturbances. In society at large, as the vertical distinction between Romans and provincials vanished, extremes of wealth and poverty, power and oppression, continued to increase. Indeed, they became enshrined in Roman law, which from this time distinguished between privileged *honestiores* and *humiliores*, ordinary Romans now vulnerable to juridical torture.[56] With their privileged legal position and immunity to torture, *milites* and veterans ranked with the *honestiores*.[57] Ever more literally, there was one law for the rich and another for the poor. Incidents of serious unrest may mark resistance to such developments.

Official responses to criminality and other deviations seen as threatening the divinely sanctioned imperial order were savage, including brutal persecution of Christians at Lyons under Marcus Aurelius.[58] This period also saw increasing use of troops for internal security, both in surveillance and in active suppression of trouble. Movements on the roads were closely monitored by soldiers such as *beneficiarii* and *stationarii*, while on occasion internal 'police actions' against bandits were required on scales which even the authorities called wars.

Valerius Marcus lived for eighteen years and was killed by bandits.
EPITAPH FROM RAVNA, MOESIA[59]

'Brigandage' had remained endemic, and was sometimes astonishingly audacious. Even senior officers travelling with their retinues were not safe from armed bandits (*latrones*). Hadrian, as legate of *legio xxii Primigenia*, had been attacked while travelling.[60] Banditry ranged from local criminality to sporadic armed revolt. For example, Spain suffered invasion by Mauri from Africa in 172, which sparked decades of local insecurity.[61] However, the law regarded any unsanctioned use of arms as effectively insurgency.[62]

Soldiers were not only the last resort in suppression of banditry, but also perhaps its most dangerous source, for many brigands were deserters or dishonourably discharged *milites*. One of the most notorious, Maternus, was a deserter turned 'bandit chieftain' who assembled a following large enough to cause substantial damage in Gaul and, allegedly, other provinces, prompting Commodus to military action. The ensuing 'War of the Deserters' (*c.* AD 186) ended with Maternus' capture and beheading – allegedly when a daring plot to infiltrate Rome and assassinate the emperor was betrayed.[63] When Severus cashiered the entire Praetorian Guard (which had recently auctioned the empire) in 193 and replaced them with loyal Danubians (Fig. 69), he expelled thousands of embittered fighting men, which did little to help already poor internal security in Italy.[64] Subsequently during Severus' reign a brigand calling himself Bulla Felix terrorized the peninsula with a regiment-sized force of 600 men, which took two years to suppress.[65] However, to civilians, 'security forces' could pose a greater danger than *latrones*.

> [Provincial governors should] take care that nothing is done by individual soldiers exploiting their position and claiming unjust advantages for themselves, which does not pertain to the communal benefit of the army.
> THE JURIST ULPIAN, IN JUSTINIAN *DIGEST*, 1.18.6.6–7[66]

Away from the frontiers or the capital, in the 'civil' provinces and in Italy (which itself became a province, an index of its declining status), people more rarely saw soldiers, but when they did, it was likely to spell trouble. Even if they behaved according to the letter of the law, serving soldiers were likely to be encountered as agents of state surveillance, or tax collection, heavy-handed law enforcement in the interests of the powerful, or in transit to some trouble-spot. They might legally requisition animals, vehicles and even people to move supplies, or require official billeting by civilians who had to feed as well as house them.

Even under orders and in sight of their officers, soldiers were widely seen as dangerous outsiders, rather than protectors. Since they were immune from civil law, there was little to stop them demanding or seizing whatever they liked, abusing civilians in myriad ways.[67] The village of Skaptopara, Thrace, was blessed by hot springs, but therefore plagued by soldiers from two nearby bases demanding 'hospitality' without paying, despite specific orders from the provincial governor that the villagers should be left in peace. In AD 238 they petitioned the emperor through 'Aurelius Purrus, a soldier of the tenth…Praetorian cohort, who lived in the same village and owned land along with them.'[68] This provides an interesting example of the complexity of relations between soldiers and local civilians. As a soldier himself, Purrus may well have been a neighbour to treat with wariness, but here he acts as patron of the villagers (who had reason to hope the emperor would heed a soldier more than peasants). He was willing to do so perhaps as much owing to rivalry between Praetorians and other soldiers, as to common interest with his neighbours.

Increasingly, serving soldiers behaved like wolves on the rampage, in ways hard to distinguish from banditry and rebellion; and increasingly, this could spill into full-scale civil war. As we have seen, at the best of times there were underlying tensions in the relationship between soldiers and the emperor, who could not simply demand obedience and enforce it through draconian punishments. Soldiers still expected emperors to demonstrate their *virtus* in war, and so their fitness to lead, and to behave as *commilitones*: aloof traditionalists were resented. It is hardly surprising that the civil wars of the 190s, and the Severans' open reliance on military power, should further encourage the arrogance and unruliness of the soldiers. The various armies became ever more important players in politics during the third century, as assassinations and civil wars swept away the Severan dynasty, and eroded the sense of loyalty to the throne as one short-lived emperor after another sought to hold power with bribes and promises to the soldiers, only to fall to their swords or their would-be successor's dagger.

There were striking examples of commanders effectively losing control of units or even entire armies. A papyrus from Dura dated *c.* 220 records large numbers of garrison troops absenting themselves without leave, and demands their recall to the standards.[69] Even more extraordinary was the 'delegation' of 1,500 men from the especially mutinous garrison of Britain, which, in 185, marched all the way to Italy to petition Commodus about the conduct of the Praetorian prefect.[70] Cassius Dio the historian had good reason to hold a jaundiced view of the soldiers. As governor of Pannonia under Severus Alexander, his attempts to enforce discipline made him unpopular, to the point where the Praetorians wanted him dead, and the emperor had to advise him to hold his second consulship outside Rome if he valued his neck.[71]

69. Tombstone of L. Septimius Valerinus, *miles* of the ninth praetorian cohort, buried at Rome, early third century. From a family given Roman citizenship by Severus, he was very likely of Danubian origin.

Such dire disciplinary problems were both cause and effect of the dynastic instability plaguing the empire much of the time from the reign of Commodus and through the third century AD. The Durene soldiers were taking advantage of political uncertainty surrounding the rule of Elagabalus. In such times, and especially during civil wars, commanders and emperors found it hard, even suicidal, to try to enforce strict discipline; as governor of Britain in the 180s, Pertinax was almost killed and then forced from the province by rebellious soldiers, and as emperor in 193 fell to the swords of the Praetorians, who then auctioned the throne.[72] *Milites* virtually became mercenaries, following the highest bidder for their swords.

Emperors had cause to fear their own soldiers, who came to have equal reason to fear each other. The flip-side of the promise of ill-gotten bribes or booty from supporting a general's bid for the purple was the likelihood of having to fight other *milites* in civil war – if the enemy leader was not assassinated first. At Lugdunum in 197, as the armies of Severus and Clodius Albinus fought for the empire, Roman-on-Roman carnage was terrible, and there was the further danger of subsequent reprisals against the losing armies.

A major factor creating tensions and fault lines among the soldiers was the shift towards local recruitment, resulting from long-term settlement of forces in the provinces. For example, hundreds of inscriptions prove that, by the third century, the regional *exercitus* of Roman Africa, of which the core was *legio III Augusta* at Lambaesis, was overwhelmingly recruited from within the provinces of Numidia and Africa Proconsularis. Soldiers became increasingly attached by blood-ties to their home provinces. During the middle empire, to wage major campaigns, instead of moving entire legions and brigaded auxiliary regiments across the empire, perhaps permanently (routine practice two centuries earlier), field armies were increasingly assembled from vexillations – temporary detachments, intended to return – drawn from many provinces. In part, this was doubtless for strategic reasons, leaving bases at least partially occupied to maintain frontier surveillance and keep potential enemies guessing about local Roman strength, a kind of 'shell-game' like that played during the Cold War with silos and missiles. However, it was also implicit recognition that the Roman military now comprised a collection of regionally based 'sub-communities' of soldiers, which could not be entirely disrupted and shifted around without risking revolts. These centrifugal tendencies could be dangerous, especially with a developing threat of major wars on multiple fronts. In tension with their Roman identity and professional pride, soldiers became understandably concerned first for their own comrades, units, families and homelands over the interests of distant *commilitones*, let alone unknown provincials.

In 238, a powerful group of provincial aristocrats attempted to exploit the strained loyalties of the army of Africa. They plotted revolt against the emperor Maximinus Thrax, ostensibly because of the economic demands he was making to fight wars in the north, and attempted to suborn the provincial garrisons by appealing to common local interests. However, on this occasion the soldiers of the province put loyalty to the unseen Thracian emperor and their distant *commilitones* first, slaughtering the rebellious magnates.[73]

That particular gamble proved a catastrophic miscalculation, but it had not been implausible. The military brotherhood had long exhibited internal rivalries, jealousies and prejudices, which had erupted in AD 69. Just as, in the modern British Army, soldiers of the elite Parachute Regiment call any soldier not qualified to wear their coveted maroon beret a 'crap-hat', and the Brigade of Guards is known to the rest of the army as 'the Woodentops', so Roman *milites* also cordially despised many of their peers. In particular, little love was lost between the pampered political troops of the Praetorian Guard in Italy and the rest of the soldiers. As we saw, regional army-groups also harboured strong views about each other. Roman aristocrats maintained a particular contempt, apparently shared by European *milites*, for eastern armies recruited from Orientals and Greeks, stereotyped as constitutionally lazy and undisciplined, even when Roman-trained – a reputation which their fighting record shows was unfair.[74] Tensions between regional armies were an important factor in the civil wars that established the Severans. They were thus a source of anxiety both to emperors and to the soldiers themselves, providing powerful motivations to emphasize solidarity, a prerequisite for continued unity of the empire and effectiveness of the armies.

All this helps explain the frequency, and implicit anxiety, of imperial exhortations to unity among their *milites*. Identity and *esprit de corps* of regiments were expressed through artefacts, especially standards, and through collective routines and rituals such as parades and sacrifices (Plate v) in the familiar built spaces of permanent bases. On such occasions identification of Roman soldiers with the emperor was reaffirmed through collective oath-taking and sacrifice to the imperial cult, and through receipt of propaganda-charged coinage on paydays. Emperors from Commodus onwards issued coins bearing legends such as 'loyalty of the armies', and 'harmony of the soldiers' (Fig. 70).[75] These coins reveal abiding fears over the fragility of the soldiers' loyalty to the ruler, and to each other.

70. Coin of Commodus with the fashionable late-second-century shaggy beard. Partly an expression of aristocratic fashions for things Greek, it also conveniently reflected the Germanic beard style adopted by the emperor's *commilitones*. Right, the reverse of the same coin, reflecting imperial anxieties about the soldiers: the emperor addresses the troops (*ad locutio*), above the legend *FIDES EXERCIT*, 'loyalty of the armies'.

Besides exhortations from above, emperors were also obliged to woo the good opinion of their *milites* in the soldiers' own terms. A fundamental of soldierly identity was its material expression through recognizable common dress and accoutrements – not least the right to wear a sword in public. 'Military dress code' seems in large measure to have been driven by rankers and junior officers; emperors, increasingly required to be seen to be good *commilitones* (p. 170), were thus themselves obliged to wear it in war.

Events in Africa in 238 show that these measures could still be successful in persuading soldiers of regional armies to subordinate their local interests to those of their unseen emperor and *commilitones* on the other side of the empire. However, the events of the following decades would see pan-soldierly solidarity crumble into military chaos.

Yet despite these tensions, the soldiers of *c.* 160–230 remained well trained, highly motivated and well equipped (not least with improved swords), and were more numerous than they had been even since the establishment of imperial rule. They were still capable of undertaking massive campaigns, and were better able to face foes such as the once-intractable Parthians on equal terms on the battlefield. The Roman art and science of war was as sophisticated as ever. Another trend gathering pace during the third century was growing professionalization of the officer corps, leading to exclusion of senators from military commands, and their replacement by equestrian career soldiers.[76]

So why, then, by 260 did Rome find itself in danger of complete military collapse and political disintegration?[77] Part of the answer clearly lies in the internal stresses and fault-lines described above. Yet, as ever, to understand developments in the empire, we need to consider it in the context of its neighbours, friends and foes. Both in the east and in the north, long-term Roman bellicosity was beginning to reap what it had sown.

## The double-edged sword: Arsacid Parthia to Sasanid Persia

In the second century, Parthia remained the only major independent power surviving on Rome's immediate borders. The two states coexisted for 300 years.[78] Most of the time the Parthians were relatively unaggressive, partly because they had other preoccupations, including fractious dynastic politics and their frontier with Central Asia, where Parthia was more exposed to the depredations of mounted nomads than the Romans. The 'feudal' military organization of the Parthian state (its armies primarily comprised contingents summoned from sub-rulers and cities for royal service as required) also meant that professional standing Roman armies could expect to defeat any Parthian invasion of her Levantine provinces. Conversely, the fate of Crassus and the experiences of Mark Antony made Rome's early emperors wary of again risking pitting legionaries against horse-archers and heavy lancers on parched plains in any renewed direct invasion of Parthia (Fig. 71). Much of the tension between the empires was therefore played out through a proxy struggle for control of the buffer-state of Armenia. The result, until the second century, was effective strategic stalemate, relations veering between cordiality, 'cold war' and combat.[79] But the following hundred years were punctuated by a series of devastating Roman invasions of Mesopotamia.

This shift from stalemate to Roman aggression was facilitated by a gradual but effective process of adaptation of Rome's eastern armies to the exigencies of the environment of eastern Syria and Mesopotamia. Already expert at siege warfare and logistics, Rome began to supplement the eastern legions with locally raised horse-archers during the first century AD, and by the third century with heavily armoured lancers, as she developed tactics allowing her to face Parthian armies on their native dry steppe on more equal terms. As Rome grew increasingly confident of success in the field, given the continued bellicosity of imperial and soldierly ideology, it became inevitable that invasions of Parthia would be attempted.

Aggression was not entirely one-sided. Parthian kings did on occasion initiate open war with Rome, or engage in opportunistic intrigue. The sack of

Ctesiphon in 165 could be presented as just retribution for Parthian attacks. Severus' first Parthian war was a deterrent countermeasure to the Parthian king's offer of military assistance to a rival contender for the imperial throne. However, Trajan, Marcus' generals, Severus and Caracalla repeatedly used Parthia as a military punchbag, a place for emperors and soldiers to gain glory and loot, and to try to seize new provinces through outright military aggression. Caracalla especially desired conquests, making Armenia a province and attacking Media, in efforts to eclipse his father Septimius Severus, as well as Trajan, and especially Alexander, whom he idolized.[80]

71. Middle Eastern terracotta figurine depicting a Parthian horse-archer (now in the British Museum).

Yet these repeated invasions were largely confined to Mesopotamia and saw only limited incursions into the yet vaster Parthian territory of Iran.

In military and political terms, the results of these invasions were, at best, mixed. Roman armies sacked the Parthian capital of Ctesiphon three times in a century, bringing sought-after loot and glory. New provinces were created in northern Mesopotamia, advancing the Roman frontier to the Tigris. However, while Rome also repeatedly occupied Babylonia to the south, she failed ever to hold it more than briefly, proving unable to establish peaceful rule, or even effective military control. It is worth pausing to ask why, since Alexander had rapidly conquered all of Mesopotamia and Iran, and more. It is in some ways surprising, since a region like Babylonia was long urbanized and also had a significant legacy of Hellenistic culture from Seleucid times, including important Greek cities. We might expect that Rome should have been able to apply here the combination of sword and open hand that had been so effective in building her empire, including in neighbouring Syria. Yet Babylonia proved unreceptive, indeed highly resistant, to Roman power.

The answer may lie in the relatively loose, devolved structure of the Arsacid empire, combined with its sheer scale. Mesopotamia was already an enormous area for even Rome's armies to seek to swallow in one go; there were simply not the resources immediately to invade the Iranian plateau as well, to extirpate the Arsacid state. Consequently, even when the Roman emperor occupied Ctesiphon, Parthian power still lurked beyond the Zagros mountains, chastened but still potent. And if Parthia's decentralized, 'feudal' structure made it hard for the Arsacid king to face concentrated Roman military power and professionalism, it equally made things difficult for the Romans, since the semi-autonomous cities and statelets (such as Hatra) and communities (not least, the Jews) of western Parthia were able and willing to resist on their own account. Many had reason to prefer the relatively light touch of Parthian suzerainty to heavier-handed Roman rule; repeated invasion can hardly have endeared Rome to them.

During Roman occupations, the continued looming presence of Parthian power to the east, and the possibility that it would return to Mesopotamia – as it had before – gave heart to the peoples of Babylonia and encouraged resistance, making Rome's grasp tenuous. For these reasons (which so closely parallel those bedevilling the vainglorious Anglo-American occupation of Iraq from 2003, similarly overshadowed by proximity of a hostile Iran), insurgency and outright revolt always assailed the Roman occupiers. In this light, it is Alexander's success in the region, not Roman failure, which is the anomaly requiring explanation; but that is a different story.

72. Overthrowing the Arsacids, literally, on a third-century rock relief at Firuzabad, Iran. The first Sasanid king, Ardashir, knocks the last Arsacid ruler from the saddle with his lance (top), while his son, the future Shapur the Great, defeats the Parthian Grand Vizier. Note the laminated limb armour worn by the Parthians, and the Sasanids' mail shirts.

If successful as looting expeditions, in the longer term the Roman invasions of Mesopotamia had unforeseen geopolitical consequences, which proved catastrophic, and near-fatal, for Rome in the east. For while they did bring glory and expand Roman territory – although much more modestly than Roman ambitions intended – repeated Parthian humiliation accidentally triggered unwelcome 'regime change'. It fatally weakened the dwindling prestige and power of the Arsacid royal house, which then fell to revolt in Iran. The result during the 220s was its replacement by the new Iranian Sasanid dynasty, which laid claim to the heritage of the Achaemenid Persian empire (Fig. 72).[81]

Rome's actions in Parthia demonstrate the limitations of the sword, and what happened when she overreached with it, while failing to complement it with the open hand. If 'one of the great laws of [modern] war is Never Invade Russia',[82] that of Roman imperial warfare should have been 'never invade Mesopotamia'.

From the start the Sasanian military demonstrated not only aggression, military skill and substantial resources in the field, but also the ability to besiege cities; it took the formidable Arab city of Hatra, whose walls and artillery had defied Trajan and Severus, and complex Sasanian siegeworks have been studied in detail at Dura-Europos, which the new Iranian power also destroyed.[83] Sasanian kings still substantially relied on levies summoned from subject rulers and cities to assemble their armies, but the ability to prosecute sieges implies that they also retained a significant body of professional soldiers and military engineers. Iranian morale was also sustained by powerful political and military ideology, forged from resentment of recent Parthian humiliations at Rome's hands, and renewed imperial ambitions. Sasanid kings proclaimed their intention of reconquering the territories once ruled by Xerxes – effectively the entire Roman east.[84] Sasanian ideology also came to be underpinned by a monotheistic state religion: resurgent, sometimes militant and intolerant Zoroastrianism.[85]

Sasanian Iran was to prove a far more formidable danger than Parthia. It soon attacked, intending at least to drive the Romans from the gains made under the Severans, and faced counter-invasion by the last emperor of that house, Severus Alexander, in 231. After initial success, with Roman troops ravaging northwestern Iran, the emperor's central force was mauled by Ardashir's horsearchers and cataphracts at Ctesiphon in a near-repeat of Carrhae.[86] Alexander escaped, but his *virtus* was undermined, and with it the loyalty of his *milites*. When he faced war with the Germanic Alamanni in 234 he could not control his men, and was assassinated by soldiers incited by their officers. Once more the ruling dynasty was extinct, and Rome was again plunged into debilitating internal turmoil, just as her enemies had become far more dangerous, not only in the east, but the north as well.

## The double-edged sword: Rome and the Germans

From the mouth of the Rhine to the Middle Danube, and by the third century on the northwest shores of the Black Sea, dwelt Germanic peoples. Roman propaganda portrayed the '*Germani*' as archetypal barbarians, savages, if occasionally noble ones.[87] Imperial ideology fixed them as timeless and unchanging primitives, so that in the mid-fourth century Ammianus could still apparently be surprised at the sophistication of German farmhouses burned by Roman troops.[88] His reaction indicated how far evolving realities had diverged from Roman prejudices. For it was the stereotypes, not the Germans, which were timeless, and became dangerously out of step with reality. Independent archaeological testimony confirms a dynamic, more sophisticated and altogether more interesting picture of early Germanic societies.

By the outbreak of the Marcomannic Wars in the 160s, Romans and Germans had been in direct contact across Rhine and Danube for more than two centuries. The two sides exchanged more than blows. Regions facing the Roman frontiers were obviously open to direct interaction, and were of immediate importance to the Romans, who regarded neighbouring groups, even if not directly under Roman rule, as within the imperial sphere of interest. Rome sought to influence them as far as possible, in time-honoured fashion selectively supporting some leaders and peoples at the expense of others. There were also evidently important connections with the deep hinterlands, coastwise to Scandinavia, and overland from the Middle Danube frontier to the Baltic. The latter, especially, were to an extent commercial, bringing coveted amber to the empire. Roman artefacts also flowed into Barbaricum. These largely comprised luxury items, such as silver drinking vessels, silver coins, and not least during the second and third centuries AD, large numbers of weapons, primarily swords. The nature and episodic history of Roman export activity suggests that much comprised state-controlled political subsidy rather than commerce.

Excavation of settlements, cemeteries and religious sites have produced Roman imports, helping document and date as-yet dimly understood internal dynamics at work in central Europe and Scandinavia, which, during these centuries, were transforming many Germanic societies. In processes similar to those which had characterized later Iron Age Gaul, more sophisticated agricultural regimes developed and populations expanded.[89] Well before the great migrations that surrounded the collapse of the Roman west, some peoples were also on the move. In particular, from the first century AD, the ancestors of the Goths slowly migrated from Baltic Poland towards the Black Sea, driven, probably, by stresses arising from population growth.[90] Other groups responded to the opportunities or demands of economic and demographic change by developing new, larger-scale, more hierarchical political structures.

Doubtless, many of these changes were down to regional social, cultural and environmental factors but, equally surely, they were catalysed and guided by proximity to the Roman empire. The wealth of the provinces was a standing temptation to plunder-loving warriors. Some may also have sought profitable and honourable service in the Roman *auxilia*, although Free Germans are hardly documented in regular Roman service at this period.[91] However, during the third century, Rome increasingly raised barbarian levies, for example of Goths from beyond the Lower Danube, to serve in its wars.[92] If some eventually made it home, they took their acquired experience, expertise and – presumably – arms back with them.

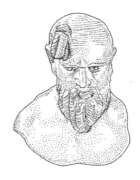

73. A bearded male with 'Swabian' topknot, a characteristic German hairstyle. Bronze cauldron mount, buried with other Roman-made items, including arms, in the grave of a 'friendly barbarian king' interred north of the Roman frontier at Mušov, Czech Republic, later second century AD.

As in Parthia, Rome's active interference beyond her northern frontiers had unforeseen as well as intended consequences. Subsidies, gifts and direct support to friendly barbarians in a band of client states roughly 100 km (60 miles) deep along the frontier (Fig. 73) had knock-on effects for those beyond them, who either became victims of Rome's clients, or potentially targeted them for their acquired wealth.[93]

It has long been thought that after the Augustan period Rome's influence in far Germania was projected solely through such political and economic means, and that the sword no longer reached very far from the Rhine or Danube. However, dramatic finds of battlefield debris far beyond the frontier, at Kalefeld south of Hannover in Germany, seem to attest a substantial Roman force, complete with artillery, attacking Germanic defenders on a hilltop.[94] Even more intriguingly, the Romans were coming from the north, suggesting they were returning from an expedition perhaps once more as far as the Elbe. This substantial engagement took place at the end of the second, or during the first half of the third century AD. The empire's arm was still long.

During the middle imperial period, Rome witnessed development beyond her frontiers of major new confederations, as existing Germanic tribes began to cooperate on a larger scale, especially in the aftermath of the Marcomannic Wars, themselves probably a symptom of the stresses and changes in Free Germany. The Marcomanni of Bohemia were long established, but during the first half of the third century long-familiar Germanic tribal groupings like the Cherusci and Chatti were subsumed into four new larger groupings: Franks and Alamanni on the Rhine, and Saxons and Burgundians to their east. Rather than unified states, these were loose confederations built from the old 'tribal' units, with multiple kings and over-kings.[95] Rome was largely indirectly responsible for their concatenation, doubtless partly for mutual protection in the face of Roman military power. Germans nearer the frontiers were learning the Roman art of war, developing into much more formidable military powers, as political organization developed too. Beyond Dacia and the lower Danube frontier, the Goths also appeared on Rome's radar during the earlier third century AD.

These are 'edge of empire' effects of a kind seen in other historical contexts, where the presence and actions of an imperial power have profound, unanticipated impacts on surrounding societies, not only immediate neighbours but also, down the line, more distant groups perhaps even beyond imperial ken. Some of the most dramatic evidence for the long reach of Rome comprises Roman swords, recovered from distant Barbaricum. Some of these blades occur in graves, but the largest numbers occur in the remarkable bog-offerings of the western Baltic.

One find in particular, at Illerup in Denmark, has a fascinating story to tell.[96] Here a remarkable lake-deposit of swords, belts, shields, spears and other gear is thought to represent an offering to the gods of the equipment of an entire small army of several hundred men, drawn from what are now Norway and Sweden, defeated and despoiled around 200: the fate of the warriors themselves is unknown. Here, as elsewhere, most of the equipment is of regional design, but the sword-blades are Roman, details of their pattern-welded manufacture beautifully preserved in the airless lakebed. A number of them show Roman stamps, and inlaid figures of gods and eagles. Some retain their Roman hilts (Plates VII, VIII, IX).

It may not simply have been arms that reached the Baltic, but also Roman military methods. Evidence from Illerup and elsewhere betrays the influence of the Roman art of war even in these distant lands. It has been suggested that the recovered equipment implies that southern Scandinavian armies were becoming larger, and more regularly organized, uniformly armed and equipped, specifically following Roman models brought back by veterans returning from imperial service.[97] Certainly, substantial change might only need an influential individual or two to spend some years fighting for Rome, and to return with a boatload of swords and a head full of ideas ... Whatever the mechanism, the bog finds betray increasing military sophistication, distantly echoing the empire.[98]

Clearly, the excellent new Roman pattern-welded blades were much sought after by Germanic warriors. But what are so many doing here? They cannot plausibly all be booty from the Marcomannic or other wars. Many, probably most, were sent to Free Germany. Do they represent commercial export of weapons? Swords are not the only Roman items going north at the time; we also see drinking gear and other luxuries, and good silver coins, some of which were in the purses of the defeated of Illerup. However, trading in advanced weapons – pattern-welded swords then, or Kalashnikov assault rifles now – is something governments seek to control.[99] Illegal arms exports were evidently a recurrent problem, since Rome maintained laws banning them.[100] Yet such measures did not preclude state-sponsored weapon exports. A clue is provided by the nature and chronology of Roman exports to Barbaricum, swords and other goods. They are selective (luxuries, arms, bullion), episodic and regionalized, hard to explain in terms of trade or smuggling.[101] They are more likely an archaeological reflection of state policy, of monetary subsidy, diplomatic gifts and Roman arms – perhaps even accompanied by 'military advisors?' – sent at certain times to favoured groups as far away as Denmark: finery for friendly rulers, and silver and weapons for their retainers. It may be that an apparent second-century principality apparently centred on Himlingøje in eastern Denmark, which perhaps for a while dominated the western Baltic, was a distant Roman client state. Military and political subsidies to selected northern groups were apparently used during, for example, the Marcomannic Wars, in an attempt to reduce military pressure on the Middle Danube by fomenting wars in the rear of the groups fighting Rome. Here was another means of projecting imperial power: wielding the sword by proxy.

If inspired, sometimes even actively incited, by Rome, increasingly sophisticated barbarian military capabilities were made possible by more complex social organization, itself arising from population growth and agricultural development. The result of these processes was the rise, in the decades after the great Illerup deposit of AD 200, of those great new barbarian confederacies that would subsequently batter, and finally overwhelm, Rome's northern frontiers.

During the early third century, substantial parts of the developing Germanic world – notably Gothic statelets abutting the Black Sea – seem to have become comparable in population density, economic productivity and social complexity to many areas of western Europe, which Rome had successfully annexed 200–300 years earlier. These changes prompt an intriguing counterfactual question. Rome had expanded to incorporate all settled agricultural peoples producing surpluses which could sustain occupying armies, and which possessed dominant 'elites' with whom she could negotiate. Her expansion probably halted in the Rhine basin because these circumstances did not then prevail across Germania to the east, although Rome retained her aggressive ideology and continued to seize opportunities to expand wherever they presented, for example in Dacia and the Middle East. So, if during the second and third centuries, many Germanic groups from the Baltic to the Black Sea were becoming socioeconomically comparable to those of (say) northern Gaul in Caesar's time, and some of them were already ruled by Roman client kings, why was there no second wave of expansion into this newly 'developing' Barbaricum, advancing the eagles to the Don, before the nascent barbarian confederacies attacked Rome?

Certainly, some of the time, Rome still exhibited the military capacity to attempt expansionist wars: Severus assembled major armies for attempts in Parthia and in Caledonia. However, Rome's internal instability often ruled this out, repeatedly wasting manpower and resources in civil wars. Above all, from the 230s Rome had to concentrate massive resources against Iran just to survive: the Sasanian threat was so great that it led to wholesale restructuring of the empire. Perhaps by the time opportunity arose in the north, crisis in the east made Rome unable to take advantage of it.

Maybe also the degree of change in Free Germany can be exaggerated, and it remained too much like the unruly interior of Hispania, which took 200 years to subdue. Romans were also now more aware of the endless extent of Eurasia, and perhaps consequently more cautious about advancing beyond the key arteries of Rhine and Danube. Experience had shown Sarmatian horsepeoples to be intractable as subjects. However, if some third-century Germans had become more like the Gauls, it may be that the Romans failed to recognize their opportunity.

As Ammianus was startled by the sophistication of German houses, so most Roman decision-makers – emperors and generals – may simply have been unable to perceive the changes in Free Germany or their potential significance, blinded by their own ideology, rhetoric and patterns of thought. On first encounter many Germanic groups may indeed have been too 'primitive' to annexe, but Romans continued to think of them as such, despite radically changing realities, and continued diplomatic and intelligence contacts. Perhaps they made the classic mistake of believing their own propaganda.[102]

Whatever the explanation, by the 230s the reality was that emperors and soldiers had inadvertently helped precipitate the simultaneous appearance of major new powers on both the northern and eastern frontiers, and thereafter permanently faced the threat of major wars on two fronts.

However, the interactions leading to this situation were not simply bloody confrontations. As we saw in the case of Roman swords in Barbaricum, they also represented cross-border influence and convergence in the sphere of military affairs. In fact swords were just one strand in a complex, multidirectional web of martial exchanges, which proved mutually transformative to all the warring peoples of the middle imperial era. We can start to unravel this through a closer look at the archaeology of Roman soldiers' equipment.

### The 'barbarian connection'

There is one further major twist to the story of the *milites* of the middle empire and their developing identity, to be told primarily through their evolving arms and equipment. And it provides answers to interesting questions about those arms: where did the new designs of the 'Antonine revolution' come from; and why did this revolution occur at all?

Some features of middle imperial equipment represented direct continuity from early imperial times: incremental developments (for example mail and scale armour designs), or innovations apparently made within the Roman provinces, above all pattern-welding technology for swords. Pattern welding was perhaps developed in areas like Gaul with major troop concentrations and a long tradition of ironworking, but we should here note our continued relative ignorance of the archaeology of the eastern armies.

Other changes relate to wider cultural trends in the Roman world of the time. For example, new sword-chape designs, some large and round in form, others representing Greek volute-topped 'pelta' shields (see Plate x), seem to be a deliberate harking-back to the similar chapes of much earlier *xiphos* swords. The simultaneous shifting of Roman scabbards from right to left noted above (p. 188), now suspended from a prominent baldric, may also in part have been encouraged by a fashion for 'looking Greek' – or, perhaps, Trojan, as Romans claimed connections with the world of the earliest Greeks through their supposed Trojan ancestry (Plate 11). It is no coincidence that these developments occurred during that era of Hellenophile antiquarianism in Roman culture known as the 'Second Sophistic', which had its military counterpart in the fascination of emperors, especially Caracalla, with Alexander the Great and his invincible phalanx.[103] The Macedonian phalanx was 'revived' in some form at this period: the tombstone of a legionary 'trainee phalangite' has been found at Apamea in Syria.[104] Other innovations of the 'Antonine revolution' represent striking discontinuities, however, differing completely from previous Roman (or Greek) arms. A notable example is the ring-pommel sword, its all-iron hilt unlike any previous Roman type (Fig. 65). However, swords and daggers with ring pommels had been used for centuries by the Sarmatians and other Iranian-speaking groups.

The Sarmatian horse-peoples of the western steppelands, such as the Roxolani, Iazyges and Alans, comprised one of Rome's greatest groups of neighbours and enemies. Romans encountered them from the Hungarian plain and the shores of the Black Sea to the Caucasus and the fringes of the Parthian world.[105] It is beyond reasonable doubt that the Romans imitated Sarmatian arms, including ring-pommel swords. Sarmatian origins may also be suggested for the Roman scabbard slide and baldric system, clearly a minimal adaptation of types already standard across the Eurasian steppe to China by this period.[106] Sarmatian scabbard slides are seen on Trajan's Column,[107] and an actual Han Chinese jade example has been found along with items from the Roman and steppe worlds in a first-century Thracian burial at Chatalka, Bulgaria.[108] The scabbard slide was developed for horsemen, allowing a long sword to be slung low from a waist-belt, six-gun style; the Romans retained the basic design, including the belt-fastener and pendant strap-end, but made it suitable for foot soldiers, raising the sword by putting its belt over the shoulder as a baldric.

Further candidates for Roman innovations of steppe origin are the new, simple cast openwork fittings for belts and horse-harness (Plate x). These likewise have excellent Sarmatian parallels (although vague dating of much

Sarmatian archaeology makes it currently hard to prove they existed earlier than the Roman versions). The *draco*, a dragon-headed windsock-standard, also appears in Roman service after it was encountered in use by Sarmatians, and had passed to the Dacians (Fig. 62).[109] Introduction of cavalry armed with long lances, probably in the later first century AD,[110] was also at least encouraged by conflict with lance-armed Sarmatians.

The two-handed lance prevented use of a shield, which Sarmatians compensated for with armour covering the whole rider and even his horse; again, Roman use of such armour might have been copied from them. Indeed, the impact of the Sarmatians on Roman equipment at this period is powerful enough for us to talk of substantial 'Sarmatization' of Roman military culture.[111] However, this is far from being the whole story.

74. Tombstone of the horse-archer Maris of the '*ala* of Parthians and Arabs', buried at Mainz in the first century AD. His servant stands ready to replenish his arrows.

There is one other potentially very important foreign source of inspiration for the changes of the 'Antonine revolution'. Many aspects of middle imperial equipment attributed to Sarmatian origins may equally or instead have entered Roman service across the Euphrates. The Romans encountered Parthian armoured, lance-armed cavalry long before they encountered the Sarmatians. They also, of course, faced Parthian horse-archers. It is clear that middle imperial Roman archery equipment and shooting methods were primarily drawn from the east. This comprised not only powerful composite bows, but by the third century, probable use of the thumb-ring for shooting 'Mongolian style'. In this technique, rather than being drawn with the first two fingers ('Mediterranean release'), the bowstring is drawn by the right thumb, the ball of the thumb being protected by a broad ring.[112] Such archery tackle and shooting methods originated in Central Asia, but were finely honed across the Parthian world and Syria. The emperors recruited Parthian exiles and Syrians as auxiliary archers from an early date, men like Maris, soldier of a mixed Parthian and Arab horse-archer unit already on the Rhine in the mid-first century AD (Fig. 74).[113]

As yet we know very little of Partho-Sasanian swords archaeologically, but several blades excavated in northern Iran are apparently of later Parthian date (Fig. 75).[114] Their hilts are very different from Roman weapons in having an iron-cross guard, a feature common with Sarmatian ring-pommel weapons, but sometimes this is extended into long quillons prefiguring medieval broadswords. Their blades mostly taper gently to a long sharp point (and so are suited for thrust as well as cut); lacking fullers or midrib, they are apparently of 'lens' section, ranging from 570 to 780 mm (22½ to 31 in) in length, excluding hilt. The similarity of these blade-forms to middle imperial Roman types is apparent. The known blades have not been analysed for composition and manufacturing techniques, but Pliny recorded that Parthian steel was surpassed in quality only by 'Seric' (Chinese), suggesting that Romans examined Parthian weapons closely.[115]

Representations also show that scabbard slides, and sword belts with fittings forming clear potential prototypes for the new Roman sword-suspension system, were used in Parthia at least as early as they appeared on the Danubian frontier, and could have entered Roman use through both routes. Early Sasanian reliefs also show Iranians with ring-buckle belts and swagged strap-ends, both prominent features of third-century Roman military dress without Sarmatian parallels (compare Figs 66 and 76). As a source of new technology, techniques and styles, the Euphrates frontier was probably as significant as the Danube, but this remains a story yet to be told in detail.

Early Germanic military equipment seems to have offered little to tempt Roman imitation; however, basic dress and grooming were another matter. It is quite clear that the ensemble of long trousers, long-sleeved tunic and square cloak worn by third-century Roman troops (p. 189) represented direct adoption of general 'northern male barbarian' dress, with minimal adaptation beyond 'Romanizing' its colours. (Given the apparent practicality of long garments in the central European climate, it is a tribute to Roman conservatism in dress, at least, that it took *milites* so long to abandon Mediterranean garments.) The 'new' Roman ensemble had long been worn by Gauls, Germans, Dacians and others around the Black Sea. Indeed, remarkably close precursors for middle imperial Roman military dress are seen on first-century Bosporan tombstones from the Crimea – which also portray prototypes for the middle imperial Roman broad-oval shield, in a zone where Roman troops operated.[116]

It is especially striking how similar the dress of Germans during the Marcomannic Wars of the 160s–170s, represented on the Column of Marcus, is to that of Roman soldiers on tombstones of the succeeding decades.[117] Even more striking is the similarity in shaggy hair- and beard-styles, on the column

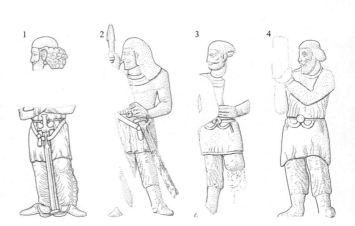

75. *Above right.* Reconstruction of a late Parthian sword, based on finds of blades from Dailaman, Gilan province, northern Iran. (Scale 1:8)

76. *Right.* Representations of sword-belts and scabbard slides, ring-buckles and swagged waist belts in the early Sasanian empire, from royal reliefs at Bishapur, Iran.

and other contemporary depictions, between Germanic warriors, Roman soldiers and emperors during the later second century AD (Figs 58, 70). Within the empire, emperors, officers and *milites* tended to wear the same hair- and beard-styles. The question is, who was imitating whom? It is often assumed that soldiers, like other privileged Roman males, followed imperial fashion leads, and began sporting beards from the time of Hadrian, when they became *de rigueur* among the elite as part of a wider renaissance of Greek culture.[118] However, there is good reason to suggest that imitation was in the opposite direction – emperors dressed their hair according to the fashion of their soldiers, as part of their persona as *commilito*, 'fellow-soldier'. Marcus Aurelius doubtless favoured a beard as a lover of Greek philosophy, but may have grown it long and shaggy in solidarity with the fashion of his *milites*. Severus – no philosopher he! – did likewise. In turn, the soldiers probably took the fashion for beards from the peoples they fought – and increasingly recruited from. In the later second century, this meant, not least, Danube Germans.

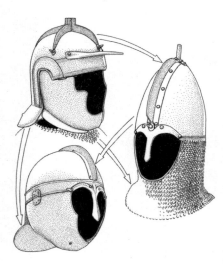

77. Top left, the skull reinforcements of mid-imperial Roman helmets and iron mail appear to have been copied by the Sasanians. They feature on the otherwise distinctive helmet of composite construction worn by a Sasanian soldier killed at Dura-Europos *c.* 256 (*right*). Reciprocally, the radically new helmets that Roman soldiers suddenly started wearing in the fourth century (*bottom left*) were clearly inspired by this Partho-Sasanian design.

The flow of military culture was no simple one-way current. The empire's neighbours adopted aspects of Roman arms and warfare too, just as the Hellenistic world had. Palmyrenes depicted their gods wearing Roman Mainz-type swords, and Nabatean Arab nobles could depict Pompeii-type weapons on an altar.[119] Sarmatians adopted iron mail, probably from the Romans, as an alternative to hide or scale defences.[120] Mail was also adopted in the Partho-Sasanian world, appearing on an early Sasanian royal relief (Fig. 72). An early Sasanian soldier found at Dura wore a mail shirt, and the helmet found near him sported a mail neck-defence. It also bore an additional reinforcing plate from crown to nose-guard, which seems to imitate longstanding features of Roman helmets (Fig. 77). Sasanian siege capability probably drew on conquered Hatrene and renegade Roman expertise.[121] Later in date, Sasanian linear defences against Central Asiatic peoples may have imitated Roman frontier systems.[122] And we have seen how even distant Germans acquired Roman sword-blades in massive numbers.

However, the flow of innovation and change was mostly into the Roman empire, for the reason identified by Polybius 300 years earlier: Roman ideological openness to accepting, and incorporating as their own, both foreign ideas and people, in civil contexts and not least in their armies and martial culture. In the later second century especially, as Romans slaughtered Danube Germans and Sarmatians, they also recruited them in thousands: for example in 175 some 5,500 Sarmatians – the equivalent of eleven auxiliary regiments – were drafted to Britain (Fig. 78).[123] Thus eastern and Sarmatian arms, and the German dress ensemble and hairstyles, entered Roman military usage on the backs and in the hands of frontier provincials, barbarian allies and recruits, as well as through booty. At the same time, traits and techniques were transmitted from the empire by plunder, prisoners of war, exiles and renegades, as well as, perhaps, veterans of barbarian origin going home.

78. Probable tombstone from Chester, likely to be that of a Sarmatian auxiliary, with a dragon-headed windsock standard streaming behind him. It may represent one of the thousands of Sarmatian soldiers sent to Britain in 175.

†

The reality of Rome's frontier zones, then, was not only violence, but also powerful cultural convergence, especially between Roman *milites* and the 'barbarians' beyond. Paradoxically, while policing and marking out their boundaries and differences between societies, the fighting men facing each other also came to have much in common, attested by convergences, exchanges and commonalities of kit. Warring peoples selectively adopted and adapted each other's equipment and tactics in all directions, across a vast zone from the North Sea to the Ukraine and the Syrian desert. These exchanges went beyond martial equipment and practices, also extending to outlook and values. With migrations, cross-recruitment, exiles and desertions, the men facing each other across Rhine, Danube and dry steppe became increasingly similar, in some respects sharing more with their ostensible foes than with the rest of their own populations.

Convergence of martial cultures is one of the most important expressions of a deeper truth about frontiers. In many respects they are not lines marking political and cultural boundaries, but deep zones straddling them; not edges, but centres of intensive interaction, violent and otherwise, with profound effects on both sides. The connections and frame of reference of the Roman frontier zone lay beyond the empire as much as with the provincial hinterland, and more so than with the city of Rome itself.[124]

Nevertheless, although they converged – to some extent, *because* they were converging on things like the most effective weapons in the pool available in their shared world – the confronting groups were also keen to retain and emphasize their distinctiveness. So Scandinavians may have prized Roman sword-blades, yet 'Germanized' the appearance of their hilts and scabbard fittings.[125] Sasanians used mail on helmets in very un-Roman ways, while Roman *milites* gave their new barbarian-style dress Greco-Roman coloration to express their traditional identity through it.

Within the community of Roman *milites*, recipients of so many recruits and new items of equipment from such diverse frontier-provincial and foreign origins, the tendency was to homogenize their material culture, to express their shared identity as soldiers of Rome. During the second century, there was general internal convergence on what had been auxiliary equipment, largely derived from the martial gear of the peoples of those frontier zones from Gaul to Thrace which had been fully 'domesticated'; like the provincial recruits who introduced it to the armies, such equipment had been naturalized as 'Roman'.[126] Arrian, himself a commander in Hadrian's time, commented on this process in his *Tactical Handbook*:

> The Romans are worthy to be praised because they do not embrace [only] their own native things. Thus, having chosen noble things from everywhere, they made them their own. You would find that they take some armaments from others – and indeed they are called 'Roman', because the Romans especially use them. [They take] soldierly exercises from others...[127]

This process reflected the reality that legionaries and auxiliaries increasingly shared similar backgrounds and homelands; many legionaries were sons of provincial auxiliaries, and auxiliaries were, increasingly, Roman citizens even on recruitment. However, as we have seen, this shared background was rooted in frontier lands developing provincial-Roman cultures increasingly divergent from that of 'core' Greco-Roman civil society. Northern limb-covering dress was not only warmer for central European winters; it also fitted with European provincial/barbarian values, and eastern traditions of bodily modesty.

Overall, evolution of Roman martial culture could be seen as military 'Romanization' of the frontier provinces: from northern Britain to the Euphrates a vast ethnic diversity came to share an overtly Roman identity and common culture as *milites*. Yet, even though these men were, or were becoming, good Romans, changes in the composition of soldierly culture – not least the 'Antonine revolution' in equipment, with the shift in its basis from Mediterranean to other cultural traditions – could equally be perceived by civilians of the core provinces as 'provincialization' or even 'barbarization' of the armies.

From the soldiers' viewpoint, this evolution of Roman martial material culture represented 'barbarization' no more than had the introduction of the *gladius Hispaniensis*. Rather it expressed continuity of a quintessential Roman tradition: absorption of foreigners and foreign ways into Roman-ness. The soldiers were one of the most important, and most self-consciously Roman, communities of the multiple, diverse societies which comprised the empire. Yet many other Romans, high and low, increasingly saw them not just as dangerous oppressors, but as aliens, little distinguishable from barbarians.

For all their purple-embroidered white tunics and the Classical motifs on their arms, to Italians and many provincials, middle imperial soldiers looked startlingly outlandish (sic). Even legionaries increasingly appeared to dress like the 'barbarians' beyond the frontier zones whence most soldiers came. And this was before they opened their mouths or otherwise displayed boorish soldierly arrogance; for they also sounded alien. When they spoke Latin, ordinary soldiers employed the *sermo militaris*, effectively a special martial dialect, incorporating slang and technical vocabulary derived from other languages; for example, much equestrian terminology was Celtic in origin.[128] Further, many spoke it as a second language with 'barbarous' accents, and some barely spoke it at all, especially in the east, where Greek was the *lingua franca*.

It is then little wonder that, when Severus arrived in Rome in 193 as victor of the civil war, 'filling the city with a throng of motley soldiers most savage in appearance, most terrifying in speech, and most boorish in conversation', as Cassio Dio records,[129] the urban populace did not see his triumphant Pannonian *milites* as 'our boys', but as little better than barbarians themselves. Doubtless, some of them were in fact first-generation barbarian recruits-becoming-Romans. The name of L. Septimius Valerinus, a *miles* commemorated at Rome, indicates that he or probably his father had received citizenship from Severus; he himself was one of Severus' new Danubian Praetorians (Fig. 69). Some such men were likely sons and grandsons of the Germans shown being slaughtered on the Column of Marcus. Yet this did not stop them feeling – or being – 'good Romans'. Soldiering had become a separate world, and most *milites* strangers to the metropolis. Here is an index of how far 'military Rome' had diverged from that of the civil 'core' provinces.

## Third-century crisis: 'imperial blowback'

> For the holy goddess Victoria [this altar is set up] because on 24 and 25 April [AD 260] the barbarian people the Semnoni or Iouthungi were attacked and expelled by *milites* of the province of Raetia and the *Germaniciani* [soldiers from Upper Germany?] and also of the *populares* [provincial militia?]. Many thousands of captured Italians were freed…
>
> INSCRIPTION ON AN ALTAR, AUGSBURG[130]

The new perils besetting Rome during the third century AD partly resulted from vast processes beyond her control, but were largely shaped by her sustained military aggression, yet failure to absorb the peoples she attacked or sought to manipulate. Through continued pursuit of the expansionist ideology of the past, during the second and earlier third centuries AD Roman leaders and soldiers inadvertently helped create powerful new enemies on multiple fronts. Through unanticipated effects on others, Roman martial spirit became a liability as much as an asset.

Even the might of the Roman military system proved unable to cope with simultaneous wars in north and east. Catastrophic defeats led to the destruction of substantial parts of the evolved Augustan provincial military structure, and opened up the regional fissures which already existed between army groups, as soldiers and commanders, faced as they were with multiple incursions such as that recorded on the remarkable altar inscription found at Augsburg in Germany (p. 219), looked first to secure themselves and their home provinces.

The murder of Severus Alexander in AD 235 was followed by a seemingly unstoppable downward spiral of foreign disasters, imperial assassinations and civil wars. Resisting a major Sasanian invasion in 244, at the battle of Mišīk[131] the emperor Gordian III was killed, or soon after assassinated, and succeeded by his Praetorian prefect, Philip, who negotiated a disadvantageous peace with the capable and ambitious new Sasanian king, Shapur I. Philip lived long enough to preside over Rome's millennium celebrations in 248, but was in turn murdered and replaced by Decius, governor of Dacia, whose bid for the throne exposed the Danube provinces to attack by the Goths, themselves under pressure from the Sarmatian Alans. Decius died fighting the barbarians in 251; and so it went on. Valerian, emperor from 253, faced wars from the North Sea to Mesopotamia, where he endured the unpredecented humiliation of capture by Shapur I (Fig. 79). While the Goths still threatened the lower Danube, on the Rhine and upper Danube, the Franks and Alamanni,[132] recently coalesced Germanic confederations, burst into the empire in deep-penetrating, devastating invasions. By 260 they would reach as far as Spain and the Po valley. Meanwhile, during the 250s Shapur I repeatedly invaded Syria. Valerian went east to face the Sasanians, leaving his son Gallienus to rule in Europe. Gallienus beat back the Alamanni, but when forced to tackle rebel commanders on the Danube, faced a more serious revolt in Gaul. Here his general Postumus made a bid for the throne, and in successfully defending the Rhine against the Germans, won the loyalty of the provincial armies. Crucially, the governors of Spain and Britain transferred their loyalty to him. Around the same time, Gallienus learned of his father's defeat and capture at Edessa by Rome's Sasanid nemesis, Shapur I.

In 260, Gallienus found himself ruler of only part of the empire. Roman power collapsed in the east, which would have fallen under Sasanian rule had it not been for the remarkable boldness and success of Rome's Syrian subjects the

Palmyrenes, who not only checked the Persians but, by 270, expanded their own hegemony over Syria, Anatolia and even Egypt. By then Postumus' successful revolt in the west had established in effect a breakaway Roman state, complete with its own duplicate senate and Praetorian Guard, known as the 'Gallic empire'.

Gallienus, based in the Danube lands, embarked on military preparations for the colossal task of defeating rebels and usurpers, expelling and neutralizing all foreign enemies, rebuilding smashed armies and frontiers, re-establishing imperial authority over the provinces, and getting the fiscal system operational again to maintain the regime and the soldiers. He is often credited with developing a new cavalry force, which formed an important nucleus of later 'mobile field armies'. Gallienus continued to struggle with barbarian invasions, which even reached Athens, until his assassination in 268. The following year saw a further, vast invasion of the Balkans by the Goths, who were now determined on permanent settlement inside the empire. It has been said, with reason, that these years were the darkest Rome had endured since the aftermath of Cannae.

In the 260s Rome, riven by bloody internal wars and assailed on all sides by foreign enemies, was fragmenting as Alexander's empire had done, and looked doomed to oblivion. It must have seemed to contemporaries that only a miracle could save it. Against all the odds, the swords of the soldiers would perform one.

79. Shapur I triumphant over two Roman emperors, Naqsh-e-Rustam, Iran. Philip grovels before Shapur, who holds the captured Valerian by the wrists. Note Shapur's long sword, attached to his belt by a scabbard slide.

# Empire of the Soldiers
## Forging the Dominate 269–376

### 'Decline and fall'?

An unprecedented concatenation of foreign invasions and internal wars during the 250s and 260s saw Roman armies and imperial prestige shattered, and the empire fragment. Yet imperial power survived. By the 280s the soldiers had reunified the provinces and driven out foreign enemies. Over the next three centuries and more, Roman *milites* continued to perform impressive feats of arms, some comparable with anything achieved by their forebears under Scipio or Caesar.

While they proved unable to conquer the major new powers arising around the frontiers, for the most part the soldiers successfully confronted a constellation of powerful foes, collectively more formidable than those faced by their predecessors in the early empire, which had itself arisen largely as a result of the wielding of the Roman sword. Rome's *milites* showed that they were still able to win wars and major battles – while also still enforcing the authority of emperors, and protecting the aristocrats who controlled civil society. Late Roman *milites* could be as tough as ever, and only in this late period were they commanded by a fully professional career officer corps.

The reformed late Roman imperial state was even more directly a creation by the soldiers, for the soldiers, than the later republic or early empire had been. Also more overtly militarized than ever before, the provinces were never more openly run as a resource base to supply *milites* and imperial courts, in their continued symbiosis with the landed aristocracies. Yet the soldiers also still indulged in mutiny, civil wars and abuse of civilians. Rome's *milites* continued to venerate the traditions and battlefield feats of their forebears, and as late as the sixth century some were still in units called legions. Indeed, far beyond this period, there were powerful, regular armies composed of soldiers who still called themselves Romans, and were trained on the same disciplinary principles as early imperial *milites*. Deciding when it ceases to be meaningful to continue the story of the *Roman* sword, either as metaphor for the martial power of a still recognizably Roman state, or as artefact in the hands of still recognizably Roman soldiers, is a somewhat arbitrary judgment. Here, for reasons that will become apparent, I choose the end of the reign of the emperor Justinian in 565.

Such a picture of several further centuries, at least, of (in their own terms) successful maintenance of Roman martial power may come as something of a surprise, since popular histories, and even many academic writings, tend to treat the era after the third century as simply a gloomy epilogue of fading glory – if they don't ignore it entirely.[1] Many interest themselves solely in the earlier 'shiny war-machine' in the ascendant. Everything thereafter (if the rot is not deemed to have set in with Septimius Severus, or even the Marcomannic Wars) is considered to be of less interest, a twilight world assessed in terms of decline, defeat and decay owing to decadence and demoralization, in which traditional Roman virtues were vanishing, armies and empire staggering through the disastrous third century only to be overwhelmed in the fourth and fifth by barbarian vigour from the north. Such prejudices are even built into the basic terms used for the era: whereas Anglophone scholars talk of the 'early' and 'late' Roman empire, in other European languages the 'high empire' from Augustus to the Antonine emperors is followed by the 'low empire' of the fourth and fifth centuries.

There are of course reasons behind such takes on the past, put into canonical form in the eighteenth century by Gibbon's iconic *Decline and Fall of the Roman Empire*. For centuries before Gibbon picked up his pen, scholars and soldiers had been poring over the rediscovered 'military manual' of Vegetius, written around the end of the fourth century, which became hugely influential.[2] Vegetius cried out for reform of armies in which, he gloomily claimed, soldiers had abandoned traditional Roman arms and discipline, in the sense of proper, old-style training, and no longer bothered to wear adequate armour. Indeed the 400s did see the last Roman *milites* on the Rhine, the western armies did disintegrate during the fifth century, and Roman rule in Europe did largely collapse. Failure of the armies, no longer able to stem the barbarian tide, has long been a major pillar of explanations of the 'fall of the Roman empire', alongside, and intimately related to, notions of internal moral decay of a once-great civilization.

This compelling, epic story of the last, degenerate Roman soldiers going down under the onslaught of barbarian swords remains central to the grand historical narrative of western Europe. The histories of many modern states, not least England and France, are considered to start with barbarian settlement following Roman imperial collapse. The problem with this familiar picture is that it is a great morality tale, but poor history. It is at best highly selective, western-Eurocentric, and in key respects is simply wrong.

In contrast to 'decline and fall', the story of unbroken martial power and gradual transformation with which I opened this chapter is itself also admittedly a 'spun' account, this time with an eastern Roman bias presented in opposition to the entrenched Western perspective. However, I argue it is a more accurate overall picture of the later history of Roman arms than the conventional tale of 'decline and fall'. For the latter airbrushes out the eastern half of the empire, the richer and, increasingly in this period, stronger half, which did not collapse at all, long remaining a major military power. In fact, alongside his account of the collapse of the Roman west, a major portion of Gibbon's great work is concerned with the further thousand-year history of the surviving eastern Roman empire, as it evolved into the Orthodox Christian medieval state we call the Byzantine empire – although, until the fall of its capital Constantinople to the Ottoman Turks in 1453, its Greek-speaking rulers and people called themselves *Rhomaioi*: Romans. It is perverse, then, to demean the long medieval history of the eastern empire as 'decline and fall'.[3] Further, there is also good reason to argue that the traditional story of the 'fall of the west' seriously misrepresents the history of the western empire and its soldiers as well. In the late empire, soldiers and the sword were as central as ever to the unfolding history of the Roman world.

The story of the later empire is, as before, of self-conscious continuity underlying never-ending changes. However, by the sixth century the changes were so profound that we cease to feel the term 'Roman' can meaningfully be applied, and use 'Byzantine' instead. Already in the mid-fourth century, these trends were visibly in train.

### Constantius II enters Rome, 357

In spring 357, escorted by imperial soldiers and military standards, Constantius II, senior ruler of the united empire, entered the City of Rome where the senate still sat, and consuls still gave their names to the years. Over the following days, like so many earlier emperors, he joined the people in enjoying chariot races in the Circus Maximus, where they indulged their time-honoured right to irreverent freedom of speech. So far, so traditional. However, the details of this imperial visitation, recorded by the historian Ammianus, starkly reveal how profoundly Rome, her emperors and her soldiers had changed since the days of Augustus. Constantius arrived less as victorious general or aristocratic magistrate of the Roman people, but rather as quasi-divine being:

> He himself sat alone upon a golden car in the resplendent blaze of precious stones…he was surrounded by dragon[standard]s, woven out of purple thread and bound to the golden and jewelled tops of spears, hissing as if roused with anger, and leaving their tails winding in the wind. And there marched on either side twin lines of infantrymen with shields and crests gleaming with glittering rays, clad in shining mail; and scattered among them were the full-armoured cavalry (whom they call *clibanarii*), all masked, furnished with protecting breastplates and girt with iron belts, so that you might have supposed them statues polished by the hand of Praxiteles, not men. Thin circles of iron plates, fitted to the curves of their bodies, completely covered their limbs…being saluted as Augustus with

favouring shouts, while hills and shores thundered out the roar, he never stirred, but showed himself as calm and imperturbable. ...For he both stooped when passing through lofty gates (although he was very short), and as if his neck were in a vice, he kept the gaze of his eyes straight ahead...but (as if he were a clay figure) neither did he nod when the wheel jolted, nor was he ever seen to spit, or to wipe or rub his face or nose, or move his hands about...[4]

For the people of the City to see the emperor at all was increasingly rare. This was the first time Constantius had ever set eyes on the ancient capital. Still a hallowed symbol, Rome had become a backwater. Wars and politics – including the making of emperors – were now played out elsewhere.

During campaigning seasons emperors were often on the move with the *comitatenses*, soldiers of the new mobile field armies, waging foreign war or suppressing usurpers. Constantius, an experienced soldier if no great general, had recently had to extricate himself from a war with the Sasanians to storm westwards and deal with Magnentius, a rival in Gaul, in a civil war which killed, yet again, thousands of Roman troops. The defeated usurper reportedly killed himself in the traditional way, by falling on his sword.

Probably more to watch their own soldiers than foreign enemies, emperors now wintered not in Rome but in major cities near the frontiers or on the strategic routes across the empire, from Trier and Milan in the west to Antioch in the east. Rapidly becoming most important of all was a new imperial capital, Constantinople, in 357 still being built on the site of the old Greek city of Byzantium, where the main land route between the Danube and the east crossed the narrow straits linking the Mediterranean and the Black Sea. Strategically placed to send armies east or west, it also blocked invaders seeking to cross the empire. Constantinople was founded by Constantius' father, Constantine the Great, who died the first Christian emperor. From the start *Constantinopolis* (the City of Constantine) was to be both a new, second Rome, and a Christian city of the Greek-speaking east. Henceforth the empire had two symbolic poles, old and new Rome. This was another profound change: Constantius was a Christian ruler of an increasingly Christianized (but still substantially pagan) empire. One of the staunchest remaining bastions of paganism was the soldiery who, in 357, escorted the emperor into old Rome.

Our vivid account of the imperial arrival was written by Ammianus Marcellinus, himself a pagan military officer. A Greek-speaking eastern Roman, probably a Syrian, he served in a military which, for a century beginning with the reign of Gallienus, had been dominated by the tough soldiers of Illyricum, the Danube provinces, recruited from Balkan provincials and neighbouring barbarians. For it was these Illyriciani – both ordinary *milites*, and the ill-educated but hard-bitten and thoroughly professional officers and soldier-emperors who arose from their ranks – who saved the empire following the disasters of the mid-third century (Fig. 80). Fourth-century emperors, Constantine and Constantius II included, were still usually of Illyrian origin.

80. The emperor Galerius addresses his soldiers. These tough Danubian Illyriciani sport helmets with nasals and dragon standards reflecting Sarmatian and Partho-Sasanian influence. Partial restoration of a damaged relief from the Arch of Galerius, Thessaloniki, Greece.

## Restoring the world, 269–84

As we saw, during the 250s and 260s, military disaster overwhelmed the empire, which began to break up (p. 220). By 269 the Agri Decumates beyond the upper Rhine had been abandoned. A massive invasion of the Balkans in 269, by Goths intent on settlement, looked set to drive Roman authority even further south. However, Rome's Balkan soldiers, under Claudius II, himself an Illyrian, achieved remarkable feats of arms against these invaders. The Goths moved in two separate bodies. By fast and skilful manoeuvre, Claudius' troops got between them, annihilated the second wave, and then intercepted and destroyed the retreating first contingent, inflicting a defeat so devastating that the Goths were little further problem for a century. Now surnamed Gothicus in honour of his success, Claudius was preparing to consolidate the restoration of the Danube frontier, by taking on the Germans attacking Pannonia, when he died suddenly (270). He was the only emperor of the period to perish in his bed – succumbing to plague.

The Danubian *milites* raised another of their own to the purple, Claudius' trusted general Aurelian. He quickly drove the Germans out of Pannonia, and shortened the Danube-zone frontier significantly by abandoning Dacia. By 271, a ruler of the central rump of the empire was finally in a position to go on the offensive to reacquire the lost provinces in east and west. Aurelian opted to recover the richer and more populous east first, especially since the Gallic empire was preoccupied with internal squabbles. While a second force seized Egypt, Aurelian's soldiers rapidly retook Anatolia, defeated the Palmyrenes in Syria and rushed across steppe and desert to besiege Palmyra itself (272). The city's famed queen Zenobia was captured and a garrison installed, but rebels massacred the Roman troops, and Aurelian tore back from Thrace to avenge them. Palmyra was sacked, and permanently broken as a major city.

Aurelian then rapidly marched his soldiers west again, right across the Roman world, to deal with the Gallic empire, the last emperor of which, Tetricus, surrendered during battle (273). In less than three years Aurelian had reunited the empire. By any standards, he was a remarkable commander. His speed in war and ruthlessness in politics were worthy of Caesar, and earned him the nickname *manu ad ferrum*, 'hand-on-hilt', yet Aurelian was also politically astute, sparing both Zenobia and Tetricus as living monuments to his triumphs. But he could not have achieved his victories without equally remarkable soldiers.

The terrible wars of the mid-third century shattered much of Rome's existing military organization; many regiments disappear from history at this time. Yet the campaigns of Claudius and Aurelian show that these conflicts also forged the tough, highly motivated soldiers and officers of the Danubian armies into skilled and experienced forces, capable of undertaking campaigns as audacious and far-ranging as those of any previous generation of Roman soldiers.

In 275 Aurelian was preparing to return east to face the Sasanians when he, like so many recent emperors, was murdered by disgruntled officers. The habit of military assassination was hard to shake off, and no ruler was safe. After the deaths of several more short-lived rulers, Aurelian's general Probus, another Illyrian soldier, ascended the throne. He successfully defeated renewed Alamannic and Frankish attacks across the Rhine, although not before they had devastated and permanently damaged the economy of northern Gaul. He also defeated the Germanic Vandals on the Danube, and achieved a truce with the Sasanians (Rome's nemesis Shapur had died in 272). Yet once again, success did not bring security to the emperor. Probus upset his Pannonian *milites* by using them on land reclamation work, and in 282 they lynched him. All too easily, the wolves still turned.

Danubian officers continued to monopolize the throne, because Illyrian soldiers dominated the armies, which now routinely appointed emperors by acclamation at the behest of supporting cliques comprised of fellow officers. Civilian politicians rarely had any say. Probus' successor, Carus, taking advantage of Sasanian preoccupation with provincial risings and dynastic revolts of their own, was able to lead Rome's resurgent armies on a successful invasion of Mesopotamia, and once again sacked Ctesiphon, for the first time since the fall of Parthia. However, as ever this proved a Pyrrhic victory, and Carus was apparently assassinated. As the army retreated, so was his son Numerianus. After personally killing Numerianus' assassin, yet another Danubian officer was proclaimed emperor: Diocletian.

In little more than a couple of decades, then, Illyrian soldiers, officers and the emperors they proclaimed halted the break-up of the empire, reunited it under central rule, drove out the barbarians and were even taking the offensive against Persia. It was a military achievement to rank with the Second Punic War. The existence of the later Roman empire, and the fact that it finally fragmented into successor states in the fifth century rather than 200 years earlier, was down to the determination, courage and ruthless brutality of the Illyriciani.

It is worth pausing to ask why the Illyriciani made such stupendous efforts to reunite the empire. Their homelands were perhaps the most vulnerable of all to mass barbarian onslaught, so why expend their energies reconquering distant Palmyra or Gaul? Multiple factors were at work, not least their powerful ideology as Roman *milites*. Following the eagles, all *milites* shared a cosmological belief in the divinely sanctioned place of Rome, and took pride in wielding the sword on its behalf. However, exposed to a lifetime of major wars, the martial traditions of the Danubian armies were especially finely honed. Their long-standing contempt for rival *milites* on other frontiers can only have been deepened by the events of 250–70, boosting their self-worth and perhaps – egged on by ambitious commanders – a sense of special destiny as saviours of the empire. Further, they were well placed geographically to reunite the state. Also, as ever soldiers sought glory and the chance for plunder, satiated in the sack of Palmyra – which raises the issue of more fundamental self-interest.

The lands from Pannonia on the middle reaches of the Danube to Thrace near its mouth remained among Rome's most important military recruiting grounds, because they were populous and retained their martial traditions, but were also relatively poor. In their development resembling more the militarized Batavi (p. 145) than the civil core of the empire, the peoples of these lands arguably formed the core of 'military Rome'. The eastern armies had been shattered, while those of the Gallic empire, with rich lands behind them, were self-sufficient and had less need of the rest of the provinces. The Danubian armies could recruit their manpower locally, but they needed the money and material resources of the richer provinces to maintain their existence. Reunification of the empire by the Illyriciani was, then, the result of a powerful combination of ideology and self-interest. They did it because of, not despite, their vulnerability.

Yet if the Illyriciani reunited the empire, it seemed that stability and harmony among their own ranks remained as elusive as under the later Severans, fifty years, at least eighteen emperors, and dozens of pretenders earlier. Narrowly defeating Carus' other son Carinus in civil war, Diocletian achieved sole power in 285. Given recent history, it must have seemed just a matter of time before he, too, fell to his soldiers' swords, or an assassin's dagger.

The problem was not only the arrogance and greed of soldiers who had, too often, tasted the bribes of would-be emperors, and the blood of those on the throne. There were underlying structural, strategic reasons for military and political instability. For a century, Rome had faced a changed reality: continual danger of simultaneous major invasions on Rhine, Danube and Euphrates. A single emperor could only deal with one front at a time and, especially when he withdrew troops from one frontier in order to gather a field army for war on another, he left remaining soldiers and home communities feeling vulnerable, and often in real danger. All too easily they might support ambitious local commanders in a bid for the purple, on the promise of putting local defence first. This was the dilemma that Diocletian faced – and, for a time, resolved.

## Forging the Dominate 284–361

It turned out that Diocletian reigned for twenty years, giving him time to apply his political and administrative skills to restabilizing the empire and the armies. In this, he performed a feat comparable to that of Augustus 300 years before; indeed, arguably greater, since Augustus faced fewer serious foreign threats. Neither Augustus nor Diocletian was a great general, but both proved talented politicians, and both were lucky to survive long enough to succeed. Both broke cycles of civil war, reformed the state from the ground up using revolutionary measures presented as restoring Roman traditions, and both profoundly reorganized the military. However, there the similarities end. Augustus had the huge initial advantages of a senatorial pedigree and Caesar's inheritance; Diocletian was an uneducated Danubian peasant soldier who rose to the purple by sheer ability and opportunism.

Diocletian's new order, today known as the Dominate, did not seek to undo the autocracy which had prevailed since Severus; there was no renewed pretence of 'restoring the republic', which now belonged to revered but distant history. He rose to power as a military strongman, and the new regime would reflect his background; the late Roman state was overtly militarized. However, Diocletian did seek to make the new autocracy less solely and obviously dependent on the swords of his soldiers than had been the case in recent decades. He sought to do this through religious ideology and associated awe-inspiring pomp. Diocletian drew on both hallowed tradition – he set about restoring the prestige of the traditional state gods, using soldiers to persecute 'atheistic' Christians and purging them from the armies (Fig. 81) – and also contemporary developments, in which emperors increasingly presented themselves as divine.

Previous emperors had extended the logic of the longstanding imperial cult, which had seen provincials following Hellenistic tradition in expressing loyalty to the ruler by offering him divine honours. Emperors now styled themselves living gods, and everything associated with them was couched in the language of religion (the imperial court was the 'sacred *comitatus*' and even imperial coinage had long since become the 'divine coinage of the emperors').[5] Court dress became increasingly gorgeous, ceremonial ever grander and more

81. *Milites* making an arrest on an early fourth-century Christian sarcophagus from Rome. They show the distinctive appearance of soldiers on the streets of Roman cities at the time: close-fitting trousers, long-sleeved tunics, cloaks held on by 'crossbow' brooches and Danubian 'pill-box' caps. The stubbly beards of the later third century were giving way to shaven chins again in the fourth.

obsequious. Those allowed into the sacred presence were expected to prostrate themselves in the face of the divine. In this, the new regime imitated and sought to rival the Asiatic splendour of the Sasanian royal court, imposing authority through awe and sacrosanctity. The theatre of imperial pageantry was further refined from the reign of Constantine, who wore a pearl diadem, even if, in adopting Christianity as the new state religion, he had to give up being an actual living god and be satisfied with being the mere equal of the apostles, and God's viceroy on earth.

Such, then, was the public face of the later Roman emperors, a far cry from Augustus presenting himself as simply first among senators. Doubtless spectacular display and assertions of divine sanction impressed many provincials and simple soldiers, but others remained fully aware that the emperor was just another man, with wars to be fought, foreign enemies to face and political interests – not least those of their *milites* – to satisfy.

Diocletian sought to resolve the chronic problem of too many strategic threats for one ruler by creating a college of co-emperors, all fellow Danubians. Drawing on the experience of the 'good' Antonine emperors, who had (until Marcus) lacked sons and so adopted proven men as heirs, Diocletian's idea was to appoint a trusted general as co-Augustus, and for each of them to appoint a promising younger officer as deputy and heir-apparent, with the title of Caesar. This college of four emperors (the Tetrarchy) would constitute a group of allied commanders, each responsible for part of the empire, and able to deal promptly with regional threats, foreign or internal (Fig. 82).

Collegiate command proved effective in halting the cycle of rebellions and stabilizing the frontiers, including that with ever-dangerous Persia. In the east, the Caesar Galerius, learning from another almost Carrhae-style defeat by Sasanian cavalry during their invasion of Syria in 295, counterattacked the following year and won a decisive victory over the Shah Narses in Armenia, capturing his family.[6]

Diocletian's clever scheme worked well for a while; uniquely among emperors, he was even able to retire, obliging his co-Augustus to follow suit. The two newly promoted *Augusti* were in turn to appoint new Caesars. However, his scheme ignored the fact that some of his colleagues had sons. The Tetrarchy dissolved into new usurpations and civil wars, resulting in the ultimate triumph of Constantine, son of Constantius I, Diocletian's other Caesar. Constantine won a decisive battle at the Milvian Bridge outside Rome in 312, a victory he attributed to the Christian God.

Sole emperor by 324, Constantine consolidated a new dynasty, appointing his sons as regional rulers, and bequeathing the empire to them jointly on his death in 337. The brothers fought each other and new usurpers until Constantius II was last man standing. Inevitably, like his predecessors, he then faced the dilemma that he could not be everywhere to deal with foreign dangers and simultaneous unrest elsewhere, which would tempt soldiers, generals and magnates to raise further imperial pretenders. On crushing Magnentius (p. 225) he felt obliged to appoint as Caesars his last surviving male blood-relatives, Gallus and Julian. However, he regarded these, too, as potentially dangerous rebels – understandably, given his experiences with usurpers and his own fratricidal clan: he had himself had the youths' family murdered. Gallus was soon executed, while his half-brother Julian, then sent to Gaul as Caesar, faced a lethal dilemma. Whether he failed or succeeded as ruler and commander, he would inevitably trigger Constantius' wrathful paranoia.

Julian proved a talented commander, exemplified in his victory over the Alamanni at Strasbourg (below). He was successful enough that his soldiers, whether spontaneously or owing to manipulation, soon proclaimed him Augustus – i.e. given equal status with Constantius – exactly what the senior emperor dreaded. Yet another civil war looked inevitable. Julian led his soldiers in a lightning dash down the Danube, intending a pre-emptive strike. Bloodshed was only avoided because Constantius died before the armies clashed. Rome never would find reliable means of ensuring smooth imperial succession, or stable control of the soldiers.

82. The Tetrarchs: Diocletian and his three co-emperors, in a statue group from Constantinople, now in Venice. The message is military strength and fraternal solidarity; the faces of the emperors are indistinguishable. They wear the 'pillbox' military hat of the time, and sport eagle-headed swords and scabbards with slides.

If third-century Illyrian soldiers were arguably as tough and effective as Roman troops had ever been, fourth-century *milites* are often seen as increasingly barbarized, and declining in capability. Certainly, by the 350s, Roman troops had changed further in appearance. Ammianus' account of Constantius' military escort into Rome (p. 224) could almost be describing Sarmatian or Sasanian warriors.[7] How effective were such soldiers in battle? Julian's military exploits in Gaul, especially against the Germans at Strasbourg (Argentoratum), vividly illustrate fourth-century *milites* in action.[8]

In Gaul in 357, while Constantius was entering Rome, Julian was facing a dangerous army of Alamanni, concentrating on the Roman side of the Rhine at Argentoratum.[9] The previous year, Roman forces had ravaged the lands beyond the Rhine, but now the Germans were back on the offensive. They had just thwarted a planned Roman pincer attack by Julian's army, coordinating with another force based in Italy, which the Germans had defeated and sent reeling home.[10] Elated, they now sought to defeat Julian as well. He had a force of just 13,000 troops, a secret betrayed to the Germans by a Roman deserter. His apparent weakness, and their recent successes against other Roman soldiers, prompted the Alamanni to demand Julian cede the lands they had conquered 'by their courage and the sword'. Julian, whose troops were few but of high quality, including cataphracts, determined to fight, accepting advice that he should seize the opportunity while the barbarians were concentrated; if he let them scatter to plunder again, he was warned his soldiers would mutiny at missing their chance of glory and perhaps lynch him. According to the historian Ammianus, in time-honoured manner Julian exhorted his *commilitones* to battle, and they clashed spears on shields in approval.

The Germans had established a camp, and dug field entrenchments. As the Romans approached, the Alamannic army, warned by scouts, drew up for battle in wedge formations. Observing that Julian placed his heavy lancers on the right, they placed their own best horse to face them, interspersed with infantry who might be able to neutralize the advantage of the Romans' heavy armour by stabbing their mounts. Reportedly 35,000 strong, the German army outnumbered Julian's force almost 3:1. Commanded by two Alamannic kings, Chnodomar and his nephew Serapio, this was no barbarian mob but, with foot and horse, scouts, and responsive tactical battle formations controlled by standards and war-horns, a complex and fairly disciplined army of men from societies that had learned much from generations of fighting against – and sometimes for – the Romans.[11]

After a long morning march to establish contact with the Germanic army, Julian tried to get his men to make camp and rest overnight before engaging, but they demanded immediate battle, and Julian gave way.[12] His soldiers advanced, and encountered contingents of Alamanni hiding in trenches intending to take the Romans by surprise. The German leaders were confident of victory, but their men demanded they dismount so that they could not flee if things went wrong. The lines collided, dust clouds rose, and in the ensuing fighting the Roman heavy cavalry began to break. Julian dashed to the scene and restored the line. Meanwhile the Roman infantry raised their war-cry, the crescendoing *barritus*, and after prolonged hand-to-hand fighting with javelins, spears and swords – Ammianus describes the Romans as both slashing and 'with…*gladii* [sic] pierc[ing] the enemy's sides'[13] – the Alamanni broke and fled. The victorious Romans pursued and slaughtered them, and when, their swords blunted or, 'as happens sometimes,' says Ammianus, bent while hacking at the fleeing foe, they grabbed German arms and continued to kill. The victorious Romans left mounds of dead and drove the fugitives into the river, where those who could not escape using shields as floats were shot or drowned. Ammianus records Roman losses as a mere 243 killed, the Alamanni losing 6,000 dead counted on the field, plus unknown thousands drowned. Chnodomar was taken alive, and sent to Constantius, while Julian crossed the Rhine on yet another punitive campaign.

As ever with such historical accounts, we need to be cautious about taking all details as fact (Ammianus was a partisan of Julian's, praising his tactical leadership and glossing over his less sure strategic grasp),[14] but the general outline is plausible enough, including casualty figures: with wounded the Roman total was probably more like 1,000, the disproportionate German losses consistent with slaughter of fugitives during a rout. There is no reason to doubt that the Germans of the new confederacies really were much more sophisticated in war than their ancestors had been; at the same time, it is also equally clear from victories like Julian's at Strasbourg that Roman arms really were still more effective. Roman armies could still take on larger numbers of barbarians and win because, except now in numbers, they usually remained superior in all other areas: equipment, training, the discipline and morale of soldiers, the tactical, strategic and logistical skills available to commanders and the resource base behind armies. In general terms, most of the fourth century saw Roman success in maintaining the integrity and power of the empire against its enemies. But the gap was narrowing, and in the east Rome and Persia remained closely balanced. If Romans could still usually expect to win pitched battles against barbarians, the prelude to Strasbourg showed that they found it harder and harder to keep the provinces entirely free of marauding invaders.

## Soldiers, swords and fortifications

Our knowledge of soldiers as individuals, and archaeological data on the dress and equipment that helped create their professional identities, is poorer during the late empire than it was for middle imperial times, and becomes thinner still for the fifth century. This is partly due to relative lack of research (especially in the east), but mostly it is down to changes in the armies, and among the soldiers themselves. In the later period, few soldiers chose to commemorate themselves or their comrades via inscribed or figured tombstones, so we lack the numerous inscriptions and epitaphs that so illuminate the lives of individual *milites* of the Principate. Few late 'official' representations of soldiers survive either. At the same time, fewer troops were based in permanent frontier bases of the kind that produce such rich archaeological finds for the early imperial period. Those that were occupied produce fewer finds, not because soldiers had less equipment, but because it was less likely to become buried. Part of this represents changes in behaviour and beliefs; there are also noticeably fewer swords deposited in rivers than before. That said, we do have striking reliefs, mosaics and paintings showing soldiers, some informative grave-groups, and important finds of Roman weapons from Barbaricum. We also have, in the writings of Ammianus, accounts of soldiers in action as vivid and well-informed as any from earlier centuries.[15] To the late empire also belong other important texts more problematic to interpret, notably the late fourth-century work of Vegetius referred to above: the *Epitoma Rei Militaris* (*Epitome of Military Science*). This purports to present to a contemporary audience the allegedly superior ways in which Roman soldiers were once equipped, trained and fought – a regime which, in his day, Vegetius complained, no longer applied.

Not least as a result of the pervasive influence of Vegetius' opinions, the later empire is widely thought of as a period of decline in the quality of Roman soldiers and their arms. Yet our evidence of military equipment, organization and the general record of fighting efficiency during the fourth century provides little support for any such notion.[16] In equipment, we still see the familiar pattern of continuity and incremental evolution with some striking innovations, for example in projectile weapons. Infantry were provided with fearsome new barbed, lead-weighted darts called *plumbatae* or *martiobarbuli*, while engineers continued to develop torsion artillery; this was the age of the single-armed, stone-throwing *onager*.[17]

On the other hand, there was much continuity from the past, not least in soldiers' dress, which well into the 300s maintained the general style and colours of the previous century (see Fig. 94). The symbolic waist belt, the *cingulum*, became highly elaborate, often broad with showy metal fittings, including characteristic buckles bearing opposed animal heads. Emphasis was also placed on the cloak-brooch, especially the so-called crossbow type, apparently exclusively military (Fig. 83). Soldiers now often sported a 'pill-box' hat, in origin a Danubian fashion (Figs 81, 82).

Most fourth- and fifth-century Roman swords are known from bogs and graves of northern Barbaricum, although some come from German-style graves of soldiers buried within the empire.[18] What we know about later Roman swords currently applies almost exclusively to the western empire, as we have effectively no swords from the late Roman east, and know little about Sarmatian sword designs and technologies of the fourth to sixth centuries, and possible further exchanges in sword design and technology across the eastern frontiers.[19] Only a couple of swords ascribed to the early Sasanian empire are known,[20] but this meagre material record is partially compensated by many detailed depictions, especially on royal rock reliefs (see Fig. 79). The two known weapons, with wide cross-guards and slender double-edged blades with no fullers or midrib, tapering slightly towards an elongated point, are barely distinguishable from blades ascribed to late Parthian times (p. 214, Fig. 75), and are generally similar to contemporary Roman weapons (below). The blade lengths, 700 and 720 mm (27.5 and 28.5 in), are consistent with the size of such weapons shown on Sasanian reliefs, which reveal discoid 'mushroom' pommels and flaring square-ended scabbards suspended via a slide from a hip-belt, also continuing Parthian-era practice (Figs 79, 84). Additionally, the reliefs feature much longer-handled, apparently two-handed, weapons, a badly damaged example of which has apparently been found, with a blade of 860 mm (2 ft 10 in).[21]

Roman sword hilts remained tripartite into the fourth century, while blades continued to grow in length. During the course of the fourth century average blade length seems to have drifted upwards past the 800 mm mark (c. 2 ft 7½ in), before returning slightly below it during the fifth. Lengthening blades may reflect improving confidence in their strength, with accumulating experience in pattern-welding, which continued to be the common method of manufacture. It also corresponds to the increased importance of cavalry combat in the west during the rise and fall of the Huns (p. 264).

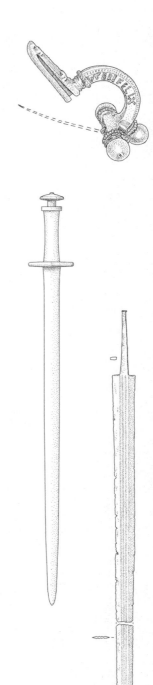

83. *Above right.* A fourth-century military 'crossbow' brooch from Aquincum, Hungary. A silver presentation piece bearing the motto *VTERE FELIX* ('use with good fortune'), shown at about the angle it was worn, prominently at the right shoulder.

84. *Centre.* Reconstruction of an early Sasanian sword, based on two actual examples from northern Iran, a jade disc-pommel from Dura-Europos (buried c. 256) and depictions of swords on early Sasanian rock reliefs. (Scale 1:8)

85. *Below right.* The fourth-century Ejsbøl-type Roman sword: an example from the Danish bog offering at Ejsbøl itself, shown as found, 'ritually killed', its edges hacked, point damaged, snapped in two, and thrown into the bog. (Scale 1:8)

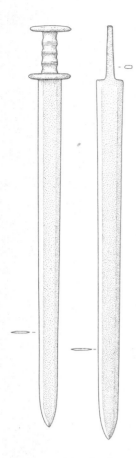

86. Restorations of early examples of Miks' Illerup-Wyhl family of later Roman swords. The Illerup C variant (left) is represented by a sword from the Danish bog-find at Nydam (later third or fourth century), the hilt reportedly of horn. During the fourth century these forms were increasingly displaced by the wider Wyhl variant (right), exemplified by a blade deposited hiltless and broken at Ejsbøl around 300. (Scale 1:8)

In form, fourth-century blades appear to represent general continuity of the two kinds established during the third: the relatively narrower Straubing-Nydam family and the generally broader and flatter Lauriacum-Hromówka types.

The narrower Straubing-Nydam tradition saw direct continuity into the late empire through the 'Ejsbøl' variant, which lasted from the later third through the fourth century (Fig. 85). Otherwise, it seems that the turmoil of the late third century, the establishment of the Dominate and, perhaps above all, state takeover of the arms industry by the early fourth, led to a new range of variants on the two established themes. Swords were probably made in most of the new imperial *fabricae* (page 246), although we know of three specialist sword factories called *spatharia*, two of which were in Gaul, for centuries a centre of excellence in arms manufacture (p. 149).

Both wider and narrower variants now tended to exhibit parallel edges or at most subtle tapering, leading to a 'gothic-arch' point, and both families shared similar cross-sectional geometries (mostly now fullered or flat-surfaced), and so are mainly distinguishable through their proportions. Alongside the continuing Ejsbøl variant, the narrower Straubing-Nydam tradition gave rise to the 'Illerup-Wyhl' family, among which blades tend to get wider in the fifth century (a trend away from the 'Illerup C' (Fig. 86, left) towards the 'Wyhl' variant more than 50 mm (2 in) wide (Fig. 86, right).[22]

In the early fourth century the Lauriacum-Hromówka tradition seems to have spawned the wide 'Osterburken-Kemathen' forms, which lasted through the fifth century. Some of these have a point so obtuse as to be virtually non-existent, and therefore look to be dedicated slashing weapons (Fig. 87).[23] Osterburken-Kemathen blades were 60–77 mm (2¼–3 in) wide. The relatively small number of very wide blades (Kemathen variants) were among the broadest of all Roman sword types. Most (Osterburken variants), however, were in the 60–65 mm range.

By the fifth century, the hilts of Roman swords changed in form, radically altering the appearance of the sheathed weapon. The traditional design, usually with rounded guard and pommel, was replaced by shapes more reminiscent of barbarian and Sasanian weapons. For example, the pommel of the sword worn by Stilicho in the surviving ivory portrait of the great general (c. AD 400) shows strong similarities with Sasanian weapons depicted in Iranian reliefs (Fig. 88). At the same period the sword, still suspended via a scabbard slide, had returned to being carried on a waist-belt, at least by officers. This was how the scabbard slide had originally been used, and still was, on the steppe and in Iran – worn like a six-gun, waist-high on the right, with the scabbard slung low on the left hip – and may be another feature reflecting the growing prestige of the mounted soldier in the Roman world at the time.

Sword and spear were still used with broad, dished oval shields, fragmentary painted examples of which have been found in Egypt (Plate xii).[24] Late shield blazons were unit-specific, and comprised bold geometric patterns of rings and stars, figures of gods or Hercules, eagles, wolf's heads etc., in motifs reflecting contemporary animal-head belt buckles and *draco* standards.[25]

Archaeologically, we know little of armour, although we have some finds.[26] At first sight this chimes with Vegetius' well-known assertion that, by his time, Roman soldiers had largely abandoned heavy armour. However, we equally lack swords and other arms from within the empire, so the dearth of finds is explicable in terms of non-burial rather than non-use, and the many state *fabricae* producing armour were still in commission. Other texts suggest that, throughout, most troops wore mail, perhaps scale, while heavy cavalry, as Ammianus described (p. 224), still used laminated limb defences. Vegetius – evidently not a soldier – exaggerated the decline in armour use to justify his own case for reactionary reforms; perhaps some units became more lightly equipped, or he wrote during a time of major shortage in equipment following the massive losses at Adrianople.[27]

The fourth-century Roman panoply included one area of prominent, startling, revolutionary innovation: helmet design. This shows total discontinuity from the past. We now have considerable numbers of dated Roman helmet finds from the early fourth to early fifth centuries. All of iron, they look so alien to imperial traditions that, if it were not for the inscriptions on some, and the

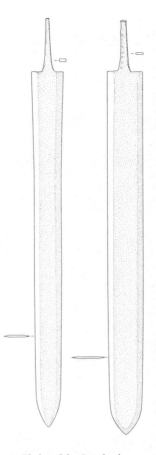

87. Blades of the Osterburken-Kemathen family of swords, fourth to fifth centuries. Left, reconstruction of a snapped example of the 'Osterburken tendency' from the Nydam bog-find, probably later fourth century. Right, reconstruction of a slightly damaged example of the 'Kemathen tendency' of ultra-wide blades of the end of the fourth to first half of the fifth century, from a metalwork hoard at (confusingly) Osterburken, Germany. (Scale 1:8)

unambiguous findspots of others, we would probably not have recognized them as Roman. Instead of the traditional Roman single-piece helmet skull or bowl with integral neck-guard, the skulls are all composite.[28] They are made in two halves (each either a single plate, or three riveted plates), riveted to a fore-and-aft 'ridge'-piece. To this assembly, a separate neck-guard and cheek-pieces were attached, rarely with hinges, usually with leather straps. Some – especially those with multi-plate skulls and larger cheekpieces, regarded as cavalry helmets – sported an additional defence, unprecedented in Roman armour: a nose-guard, riveted to the front of the helmet via laterally projecting 'eyebrows' (Fig. 77, bottom). Many such helmets were originally covered with silver plating, the more elaborate with repoussé decoration, sometimes gilded, and a few splendid examples were even set with glass-imitation gemstones (Plate XI). These last, especially, look more like something out of Arthurian epic or Wagnerian opera than our expectations of Roman equipment.

Such helmets constitute the most prominent evidence for continued foreign influence on Roman arms. The gaudy splendour of the finest, especially use of bullion and 'gems', fits with continued Sarmatian influence.[29] However, it should also be noted that at the siege of Amida (p. 240), Shapur II wore a golden head-dress or helmet set with jewels,[30] while the basic design of late Roman helmet bowls, and the T-shaped nasal, were certainly Partho-Sasanian in origin. A 'Persian' helmet buried during the siege of Dura-Europos c. AD 256 provides a clear prototype for the construction of the new Roman helmets, which appeared

88. Ivory portrait of Stilicho, the great western Roman general of the early fifth century AD. Note his (doubtless gold) crossbow brooch, bossed oval shield with portraits of the emperors Honorius and Arcadius, and his sword. The form of the hilt, the fact that the scabbard is now worn on a waist-belt, and indeed the elaborately patterned textiles of his clothing, all point towards Sasanian influence on late Roman military fashions.

some decades later (see Fig. 77).[31] Roman armourers simply tinkered with the skull design, and replaced the hanging mail with the plate cheek and neck protection Roman *milites* favoured.

Such apparent further visual 'barbarization' was still in the spirit of Roman tradition, imitating the arms of respected and feared foreign enemies, and integrating them into the ever-evolving definition of Roman military culture. Danubian troops and their fashions still predominated, providing the main route for continued Sarmatian influence while, from the later fourth century, the Huns appeared as a new factor, bringing to prominence, and enhancing the prestige of, the bow. However, Persia, Rome's most consistently important and powerful enemy throughout the era, so influential on the culture of the imperial court, also strongly influenced soldierly culture, and not only in helmet design. Like earlier ring-buckles, common fourth-century animal-headed Roman military belt buckles also find parallels, and perhaps their origin, in the Partho-Sasanian world, where similar buckles are known.[32] In Diocletian's price edict of 301, military belts are called *zona Babulonica*, 'Babylonian belts'.[33]

†

If arms and equipment reflect continuity and change in soldiers and soldiering, other major material developments in the later Roman world provide an even more dramatic index of radical shifts in the nature and distribution of martial violence. For it was during this period that, in effect, the castle was introduced to Europe.

In the east, fortified cities, and military fortresses in the true meaning of the term – strongholds designed to withstand formal siege through careful siting and formidable constructed defences – had been features of the landscape for centuries, and continued to be gradually refined in a slow 'arms race' between architects and siege engineers, especially as the Sasanians proved far more adept at sieges than the Parthians. However, in the European provinces, they hardly existed until the third century. The walls of western cities were primarily status symbols, often over-long and of limited military value. The soldiers usually guaranteed freedom from war, so viable urban defences had been unnecessary and valley locations for towns favoured for convenience and for gravity-fed water supplies. Similarly, as we saw, since commanders routinely expected to fight European foes in the open, preferably on enemy territory, military bases had been designed to foil surprise attack, not withstand prolonged investment; northern barbarians had no siege capabilities, although they might storm a wall if sentries dozed.

Third-century invasions across Rhine and Danube changed all this. Despite success in the field, the Illyrian emperors knew they could no longer hope to secure all the frontiers all of the time. Even as he triumphantly rampaged across the empire with his mobile field army, Aurelian ordered the massive re-fortification of Rome itself. From the later third century, European cities were surrounded by eastern-style defences, with strong gates, higher walls and projecting towers that made attackers vulnerable to crossfire. Such walls were easier to defend but, often following much reduced circuits dictated by tactical priorities, marked radical shrinkage in urban areas. Many such wall circuits would continue to be maintained thereafter into late medieval times.

European military bases also became strongly fortified for the first time. Familiar 'playing card' plans gave way to squares (Fig. 89) or irregular contour-hugging forms, with high walls and projecting towers. Some sites were reduced in size to make them defensible with smaller garrisons. Many looked like medieval castles (Fig. 90), and some would later be reused as such. Most military strongholds remained in the old frontier zones, but some were also built far to the rear, for example along the roads of Gaul,[34] while fortified naval bases were built to counter sea-raiders around the coasts of Britain and Gaul.

Paradoxically, strong walls were introduced in Europe not because the barbarians had acquired siege capabilities, but because they had not. City circuits provided sanctuary for the civil population, while the new military stations provided additional bases for communications, supply and accommodation of Roman troops. Their powerful defences allowed them to be secured by relatively small garrisons, freeing most troops for field operations, while making it harder for barbarians to roam the countryside at will. However, they were also tacit admissions that the countryside might no longer be safe from foreign attack, and people and property outside these sanctuaries remained vulnerable. Even if beaten off, repeated invasions might gradually erode the economic base on which the empire, and the soldiers themselves, relied. Some areas, such as the devastated villa landscapes of northern Gaul, had already been irreparably damaged, although most regions, including some near the frontiers such as the Moselle valley around Trier, remained prosperous far into the fourth century.

## Effectiveness and organization of the armies

> When [Constantius] came near the walls [of Amida] and surveyed only a heap of ashes, he wept and groaned aloud as he thought of the calamities the wretched city had endured. And Ursulus, the state-treasurer...cried: 'Behold with what courage the cities are defended by our soldiers, for whose abundance of pay the wealth of the empire is already becoming insufficient.'
> AMMIANUS 20.11.5[35]

For the reasons indicated above (p. 233), despite the importance of soldiers in later Roman society, we know less about individuals in this period. In literary sources such as Ammianus, ordinary *milites* remain as anonymous as ever, and

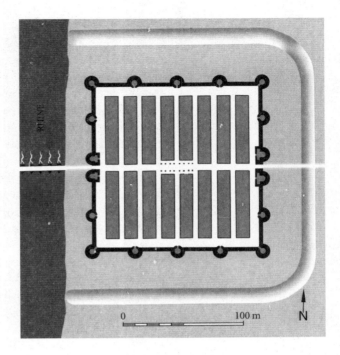

89. Plan of *Divitia*, late Roman bridgehead-fort across the Rhine opposite Cologne, Germany. Its powerful tower-studded perimeter defences prefigure the castles of medieval Europe. Its internal layout, two rows of near-identical blocks, also differs from more differentiated earlier Roman forts, while resembling recently explored Sasanian frontier bases; but who was imitating whom?

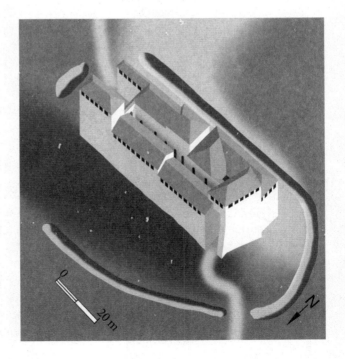

90. The small fourth-century defended Roman military station built on a knoll at Bürgle-bei-Gundremmingen in Germany looks more like a medieval castle than the familiar 'Roman fort'.

91. A rare example of a funerary *stela* depicting a named fourth-century soldier, Lepontius, who was buried at Strasbourg. This relatively crude carving shows his sword and other arms, helmet, cloak-brooch and apparently Gallic cockerel standard.

there are far fewer inscriptions by or for the soldiers themselves; some monuments do exist, but they are less informative than before, for example the stone of Lepontius, found at Strasbourg (Fig. 91).[36] However, we can say much about soldiers collectively, from the histories and not least from late-Roman law codes, which record or imply much about their activities and behaviour.

Notwithstanding comments such as that made by Ursulus in AD 359 (quoted by Ammianus above) and the strictures of Vegetius some decades later, from their performance in war there is no real sign that Roman soldiers declined in discipline, training or fighting ability through the fourth century, and much later in the east. Ursulus' comment was particularly unfair, given Ammianus' testimony of the Amida garrison's spirited defence against the Sasanians. His eyewitness account of the seventy-three-day siege by Shapur II, from which he was lucky to escape with his life, constitutes one of the most vivid of all accounts of ancient warfare.[37] Indeed, the injustice of Ursulus' comment was underlined by the fact that Constantius ordered the setting up of an unusual memorial at Edessa to the ferocious bravery of the Gallic soldiers of the Amida garrison, who had staged a daring night attack on Shapur II's camp: statues of their *campidoctores,* the 'drill sergeants' who had led them.[38] Other *milites* later ensured that Ursulus paid for his calumny with his life.[39]

In foreign wars, fourth-century *milites* often faced a harder task than those of the early empire, and were inevitably more often on the back foot. After the disaster at Adrianople in 378 (p. 261), they also permanently declined in numbers, especially in the west, where the state could not replace either the men or accumulated experience lost, so that under-resourced frontier units had to be drafted in to fill gaps in the *comitatenses.* Henceforth, western units doubtless did grow more variable in quality, but remained capable and feared by their foes.

The fourth and fifth centuries are often thought to have seen deep 'barbarization' of the soldiers, as they apparently became more and more reliant on recruiting Germans, Sarmatians and others to fill their ranks. There are some striking indications of barbarian habits entering Roman military usage. The late Roman warcry, the *barritus,* was adopted from the Germans.[40] Julian, when proclaimed Augustus by his troops, was raised aloft on an infantry shield – something Tacitus records as a Batavian custom on electing leaders – and crowned with a torc provided by a standard-bearer.[41] As we saw, Roman arms were also still 'Sarmatizing' and 'Persianizing', yet overall, the changes represented continuity of the long tradition of absorbing foreign ways into a self-consciously Roman martial culture that remained distinctive, vigorous and arrogantly proud. Rather than 'barbarizing' the Roman military, many barbarians were still being successfully incorporated into it; but in accommodating them, evolving military 'Romanness' continued its divergence from that of the civil provinces.

Perhaps more important than supposed barbarization were other internal changes to the culture and structure of the community of *milites*. An ostensibly fundamental break with the past was abandonment of the traditional Roman gods for Christianity. The course of this is symbolized in the struggle over the ancient statue of Victory that Augustus had set up in the Roman senate house centuries earlier. It seems that Constantius removed it on visiting Rome in 357, but Julian, who reverted to paganism, restored it; Gratian removed it again in 382, over the protests of the still-largely pagan senators, but it was restored under the usurper Eugenius in 392. It was probably removed again under Theodosius, but apparently restored yet again by Stilicho; it is not mentioned thereafter, and was likely a victim of the sack of Rome in 410.[42] As espousal of Christianity gradually became essential for advancement in imperial service, so the military (while remaining substantially pagan to the end of the fourth century) began to accept officers and soldiers who were openly Christian. This apparently momentous change was effected with surprisingly little sign of internal stress. At one level, as in wider society (p. 255) it 'simply' involved changing the name of the main divine figures at the heart of imperial ideology from the Capitoline triad (Jupiter, Juno and Minerva) to the Holy Trinity. Conversion, especially for soldiers, was facilitated by Christians reciprocally accepting rationalizations of their faith, permitting armed violence, if not actively lauding killing for Jesus (although this doubtless became easier where enemies like Goths joined 'heretical' Christian sects).[43] Further, abandoning the old beliefs did not also require rejecting the mythology or historical achievements of pagan Rome, which remained cultural treasures essential to the education of Christian gentlemen, and the ideological motivation of Roman soldiers.

Another fundamental change to the military was structural: the development, at last, of a fully professional officer corps. This began to evolve during the third century, as senators were gradually excluded from the military commands that, in traditional careers, they had alternated with civil posts. Increasingly soldiers were led by capable career officers of much humbler origin, who rose by courage, capability or ruthlessness, some to the very top as Praetorian prefect, and often thence (by acclamation or assassination) to the purple itself. Given the more meritocratic ethos of the late military, command was no longer solely the preserve of the established imperial elite; the capable could claw their way upwards from the ranks in a manner impossible in Augustan times. First- and second-generation barbarian immigrants were prominent in the armies, and not just as ordinary *milites* and unit commanders. A number of successful generals were barbarian-born (mostly Germans, but including a Sarmatian Master of the Soldiers);[44] others were Classically educated sons of immigrants.[45] The throne itself remained a step too far for such parvenus, although from the end of the fourth century, a few generalissimos of barbarian descent such as Stilicho, Roman-born son of a Vandal officer, came to be effective rulers of the west, nominally under puppet emperors.

The responsibilities of the Praetorian prefect had expanded during the third century from guard commander to effective grand vizier of all military and civil affairs under the emperor. However, because this office posed such danger to the emperor, Constantine cut it down to size, removing its military duties, abolishing the Praetorians and replacing them with new guards units. The armies came to be overseen by field-marshals known as Masters of the Soldiers (*magistri militum*). Smaller battle groups of *comitatenses* might also be commanded by lesser generals, with the title 'companion [of the emperor]' (*comes,* plural *comites;* hence French *comte,* 'count'). Frontier troops were no longer commanded by provincial governors; each frontier army came under a separate general, or *dux* ('leader'; hence medieval 'duke'). Constantine's reign saw completion of the separation of military command and civil governance.

Military and civil were henceforth parallel but separate worlds in a way unthinkable in the republic. Not only ordinary soldiers, but also many officers, whether of barbarian or indeed provincial origin, now lacked the Classical education, family contacts, and inculcation into civil politics that senatorial generals had once had as their birthright. The period saw the evolution of an even more sharply delineated military caste, now comprising officers as well as soldiers, with its own laws, increasingly considered by most people in the empire as threat as much as protector. 'Military Rome' continued to diverge from 'civil Rome'.

Relations with the civil population were as troubled as ever, soldiers being feared for their arrogance and brutal venality. Libanius, writing in the later fourth century of his native Antioch in Syria, recorded the hazards facing market traders roughed up by soldiers, who dare not fight back for fear of being hauled off to the camp, where they would have to buy their way out of being beaten to death.[46]

Fourth-century armies were structured and commanded in ways distinctively different from those of the Principate.[47] The disasters of the later third century had destroyed much of the fabric of the armies, which had evolved incrementally since the Augustan reforms. Also, in rebuilding the military, emperors from Gallienus to Diocletian and Constantine faced a radically changed strategic environment. The historian Peter Heather convincingly argues that the rise of Sasanian Iran, in particular, posed a danger so great that it triggered massive restructuring, not just of Rome's military, but of the entire imperial system.[48]

The result was extensively reconfigured armies. They still included legions and auxiliaries, but alongside new-style formations such as the cavalry *cuneus* ('wedge'), and established regiments actually named *vexillatio* (hitherto meaning a temporary detachment, a term like the modern 'task force'), *equites* or *auxilia* (until this time collective terms for units of 'horse' and 'auxiliaries', that is, the old *cohortes* and *alae*). Some were raised from scratch, others, as the name *vexillatio* implies, apparently formed round the cadre of detachments from old units, now made permanently autonomous.[49]

92. A small copper coin of Constantine the Great with the legend *gloria exercitūs*, 'glory of the army', singular. It dates to the 330s, in the latter part of his reign when, exceptionally, there was only one Augustus and supreme commander.

Overall, the legion of heavy infantry no longer dominated the Roman order of battle; such formations were now smaller – perhaps normally only 1,000 men, though the debate rages – and the later armies certainly had a higher proportion of cavalry than before, although infantry remained vital to Roman warfare.[50] Fourth-century armies arguably had an improved balance of steady infantry and mounted striking power.

The armies remained divided into two fundamental groupings, but the new boundary cut across the old legionary/auxiliary division. The major distinction now lay between so-called 'frontier troops' and 'field army troops'. The former, at least in later times called *limitanei* or *ripenses* (soldiers of the frontiers or the river-banks), became second-grade forces, although they remained more effective than the peasant militia as which they are sometimes derided.[51] Many such formations were survivors from the Principate. Field army troops, the *comitatenses* (derived from *comitatus*, the body of *comites* or 'companions' directly surrounding the emperor), were better paid, better equipped, and provided with the best recruits.[52] Evidence is sparse and ambiguous enough to fuel continual debate over how far there was continuity from the new mobile force wielded by Aurelian to the *comitatenses* of Constantine and after, and especially over the degree to which Diocletian had sought to return to primarily frontier-based forces.[53]

Beyond this new military 'class distinction', the armies remained multiple and segmented in other ways, notwithstanding Constantine's coin-types exceptionally celebrating *gloria exercitūs*, 'glory of the army', singular, dating from the few years when he was sole emperor (Fig. 92). During almost all the rest of the period there were multiple emperors (whether by appointment or usurpation), with military command structures duplicated at each court, each controlling multiple armies. Standing garrisons of one or more provinces were grouped into frontier armies, while the *comitatenses* were also split between the emperors, and increasingly subdivided into troops directly attendant on each emperor, and strategic regional field armies. There were also smaller *ad hoc* groupings of *comitatenses*, such as that sent to deal with the so-called 'Barbarian Conspiracy' in Britain in 367, or the modest standing force later established in the island.[54]

A major point of uncertainty is the actual size of the later Roman military.[55] A seductively precise, and (to me) plausible total figure for the military under Diocletian, cited by the sixth-century author John Lydus, is 435,266, including 45,562 fleet personnel.[56] Other ancient authorities offer figures for the late armies up to 645,000.[57] However, these numbers come from sources written long after the period. We also have the remarkable *Notitia Dignitatum*, apparently an official handbook of offices of state and military commands, which lists significantly larger numbers of units than the early empire. However, this problematic text is no simple snapshot of the order of battle at a single moment, but a palimpsest of superimposed and inconsistent revisions, perhaps intended to record what should exist rather than what actually did when the handbook was last revised in the earlier fifth century. Beyond such problems, we have to make two distinctions: establishment figures (i.e. planned unit sizes) and actual strengths. There is good reason to suggest that regimental establishment figures were significantly smaller than under the early empire. For example, Ammianus mentions two Illyrian cavalry units in the east totalling 700 horse; but were these whole units, and up to strength?[58] There is evidence that some establishment figures may have been drastically reduced in the later period. Frontier units and those in quiet backwaters may well have been formally scaled down, through non-replacement of losses even if they did not actively lose men to reinforce the *comitatenses*, especially as recruits became ever harder to find in the fifth century; establishment of frontier legions, at least, apparently declined to around 1,000 men.[59] Further, individual references to unit sizes suggest many units were actually considerably weaker even than their theoretical establishments, while strength returns may also have been deliberately exaggerated (p. 253). Generally, it seems unlikely that an empire that – with difficulty – could pay and sustain around 450,000 troops in AD 200, could 150 years later support significantly larger numbers. The productive capacity of the empire was not significantly greater, and may have shrunk from second-century levels. On balance, it seems likely that the fourth-century military was similar in total size to those of Severan times, as the reported Tetrarchic figure suggests; and that the probably real major increases under the Tetrarchy and Constantine were simply restoring the catastrophic losses of the mid-third century.

Contemporaries may also have perceived the military as larger because it was increasingly visible; more *milites* operated further from the frontiers more of the time, with *comitatenses* regularly wintering in provincial cities (relatively novel for Roman Europe). Another reason the military seemed bigger was extension of the notion of *militia*, 'military service'. During the early empire, provincial governors and imperial financial officials employed some soldiers not only as bodyguards, but as clerks, accountants, and so on. By the Dominate, when imperial bureaucracy mushroomed, so did the number of imperial officials, many of whose jobs continued officially to rate as *militia*. They wore uniform and had the legal privileges of soldiers, even though they were civil servants, not combatants (Fig. 93). This marked further militarization of the state, but also dilution of the meaning of *miles*.

93. Paintings from the tomb of a fourth-century official buried at Silistra in Bulgaria. He wears military uniform: servants bring his belt of *militia* and his cloak with 'crossbow' brooch.

The notion that almost any kind of imperial service performed by free men could be classed as *militia* was also seen in arms manufacture. It was apparently during the reign of Diocletian that the state 'nationalized' arms production.[60] A new system of centralized state factories, *fabricae*, was created, located at major cities across the empire. The *Notitia* lists their locations and outputs (including specialist sword-factories: p. 149). It seems that all civilian armourers were conscripted into the new factories, which were probably built around cadres of legionary *fabrica* personnel. Certainly they were run on military lines. Henceforth arms workers, *fabricenses*, were technically *milites*, with military-style ranks, although (like civil servants) they were not directly part of the fighting forces.[61] We know something about the arms-workers (*fabricenses*) as individuals from epitaphs, and collectively from laws regulating their working conditions and behaviour, which could be riotous.[62] Across the empire there were doubtless many thousands of *fabricenses*, who when not at their forges were presumably seen wearing military dress on the streets of the many major cities in which they were stationed, adding to the martial aspect of the late imperial service.

There was another reason why soldiers were so often visible in the interior of the later empire. When 'mobile field armies' originated in the third century, they were intended by the rulers of the central empire for waging both foreign and civil war: to expel invaders, and crush both provincial rebels and usurpers leading 'renegade' *milites*. In practice, despite the general stability achieved by Diocletian, their double mission remained unchanged. Doubtless the permanent *comitatenses* as developed by Constantine still dreamed primarily of gaining glory through victory over foreign foes, but in reality their primary task remained, as ever, regime protection, and their deployments, often far back from the frontiers, for internal security as much as imperial defence.[63]

If the earlier third century saw the soldiers help tear the Roman world to pieces, its later decades witnessed how they, and emperors who emerged from their ranks, entirely seized the state, reunited the empire and reformed it, largely in their own image. Diocletian's Tetrarchy marked the zenith of 'military Rome', establishing the frontier-Roman culture and values of the soldiers – especially those of the Illyriciani – in the imperial court. As they brought a military mindset to revolutionizing government, so their approach to imperial propaganda art also displaced the Classicizing tastes of the old imperial aristocracy with the bolder, less naturalistic provincial styles hitherto employed on frontier soldiers' tombstones. Imperial portraits no longer depicted recognizable individuals. From their faces, on coins or in the remarkable statue-group, now in Venice, it is not possible to distinguish the Tetrarchs (Fig. 82). Quite the opposite: the simple message, hammered home by the embracing pose of the malproportioned figures, is of solidarity between tough soldier-emperors, who sport eagle-headed swords and Danubian military pill-box caps. The triumph of military Rome thereafter saw its influence spread through Roman society, as imperial service in general became *militia*, and soldierly dress-styles – hose, *cingulum*, cross-bow brooch – spread as the visible mark of power.

As military Rome came to dominate, so politically powerful soldiers interacted routinely with aristocrats and officials of civilian background. With the centre of gravity of the armies also moving back from the frontiers on the rise of the *comitatenses*, the military frontier communities, especially from Britain to the Black Sea, which had formed the core of the distinctively martial strand of 'Roman-ness', became depleted, poorer and increasingly vulnerable to barbarian attack. While *milites* continued aggressively to assert their distinctiveness, the autonomy of military Rome eroded, as it became partly reintegrated into mainstream Roman culture.

### The fourth-century empire: dynamic stability

What was it like, the fourth-century Roman empire to which soldiers were so central, and over which they watched? What were the relationships between *milites* and the rest? It is hard to resist the temptation to interpret the fourth-century empire in the light of the chaos that preceded it and especially of what we know (or think) followed in the fifth century – and so to assume that, even if for the most part the soldiers held the Persians and barbarians in check, the empire was already sliding towards collapse. In Anglophone scholarship, this was the line taken by the historian A. H. M. Jones in his magisterial accounts of the era, written in the 1960s, which long remained influential. He saw the fourth century as a period of growing malaise, in which massive expansion of the military combined with unchecked growth in the wealth and power of the dominant aristocracy at the expense of the rural masses, who became impoverished and died in droves, apathetic and disaffected, critically undermining the ability of the more vulnerable west to resist the barbarian pressure that followed during the fifth century.[64] Similarly, the historian Ramsay MacMullen also argued that corruption at the top of fourth-century society was massive in scale, and catastrophic in consequences.[65]

However, Jones seems to have greatly overestimated the size of the military while, more broadly, a new generation of historians, notably Brian Ward-Perkins and Peter Heather, have challenged Jones's picture of a deeply dysfunctional fourth-century society.[66] Heather's account, in particular, offers a detailed and compelling new view of the empire in the fourth century and beyond, which forms an excellent basis for discussion here. Archaeology has had a key role in generating these revised views of the period, recent surveys revealing that, far from being impoverished and depopulated, at least some late-Roman regions, from the fourth-century villa belt of Britain to fifth-century village landscapes in Syria, were more populous and materially prosperous than ever. Heather goes further, arguing that Jones was influenced by Marxist thinking into seriously exaggerating the extent and significance of oppression and distress among the lower orders. He makes a compelling alternative case that, while no bed of roses for the majority, the fourth-century empire was generally stable and viable until dismembered by foreign swords in the fifth, the western empire actually expiring quite suddenly.[67]

So who is right? If archaeology reveals that some areas flourished remarkably after 300, it also confirms that others, such as tracts of northern Gaul, were indeed devastated. This mixed archaeological picture, combined with the limitations of surviving textual evidence (overwhelmingly written from the standpoints of aristocrats and of the state) makes it hard to assess the net results of (probably patchy) resumed net economic growth on the one hand, and of deepening social and economic polarization on the other. However, stimulating though it is, to me Heather's critique of Jones' view swings the pendulum much further the other way than is warranted by the evidence he offers. If Jones may be accused of seeing the era through a Marxist prism, then the new alternative reciprocally smacks of a comfortable capitalist view, notably 'relaxed' about the impact and import of extreme asymmetries of wealth and power. It seems to me that the picture we get from contemporary writings, not least the implications of surviving laws of the time, really does look grim for the majority, in many areas, most of the time – an impression which the new archaeological survey evidence qualifies, but does not negate. The evidence suggests that ever-deepening domination by (to adapt Eisenhower's phrase) the 'military-aristocratic complex' had grave social consequences for the majority outside the charmed circle of the privileged and their patronage.

Disparities of both wealth and power had never been more extreme. This was the long-term outcome of the core 'pact of empire' between the powerful landowners who dominated provincial societies on the one side, and on the other the emperor and his soldiers, who guaranteed the security of the magnates in return for their ensuring local civic order, and delivering gold and grain to imperial coffers and recruits to the armies. Taxation and state consumption were central to the dynamics of the empire.

Of course, everyone moans about taxes and will avoid paying them if they can, but late Roman texts suggest matters were far worse than that. In an autocracy run by and for the emperor and his cronies, there were no institutional or constitutional checks on expenditure; voteless taxpayers had no official means of redress apart from petitioning the imperial court for relief from their burdens. Fundamentally, too many of the people perceived that too much was being demanded of them from above: many would not, many could not pay. We hear of deserted lands, sometimes because peasants have fled. Most startlingly, we hear of less well-off landowners seeking to avoid service as town councillors, even abandoning their property and fleeing what had ceased to be a social privilege, but had become an intolerable burden: accepting personal financial liability for ensuring collection of state revenues. Increasingly, the state sought to force people to take on such duties, and to extract the goods, gold, men and services it demanded by draconian laws and by threatening the sword.

During the war-torn third century, the militarized state had kept itself going by *ad hoc* requisitions of materiel, conscription and corvée labour. With the return of stability there was a substantial reversion to monetary taxation, but requisitions of food and basic materials, and state-imposed service such as transporting levied goods, became institutionalized. Reflecting their military mindset, soldier-emperors from Diocletian onwards sought to run the empire as a vast military logistics operation. Rulers made strenuous efforts at social control and coercion, through official religion and state propaganda, and through attempts to regulate life and work, at times including attempts to control prices and wage rates. To try to stop people fleeing disagreeable lives, many professions – including soldiering – were made legally hereditary. Some, such as arms production, were taken into direct state control, as we have seen above. Unsurprisingly, many people sought to escape the ruinous burdens imposed on them.

These changes may not have occurred because, in simplistic modern terms, the real cost of defending the empire from proliferating foreign enemies had grown greater than its economic ability to meet it. Perhaps that had been a real danger during the chaos of the third century, but the fourth-century empire was by no means impoverished. We simply do not have the data to quantify precisely the balance between the scale of the economy and the scale of resource levied for state purposes – primarily military – during this period. There is, however, reason to conclude that there was ceaseless pressure for state demands to drift upwards, to the point where taxpayers defaulted or took to sedition. The only tacit brakes on budgets were the reality that receipts often did not fulfil demands, and nagging anxiety that, ultimately, the provincials would be goaded beyond endurance (and their own fear of the sword) into open revolt.

The idea that the later Roman military was inflated to enormous size, more for the glory of the regime than for the real needs of frontier defence, goes back to the attacks of the Christian propagandist Lactantius on Diocletian and all his works.[68] At times, the size of the military budget may indeed not have been rationally proportionate to current or likely future tasks in war. It has recently been argued that for much of the fourth century the scale of the 'German threat' on the Rhine frontier, at least, was deliberately exaggerated by the state, to justify the size of the army and bureaucracy.[69] Emperors certainly had little incentive to undermine their own power and status by retrenchment, while their *milites* would hardly take kindly to 'defence cuts'.

Yet in practice, it is impossible for us to assess at this remove what imperial defensive needs 'truly' were. It probably couldn't have been assessed objectively at the time anyway; even with developed arts of strategic and financial analysis, modern states grapple endlessly with the same problems. For, in the fourth century as in the twenty-first, perceived or actual needs changed unpredictably from year to year as unforeseen crises blew up, or threats suddenly dissipated (as with the rise and fall of the Hunnic empire, below). In times of peace, people could point to past crises and argue (as Vegetius did, and generals still do), that 'if you desire peace, prepare for war'.[70] Such claims were plausible enough: for even if all was quiet on the Rhine, soldiers could at any time be needed for war on the Danube or in Mesopotamia. In times of crisis, of course emperors and generals needed every man they could get. Overall, both realities and rhetoric of imperial defence led to unending upward pressure on the military budget, which tended to inflate to as much as could be supported from the resources extractable from the empire short of provoking popular risings. There was little to stop it doing so, in a world where taxpayers could not vote the government out.

However, in any case, what was being demanded from the populations of the empire was not simply the cost of maintaining the soldiers as a bulwark against foreign enemies. It was vastly more than that. To begin with, if less incessantly than in the third century, emperors and soldiers still periodically wasted lives and treasure in fighting each other. Then there were the costs of (usually multiple) imperial courts, which required ever more pomp and splendour to project a quasi-divine image of rulership. There were also more and more intermediaries between taxpayers and imperial courts and armies, in the burgeoning civil service departments and the tax-collection system itself. Diocletian's reforms created larger numbers of smaller provinces, grouped into dioceses that themselves formed great regional prefectures, requiring additional tiers of administrators.[71] This was largely a result of the difficulties the emperors had faced since the chaos of the third century in extracting wealth and resources from the provincials.[72] They sought to enforce compliance through closer surveillance and regulation by larger numbers of salaried state officials, aiming to create something approaching a 'command economy'. To supplement their salaries, many officials also took traditional-style 'commissions' on funds passing through their hands (rake-offs regarded as legitimate perks of state service).[73]

All this was made even worse by grossly unfair social distribution of the tax burden. In particular, the fourth century saw an important shift in the nature of the imperial pact between emperors and the landowning class. Many magnates became ever more intimately engaged with the expanding state structure rather than with their provincial communities, increasingly escaping the burdens of service as city councillors (who ran the provinces at the local level) by becoming imperial officials themselves. Or, even more desirably, they lobbied for honorary rank, which brought the prestige and privileges of service – not least tax exemptions – without the tiresome workload. The increasingly onerous duties of extracting taxes from the population still had to be carried out by someone, and so local civil administration was dumped onto smaller property owners less able to undertake the personal financial liabilities involved. Those magnates inside the charmed circle thus fed at the imperial trough without having to contribute to it – and could use their protected wealth and position to extract huge private rent revenues from vast portfolios of estates across the empire, while snapping up ever more land, some living more grandly than early emperors.[74] Exploitation reduced many peasants to proto-serfs, *coloni* legally tied to the land. A greater and greater proportion of the wealth of the empire was concentrated in fewer and fewer hands.

Another important novel factor in the fourth-century imperial equation was the newly established state-sponsored Church. Whether Christianity spiritually strengthened the empire or, as Gibbon thought, sapped its moral vigour is an arguable point, but lands, goods and people poured into its largely tax-exempt control, while bishoprics would come to provide alternative power-bases for aristocrats.

Further, at all stages from the collection of taxes to their expenditure on imperial courts, civil service or soldiers, there were additional practices that even insiders regarded as outright extortion, fraud or profiteering. As guarantors of, and participants in, this system, the soldiers were among its beneficiaries, through pay, donatives and by helping themselves. Soldiers were still widely used in policing roles and in the tax system as guards and overseers of the process. These men, and many others now urban-based and billeted on civilians, in time-honoured manner ensured they got their slice of the action by direct extortion. Some even levied fictional 'taxes' on civilians, using official-sounding terminology, which, in Ramsay MacMullen's lovely phrase, betrayed their 'intimate acquaintance with the sonorities of bureaucratic rapacity'.[75] However, other *milites* were among the victims of the system since, it seems, much of what was levied for the armies, perhaps especially the frontier garrisons, never got through to them. Besides rake-offs at collection and in transit to the military, even more was pocketed within the armies themselves.

There were, as we have seen, pressures to maximize the numbers of *milites*. There is routinely a difference between the theoretical strength of any military and the numbers of men actually available for war. Even in peacetime it is difficult to keep recruitment and training in balance with losses owing to death, desertion or discharge, to ensure all units are up to strength all the time; some shortfall is normal.[76] However, in the case of the late Roman military, there were three figures to consider: how many soldiers and warhorses the armies should have had on paper; the numbers generals believed they had; and the numbers that really existed. There may sometimes have been substantial discrepancies between the latter two figures, due to corruption inside the military.

We have some startling evidence of venality within the later armies, and also of extreme undermanning. A remarkable case of a corrupt commander occurs in the letters of Synesius, a bishop in early fifth-century Cyrenaica, Africa. He records how Cerealis sold all the horses of the *Balagritae*, turning a regiment of horse-archers into foot-archers![77] Another means of military profiteering was keeping dead men on the regimental rolls and pocketing the pay of non-existent soldiers. Did higher authority know, as Synesius records, that the *Unnigardae* cavalry regiment actually comprised only forty men?[78] These extreme examples were in a peripheral province, surely untypical of regions under the direct eye of senior commanders, but we simply don't know the extent of corrupt practices conducted in more subtle ways. Nevertheless, the Cyrenaican cases underline doubts about the actual – as opposed to paper – strength of the late Roman military. If units were starved of recruits, equipment and supplies owing to corruption, some soldiers doubtless paid for others' profits with their lives.

In such a system, levels of state demand drifted upwards beyond what tax-payers were able, or at least willing, to pay, despite imperial exhortations or threats. Ammianus claims that Julian, while Caesar in Gaul, experimented with a major reduction in levels of annual tax demanded from 25 to 7 gold *solidi* per head: allegedly, state coffers were still adequately filled, because more provincials could and did pay up.[79] However, there was little motivation for most emperors to do much about the problems: rather the opposite. Traditions of patronage, and the mutual dependency of insiders, encouraged turning a blind eye to the consequences of, if not actually conniving at, abuses.

†

In an important sense, it was immaterial whether provincials at large could afford to pay their taxes or not. They were living under an increasingly oppressive autocracy, which redistributed an ever-increasing proportion of the empire's wealth to its own coffers and those of its cronies. Modern studies show that people's perceptions of self-worth and quality of life depend less on their absolute wealth than on their relative prosperity, their sense of freedom and just treatment.[80] Many Roman provincials may indeed have been materially better off than their pre-Roman ancestors, with factory-made pots or even glass in their windows, recipients of the 'trickle-down' benefits of aggregate imperial prosperity.[81] But this does not mean they were happy with their lot, or entirely passive. They were living in a world where there was, literally, one law for the rich and another for the poor. The later Roman empire sought to cage its population. Even if gilded, a cage is still a cage.

As ever, the empire's rulers sought to reconcile the population to their lot by a combination of means, not least ideological indoctrination. However, under the Dominate, the established order relied less than before on winning the acquiescence of the masses by bread and circuses, and ever more on indoctrination, intimidation and the sword.

Imperial propaganda and ceremonial presenting the *status quo* as divinely ordained, inevitable and eternal, demanded acceptance, or at least acquiescence. Peter Heather vividly portrays Rome as a 'one-party state', which, by AD 350, had for centuries been brainwashing populations who had access to no competing ideology.[82] Slaves, the poor and the marginalized doubtless resented their lot, but anything other than the rule of Rome was almost literally unthinkable. However, the religious cult at the heart of imperial ideology underwent revolution.

Alongside, and increasingly instead of, Rome's traditional gods, third-century military emperors such as Aurelian experimented with the quasi-monotheistic imperial cult of Sol Invictus, 'the unconquered Sun', especially appealing to soldiers. Diocletian tried to restore veneration of Rome's traditional deities by propaganda and compulsion, one of several emperors to order violent retribution against those who would not conform to the imperial cult, as loyalty to the Roman order was expressed through required acts of religious worship. Such *refuseniks*, especially Christians, were seen as atheists whose behaviour threatened divine wrath. Endangering the state and the common good, they faced persecution or death. The armies were purged of Christians, and *milites* used as agents of persecution (see Fig. 81).

Constantine then took the radical step of abandoning the traditional gods entirely, adopting Christian monotheism as the new state cult.[83] By 400, traditional religions were being suppressed, while Christian mobs were making violent attacks on pagan targets, and not least on each other ('heretics'). 'Subversive' Christianity was transformed into a religion of state authority, the stern Christ *Pantokrator*, 'Ruler of Everything', replacing Jupiter in a religious revolution, which, overall, passed off relatively peacefully.[84] This was less a miracle than a logical progression in an empire long increasingly inclining towards monotheism,[85] with a dangerous new neighbour possessing a strong religious ideology.[86] Constantine's religious revolution was partly in imitation of the perceived success of the Zoroastrian 'state church' of Sasanian Iran as an instrument of imperial power.[87] Christian emperors then gave conversion a massive boost by making it a requirement for advancement in imperial service.[88] Rome ruled, then, because God willed it so; resistance was not just criminal, but sacrilegious, when the emperor was himself a living god (under the Tetrarchy) or (from Constantine) divine viceroy. *Religio* – reverence for authority, earthly as much as divine – remained a central tool of political control.

Then there was the majesty of the law. Maintenance of wealth and power of landowners formally depended on an inequitable legal system backed by imperial swords.[89] Within Roman law, always primarily concerned with upholding order and property rights, inequalities within the citizen body between *honestiores* and *humiliores* had become institutionalized (p. 199). Christianity brought an end to gladiatorial combat and crucifixion, but those who fell foul of the powerful faced increased juridical savagery in other forms, from mutilation to death by torture, with public punishment of violent criminals and suspension of bodies on gibbets at the scene of the crime.[90]

The great magnates did not only rely on the biased legal system to enforce their will. They also increasingly retained private bodies of armed men for less formal direct action.[91] Sometimes they pushed strong-arm tactics too far. In 384, Scirtius of Praeneste went to law to try to get back an estate he claimed had been forcibly seized by henchmen of the senator Q. Clodius Hermogenianus Olybrius. It transpired that the senator's 'agents' had also imprisoned the entire city council of Praeneste to prevent them testifying on Scirtius' behalf.[92]

The swords of the soldiers remained the ultimate deterrent in this formidable arsenal of oppression, often encountered on city streets and highways, and sometimes unleashed on deviants and dissidents, during religious persecutions or times of unrest.

Overall it seems that combined ideological indoctrination, the law and the shadows of cudgel, whip and sword constituted a grimly effective system of domination, generally successful in keeping the fourth-century empire operating. Emperors aspired to something resembling a totalitarian state and magnates behaved like Mafia dons, yet – while dangerous and frightening – Scirtius' world in 384 was nothing like Winston Smith's in *1984*, Orwell's 'jackboot stamping on a human face – forever'. Lacking the techniques or technologies for communication, surveillance, data storage and processing available today for really invasive social control, the later Roman empire was nowhere near as efficient as the totalitarian regime Orwell depicted, or the real ones on which it was based.

Severe laws specifying savage punishments for deviants were promulgated repeatedly, perhaps because emperors wanted to be seen to be vigilant – or because laws were not very effective. Lacking means for rigorous enforcement, the state was reduced to trying to coerce compliance through terror.

In practice, the fourth-century Dominate worked partly because it was open to some negotiation and widespread manipulation, and vulnerable to evasion. People actually stood some chance of avoiding their burdens, or escaping the net entirely. Communities appealed to the emperor for relief, individuals sought protection of powerful patrons, made false tax returns or engaged in other forms of passive resistance. Others simply bolted, seeking a new life elsewhere; there was a reasonable hope the authorities couldn't trace them or, lacking photos or fingerprints, identify them with certainty. Some hard-pressed town councillors abandoned their properties and illegally sought refuge in the armies. Other fugitives added to the endemic problem of brigandage, which might spill over into political violence.

The question of how far there was popular violent resistance to the late imperial order remains hotly debated. Serious non-military risings occurred in some parts of empire, notably in Gaul, where the enigmatic Bagaudae were episodically enough of a problem to require internal military campaigns to suppress them. These may have been popular risings triggered by breakdown of traditional patronage structures that bound farmers and landowners, as the latter became ever more overbearing.[93] While playing down the scale and significance

94. A fourth-century *miles* (soldier or imperial official, but either way in military dress) beating a servant, from the mosaics in the great villa at Piazza Armerina, Sicily. A perhaps unique visual depiction of the violence soldiers routinely dealt to Roman civilians.

of such trouble as no worse in the fourth century than before, Peter Heather concedes that if most later Roman peasants did not actually rebel, neither did they feel much commitment to the state.[94] Whatever the actual level and nature of internal violence, with no clear boundary between 'criminal' brigandage and political insurgency, and likely large-scale alienation of the population, the behaviour of the authorities reflects their anxieties about resistance to the imperial order. The stability of the fourth-century empire was in part a balance of the heightened mutual fear of rulers and ruled (Fig. 94).

In this situation, and having themselves created the late Roman state, the soldiers were more prominent than ever in guaranteeing maintenance of the Roman imperial order against an unprecedented combination of external threats and internal pressures. Overall, during the fourth century they succeeded. Heather's argument that the fourth-century empire was stable is valid; however, this was a dynamic stability, which, like that of a speeding motorbike, required constant vigilance and active intervention to sustain – and was always potentially vulnerable to unexpected shocks from outside. These began to rain down on the frontiers from the 370s, increasing internal strains to the point that, before the century's end, the state would permanently split in two: a western empire preoccupied with fighting the northern barbarians, and an eastern state focused primarily on Sasanian Iran (Fig. 95).

To understand the long Romano-Sasanian duel, it is essential to look at the other side of the frontier as well.[95] For the course and outcome of relations between the two empires were equally dependent on the fact that Persia, like Rome, was an imperial power vulnerable to conflicts over succession to the throne and to risings in distant provinces, besides serious external threats on her other frontiers (during the third and fourth centuries, notably from the Kushan empire).[96] Hence, Rome's eastern woes during the mid-third century resulted in particular from the longevity and firm grip on power of Shapur the Great, while those of the mid-fourth century arose from the seventy-year reign of the mighty Shapur II (309–79). Conversely, Sasanid dynastic in-fighting and provincial risings between these reigns facilitated Tetrarchic Roman recovery in the east.

Shapur II also fought serious wars against increasingly powerful Arab tribal confederations. These provide yet another example of the development of peripheral powers, here threatened, manipulated and encouraged by two competing empires. With the development of Islam, rising Arab power would change world history every bit as much as the rise of the European barbarian peoples.

In Shapur II's time, the Sasanian military remained centred on its corps of lance-armed armoured cavalry, levied by the Shah in time of war from the Iranian warrior-aristocracy in particular.[97] However, they also now included substantial numbers of professional soldiers in direct royal employ, more closely resembling Roman forces than Parthian armies had. The crack imperial cavalry corps of 'Immortals' directly alluded to the Sasanids' claimed Achaemenid heritage, reviving the name of the old Persian royal guard; they also deployed war elephants, and retained a well-established siege capability, vividly described by Ammianus, who saw it first hand at Amida in 359 (p. 241). The Sasanians were equally accomplished at building fortifications, resulting in confronting systems of fortresses in the Roman frontier zone. The Sasanians also developed linear frontier systems, perhaps in part imitated from Roman practice (p. 122).

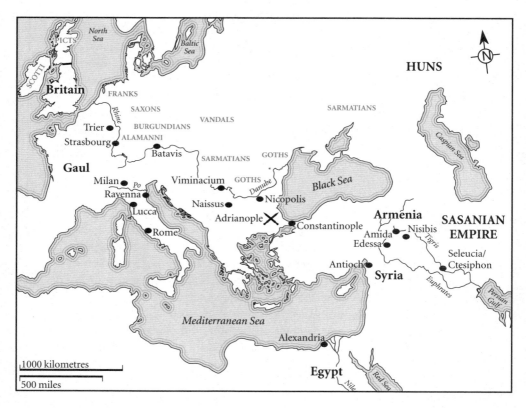

95. The Roman empire, its neighbours and enemies in the fourth and fifth centuries AD, showing regions, states, peoples and places mentioned in the text.

Sasanian armies also now included capable bodies of armoured infantry, again in convergence with Roman practice, although these were never as important as the lance-armed cavalry and mounted archers that continued to comprise the core of Sasanian military power. Fourth-century Sasanian cavalry appears to have been more heavily equipped than ever. Even the horse-archers were now armoured, while greater reliance seems to have been placed on the lancers to engage in close combat with the Romans, aiming to smash through their lines. These developments, primarily experimental responses to war with Rome, limited the endurance of men and horses and appear not to have been entirely successful against Julian (below); they did not work well against the Huns.[98]

Persian territory was invaded by Chionite Huns from Central Asia in the 350s, a peril grave enough to force the Sasanians to abandon recent gains against Rome. It took them years of fighting to restabilize their frontier with Central Asia,[99] after which Shapur returned to the attack against Rome, now including Huns among his allied contingents, besieging Nisibis in 359, and after prolonged and bitter fighting, taking Amida. Constantius II's attempts to strike back were aborted by the challenge from Julian, which, as we saw, was resolved by Constantius' death. Countering Shapur in the east would fall to Julian.

As sole emperor, Julian now dreamed of greater glory, and counter-invaded the Sasanian empire. It is unclear how far Julian was carried away by a wish to imitate Alexander, or was pursuing ostensibly more achievable war-aims. Shapur's brother Hormuz had defected to Julian, with significant elements of the Sasanian elite cavalry, so even if the Roman emperor could not conquer Persia outright, he might at least hope to achieve 'regime change', replacing a dangerous foe with a dependent puppet Shah.[100]

Like so many Roman armies before them, Julian's soldiers invaded Mesopotamia, but failed either to destroy the main Sasanian army, or to take Ctesiphon. Facing Sasanian scorched-earth strategy, the campaign ended, once again, in ignominious retreat, during which Julian was killed (363). As ever, Roman military aggression faltered in Babylonia. Shapur extracted an enormous price to let the defeated and starving Roman field-army home alive. Rome had to give up much territory and key fortress-cities in the Tigris basin.

In the fourth century, the Romans regarded Persia as the main threat; the northern barbarians were seen as a serious problem but not a mortal danger.[101] The sheer proximity of the empire, both as a rich potential target and as a powerful neighbour actively interfering through war, diplomacy and subsidy, continued to have a profound effect on Rome's European neighbours. Common interest in treating with Rome, resisting its forays or raiding its territory all encouraged the concatenation of larger political units in Barbaricum. In free northern Britain imperial intervention inadvertently helped create a stronger, more centralized barbarian power: the Picts.[102] Rome also influenced Ireland, leading by the fourth century to internal political changes, and growth in the coastal raiding of Britain by Irish 'Scotti' who would bring back booty and Romano-British slaves, including St Patrick.[103]

Fourth-century Continental peoples were affected on an even greater scale, not least the multiple emergent Gothic kingdoms west and north of the Black Sea.[104] Contrasting sharply with the 'barbarian hordes' of Roman and later stereotypes, these statelets were based on improved agricultural regimes and population densities comparable with those of the Roman provinces. They were ethnically mixed societies, economically sophisticated and militarily powerful. Ruled by Germanic-speaking groups who called themselves Goths, they were under strong Sarmatian cultural influence (particularly in military affairs), and also incorporated Dacian Carpi, conquered Greek coastal cities and communities descended from Roman provincials captured in the third century. The presence of the last brought Christianity to the Goths, and also industrial advances such as glass production. They minted no coins, but used Roman coinage extensively. Germans generally prized Roman swords, coins and drinking gear, but Gothic leaders also enjoyed many other aspects of Roman lifestyle.[105] Their kingdoms established hereditary rule, but no single overking.[106] Constantine the Great defeated them and regarded them as clients. However, a crisis in Roman-Gothic relations set in train the military events that led to disastrous damage to Roman military power and prestige and, ultimately, the end of the western imperial regime.

# Extinctions and Transformations 376–565

## Disaster at Adrianople 378

> Bellona, raging with more than her usual fury…
> AMMIANUS 31.13.1[1]

Extinction of the house of Constantine with the death of Julian did not result in civil war but a peaceful succession, probably because most leading generals were campaigning together in Mesopotamia at the time. Two more Danubian officers rose to the purple: Valentinian was acclaimed and chose to rule over the west, appointing his brother Valens co-Augustus over the east. Valentinian, often seen as the last truly effective military emperor of the west, died of apoplexy at the insolence of some barbarian ambassadors in 375, and was succeeded by his son Gratian.

In 376, vast numbers of Goths petitioned Valens for permission to cross the Lower Danube and settle on the Roman side. Valens consented. His troops were busy fighting the Sasanians, so he could not have prevented the Goths from crossing anyway. Better to accept them; there were precedents for absorbing masses from across the Danube.[2] They could farm vacant land and provide valuable troops.[3] However, abuses by Roman officials triggered a revolt, which devastated Thrace. Suddenly Valens had another huge war on his hands, so serious that he appealed to his western colleague for military assistance. Gratian was delayed by wars of his own, but in 378 was on his way to help. In August, Valens, encouraged by minor successes, impetuously ignored advice to await the western troops, and sought sole glory by attacking a Gothic force at Adrianople in Thrace.[4]

Valens' army, *comitatenses* probably supplemented with units from the army of Thrace, totalled 20,000–40,000 men and was thought to outnumber the Goths, encouraging Valens' rejection of the Gothic leader Fritigern's overtures to negotiate. The Romans had, however, suffered a disastrous double intelligence failure. They seriously underestimated the size of the encamped army facing them and – worse – had not detected another large force of Gothic cavalry that was away foraging, yet still close enough to join battle.

The Gothic camp, a wagon-laager on a hill, lay 8 Roman miles (*c.* 7 miles or 12 km) north of Adrianople. Valens compounded his errors by marching his soldiers in battle-order through the heat of the day, without food or water, intending a rapid attack. While the wilting Romans struggled to form line of battle, the Goths fired the surrounding fields to further discomfort the parched and hungry imperial soldiers with smoke. Fritigern also renewed offers to treat, stalling for time, hoping his cavalry would return. Fighting broke out when some exasperated Roman troops attacked without orders, bringing on a general engagement. The Romans, attacking the Gothic camp, were in some disorder when they were surprised and outflanked by the Gothic cavalry, assisted by a contingent of Alans. Enveloped, the Roman foot were herded together, many unable to wield their swords or raise their shields to intercept arrows, and were slaughtered. Valens perished somewhere on the field; his body was never found. According to Ammianus, no battle save Cannae was such a disastrous Roman massacre.

Adrianople was indeed a catastrophe comparable in gravity to Cannae and, in retrospect, had worse consequences than Carrhae or the defeat of Varus. It was a turning point, because it marked the end of Rome's unchallenged military ascendancy in Europe, beginning a process that would culminate a century later in extinction of the western empire. With such hindsight, it has been tempting to assume that the army, which failed so disastrously at Adrianople, was already 'declining' and 'decadent'. However, as we have seen, there is little to support this assumption. Like many military disasters, Adrianople resulted from an unforeseeable combination of factors: bad luck and misjudgment – the most high-tech armies suffer catastrophic intelligence failures – plus the kind of commander's folly seen at Carrhae. Also, Roman soldiers had always been inclined to get out of control. None of this need imply that their fighting qualities, or the effectiveness of Roman field armies, had 'declined' significantly before 378. Rather, it marked a fundamental shift in the global balance of power, which, now involving potent enemies on multiple fronts, was no longer weighted decisively in Rome's favour.

Since the third century Rome had not been able to guarantee the integrity of her frontiers, although until 378 she could still expect to win wars. At Adrianople an imperial field army had been slaughtered by a barbarian one; worse still, in a real change from the Varus disaster or those of the third century, the Romans were now unable to inflict even plausible-looking retribution on the Goths for their temerity. The result was the settlement of 382, agreed between the Goths and the new eastern emperor Theodosius. Its unprecedented terms accepted the presence of the Goths settled on Roman provincial soil as an autonomous group, retaining their own rulers and identity. They were allies (*foederati*, from *foedus*, 'treaty') who, besides furnishing recruits for regular regiments, would serve Rome in war under their own commanders. The difference from earlier alliances was that the Romans could no longer be certain that they could defeat these Goths if they went against imperial wishes – and both parties knew it.[5] Adrianople did not break the power of the imperial armies, but it permanently damaged Rome's crucial military and moral ascendancy over the barbarians in Europe.

In absolute numbers, Roman losses at Adrianople are unlikely to have been as great as at Cannae; estimates go as 'low' as 10,000, although many are higher.[6] Yet, in stark contrast to the aftermath of Cannae, Adrianople left the Roman military permanently weakened. Despite the resources of the entire empire, the state proved unable ever to make good the losses of whole regiments of seasoned professional troops destroyed by the Goths. This says something important about the fourth-century empire; internal constraints of some kind prevented recovery, during decades when the western empire had not yet suffered the serious damage to its resource-base of land, productive capacity and manpower that would push it into its final downward spiral. It was more likely a result of systemic paralysis, arising from multiple causes including corruption, misappropriation of resources, alienation and evasion of service.

Adrianople had another major long-term implication. Why were so many Goths desperate to cross the Danube in 376? It was because wolves even more fearsome than the Romans were snapping at their heels: the Huns.

### 'Exogenous shock': the Huns and their barbarian bow-waves

Imperial actions had triggered the rise of neighbours collectively too powerful to destroy. Yet Rome remained strong enough to contain them, and perhaps would have done so indefinitely but for the addition of a wildcard factor, unrelated to the dynamics of Europe, Mediterranean and Middle East: the still-unexplained eruption of the Huns. Here I largely follow Peter Heather's argument that the fall of the west was not inevitable at the time, but actually quite sudden, primarily the result of invasions from outside, triggered by the Huns.[7] This 'exogenous shock', as he terms it, proved too much for the western empire; the east, which lost the city of Rome, Italy, and its Latin heritage as it evolved into a Greek-speaking medieval Christian kingdom, gradually ceased to be Roman in anything much but name. However, if the barbarian invasions comprised catalyst and immediate cause of the fall of the western empire, they were interacting with internal dynamics that, as we saw above, had – hitherto – generated imperial stability.

A profoundly important internal development of the later fourth century, resulting from external pressures, was that Roman Europe could no longer easily draw on the resources of Roman Asia, a significant factor in its fate.

From the third century, emperors faced multiple foreign and internal dangers. Lacking high-speed communications, the empire was too vast and unwieldy for a single ruler and court to control. Various constellations of regional authority, under multiple emperors who achieved the purple by appointment, dynastic succession or the sword, became the fourth-century norm. The death of Julian in 363, which extinguished the house of Constantine, was followed by one such division of the empire, between Valentinian in the west and Valens in the east. This time the division would prove permanent, culminating in 395 with effectively a formal fission into two empires, a Latin-speaking western state based spiritually on Rome (although the imperial court now resided at Ravenna), and a Greek-speaking eastern state based on Constantinople.[8] The two Roman empires rapidly went their own ways, sometimes assisting each other, though the east was sometimes prepared to divert barbarians towards the west in the interests of protecting itself. Vastly more durable than Alexander's empire had been, the Roman empire was, finally, permanently fragmenting.

The history of the wars and invasions of Roman Europe between Adrianople and the end of the western empire in 476 is too complex to detail here, but several major events stand out. Some measure of stability was restored with the Gothic settlement of 382, until 405 when Goths attacked Italy. Then at the turn of 406–7 a massive barbarian invasion – or migration of entire peoples – erupted across the frozen Rhine.[9] The army in Britain raised several usurpers who intervened in Gaul and sought to expel the invaders, but neither these nor the official emperor at Ravenna (or rather his mostly German generals and their dwindling numbers of *milites*) could do so. Franks and Burgundians permanently established themselves in Gaul; Suevi and Vandals pushed on to Spain. After 410 Roman Britain and its armies rapidly disintegrated.

Meanwhile, the Roman world suffered another devastating blow: in 410 the City of Rome itself was sacked by Goths, led by Alaric. Of negligible military significance, this was nonetheless of earth-shattering psychological importance: the Eternal City had fallen to barbarians, with incalculable damage to imperial prestige. The Goths responsible subsequently established themselves in Gaul, before moving on to found a lasting 'Visigothic' (western Gothic) kingdom in Spain. Real strategic disaster struck in 429 when the Vandals took much of Roman Africa, on whose vast wealth Italy had long depended.[10]

Behind these movements of Germanic groups lay the growing power of the Huns. Hunnic origins and ethnic affiliations, and the reasons for their eruption onto the scene, all remain mysterious,[11] but in general terms they represent just another 'wave' of horse-archer nomads from the Asiatic steppes, in the tradition of the Sarmatians and Parthians (although they seem to have lacked heavy lancers) and of the later Turks and Mongols. The Huns struck terror into all they encountered, and, Peter Heather has convincingly argued, were even more important in the destruction of the Roman west than has hitherto been realized.

Arriving in the Black Sea region *c.* 350, multiple Hunnic groups put military pressure on the Sarmatian peoples, Goths and others of the region. One reason that the Huns had effects in eastern Europe greater than comparable prior movements by Sarmatians was that, rather than overrunning mosaics of small, low-population-density chiefdoms of earlier times, the Huns crashed into substantial barbarian proto-states. They destroyed some and reduced others to vassalage, but more sought survival by migration. Adrianople was a consequence of Goths fleeing Hunnic assaults.[12]

Sometime around 400, large numbers of Huns moved west, to the Hungarian plain,[13] a decisive move which both facilitated terrifying Hunnic raids into the Roman empire – they travelled faster than news of their coming – and also probably triggered the mass migration of other peoples across the Rhine in 406–7. This included Germanic Vandals and Suevi, but also Sarmatian Alans who appear to have fled westwards before the Huns all the way from the Carpathians.[14] The invaders even included 'hostile Pannonians', perhaps disaffected Roman provincials, oppressed peasants (and perhaps more privileged dissidents?) throwing in their lot with the barbarians, a phenomenon which may have been a factor during the earlier Gothic incursion that led to Adrianople.[15]

Dominating Barbaricum and impinging on the provinces, 'for the first time in Roman imperial history, the Huns managed to unite a large number of Rome's European neighbours into something approaching a rival imperial super-power',[16] creating their own empire, which reached its height under Attila. Like Rome and Sasanian Persia, this was a multi-ethnic empire, its tributary peoples including many Germans: Gothic became its *lingua franca*.[17] Rome now faced two huge empires – the Sasanian and the Hunnic – beyond its capacity to defeat simultaneously, let alone conquer.

They are lightly equipped for swift motion, and unexpected in action, they purposely divide suddenly into scattered bands and attack, rushing about in disorder here and there, dealing terrific slaughter…you would not hesitate to call them the most terrible of all warriors, because they fight from a distance with missiles…then they gallop over the intervening spaces and fight hand to hand with swords, regardless of their own lives; and while the enemy are guarding against wounds from the sword-thrusts, they throw strips of cloth plaited into nooses over their opponents and so entangle them that they fetter their limbs…

AMMIANUS 31.2.8–9[18]

96. One of two mid-fifth century swords found at Pannonhalma-Szélsòmalom, Hungary. The blade was of lenticular section. Such swords were current in the Hunnic empire. (Scale 1:8)

Primarily horse-archers, the Huns do not seem to have fought as lance-armed armoured cavalry (although their Sarmatian subjects did) but, as Ammianus vividly recounts, did enter close combat using lasso and sword. At the end of the fourth century a new type of blade appeared in the Danube lands, and later in other contexts as far as Spain, which leaves little doubt that it was introduced from the steppe by the Huns and their subjects (Fig. 96).[19] Its great length, blades averaging *c*. 830 mm (33 in) and sometimes exceeding 900 mm (3 ft), is also consistent with a primarily cavalry weapon. Its characteristic outline comprises twin edges, initially parallel, then curving gently towards a very elongated, near-parabolic point, resembling the Roman Illerup-Whyl type. However, its hilt includes a separate iron guard of diamond plan, like those of earlier Sarmatian-inspired ring-pommel hilts, but rather elongated like Partho-Sasanian weapons, which form perhaps the closest parallels.

Nevertheless, among the Huns prowess with the bow reigned supreme. It has recently been argued that a major part of their secret was a new asymmetric composite bow design, supposedly of exceptional power (Fig. 97).[20] Yet there seems to be no evidence that this was any kind of 'secret weapon', vastly more powerful than the sophisticated composite bows long in Partho-Sasanian and Roman use; at most, it was an incremental improvement on an already-ancient design. To be sure, like Roman might before it, Hunnic power depended on effective military technology, and warriors' personal and collective skills in its use. But Hunnic success is better seen as a result of a combination of archery and horsemanship – perhaps most especially the latter, for it was the Huns' exceptional speed and range of movement, outstripping warning of their approach, which made them terrifyingly effective.

So, I suggest that the Huns' domination in war, like that of the later Mongols, depended equally on moral ascendancy, achieved by combining speed and shock derived from their martial technology and skills, and not least endurance, with sheer bloody ruthlessness and ferocity, half-beating their foes even before contact by generating terror – again, just as the Romans had. The Huns added to their shocking reputation by acquiring

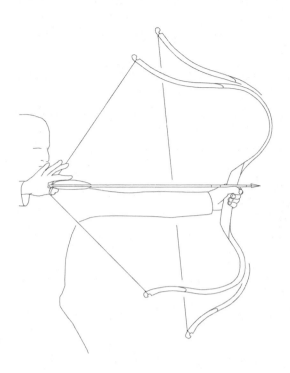

97. Reconstruction of the asymmetric Hunnic bow based on European and Asiatic finds. The archer is using a thumb-ring for the 'Mongolian release', known in western Asia by the second century. This is the moment of release, as he opens his fingers to let the bowstring snap from his thumb. The bow is also shown in its at-rest position.

other martial skills unprecedented among 'barbarians': the ability to take fortifications by siege, using machines. In the fifth century, not even major centres were safe: Attila took Naissus, Viminacium and Nicopolis in the 440s.[21] This capability probably implies that Roman-trained artillerymen and siege engineers – opportunistic renegades or prisoners under duress – served the Huns, who, in their exceptional openness to effective foreign ideas, also resembled the Romans.[22]

The deep impact of Hunnic warfare on the Roman world is seen in the temporary supremacy in Europe of the prestige of the Asiatic composite bow over the sword. The bow was the supreme symbol of political authority as well as military prowess among the Huns – gold-covered ceremonial examples have been found in Hunnic graves – a fact absorbed by the Roman world.[23] On the death of Attila, the emperor Marcian was said to have dreamed that the Hunnic king's bow had broken in two.[24] Following their own tradition of openness to effective foreign martial culture, fifth-century Romans made central to their own military skills what had hitherto been a supporting weapon. In 455 Valentinian III was murdered on the Campus Martius at Rome, when about to practise not with the sword but with the bow.[25] In the 440s, the Roman general Aetius, soon to be Attila's nemesis, 'was…a practised horseman, a skilful archer and tireless with the lance'.[26] These changes resulted from centuries of war with lancers and horse-archers across Danube and Euphrates, but especially recently, against the Huns.

Partial eclipse of the sword in Roman service came as the *milites* of the west were in the process of final dissolution. However, a curious tale survives of a man who followed the blood trail from an injured cow to the buried sword that had cut its foot. He took the weapon to Attila, who presented it as a divine sign: '…he concluded that he had been appointed ruler of the whole world and that through the sword of Mars he had been granted invincibility in war'.[27] Even if mythical, the story shows that the sword retained much of its symbolic aura for Romans – and if based on a real incident, it shows Attila knew it.

## *Milites* and *foederati*

A Frankish citizen I, but a Roman soldier under arms. I always bore my (?)weapons in war with exceptional courage.

UNNAMED SOLDIER'S EPITAPH AT AQUINCUM, BUDAPEST[28]

In the fifth century, Roman armies were usually composite forces, often including contingents from more-or-less willing allies, or mercenaries. This was time-honoured Roman practice. However, the period saw real qualitative and quantitative changes, especially in the west, with growing proportions of *foederati* – allied Germans or others, including Huns – under their own commanders, alongside dwindling numbers of regular Roman *milites*.

The *Notitia Dignitatum* (p. 246) reveals big losses to the western armies in the early fifth century AD. These may mark bigger cumulative losses than those resulting from Adrianople, amounting to perhaps 30,000 from the western *comitatenses*. Whole units vanished – and with them, traditions and continuity. Some ninety-seven new units had appeared since 395, about two-thirds promoted frontier regiments, the rest new formations, some with barbarian names.[29]

Many of these losses may have been self-inflicted, during the last disastrous civil war battle between east and west. Efforts of the eastern emperor Theodosius to crush a western usurper, Eugenius, resulted in September 394 in the battle of the Frigidus, which inflicted serious damage on the western field armies. It was followed by one final, brief reunification of the empire. Theodosius appointed his sons to succeed him: Honorius in the west and Arcadius in the east. With their accession in 395, the empire permanently split into two states.

If it had the money to support *foederati*, why couldn't the western regime raise regular units? Growing reliance on quasi-mercenaries was apparently necessitated by increasing difficulties in recruiting Roman provincials, especially in the long-demilitarized core provinces.[30] During the fifth century, the west became trapped in a spiral of military decline, as its resource base eroded away with disruption of provincial revenues and loss of vital recruiting grounds, as barbarians overran much of Gaul and the Balkans. Vandal conquest of Africa was especially catastrophic, as Rome and the western state depended on its produce and tax revenues, just as Constantinople relied on Egypt.[31] Declining internal capacity to raise and maintain *milites* thus necessitated growing reliance on *foederati*. Barbarians were all too plentiful, probably cheaper and certainly more expendable than regular soldiers, if less capable. Their developing military skills and sophistication should not be underestimated, however: as the west's own armies declined in strength, and – probably, at last – excellence, the qualitative gap narrowed.

Then, as Roman moral ascendancy declined in the decades after Adrianople, many barbarian 'allied' contingents simply did what mercenaries were already tempted to do before the Punic Wars: turn on those they were paid to defend, to extort gold or land.[32] Now the western empire lacked the ability to do much about it, apart from try to play barbarians off against each other, and call for assistance from the eastern state, which remained in a much stronger military position.

Being better placed to recruit and maintain forces for its own defence, the regime in Constantinople was able to place less reliance on barbarian allies, although it continued to use them extensively – despite massacring Goths serving in the eastern armies as a 'security measure' after Adrianople.

Were barbarians in late imperial service inherently a problem? It is often assumed that Rome's military was seriously 'barbarized', bringing dangerous dilution of imperial military traditions, not least of Roman martial *virtus*, and (given the ultimate fate of the west) serious risk of direct treachery among ethnically barbarian *milites*.[33] Some barbarian soldiers were employed under 'limited contracts', serving close to home and probably staying in close touch with their communities.[34] In 378, a returning Germanic soldier revealed the depletion of Rhine garrisons to his countrymen.[35] By Julian's time, many of Rome's most senior generals were first- or second-generation barbarian immigrants.[36] In the fifth century, command of the western armies (and often, with it, effective control of figurehead emperors at Ravenna) fell to generalissimos of barbarian ancestry, such as Stilicho. It is tempting to trace this 'rot' far back into the fourth if not the third century, when contingents of Goths and others were already serving as allies in imperial armies.

Yet this is a false picture. Surviving texts reveal that, while Germanic and other barbarian names made up a substantial proportion of both the officer corps and other ranks, Roman names were always in the majority, right into the fifth century.[37] As the historian Hugh Elton observes, Stilicho was a Roman in all but accident of paternity, in no sense a 'barbarian' except in the eyes of modern writers, and occasionally, contemporary political enemies who used his parentage against him.[38] Many barbarians sincerely wanted to become Romans, just as many from former or even current enemy states wish to become Americans today. Germans and others serving as *milites*, high or low, generally showed the same high level of loyalty to their adopted country. It is actually rare to hear in Roman sources of instances of treason among such men, despite attested visits to their original homelands, or veterans perhaps going back.[39] As ever, Roman *militia* had attractions for ambitious young warriors, offering pay, prestige, a new identity and a chance of glory. Late Roman military culture continued to evolve, and as always to absorb some of the equipment and traditions of these foreign recruits. As such, it did indeed appear ever more barbarous to provincials, yet, through the fourth century and beyond, the *milites* still remained a self-consciously Roman community. However, while fourth-century emperors still took the field and were still expected to act as *commilitones*, by the fifth century most left command to generals, relying more on their quasi-divine status for their authority. They became rather more remote from the soldiers.

Even if the damage to Rome's military prestige and loss of manpower at Adrianople meant that her European armies were less and less able to enforce her will on groups of barbarians, they could still exert severe counter-pressure on their antagonists. Barbarian groups responded by further integration, growing in relative and absolute size and military power – a process accelerated as peoples found themselves squeezed between Rome and the new Hunnic peril.[40] It seems that these processes led to the creation of the Visigoths, not in Barbaricum, but on Roman soil, as a consequence of the revolt of 395 by Goths under the war leader Alaric. It was a process of ethnogenesis among existing groups already inside the empire, who banded together under Alaric for mutual survival, in the face of threats from the twin Roman regimes.[41] Such processes put confederations like the emergent Visigoths on a less asymmetric relation of power with the emperors, reflected in their achievement of the status of *foederati*. The *foedus* implied a bargain more equal than the Roman state had normally contemplated with anyone save Parthians and Persians since the republic.

From the point of view of Roman commanders, these processes were, if undesired, by no means entirely negative. Combined Roman and allied barbarian armies could be very effective, as they proved in Gaul in 451, against Attila's Huns.

### Fall of the west, survival of the east 376–565

In the 440s, the new Hunnic empire seemed an established factor in geopolitics. But in 451, a combined army of Romans and Visigoths under Aetius defeated Attila in Gaul. Within years, even faster than it had appeared, the Hunnic empire collapsed. However, by this stage the Roman west was mostly lost to the emperors who still held court at Ravenna, and was already becoming a patchwork of emergent 'sub-Roman' or Germanic-ruled successor states. In 476 the last nominal emperor, Romulus Augustulus, was deposed and the western empire extinguished. By 500, Rome itself was part of a new Ostrogothic ('eastern Gothic') kingdom of Italy.

Nevertheless, while the Roman west disintegrated, the eastern empire survived. Whatever the favoured explanation for the fall of the western empire, it must also account for the long subsequent survival of this 'Byzantine' empire. Before Adrianople, east and west generally shared the sociopolitical structures and internal dynamics discussed above, so it is reasonable to seek the primary reasons for their divergent military fates elsewhere. There were vital economic and demographic differences; long heavily urbanized, the eastern empire was generally richer and more densely populated than the west, and so better able to sustain the lifestyle of its aristocrats, an increasingly powerful Church and the wars of its emperors. Crucially, the eastern imperial regime was also better placed to protect this logistic base, due to accidents of geography and politics, and the advantage taken of these by soldiers, military engineers and diplomats.

Although its Balkan provinces were devastated by the Hunnic storm and its western barbarian bow-waves, the Roman east otherwise escaped relatively unscathed. The great walls of Constantinople, rebuilt on a stupendous scale by Theodosius II in the early fifth century, prevented land invasion of Roman Asia from Europe, while the Black Sea, patrolled by Roman naval forces, also usually kept the barbarians out. Further east, Rome and Persia remained potentially deadly dangers to each other (and in the sixth century the Sasanians came close to destroying what by then we call the Byzantine empire), but at least had established regimes able to negotiate with each other deals potentially more enduring than those either struck with unstable barbarian regimes. There were important periods of Roman-Persian peace, and even *rapprochement*, with the empires sometimes cooperating against common barbarian dangers in the Caucasus.[42]

In contrast, the Roman west had a much longer and more exposed perimeter, and was trying to deal with a shifting pattern of barbarian confederacies, which were responding to Rome, to each other and to outside forces rooted in Central Asia, in ways which the Romans only dimly perceived. As we saw, Heather's recent overview of the period proposes that collapse of the west was not inevitable, and until remarkably late could have been prevented or substantially postponed, if military events had gone differently, as they easily might have. For example, because he was obliged to concentrate on the Hunnic threat in the 440s, Aetius was unable to restore full control of Hispania and, disastrously, lost Africa.[43] In this view, as late as the 460s there was still a possibility of pulling much of the west back together by the sword, if feasible attempts to reconquer Africa had met with better fortune. For most of the west, the end was quite sudden.[44] It was the direct result of contingent military events; however, the situation became irremediable because these events definitively destroyed the core relationships on which the imperial system relied. When the emperor and his soldiers could no longer protect them, the landowners were quick, and effectively obliged, to make other arrangements, striking deals with incoming barbarian powers, who generally wanted to maintain and enjoy Roman wealth and lifestyle rather than destroy it.[45] Instead of symbiosis with emperor and *milites*, landowners' interests were now guaranteed by payments to Germanic kings and their warbands. The result of the success of barbarian swords, and the pursuit of self-interest by provincial magnates, was 'regime change'. Grown ineffectual and redundant, western emperors and soldiers vanished together.

Such realignments allowed many aspects of Roman provincial life to continue into early medieval times, including landholding and law, the Christian church and Latin dialects already evolving into the Romance languages.[46] Except in Britannia. Here Roman power structures, including the landowning class as well as the provincial soldiery, apparently collapsed, or were transformed beyond recognition, early in the fifth century before Germanic warriors arrived in sufficient numbers to make the kinds of deals which guaranteed continuity of much of the *status quo* across Roman Europe. The result was loss of Roman culture in the former province: towns and villas vanished, Christianity and Latin virtually did. Forts on Hadrian's Wall were abandoned, or became strongholds of warbands.[47] The early medieval population came to speak Germanic dialects ancestral to English, rather than Latinate ones leading to French, Spanish, etc. The contrasting fates of Britannia and adjacent Gaul are consistent with the idea that highly stratified Roman provincial life was only stable so long as civil authority had the sword immediately to hand, in the form of imperial soldiers, or amenable barbarian warriors.

So long as the Roman dominion lasted, *milites* were maintained in many towns at the public expense to guard the *limes*. When this custom ceased, the regiments of *milites* and the *limes* were blotted out together. The unit at Batavis, however, held out. Some soldiers of this regiment had gone to Italy to fetch the final pay to their *commilitones*, and no one knew that the barbarians had slain them on the way. One day, as Saint Severinus was reading in his cell, he suddenly closed the book and began to sigh greatly and to weep. He ordered the bystanders to run out with haste to the river, which he declared was in that hour besprinkled with human blood; and straightway word was brought that the bodies of the soldiers mentioned above had been brought to land by the current of the river.

EUGIPPIUS, *THE LIFE OF ST. SEVERINUS* 20[48]

The *Life* of Saint Severinus (*c.* 410–82) preserves our last close-up historical glimpse of ordinary *milites* of the western empire, and the actual moment of dissolution of a Roman frontier garrison, at Batavis (Passau, Germany) on the

Raetian *limes* of the upper Danube, near the boundary with Noricum. Finding the bodies of their slain comrades makes the soldiers realize that no further pay will reach them from the emperor in Ravenna. They are on their own.

Apparently occurring in the third quarter of the fifth century, these events resulted in the unit dissolving, its men perhaps moving on, hoping to join surviving Roman formations or, more likely since many were doubtless locally born, shedding their uniforms and staying put. Certainly, in a subsequent passage, the 'people of Batavis', now including many from surrounding districts who had recently sought security inside the walls, no longer include anyone described as a *miles*. Under the guidance of the saint, they face threatening Alamanni in line of battle, but defeat them more by prayer than the sword. However, Severinus then urges all to move to the greater safety of Norican Lauriacum. All those who stayed behind were butchered or enslaved when Thuringians stormed Batavis.[49]

The soldiers of Batavis comprised one of many frontier regiments with long and proud histories. For it seems that their town took its name from the unit stationed there since the third century, and listed in the *Notitia Dignitatum* as the *cohors IX Batavorum*.[50] Although by then it had been Batavian in no more than name for almost three centuries, it seems that, by remarkable coincidence, this regiment of Raetian *limitanei* is the same unit about which we know so much in its earlier days, at Vindolanda around AD 100 (p. 146).

The fate of this unit documents a general process of dissolution of Rome's last western *milites* in the later fifth century. Or does it? A remarkable passage in Procopius' accounts of the wars of Justinian suggests that significant numbers of Roman frontier units in Gaul maintained their cohesion and identities for generations after the fall of the last western emperor:

> Other Roman soldiers, also, had been stationed at the frontiers of Gaul…having no means of returning to Rome, and at the same time being unwilling to yield to [the Visigoths] who were Arians, gave themselves, together with their military standards and the land which they had long been guarding for the Romans, to the *Arborychi* [probably *Armorici*, proto-Bretons] and Germans [probably here the Franks]; and they handed down to their offspring all the customs of their fathers, which were thus preserved, and this people has held them in sufficient reverence to guard them even up to my time. For even at the present day they are clearly recognized as belonging to the legions to which they were assigned when they served in ancient times, and they always carry their own standards when they enter battle, and always follow the customs of their fathers. And they preserve the dress of the Romans in every particular, even as regards their shoes.
>
> PROCOPIUS, *HISTORY OF THE WARS*, 5.12.17[51]

In Gaul, it seems, the strength of imperial military traditions outlasted the empire itself through several further generations of self-aware Roman *milites*, down to at least the mid-sixth century. Tantalizingly, we know no more of how these men saw themselves in a transformed world of barbarian kingdoms, or how much longer these relict Roman formations lasted.

While Rome's western armies stumbled towards extinction, her eastern soldiers fully maintained their strength and traditions intact. Despite devastation of the Balkans, eastern Rome was mostly protected from the northern storm by the great walls of Constantinople, its Black Sea fleets, and its gold, which could buy off barbarians. And, much of the time, it enjoyed more peaceful and stable relations with its Sasanian neighbour, for the Persians were similarly beset.

Overall, while it saw great wars between the two empires, the fourth century had been marked by strategic stalemate in the east, leading to peace and growing rapprochement during the fifth.[52] Shah Yazdegird I (r. 399–420) and Arcadius were on such good terms that the emperor appointed the Shah guardian of his son, later Theodosius II (r. 408–50).[53] Despite a brief war on the death of Yazdegird, Romano-Sasanian relations continued cooperative rather than confrontational. The new king Bahram V signed a hundred-year peace with Constantinople, which involved the Romans conceding defence of Caucasian passes to the Persians, and also agreeing to help fund their garrisoning. These developments reflected the hard reality that the two empires faced common, potentially lethal dangers, especially the Huns.

The Romans clumsily triggered renewed war by treaty-breaking fortification building in the 440s, but this was quickly settled, as both empires had their hands full with marauding barbarians: Attila in Europe and the Kidarites to Persia's north. Wars against these peoples, and Hephthalite Huns, would long preoccupy the shahs, culminating in a disastrous defeat in 484, which almost broke the Sasanian empire, and debilitated it for decades.[54]

In the east, then, Rome's soldiers and military institutions remained relatively intact down to the sixth century. However, although they still thought of themselves as Romans, the loss of the west ended exchanges with European, Latin-speaking *milites*. The culture of the soldiers of the eastern empire continued as ever to change, under the influence of interactions with Goths, Huns and Iranians.

The dissolution of the western imperial throne and its armies was not the end of the story of Roman power in the west. In 533, the emperor Justinian, having (he believed) secured his frontier with Persia, despatched a strong army under his great general Belisarius on a major expedition to start reconquering the lost western empire. The effort was remarkably successful in retaking Vandal-held Africa and, later, Byzantine soldiers would also retake parts of Spain. Italy, under the rule of Ostrogothic kings, was, of course, a major objective. The Ostrogothic state maintained much of the fabric of Roman governance, law, and civil life in the familiar shape of urban living, aqueducts, baths and so on. At first Justinian's armies met with victory, Belisarius 'retaking' Rome in 536 and the Ostrogothic capital at Ravenna in 540. However, the Ostrogoths fought on, and east Roman soldiers and resources ran short, as the Sasanians took advantage of Constantinople's 'overstretch', leading to further prolonged wars, while plague also ravaged the empire. Indecisive fighting dragged on in Italy for decades. Finally, in 554 Ostrogothic power was broken. Long term, Constantinople only succeeded in holding parts of the peninsula. Justinian's attempt to retake the west ran into the sand.

This half-bungled attempt to retake the west resulted in a terrible irony. During long years of devastating the countryside and besieging cities, Roman soldiers sent by Constantinople – some of the last generations of *milites* to serve in a military that still maintained formations called legions – inadvertently caused much more destruction of surviving Roman life and culture in Italy, and in the City of Rome itself, than the barbarians had in conquering it the previous century. It was the ultimate illustration of the double-edged nature of the Roman sword.

It is hard to offer a meaningful end-date for the history of the Roman sword, as artefact or metaphor, in west or east. If western *milites* and their living traditions vanished with the state during the fifth century, the end of the actual Roman sword in Europe is more problematic. The empire's European *fabricae* continued to churn out arms into the fifth century, so swords of Roman manufacture continued to equip the dwindling western armies. Yet they also continued to flow into barbarian hands: Alaric's Goths, who couldn't be destroyed, but might be used, were directly armed by Roman factories when, in 397, Constantinople gave him the rank of Master of the Soldiers.[55]

As the western state disintegrated, skilled swordsmiths and other armourers from the *fabricae* did not find themselves short of work in the new Europe. The Ostrogothic Italian kingdom, for example, continuing Roman practice in arms procurement as in so many other aspects, directly employed 'armifactores', many doubtless descendants of imperial *fabricenses*.[56] Thus were Roman swordmaking traditions bequeathed directly to medieval Europe. Examples of Illerup-Wyhl-type swords, both wider and narrower variants, are still known in contexts dating to around AD 500, if rarer than versions of the broader Osterburken forms. Both families of swords therefore outlasted the Roman empire in the west.[57]

98. A late Sasanian sword, with an asymmetric 'pistol grip', and new two-point suspension system, the whole cased in decorated silver plating. Late sixth to earlier seventh century, from (?)Tcheragh Ali Tepe, Iran. (Scale 1:8)

Very similar pattern-welded weapons continued to be made across Europe, but at what point did such weapons cease to be Roman swords, and become Roman-style Frankish or Anglo-Saxon weapons, in a process of convergence, continuity and oblivion? A fine pattern-welded blade was buried early in the seventh century with an Anglo-Saxon king at Sutton Hoo in eastern England. Its blazing gold hilt reflects the glittering weapons and obsession with sword-play of the epic poem *Beowulf*, set in heroic, pagan Scandinavia; the blood-red garnets set into the pommel attest tastes which spread to the Germanic world from the steppe. Yet the Roman associations of the blade may not have been entirely forgotten, for with the sword was buried a helmet clearly imitating late-Roman precursors.[58]

In the east, we don't know what fifth- to seventh-century Roman/Byzantine weapons were like; well-preserved examples have yet to be found. This is a chapter of the story yet to be written, both for swords and, to a considerable extent, for the soldiers who wielded them. By comparison with the armies of the republic or earlier empire, those of the later eastern empire remain little explored, through texts and especially through archaeology. Yet we have some vivid images of this late antique world. In 421 the Sasanian Shah Bahram v supposedly conceded the field against a Roman army when his champion, Ardazan of his elite Immortal cavalry, was defeated and killed in single combat by the Roman champion, Areobindus.[59] This incident, likely apocryphal, looked back to ancient traditions of heroic warfare shared by both empires, to Marcellus winning the *spolia opima* at Clastidium, to the Achaemenid corps of Immortals, and Sasanid traditions of mounted duelling.[60] Historical or not, it also expressed contemporary martial realities: Areobindus was a Goth, a horseman who used a Central Asiatic lasso. It also foreshadowed the future: this single combat resembles a medieval joust. It is often argued that the Sasanians, as a society dominated by landowning, aristocratic heavy cavalry, prefigured later chivalric Europe,[61] as well as the characteristics of subsequent reformed Byzantine military organization. The duel between Areobindus and Ardazan catches Rome's eastern armies on the cusp of change towards a new and different era, which was also marked by fundamental changes in their martial culture.

The 'Byzantines' called themselves Romans for almost another millennium. Eastern Roman armies sustained their structure and effectiveness until shattered in desperate wars with Iran at the end of the sixth century; wars which, in the seventh, facilitated Islamic conquests of the mutually debilitated empires in the Middle East. Sasanian Iran succumbed to Muslim armies, although the reduced Roman state survived, albeit shorn of Egypt and Syria. Through these crises and far beyond, Constantinople retained a regular military, which maintained many Janus-faced Roman military traditions of discipline, training, strategy and stratagem, but also of unruly soldiers, military coups and assassinations.[62]

99. A changing world: a mounted archer with the new type of sword and scabbard suspension, plus stirrups, on an unprovenanced Sasanian-style silver plate now in the Hermitage, St Petersburg, Russia. It probably dates to the seventh century, just after the Sasanians succumbed to the armies of Islam.

However, in the course of their struggles for survival, the state and its soldiers were transformed so completely that the label 'Roman' ceases to be useful. By the seventh century Constantinople's armies were Greek-speaking, increasingly cavalry-dominated and based on completely new, territorial organizational structures. Their ethos had also evolved into something no longer recognizably Classical, a process arguably already under way even before the last western *milites* faded away.[63]

Perhaps paradoxically, the eastern Roman soldier turns out to provide a good illustration of the recent notion that Classical civilization did not 'fall', but rather transformed by stages into that of the medieval Christian world.

These upheavals provide symbolic closure to the story of the Roman sword. The sixth century saw extinction of the last surviving formations called legions, and abandonment of Latin by the east Roman military, at which point imperial soldiers finally ceased calling themselves *milites*, and each other *commilitones*. Further, by the sixth century, the stirrup had reached the western world from Central Asia. Around the same time, from the same source, the Sasanians adopted a completely new way of carrying their swords: the ancient scabbard-slide was abandoned, replaced by two projecting mounts on one side of the scabbard, which hung from the waist belt on two pendant straps. Not least, these Sasanian scabbards held an entirely new kind of sword. Their traditional two-edged blades gave way to a pistol-gripped precursor of the single-edged scimitar and sabre (Fig. 98).[64] How far and how quickly Byzantine soldiers adopted similar equipment is yet to be determined, but by AD 700, they were fully part of a medieval world of Islamic armies (Fig. 99), and later, emergent European chivalry.

# Conclusion
## Rome and the Sword

The fate of most Roman swords was to be recycled for their metal. Others, lost in battle or some other accident, simply rusted to dust. The symbolic potency of the weapon, derived from its lethal physicality, ensured that many were ritually disposed of by Roman soldiers and barbarians alike, some as funerary accompaniments for the glorious dead, others in shrines or lakes as offerings to the gods of victory. As a result, they survived by the hundred to our own times, to be dredged up or excavated for the curious to ponder in museums. These relics still transmit their messages of power across two millennia.

Engraved on brass set into the iron and steel of the pattern-welded blade, close to the hand of the wielder, the images of Mars, Jupiter's eagle and military standards inlaid into some middle imperial swords imprint on these weapons the cosmological beliefs and values of Rome and her *milites*. *Religio* meant reverence for both divine and earthly authority, central to which became loyalty to the emperor, whose image dominates the glittering scabbard of the Sword of Tiberius. The celebrated Spanish ancestry of this blade exemplifies incorporation of the traits of foreign enemies and subjects into Roman martial culture, also seen in its final deposition in a river, by a *miles* following the rites of the northern barbarians. Like many other Roman weapons, the Sword of Tiberius was dropped into the Rhine, that military highway and stop-line of effective imperial conquest.

While Rome's sword was sometimes wielded far beyond the Rhine, Danube or Euphrates, it could not be sustained where the accompanying open hand of integration found no secure purchase. The long reach of Roman arms, sometimes wielded through proxies, is seen in the scores of imperial blades in barbarian bog-deposits like that at Illerup in Denmark. That the swords recovered there were prized by Scandinavian warriors is evident; but the fact that many were embellished according to Germanic tastes itself attests the fact that the deadly embrace between the fighting men of confronting cultures was truly a two-sided affair. We can only understand Rome's soldiers by also considering their antagonists.

These instruments of death preserved in our archaeological collections tell us all this, and much else about the men who wielded them, and the societies that produced them. The facts, events and processes they attest come to us directly from *milites*, Sasanian soldiers and barbarian warriors, filling in gaps in the testimony offered by surviving historical texts while, to a degree, bypassing their biases and filtering effects. They bring us as close as we can get to the ancient reality experienced by men like Josephus.

✝

...As if they always had weapons in their hands, [the Romans] never have any truce with warlike exercises...
JOSEPHUS JEWISH WAR 3.5.[1]

Flavius Josephus, who had fought Roman soldiers, has left us one of the most vivid descriptions of them at war, forming a precious part of the image of the legions we have built down the generations. Among the warriors and soldiers of antiquity, Roman *milites* were second to none in exhibiting exemplary courage and devotion to duty – including *devotio*, literal self-sacrifice in war, during the republic. Following the eagles of Jupiter, heavily armoured and plying the fine swords that they so prized, Rome's soldiers came to expect victory against overwhelming odds; and if worsted, would refuse to admit defeat. Preferring death to dishonour, many fought to the last to protect their standards, their homes and their country; some, *in extremis*, turned their swords on themselves. Such were the circumstances in which *milites* liked to picture themselves, bringing glory to the Roman state, achieving personal honour, wealth and fame in the hearts and memories of their comrades, to whom they were bound as blood brothers by emotional ties forged in common toil, suffering, elation and horror. Some had their deeds immortalized by historians, through whose writings they would inspire future generations of Romans, and unimagined successor societies.

This was already a highly selective view in ancient times, and has been made more so since. For 2,000 years, the Romans' remarkable feats of arms have inspired admiration among Western poets, historians, educators and politicians, and emulation among soldiers and generals. There was always the other, inseparable Janus-face of soldiers at war, acknowledged and sometimes overtly celebrated in Roman accounts, yet which modern treatments usually downplay, or airbrush out entirely. For under their eagles or hissing dragon standards, Rome's *milites* plundered, raped and slaughtered on scales outmatching almost any of their foes. Frequently outright aggressors (if ritually careful to portray their enemies as the offenders), they sacked cities, devastated landscapes and massacred or enslaved and deported entire populations at the behest of their commanders. Romans attacked some societies because they feared them, sometimes to a paranoid degree. Others they assaulted simply because they could, seeing them as sources of booty, power and glory. In such actions, Romans were not exceptional in kind. Fascination with Rome has thrown into shadow the reality that most of Rome's foes, 'civilized' soldiers or 'barbarian' warriors, were also brutal and ferocious. Indeed this created the environment that produced Roman bellicosity in the first place, something exceptional largely in degree, and especially in success. Far from being a unique trait endowed by the gods, Roman military capacity evolved in bloody struggle with others, the Romans gradually becoming *primus inter pares* – first among equals – on the battlefield.

In antiquity, provided it was in the line of duty, Romans and others generally saw plundering as laudable, indeed a key benefit of war. Abuse and slaughter of civilians were legitimate (or at worst distasteful) inevitabilities, and potentially useful if such acts also terrorized others into submission. The sons of Mars were wolves to their foes. Tasting blood on such unprecedented scales, like wolves they also sometimes turned on their own kind. From early in their history, Romans feared the two-edged sword being turned back on the Roman state, a danger that became a repeated reality, eventually destroying the republic, and periodically convulsing the empire.

As on campaign, so in other circumstances, *milites* could by turns be heroes and monsters. Imperial soldiers lived as family men and loyal friends, especially to comrades. At the same time they were fiercely competitive, rivalries between soldiers and armies sometimes becoming deadly. On duty, as keepers of the peace, they often feature in our sources as, at best, officious and above the law, more often as dangerous and malevolent: enforcers, jailers, torturers, executioners, routinely as bullies and extortioners. At worst they are glimpsed entirely out of control, collectively preying on society. Martial violence was dealt off the battlefield as much as on it.

Roman soldiers were, and were expected to be, very different from modern Western soldiers, whose behaviour is expected, at least, to be constrained by standards of justice and humanity evolved from the Christian tradition, the Enlightenment and the rise of egalitarian democracy. If fundamental features and basic practices of Roman armies prefigured and inspired our own, the soldiers in their ranks seem dangerously alien. If we seek modern parallels for *milites* in battle, in aggression, brutality and determination to die rather than surrender, Roman soldiers more closely resembled the fanaticism of the Japanese in World War II than any Western armies – highlighting the under-appreciated 'otherness' of Rome.[2]

Roman civilization and the Latin language indeed gave the Anglophone West many of its most cherished concepts, honoured institutions, or the words to describe them: legality, justice, government, constitution, republic, senate, president, military, army, soldier, courage, sacrifice, religion. Yet other, grimmer words equally derive from the legacy of Rome: empire and imperialism, domination, invasion, conquest, oppression, rape, torture, crucifixion, homicide, fratricide, suicide, genocide – and violence itself. Roman *milites* could be eagles, but it is the shadow of the wolf that lingers (Fig. 100).

100. The twin faces of Rome. Marcus Aurelius was the most cultured of emperors and is remembered as a Hellenized 'philosopher king'; but here he is presented with prisoners and severed heads by his *commilitones*, during the Marcomannic Wars.

If Western veneration of the Roman sword has led to downplaying of its inconvenient and disagreeable aspects, it has equally resulted in inadequate attention to – often outright neglect of – the times that produced it, the wider Roman society, and especially the peoples Rome encountered as friends or foes. Even hostile treatments, which identify with Rome's enemies and emphasize the horrors of her imperialism, are often in danger of inadvertently colluding with Roman triumphalists. For, by keeping the spotlight on the Roman side, and presenting their opponents as victims rather than agents in their own right, let alone perpetrators, they may distort historical reality as much as anyone.

As a result of misguided assumptions that 'Rome's secret' is to be found in her own qualities examined in virtual isolation, modern accounts often overlook other fundamental reasons for Rome's triumphs, which were just as important as martial violence and which operated in combination with it, in a mutually reinforcing, winning formula.

In a world full of skilled armourers and tough fighting men, fine swords and ferocity were not always enough for Roman victory. Many of the Romans' enemies outclassed them in some aspects of war. Romans excelled, where they truly excelled at all, in degree rather than kind. In their refusal to acknowledge defeat and their obsession with victory, they showed intense, sometimes suicidal, ideological commitment; but if they outshone others in this, it was often not by very much. Carthaginians could outdo Romans in fanaticism and brutality. Man for man, third-century BC Macedonians were probably better soldiers than contemporary legionaries, who also sometimes faced Gauls sporting superior armour. Later republican *milites* had no answer to Parthian horse-archers and armoured lancers, while four centuries later, Roman soldiers found Hunnic warfare just as difficult to deal with.

At least from the third century BC, a central factor allowing the Romans to overcome such problems was the sheer scale of the resources they commanded: virtually numberless soldiers and endless materiel allowed them to overwhelm foes or, if they could not outfight them on the field, to outlast them in war. This fundamental advantage was itself a cumulative by-product, the outcome of another, deeper characteristic of Roman culture, which, if any one thing may be claimed to be, was the truly exceptional factor giving Romans their edge. Paradoxically, this was something manifested more obviously in politics and diplomacy than on the battlefield.

What really distinguished Romans from their contemporaries was the extent of their openness to accepting others (initially, ruling aristocracies), first as subordinate allies rather than crushed subjects – unusual enough – but exceptionally, eventually as fellow Romans. Such an incentive positively encouraged loyalty, which by no means depended solely on fear of Roman retribution (although that, too, concentrated minds). This open secret of Roman power had remarkable political consequences, and equally important military outcomes. It generated an incomparably resilient and coherent system of allies, gradually absorbed into the expanding Roman state. Successful political integration of many peoples made available to republican and imperial armies their vast reserves of manpower and resources. Roman military power was as much the product as the instrument of a unification of Italy, achieved by sword and open hand together, the inseparable combination behind Roman success for centuries to follow.

The metaphorical open hand also helped continual re-creation of the sword, both figuratively and literally. For unmatched ideological openness to others, allies or enemies, also underpinned other key characteristics of Romans at war, paradoxical in people who regarded themselves as conservatives wedded to the ways of their ancestors: unusual flexibility and inclination to imitate, innovate and integrate. Most, perhaps all, ancient societies copied martial traits from their foes, but no other people matched the Romans in their degree of willingness to learn from enemies how better to fight, to copy their tactics and arms, even to recruit them, all incorporated into a continually redefined Roman martial culture and way of war. This trait made Romans exceptionally adaptable and, where outfought, best able to learn how to turn the tables.

Roughly from 200 BC to AD 200, Roman arms dominated the known world. For the first half of that period, its expansion seemed unstoppable. By the turn of the millennium it was already slowing, however, as Rome came up against oceans in the west, deserts in the south and societies to north and east she found she could neither absorb nor destroy in lands where, if weapons could reach, the open hand found no purchase. Still, against Caledonians or Marcomanni, Sarmatians or Parthians, she retained her aggressive ideology, still expected to win wars and, when opportunity presented, continued to seize new lands.

If the skilful combination of sword and open hand established the astonishing extent of Roman power, it also remained vital to its equally remarkable durability. The glories of civilization in the civil provinces – roads, cities, villas, expanding trade and economic growth, the spread of literacy and of new ideas and religions – were results of lasting rapprochement between native landowning aristocracies and the Roman state, which from the time of Augustus burgeoned into a new, universal imperial civilization. The network of the powerful that articulated this empire was created by Rome's genuine (if conditional) openness. But this order, which favoured the few over the many, had to be guaranteed by the emperor and his soldiers, and depended on them. Their compact with the landowning class was equally critical to emperor and soldiers because it guaranteed their continued access to the vast wealth and manpower of the empire, and was jealously guarded. For it was the productive capacity of the provinces and the populations of the frontier recruiting-grounds which underpinned Rome's enduring success down to the late fourth century AD in the west, and far beyond in the east, giving the Roman military the sheer momentum of being large and powerful enough to overcome any foe except Parthia/Persia. Resource superiority in turn facilitated lasting Roman moral ascendancy in war. A lengthening tradition of victories gave Romans an expectation of more, and placed her enemies at a psychological disadvantage even before battle was joined. Of course, maintaining martial momentum also required continued display of military valour sustained by traditional martial ideology, even if active participation in war was increasingly the preserve of emperors and the military communities of the frontier regions.

From the beginning martial violence shaped Roman identity, as it did those of many contemporary peoples. It played a central role in notions of masculinity, with victory equally central to state ideology in republican Rome. Out of the ruins of the republican order, the Augustan era saw the foundation of not one, but two new Roman cultures beyond the City itself. As the landowning elites led development of a demilitarized, 'globalized' Roman civilization in the core provinces, so the soldiers would come to articulate another, equally important, distinctive 'military Rome' in the bases and growing cities of the frontier provinces. Military-centred development of frontier zones provides a major example of the paradoxically constructive consequences of the Roman sword, in the aftermath of conquest. This 'military Rome' remains an under-appreciated facet of the empire's history, and of the story of her soldiers.

In the bloody process of carving out an empire, Roman military power also destroyed some states, peoples and identities, directly (for example the Eburones, the Seleucid and Ptolemaic states, and not least Carthage) or indirectly (above all, precipitating Parthian collapse). However, Roman actions also reforged others in new ways, deliberately (for example the Batavians) or inadvertently (the Jews). During the early centuries of our era, from Iran to Ireland, and from Scotland and Scandinavia to the Black Sea, Roman military and political activities also unwittingly precipitated the formation of new, larger and more dangerous polities.

In the north, the Varus disaster of AD 9 made Rome realize that peoples like the Germans were not amenable to absorption by established methods of threat and seduction. Sarmatian steppe semi-nomads proved equally intractable, and dealings with them remained largely military – with profound consequences for Roman martial culture. Nevertheless, alongside sabre-rattling and war hot and cold, emperors and the 'military Rome' of the frontiers had significant success in projecting their influence in Free Germany as far as Scandinavia, through subsidies to favoured leaders, economic exchanges and recruitment of barbarian soldiers. Rome's actions and simple proximity had knock-on effects even beyond her ken, with unforeseen and undesired consequences. In attacking some barbarian groups, and supporting others, she unwittingly encouraged them to forge new larger-scale shared identities, and bigger polities with growing military capacities, which, with the added impetus of the Huns, would ultimately overwhelm the western empire.

In the east, Rome's relations with the Parthian empire exhibited analogous patterns, with some rapprochement, mutual recruitment (for example of political exiles) and also major exchanges of martial culture. However, Rome's political interference, and especially her soldiers' repeated aggression, destabilized the Parthian empire while failing to annexe it, and inadvertently precipitated its overthrow and replacement by the far more formidable Sasanian Iran. There ensued the longest of Rome's deadly embraces with a neighbouring state, the four centuries of shared history with the Sasanians, which veered from rapprochement as the 'two eyes of the world', and profound mutual influence that reshaped both parties, to near mutual destruction.

If Rome's empire was first created by her traditional aristocracy and the soldiers they commanded, the autocratic late empire was primarily forged by and for the *milites* themselves. When third-century military crises threatened permanent fragmentation, the Danubian armies reunited the empire by force. Their soldier-emperors then reconstructed the late Roman state, guaranteeing continuity of the imperial compact with the landowners on which their continued existence depended. It was a triumph of the 'military Rome' of the frontier provinces, resulting in a militarized state, which toiled – successfully, for generations more – to keep Sasanians and northern barbarians at bay, and the disenfranchised majority down, even though still plagued by succession crises and by military revolts.

By the fourth century, Roman aggression and interference had brought into being a ring of enemies beyond the capacity of her soldiers to destroy, and only just within their abilities to keep at bay – a precarious balance shattered by the unforeseeable intervention of the Huns. In the west, when they became too weak to secure the frontiers or uphold their end of the compact with provincial landowners, soldiers and emperors eventually went down together. In the richer, more defensible east, imperial autocrats continued to be locked in a deadly embrace with soldiers and generals until none of them remained recognizably Roman in anything other than name, but had seamlessly evolved into the still-powerful, Greek-speaking Christian medieval successor-state we know as the Byzantine empire.

The *gladius*, then, was instrumental not only in carving out the Roman empire in the first place but, indirectly, was also a creative force both inside and beyond the frontiers. Beyond them the actions of Rome's soldiers inadvertently catalysed the rise of new peoples and states, which would shatter the west, and shake the east. Within the empire it gave rise to an influential strand of Roman civilization based on the community of the soldiers. Further, the *milites* were responsible for ensuring the *pax Romana*, keeping war out of the Mediterranean world to a degree envied by later societies, even if this exceptional success also involved far more violent internal repression than is often realized. But didn't the countervailing benefits of civil development still, perhaps, outweigh the hideous costs of building and maintaining Roman imperialism?

Rome remains relevant, both as civilization and military power, and many, especially in lands once under its rule or (in the case of the USA) part-modelled on it, still take Rome as a positive exemplar in arguments for our own time. Rome stands out in Western memory because of its scale and longevity, and its perceived cultural achievements. We still marvel at its material remains: the sophistication of the empire's cities, the opulence of its great residences, the regularity of its military bases, and the ambition of its engineering works, from aqueducts to frontier systems. Who could doubt that, for much of the ancient Mediterranean world and Europe, all this attests anything but a major advance in the human condition? True, much of the eastern empire had already long been urbanized, but before Rome temperate Europe was still preliterate and 'tribal'. Even acknowledging the rivers of blood that often accompanied conquest, surely dazzling subsequent provincial development marked a major net improvement? We saw at the outset that many do not accept this, seeing Rome in negative terms. For example, Jewish popular history blames Rome for expelling the Jews from their ancestral homeland, beginning two millennia of exile. Explicitly, or implicitly in the language they use, people tend to make value judgments about Rome and the sword. Specialists may not quit this field, but must engage, since these representations of the Roman past often amount at best to half-truths, where they are not outright falsehoods. Received ideas must be challenged in the light of the actual evidence, and its implications.

It has been said that it is unjust and pointless anachronism, to judge past cultures according to our own values, which earlier generations did not share. This is true, up to a point: there is a good case for aiming at complete detachment in strictly academic discourse, seeking dispassionately to describe antiquity in its own terms, as I have sought to do in writing of 'the soldiers' rather than 'the Roman Army'. But history is not 'what happened in the past'; the Greek ἱστορία (*historia*) means 'researches', presupposing a researcher. Histories are *our* interpretations of the past. At best, history is what we conclude happened, how and why, on the basis of evidence available to us, and the assumptions about human behaviour we bring to it. At worst, it is what we choose to believe the past was, which can veer into manipulated pseudohistory and nationalist or otherwise chauvinist mythology. A major example of a historical factoid (a widely disseminated falsehood commonly accepted as fact) was mentioned above: Rome's alleged responsibility for 'exiling the Jews' from Judea/Palestine. Rome committed many real atrocities, but this is simply untrue: there was no such expulsion. The 'diaspora' of major Jewish communities across the Mediterranean world and Babylonia was already long established.[3]

It is probably impossible for anyone to achieve an entirely balanced and dispassionate perspective of something as vast, complex and changing as the Roman world, which achieved such extremes of creativity and cruelty. The implications of our evidence from the Roman world are sometimes unexpected, unwelcome or uncomfortable. Thus liberals (among whom I situate myself) may find it hard to swallow that the catalogue of violence of Roman soldiers was not wholly destructive: shared military service and the crucible of war forged the new Roman and foreign identities that shaped Western history. Conversely, conservatives may find the profoundly dark realities underpinning Roman imperialism and the *pax Romana* equally uncongenial. In seeking to understand the past, we should aspire to be as open as we can to the implications of the evidence we uncover, even – especially – when these challenge cherished assumptions. At the same time, we must recognize that, even when we seek to comprehend as fully and honestly as we can what the past was really like, as human beings we cannot avoid emotional, visceral reactions to what we learn. A leading British Iron Age archaeologist once said to me: 'I *hate* the Romans'.

In my view, there clearly were positive aspects to Roman imperialism. Rome built something new, unique and stupendous across the Mediterranean and western Europe. Some, while conceding the empire was run primarily for dominant landowners, imperial court and soldiers, emphasize wider benefits. Imperial society certainly offered new opportunities for upward social mobility, permitting the ambitious to escape the confines of traditional societies. People from all levels of the social pyramid seized new opportunities to improve their lot, occasionally spectacularly. Ex-slaves became Roman citizens in remarkable numbers. Despite inherent occupational hazards, the very armies themselves provided relative prosperity, security and advancement for millions of men over time, and a living for even greater numbers of dependants.

I myself argued above that 'military Rome' was a major constructive outcome of wielding the Roman sword, driving urban and economic development of large parts of the Roman empire, paralleling the more familiar evolution of impressive urban-centred civilization in the civil provinces. Generally, apologists argue, for all its faults the Roman peace facilitated impressive economic expansion, population growth and increased prosperity, which 'trickled down' through society, making even peasants materially better off than their ancestors.[4] This is all probably true, but were these trends positive results of Roman conquest, or processes already underway at conquest – actually preconditions which permitted creation of the empire in the first place?

The east was already urbanized and rich, while population expansion and agricultural intensification in much of Europe also preceded Roman rule. Imperial unification probably facilitated further and faster growth, achieving levels of population, productivity and specialization higher than would have been possible among multiple warring polities. However, even if we credit most of this development to the *pax Romana*, there remains a grave danger of simplistic equation of greater aggregate prosperity with generally improved quality of life and happiness for the peoples of the provinces. The most durable and eye-catching archaeological remains of the Roman empire – public buildings, city walls, villas, military bases – conspire with the surviving historical record to reflect primarily the perspective of power and privilege. They still tend to dazzle Westerners. Yet our knowledge of how humans act and react tells us that where there were such extreme concentrations of wealth and power in so few hands at the glittering apex of the social pyramid, there were corresponding chasms of suffering and despair in the shadows below.

Some common people may have acquired more and better pots and metalwork, perhaps even glass in their windows, but I have seen no evidence that they were physically healthier or longer-lived, or generally happier, than their pre-Roman ancestors. Indeed, under Rome many were both relatively and absolutely worse off than Iron Age peasant farmers. Most glaringly, if many slaves won freedom, this was possible because so many millions had been enslaved in the first place; and in the republic most were never freed, but worked to death on unprecedented, quasi-industrial scales, on estates and in mines. In subsequent centuries, if some peasantries acquired window-glass and similar amenities, others (for example in northern Roman Britain) show few, if any, such signs of material betterment during imperial times.

Acquiescence to Roman rule was gained – most of the time – partly through incentives: 'bread and circuses',[5] and hopes of climbing the social ladder. The lottery of living under Roman imperialism certainly produced big winners; but 'a lottery is a taxation – upon all the fools in creation',[6] then as now working because the vast losing majority exaggerate their tiny chances of real success. Such hope served as a carrot encouraging submission to an imperial order also inculcated through ideological indoctrination (Rome as eternal, divinely sanctioned). Increasingly, however, obedience had to be enforced by oppression and coercion, threats backed with violence, directly inflicted by the landowning classes or on their behalf by a biased judicial system, an order ultimately guaranteed by the swords of the soldiers. By modern standards, all ancient societies were insecure and dangerous, but the lottery of life in the Roman world, with its vast stakes, was especially murderous – and also rigged.

The empire existed neither for the majority, nor with their consent. It was for the benefit of privileged minorities exploiting the economic output of disenfranchised urban populations, slaves and increasingly powerless peasantries. In its alliance with the civil magnates, 'military Rome' can itself be seen as predatory on both civil provinces and foreign neighbours. Predicated on striking deals with already-powerful aristocrats, Roman imperialism deepened their privileges, binding them to the regime while loosening traditional reciprocal bonds with their own subordinates, whom they increasingly dominated by coercion.

It is not even clear that the *pax Romana* brought reduced danger of violence for most. Revolts and civil wars notwithstanding, it certainly reduced levels of warfare, but other forms of violence increased, such as slavery, and dissemination of gladiatorial combats to east and west. Even raiding did not stop; it was reclassified as banditry. Provincials were now often exposed to endemic brigandage, which the state was powerless to suppress, unless it became a threat to the imperial order, when it was dealt with through savage juridical counter-violence. Indeed to many, the law and official authority presented a more immediate threat than bandits. The perils of war that had faced their ancestors were replaced by threats and oppressive violence from increasingly rapacious magnates and *milites*. The net result was less reduction, than redistribution, redefinition and reconfiguration of violence – and fear.[7]

The imperial compact between emperors, soldiers and landowners, probably continuing pre-Roman trajectories already established in many regions from southern Britain and Gaul to Italy and beyond, saw sustained increases in population and aggregate wealth, but reciprocal progressive decline in the liberties and relative status of the majority. Even as ordinary provincials became Roman citizens and, perhaps, acquired more 'consumer goods', so their labelling as *humiliores* attested the widening gap between them and the self-styled *honestiores* who dominated them. Burgeoning asymmetries of power laid the foundations for European feudalism. The powerless poor were exposed to the corrosive effects of endemic fear and routine humiliation.[8] This almost certainly had insidious effects on life less visible than, but perhaps cumulatively as destructive as, those of direct oppression.

Cross-cultural studies show that a key factor overriding mere material prosperity in human well-being – from happiness, health and vulnerability to disease, to sheer life expectancy – is one's position in the social pecking order. Relative differences in wealth and power, and especially the extent to which people feel that they have a place in society, are valued and are in control of their own lives and destinies, are far more important than absolute levels of wealth. If disparities of wealth, status and power increase, then, regardless of absolute material prosperity, life deteriorates for those at the bottom of the social pile.[9] Even bloodless crises affecting whole populations can have devastating social impacts. An extreme illustration of this is provided by what happened in Russia during the decade immediately following the collapse of Soviet Communism. These years saw rapidly increased privation and a despairing sense of collective helplessness and national humiliation, as a deeply flawed yet familiar world vanished, to be replaced by one feeling far less secure, and with much more marked and visible extremes of wealth and power. During these years, from a variety of causes – not least increased violence – Russia suffered *four million* 'excess deaths', i.e. over the numbers to be expected from foregoing or subsequent historical rates.[10] This startling statistic simply marks the tip of the iceberg of stress, suffering and demoralization of much of Russian society under traumatic circumstances. From the viewpoint of the majority, Roman conquest, and their inexorable decline into ever-deeper subordination to landed magnates backed by harsh laws and the sword, constitutes a comparable but far longer-term process, likely to have had similarly grim chronic effects on people's lives and wellbeing. The absence of internal war usually guaranteed by Rome's soldiers may well have allowed economic expansion and growth of populations to levels impossible without it, and in Europe not reached again for a thousand years. However, Rome may receive much more credit for the extent of development during the era than she deserves. In my view, Roman power harnessed, directed and significantly amplified major trends that were already under way during the last millennium BC, as, facilitated by several centuries of more favourable climatic conditions, many more European and Mediterranean Iron Age societies were able to 'take off', developing to scales capable of sustaining empires. Rome was less guardian and guarantor of general prosperity, and more gangmaster, ensuring the benefits went disproportionately to the favoured few – magnates and *milites* – while cowing the many. For the rural masses, the material benefits of imperial rule – often little more than patchy access to industrially-made pots and brooches – were outweighed by sustained erosion of their rights and autonomy, leading to apathy, despair or disaffection.

So, were there, truly, net benefits to Roman imperialism? Like other imperialisms, it depended on who you were, but most lost out.[11] To be sure, in the absence of Rome, ancient Europe and the Mediterranean would never have been havens of peace and love. However, even in a patchwork of smaller, eternally warring states might life for the majority have been better – materially poorer, but at least generally freer – without Rome? This is no pointless lament over the existence of Rome, but a 'thought experiment', which, if posing a rhetorical and ultimately unanswerable question, at least obliges us to reflect on traditional assessments of 'the glory that was Rome'. Not least, it should also give pause to those who profess to love liberty – another Latin loan-word – before singing Rome's praises. It prompts the question 'liberty for who to do what, and to whom?'

It seems to me that outright admiration for Rome is hard for any thinking person to justify. To be sure, Roman times were not an endless, universal bloodbath. In many areas, much of the time, people had opportunities for contentment and laughter. Yet much humour, like so many of Plautus' jokes, was cruel – guffawing at the sufferings of others – or anxious: laughter was believed to ward off bad luck.[12] Today some, even while acknowledging (when pressed) the horrors of the Roman sword and imperialism, and occasionally paying lip-service to the sufferings of those on whose backs the imperial edifice was raised, still focus solely on its agreeable aspects, while perhaps muttering about omelettes necessitating the breaking of eggs. At best, this lays them open to the charge of complacency. They are either not considering all the evidence, or, even less excusably, are choosing to ignore the screams of victims such as those who still lie in the buried streets of Valencia, or who once writhed on crosses along the road all the way from Capua to Rome.

My own experience, over thirty years of exploring the evidence and trying to face its implications, has been a long journey from teenage admiration of the power of 'the Roman Army' to a much darker view. I now regard Roman imperialism in much the same way that I see other important aspects of our shared history, recent totalitarian regimes and colonialisms: horrified fascination veering into revulsion. If people object to such grim assessments of Rome, they should equally reflect on the common, often unthinking, positive admiration for Roman power, either naively dazzled or selectively identifying only with the winning minority.

As we saw, Rome's achievements and military atrocities were exceptional in scale rather than nature, symptomatic of an ancient world built more openly on domination and coercion than our own: Rome was just the biggest shark in a sea full of sharks. While the Roman empire saw remarkable human achievements in economic and political development, literature and visual arts, architecture and technology, it was also a terrible place for most to live in. Yet, as a central phenomenon of Western history, shaping the destinies of all peoples from Arabia and the Sudan to Morocco, to Ireland and Scandinavia, to South Russia and Iran, it legitimately claims our special attention, and demands critical analysis, and neither simplistic admiration nor hostile dismissal.

&#8224;

Memories of Rome's imperial power, her soldiers and their arms, are undying in the West. If temporarily eclipsed by the Hunnic bow, the sword reasserted its importance during the early medieval Migration Period, or 'Dark Ages'. As we saw at Sutton Hoo, Roman-style pattern-welded weapons continued to be made, and swords and swordsmanship to be celebrated in contemporary poems such as *Beowulf*. Roman sword terminology lived on into later eras, *gladius* inspiring *glaive* and *claymore*, *spatha* leading to Italian *spada* and French *epée*.

101. A relief depicting a Pompeii-type sword with its scabbard and belt, from Pula, Croatia, late first century AD.

This was part of a more general remembering of the fabled power of imperial arms in Europe long after the demise of the Roman west, seen in Charlemagne's attempts to refound the empire. Later centuries saw many proposals and attempts to revive Roman-style armies and soldiers, including Machiavelli's sixteenth-century *Art of War* and the new Vegetius-inspired disciplined European armies of the seventeenth century, Marshal de Saxe's *Reveries* about ideal armies (1757), the Roman republican echoes of the French revolutionary armies and Napoleon's imperial eagles. Subsequently, there have been military formations called 'legions', such as Hitler's Condor Legion in Spain, while the French Foreign Legion is with us still.

The Roman soldier has also become part of modern popular culture, not least through the distorting lens of 'sword-and-sandal' movies such as *Ben-Hur*, *Spartacus*, *Gladiator* and *The Eagle*. Since the 1970s there have been growing scholarly inspired attempts at more authentic recreation of Roman martial material culture and practices. Using modern archaeological studies of actual examples, Roman arms have been reproduced. Skilled modern smiths have replicated Roman swords, including magnificent pattern-welded examples (Plate XIII). Such replica equipment has then been tried out (within ethical limits!), for weight, durability and so on. I have myself found riding a horse, shooting an arrow, wearing armour, and wielding a sword invaluable in providing fundamental physical insights simply impossible from an armchair. Equally valuable is discussing practical matters with the more serious and painstaking re-enactment groups, notably the much-imitated British-based Ermine Street Guard, who simulate imperial legionaries of the reign of Vespasian.[13]

Groups like the Ermine Street Guard stage popular public displays of Roman arms, drill and tactics. These are skilful, spectacular, stirring, informative – but, of course, necessarily bloodless. Such displays are largely subsumed into the 'Heritage industry', in which 'history' becomes just another commodity in a tautologically 'globalized world'. Via the internet you can buy your own plausible imitation of a republican Delos-type *gladius Hispaniensis*, a Mainz or Pompeii sword, or *spathae* of various kinds, made in India.[14] Or if you can afford it, you can commission a pattern-welded replica from a real swordsmith.

Like movies, all this becomes the stuff of 'Fantasy Romes', which may be educational, benign or more dangerous. Doubtless we will continue to remember the power of Rome's armies and the courage and aggression of her soldiers; but if we are to understand the empire, we must also remember those who fell to the Roman sword, or suffered in its shadow. In the Garden of Gethsemane at Jerusalem, in the imperial province of Judea, men armed with staves and swords came to arrest Jesus, for subsequent torture and execution by Roman soldiers as agents of the emperor and the local temporal authorities. Simon Peter drew his own sword and struck off the right ear of Malchus, servant of the High Priest. 'Then said Jesus unto him, "Put up again thy sword into his place: for all they that take the sword shall perish with the sword"'.[15]

The Roman world that Jesus knew was indeed largely created, maintained and ultimately destroyed by the sword. Collapse of the more strategically vulnerable western empire was largely a long-term consequence of Rome's own military aggression, and the changes she precipitated among the barbarians beyond the frontiers.[16] Likewise, the eastern empire was subsequently shaken and diminished, in the sixth century, by the Sasanians (whose rise was precipitated by Rome), then by the Arabs, a new military power created by the proximity of these warring empires. Further hacked by Crusaders' swords, it was finally extinguished by Ottoman cannon. For the West, the Roman *gladius*, as fearsome material artefact and grim metaphor, remains central to our common history.

# Timeline

| | |
|---|---|
| 753 BC | Traditional foundation date of Rome |
| 509 | Expulsion of the kings; foundation of the Roman republic |
| 508 | Foundation of democracy at Athens |
| 499? | Battle of Lake Regillus |
| 491? | Coriolanus and Volscians attack Rome |
| 396? | Destruction of Veii |
| 390? | Senonian Gauls sack Rome |
| 343–341 | First Samnite War |
| 340–338 | Latin War |
| 334–323 | Alexander the Great conquers the Persian empire, from Anatolia and Egypt to Iran and beyond |
| 332 | Death of Alexander: fragmentation of his empire into Hellenistic successor states |
| 326–304 | Second (Great) Samnite War |
| 298–290 | Third Samnite War |
| 295 | Battle of Sentinum |
| 280–275 | Pyrrhic War |
| 288 | The Mamertines seize Messana |
| 264–241 | First Punic War |
| 247 | Foundation of Arsacid dynasty: start of rise of Parthian kingdom |
| 222 | Battle of Clastidium during Roman conquest of Po valley Gauls |
| 218–201 | Second Punic War (Hannibalic War) |
| 216 | Battle of Cannae |
| 202 | Battle of Zama |
| 200–196 | War with Macedon |
| 197 | Macedonian phalanx defeated at Cynoscephalae |
| 192–189 | War against Seleucid empire |
| 190 | Seleucid army defeated at Magnesia |
| 181 | Start of Celtiberian Wars |
| 167 | Battle of Pydna |
| 166 | Romans abolish Macedonian kingdom |
| 149–146 | Third Punic War |
| 146 | War with Achaean Greeks: destruction of Corinth and Carthage |
| 133 | End of Third Celtiberian War. Pergamum bequeathed to Rome. Assassination of Ti. Gracchus |
| 121 | Assassination of C. Gracchus |
| 113 | Appearance of the Cimbri and Teutones |
| 105 | Cimbri and Teutones annihilate Roman armies at Arausio |

# Notes

### Preface, pp. 6–11

1. Caesar *Gallic War* 2.7–10.
2. The armies of the early Chinese empires were also very large and sophisticated: Lewis 2007 pp. 30–50; Rosenstein 2009.
3. Cf. Italian *soldi*, 'money'.
4. Beard 2007. On imperial triumphs, much rarer than republican ones – thirteen between 31 BC and AD 235 – see Campbell 1984 pp. 133–42.
5. For an exhaustive recent study of Roman swords, see Miks 2007. Good introductory treatments of the 'Roman Army' are widely available, for example Keppie 1984 for the republic, and Goldsworthy 2003, Le Bohec 1994 or Webster 1985 for the earlier empire. For the later Roman/Byzantine armies see Southern and Dixon 1996, Le Bohec 2006 and Treadgold 1995. See also Erdkamp 2007.
6. The literature on forts and frontiers is vast. Western forts: Johnson 1983; Bidwell 2007; for example, Inchtuthil legionary base: Pitts and St Joseph 1985; Elginhaugh auxiliary fort: Hanson 2007. On frontiers: Whittaker 1994; the example of Hadrian's Wall in Britain: Breeze and Dobson 2000.
7. Intelligence: Austin and Rankov 1995; Sheldon 2005.
8. Caesar *Gallic War* 2.19–28.

### Introduction:
### Swords and Soldiers, pp. 14–37

1. From http://classics.mit.edu/Virgil/aeneid.html.
2. For example 'The *pax Augusta*, which has spread to the regions of the east and the west and to the bounds of the north and of the south, preserves every corner of the world safe from the fear of brigandage', Velleius Paterculus 2.126.3.
3. For example Woolf 1998; Wallace-Hadrill 2008.
4. For the Jewish perspective on the Roman military as an alien army of occupation: Isaac 1992.
5. Josephus *Jewish War* 5.2–6.9.3.

'…the siege of Jerusalem was probably the greatest single slaughter in ancient history', Lendon 2005 p. 256.

6. In scare-quotes because the idea Britain was Celtic is a modern one, although its multiple societies were certainly related to the people actually called Celts in regions such as Gaul (France): James 1999; Collis 2003.
7. Trans. Canon Roberts, 1912, *Livy, History of Rome*, London, Dent. An alternative account (Aulus Gellius 9.13) says Manlius also took his head.
8. This is not intended to be a monograph on the archaeology of the Roman sword, for which see Miks 2007.
9. Death of Archimedes: Livy, 25.31; Valerius Maximus 8.7 and Plutarch *Parallel Lives: Marcellus* 19.4, which specifies that he was killed by a sword.
10. Plutarch *Parallel Lives: Antony*, 76–77. However, outside civil war, it was rare for commanders to commit suicide in the later republic or empire. Varus was an exception: Goldsworthy 1996 p. 165 fn. 87.
11. Josephus *Jewish War* 7.9.1–2.
12. The survivors of Cotta's and Sabinus' force, defeated by the Eburones at Atuatuca in 54 BC in Caesar's worst setback during the conquest of Gaul, committed suicide: Caesar *Gallic War*, 5.37. In AD 47, 400 Romans cut off by Frisians preferred suicide to surrender: Tacitus *Annals* 4.73; Goldsworthy 1996 p. 262.
13. The *Oxford English Dictionary* defines violence as 'The exercise of physical force so as to inflict injury on, or cause damage to, persons or property; action or conduct characterized by this; treatment or usage tending to cause bodily injury or forcibly interfering with personal freedom'.
14. Juvenal 16.10–13, 24–25. The Vindolanda tablets include a letter of complaint by a civilian whom a soldier had 'beaten [with] rods',

Bowman and Thomas 1994, p. 344. Some soldiers carried a knobbed staff that could be used offensively: Speidel 1993.

15. Horace *Satires* 1.2.41; 1.3.119; in the Bible, used on Jesus: Mark 15.15.

16. '…Roman government depended largely on force and its handmaiden, fear', Lendon 1997 p. 3.

17. Quoted in Dalrymple 1994 pp. 266–67.

18. For example crossed broadswords in the badge of the British Army, and sabres in those of US Army 'Cavalry' units.

19. Special swords are used in Spanish bullfighting, and some Sasanian hunting scenes show kings killing lions with the sword, but these are allegories of royal power and courage rather than depictions of reality, unless the lions were heavily drugged.

20. Battle-axes were known but little used in the Roman era (Bishop and Coulston 2006 p. 205, fig. 133) and have rarely challenged the primacy of the sword even when they were employed, as in the Viking era. Neither did they offer the option of thrusting.

21. Leaving aside team operated machines such as catapults or warships.

22. See, for example, Künzl 1996 for discussion of decoration on early imperial *gladii*. Also Künzl 2008.

23. On the phenomenon in prehistoric Europe, see Bradley 1998.

24. Many of the weapons illustrated are from rivers, lakes or bogs.

25. Livy 5.34–49.

26. The sword as metaphorical opposite of peace: for example Matthew 10.34. St Paul uses multiple armour and sword metaphors (*Epistle to the Ephesians* 6).

27. Trans. C. D. Yonge, 1888, *Cicero's Tusculan Disputations*, New York, Harper.

28. The axe appears not to have been used for execution.

29. 'To have simple *imperium* is to have power of the sword (*potestas gladii*)

to punish the wicked…', Ulpian, in Justinian *Digest* 2.1.3; 'Those who rule entire provinces have full power of the sword (*ius gladii*)…' Justinian *Digest* 1.18.6.8: (trans. Mommsen *et al.* 1985). Roman practice is presumably the source of the familiar personification of Justice as blindfolded with sword and scales, but this is post-Roman: *Iustitia* was most often personified on Roman coins with sceptre and *patera*.

30. Suetonius *Twelve Caesars: Vitellius* 8.1.

31. The sword symbolizing unsanctioned violence: Horace *Satires* 2.3.276; or dangerous armed individuals: Cicero *Phillipics* 2.106.

32. Skinner 2005 p. 210.

33. Hallett and Skinner 1997; Walters 1997; Skinner 2005. On the relationship of power to violence and sex in Roman culture, see now Mattingly 2010 pp. 94–121.

34. Plautus *Pseudolus* 4.7.85. These were part of a much wider repertoire of military metaphors for love and sex in the writings of Plautus and other authors, where wooing and seduction were described in the language of military service (*militia amoris*), campaign and, not least, siege. Latin military vocabulary for sieges distinguished blockade (*obsidio*) from assault (*oppugnatio*): Cloud 1993; Roth 2006. The earliest English usage of the term *vagina* for the female sexual organ recorded in the *Oxford English Dictionary* is as late as 1682.

35. Sometimes comprising the title: for example, Peddie 1994. 'Roman military machine': Tomlin 1999; Brewer 2002.

36. *Contra* the 'machine metaphor', see Goldsworthy 1996 pp. 283–85; James 2002. It may well be asked, if the twin notions of 'the Roman Army: war machine' are so glaringly inappropriate, where, then, did they come from? In short, I believe that what happened was this: since the Roman army has

been seen as directly ancestral to modern armed forces, used since the Renaissance as a model for new state armies, there has been a tendency to assume that, conversely, 'the Roman Army' must have been essentially like modern forces – a *non sequitur*.

37. Pronounced '*mee*–lays' and 'mill–*ee*–tays' respectively.

38. Pronounced 'ex–*er*–kitooss', the singular –oo– as in 'book', the plural –oo– as in 'boot'.

39. For example Hadrian issued coins (*sestertii*) for the various provincial armies he inspected: EXERCITUS BRITANNICUS, EXERCITUS DACICUS, EXERCITUS MAURETANICUS, EXERCITUS SYRIACUS, etc.

40. There were a few exceptions, of imperial coins referring to 'the army' singular and unspecified, but often (as with the earliest examples from the civil wars of AD 69) these are appealing to the section of the military currently loyal to the man on the coin. Elagabalus and Philip the Arab minted *Fides exercitus* ('loyalty of the army') coins, while Constantine's *gloria exercitus* ('glory of the army') issues significantly belong to the 330s, the years late in his reign when the whole empire was finally under his sole rule; so, relatively briefly, his was the only army. The fleets were treated as units of soldiers; there was no separate 'Roman navy' either.

41. A notion originally developed in the context of understanding nationalisms (Anderson 1991), but usefully applicable to other groupings, including large armies.

42. This is no mere fashionable revisionism or 'deconstruction' for its own sake. All fields of study need, from time to time, to re-examine and overhaul their basic concepts, and be prepared to abandon the inadequate and outdated for better ones that may radically shift, and improve, our perspective.

43. How far modern reality actually diverges from this ideal is another question.

44. The famous inventor Heron of Alexandria wrote a book on the subject, *Automata*, among other works on ingenious machinery. Complex mechanisms provided fashionable toys for the rich: Petronius *Satyricon* 54.4.

45. Slaves were conceptualized as living tools by Aristotle (*Politics*, 1.4), and more literally treated as such by Romans. For example Cato recommends sale of defective livestock, worn-out equipment, and old or sick slaves, listed in that order: *On Agriculture* 2.7.

46. For example over the young imperial prince Gaius. From his miniature military uniform the soldiers gave him his nickname, 'little boots': Caligula (Suetonius *Twelve Caesars: Gaius* 9).

47. Since morale remains so crucial even to the most mechanized force, it is moot how far even modern armies are usefully termed 'war-machines'.

48. Trans. B. O. Foster 1922, *Livy, History of Rome,* vol. II, Loeb Classical Library, Cambridge MA, Harvard University Press.

49. According to Pliny the Elder (*Natural History* 10.16), the eagle legionary standard was introduced only in 104 BC under Marius, replacing wolf, minotaur, horse and bull standards. A *denarius* of 82 BC is its earliest representation (Fig. 3): Bishop and Coulston 2006 p. 68.

50. Caesar *Gallic War,* 4.25.

51. Polybius 6.22. It is not clear that the animal skins worn by later standard bearers and military musicians actually included wolves, alongside bears and lions.

52. Horace *Epistles* 2.2.37–40.

53. Livy 1.4.

54. Livy 1.7.

55. Petronius *Satyricon* 62 (first century AD).

56. Suetonius *Twelve Caesars: Tiberius* 25.1.

57. On the difficulties Greek, even Spartan, officers had in enforcing obedience in action, see Lendon 2005 pp. 71–77.

58. On the competitive nature of Roman armies: Lendon 1997, especially pp. 237–66.

59. For example the general Decius, before explaining his plan to his soldiers, told them that they needed to keep silent while listening, 'without any of the usual soldiers' acclaim', Livy 7.35.

60. Cf. Kipling's poem 'Tommy' for similar sentiments about soldiers in Victorian Britain.

61. Livy 1. 19. No trace survives of the republican temple, which stood on the road between the Basilica Aemilia and the Curia Julia.

62. Goldsworthy 1996 ch. 2 for an example of this.

63. The use of the image of the two-edged sword to connote double danger is, however, apparently post-medieval, at least in English. The earliest recorded usage known to me is by Thomas More in 1535 (Ackroyd 1998 pp. 377–84). See also Dryden's 1687 *The Hind & the Panther* III. 192, referring to ambiguous oracles: 'Your Delphic sword…Is double-edged and cuts on either side.'

64. For an account of the development of Roman swords in the context of military equipment as a whole, see Bishop and Coulston 2006. There is now a vast two-volume German monograph on Roman swords: Miks 2007. Concentrating on the imperial era, although also covering the republican background, it catalogues and discusses known Roman sword finds. Essential for specialists, it is not for the faint-hearted! Another very important publication on the superb mid-late imperial swords from Illerup, and others from 'barbarian' territory (Barbaricum), also appeared the same year: Biborski and Ilkjaer 2007.

65. Varro *On the Latin Language* 5.116;

Bishop and Coulston 2006 p. 54.

66. Tacitus *Annals* 12.35. Trans. by author.

67. Bishop and Coulston 2006 p. 41.

68. Columella *On Agriculture*, 12.22.1; Pliny the Elder *Natural History* 23.139; related to English 'spade' and the diminutive *spatula*: Celsus 8.15.4; 7.10.

69. Apuleius *The Golden Ass* (*Metamorphoses*) 1.4; 9.40.

70. Youtie and Winter 1951 no. 467.

71. Tomlin 1999 128–29.

72. Vegetius 2.15. Miks has proposed calling all swords with blades (excluding hilt) in the range 350/400–500 mm *gladii*, those over 600 mm *spathae*, and those 500–600 mm *semispathae*: Miks 2007 p. 435. This has the virtue of neatness but (although he notes the need for some flexibility in this) may potentially confuse. The scheme excludes from the category '*gladius*' those archaeological examples of longer weapons of the later republican era, which most specialists agree represent the *gladius Hispaniensis* of the texts (although Miks does indeed argue, to me unconvincingly, that these are misidentified: Miks 2007 pp. 435–36).

73. See note 64.

74. Purdue 2000 p. 135.

75. The bird-headed '*parazonium*', possibly of Hellenistic Greek inspiration: Barnett 1983. The only archaeological example is of unknown provenance: Miks 2007 A203.

76. A possible example was found at Carlisle: McCarthy 2002 fig. 33. A wooden sword, of gladiatorial rather than military pattern, was found at the Roman fort of Oberaden, Germany: von Schnurbein 1979.

77. Martial *Book of Spectacles* 31 (Coleman's numbering).

78. Except for a coin image of the one-armed M. Sergius, I know of no evidence for left-handed weapon use in Roman times. It would disrupt shield formations.

Ancient left-handed soldiers presumably just had to learn to fight right-handed.

79. Petronius *Satyricon* 80, for unarmoured men drawing swords, one wrapping his cloak round his arm and dropping into a fighting crouch.

80. Vegetius 1.12. Bishop and Coulston 2006 p. 56.

81. Plutarch *Parallel Lives: Caesar* 45; *Pompey* 69. During the battle, the Pompeians also aimed for the face: one of Caesar's centurions was killed by a sword thrust through the mouth, which emerged from the back of his neck: Plutarch *Parallel Lives: Caesar* 44.

82. Trans. E. Cary, 1950, *The Roman Antiquities of Dionysius of Halicarnassus, Books XI–XX*, Loeb Classical Library, Cambridge MA, Harvard University Press; Pleiner 1993 p. 26.

83. Polybius 2.33. Trans. E. S. Shuckburgh, 1889, *The Histories of Polybius*, London and New York, Macmillan.

84. At Telamon, 225 BC, Polybius reports that Gallic swords bent in both planes, and had to be stamped flat: (2.33.3). Metal analysis showing the actually variable quality of La Tène swords: Pleiner 1993 pp. 156–59. Repeated references to Gallic and British swords being purely slashing weapons lacking points for thrusting: for example Polybius 2:30 on Gallic swords; Tacitus *Agricola* 36 on Caledonian British weapons. For archaeological finds see Pleiner 1993; Stead 2005.

85. Polybius 3.114: 'For that of the *Roman can thrust with as deadly effect as it can cut* while the Gallic sword can only cut, and that requires some room' (my emphases). Adapted from trans. E. S. Shuckburgh, 1889, *The Histories of Polybius*, London and New York, Macmillan.

86. From the Etrusco-Roman François tomb to Adamklissi and Column of Marcus (Figs 17, 53 and 58). A statue

in the British Museum of Mithras killing the celestial bull shows him using a reversed sword in this manner.

### Prelude, pp. 38–41

1. Punic = Phoenician.
2. Polybius saw with his own eyes Roman soldiers played dice on famous paintings: Polybius 39.13.
3. Polybius 29.27; Livy 45.12.
4. John Mann saw the republic as struggling to keep pace with the incredible success of its soldiers: Mann 1974 p. 509.
5. Erdkamp 1998.
6. Trans E. Sage 1935, *Livy, History of Rome, Books XXXI–XXXIV*, Loeb Classical Library, Cambridge MA, Harvard University Press; London, Heinemann.
7. See especially Harris 1985 for emphasis on Roman aggressiveness in the republic.
8. Livy 1.16. Trans. Rev. Canon Roberts, 1912, *Livy's History of Rome*, New York, Dent.
9. Pers. comm.
10. Livy 5.21–23.
11. Walbank 2002.
12. Polybius 1.1.
13. As Pyrrhus of Epirus had also already discovered before Hannibal (pp. 60–61).
14. My understanding of the political dimension of the rise of Roman power, the 'open hand', is based primarily on the ideas of Nicola Terrenato, which still await full publication, but see Terrenato 1998a, 1998b, 2001; Terrenato 2007a.

### Chapter 1 Forging the Roman Sword: The Republic to 270 BC, pp. 42–69

1. Livy 10.27–29.
2. Then regarded as beyond Italy, which stopped at the Apennines. The Po plain became part of Italy during imperial times.
3. Livy, 10.26.14–15.
4. Livy, 10.26.11.
5. Livy, 10.27.
6. Livy. 10.27.8–9. Trans B. O. Foster 1926, *Livy, History of Rome*

*Books VIII–X*, Cambridge MA, Harvard University Press; London, Heinemann.
7. 340 BC: Livy, 8.9.
8. Livy 10.28–29. Trans B. O. Foster 1926, *Livy, History of Rome Books VIII–X*, Cambridge MA, Harvard University Press; London, Heinemann.
9. Livy 10.29.11–15. Trans B. O. Foster 1926, *Livy, History of Rome Books VIII–X*, Cambridge MA, Harvard University Press; London, Heinemann.
10. Livy 10.30.8–10. Trans B. O. Foster 1926, *Livy, History of Rome Books VIII–X*, Cambridge MA, Harvard University Press; London, Heinemann.
11. This is a common omission in ancient battle accounts. The actual field of Sentinum remains, to my knowledge, unlocated.
12. Livy 10.26, 30.
13. Livy 8.9.
14. Keegan 1988 pp. 35–41.
15. Miks 2007 pp. 30–33, 435.
16. All blade lengths given exclude the tang.
17. Livy 2.46.
18. Cornell 1995 pp. 135–41.
19. Debris from the manufacture of a batch of Iron Age chariot fittings at Gussage All Saints in Britain fits with the notion of itinerant specialists moving from commission to commission: Wainwright 1979; Foster 1980.
20. Bishop and Coulston 2006 p. 233; Roman production in Carthago Nova, Spain, 210 BC: Livy 26.47.2; production in Carthage itself during the Third Punic War: Appian *Punic Wars* 8.93.
21. Bishop and Coulston 2006 p. 232. More information survives for the early imperial period.
22. The earliest detailed references are in the context of the Pyrrhic Wars, which alternately have the Romans copying the regular layout of Pyrrhus' camp after Malventum (Frontinus *Stratagems* 4.1.14), and Pyrrhus marvelling at the order of a Roman camp (Plutarch *Parallel*

*Lives: Pyrrhus* 16.4–5). However, Philip v of Macedon is supposed to have said effectively the same things as Pyrrhus *c.* 200 BC, suggesting the same story became attached to more than one of Rome's enemies (Livy 31.34.1–5). One or the other Pyrrhic references is presumably garbled, but both suggest the Romans went into the Punic Wars using marching camps.

23. Goldsworthy 1996 p. 113.
24. Polybius 6.26–36.
25. Livy contrasts the actions and personalities of the two consuls, in ways perhaps coloured by traditional patrician bias against plebeian magistrates.
26. For example Polybius 2.33.
27. This is roughly consistent with archaeological evidence. There seem to have been a group of Iron Age villages, which began to coalesce into something recognizable as a city-state by the seventh century BC.
28. Treherne 1995.
29. For some skeletal data, Robb 1997.
30. Lendon 1997 p. 32; Péristiany 1966.
31. Vendettas that plagued Sicily, and still plague Albania.
32. Smith 2006.
33. Motta and Terrenato 2006.
34. Where it still often remains incomplete even now, citizens retaining the right to use 'reasonable force', even lethal violence, to protect their lives and property, notably in the USA.
35. Harries 2007.
36. The Latin term *latro* originally meant 'mercenary', but in line with this change came to mean exclusively 'bandit': Grünewald 2004 p. 5.
37. For example one P. Valerius, possibly P. Valerius Publicola, and his 'companions of war', a personal war-band on an inscription of *c.* 500 BC from Satricum: Cornell 1995 p. 144.
38. Livy 2.48–49; an early manifestation of what became a tradition of particular senatorial families tending to monopolize

dealings with particular foreign enemies, first on the battlefield, later as patrons of the conquered.
39. Livy 2.34–40.
40. Eckstein 2006 also argues that Rome was not exceptional in kind, but downplays the role of the sword too far.
41. Eckstein 2006 p.85. On Alexander's conquests as spear-won land: Diodorus Siculus 17.17.2.
42. Fetial priests and ritual procedure for declaring war: Livy 1.32.13–14.
43. This reflects the 'contractual' nature of Roman religion (seeking to strike quasi-legal reciprocal deals with deities, of offerings or temples in return for their favour), and the importance of fear – here fear of the gods – in Roman culture.
44. So also Eckstein 2006, but see note 40. Like many 'new' ideas, the importance of Rome's skill at making and managing alliance networks has been identified before, but has been widely overlooked. Carl von Clausewitz wrote: 'Rome …became great more through the alliances which it formed, and through which neighbouring peoples by degrees became amalgamated with it into one whole, than through actual conquests. It was only after having spread itself in this manner all over Southern Italy, that it began to advance as a really conquering power', *On War* (*Vom Kriege*), 1832, 8.3, trans. by J.J. Graham 1873, London, N. Trübner and Company.
45. See p. 41 and its note 14. Eckstein's emphasis on relations at state level also sees alliances as crucial, but because it is an International Relations perspective, it is too 'presentist' and pays far too little attention to what seem to me the crucial factors of socio-political dynamics within polities, which were very unlike modern nation-states, notably quasi-private aristocratic interactions across the boundaries between them.
46. Migration of the *gens Claudia*: Livy 2.16.3–5. Exile of the perhaps

legendary Coriolanus: Livy 2.35–40.
47. For example Spurius Maelius, a rich Roman with 'friends and dependants' in Etruria: Livy 4.12 or 13. Campanians 'who were connected [to the Romans] by personal ties of hospitality and kinship': Livy 8.3.
48. Terrenato's 'elite negotiation model': see p. 41 and its note 14.
49. Livy 4.9–10.
50. A good example is provided by Tusculum: Livy 6.26.
51. Livy 7.29–31.
52. Livy 2.31–33.
53. Livy 6.38.
54. Livy 4.49–50; 7.12–14.
55. Livy 7.38–42.
56. For example the *Lex Julia de vi publica*: Justinian, *Digest* 68.6.1. Harries 2007 pp. 106–11.
57. For Romulus establishing the *pomerium*: Tacitus *Annals* 12.24. On the *pomerium* in principle, see Varro *On the Latin Language* 5.143. On the nature of the *pomerium*, and its periodic extension: Livy 1.44.
58. A manubial temple founded 296 BC (Livy 10.19.17), at the moment I suggest Roman ferocity was reaching its zenith.
59. *Tubilustrium* (23 March), and *armilustrium* (19 October), ritual 'decontamination' of the army and its weapons after contact with blood and strangers: Scullard 1981 pp. 94–95, 195.
60. In commemoration of which they renamed *Malventum* ('bad-winds') *Beneventum* ('good-winds').
61. Trans. E. S. Shuckburgh, 1889, *The Histories of Polybius*, London and New York, Macmillan.
62. Harris has commented on Romans' extreme levels of ferocity combined with high level of political culture: Harris 1985 p. 53.
63. Welch 2006 p. 7.

**Chapter 2 Obsessed with Victory: The Imperial Republic 270–30 BC, pp. 70–115**

1. Trans. E. S. Shuckburgh, 1889, *The Histories of Polybius*, London

and New York, Macmillan.

2. Polybius 3.110–17, Livy 22.44–51. For an attempt to provide a detailed 'Keeganesque' (Keegan 1988) account of the battle, see Daly 2002.
3. Polybius 1.7.1–4.
4. Polybius 3.90.
5. Polybius 18.28.
6. 'Higher level tactics' or 'Grand Tactical manoeuvres': Sabin 1996.
7. Polybius 18.28.
8. Polybius 1.21, 37.
9. Frontinus *Stratagems* 3.18.2; Livy 26.11.
10. Polybius 15.13.
11. *Candide,* chapter 23.
12. Polybius 6.25. Trans. E. S. Shuckburgh, 1889, *The Histories of Polybius,* London and New York, Macmillan.
13. Polybius 1.21.
14. Polybius Fragment 22 (see note 22 below).
15. On the origins of the '*gladius Hispaniensis*' see Connolly 1997; Quesada Sanz 1997. Miks disputes the identification of the archaeological examples with the *gladius Hispaniensis* of the texts (Miks 2007 pp. 435–36), but his arguments that the origins of the early imperial 'Mainz'-type sword are Greco-Italic, and that it is an evolutionary descendant of the *xiphos,* are unconvincing – especially regarding the difficulty of explaining why the later republican weapon was described as 'Spanish'.
16. Delos sword: Siebert 1987; Šmihel: Horvat 1997; Bishop and Coulston 2006 p. 56. Examples from Vrhnika, Caminreal and Alesia: Rapin 2001. Also Jericho: Stiebel 2004 p. 230.
17. Miks takes a more cautious position on the nature and evolution of the *gladius Hispaniensis* than is outlined here (Miks 2007).
18. The Delos dimensions, especially width, are narrow estimates as it is still in its scabbard.
19. Bishop and Coulston 2006 pp. 82–83.

20. As Livy describes: 22.46.5.
21. Ring-mounted scabbards were also used in fifth-century Greece, for example appearing on a red-figure vessel of *c.* 460 BC (Miks 2007 Abb.6.E. and see Fig. 16), but the combination with a metal frame-scabbard still seems to be specifically Iberian, especially given the association with the unambiguously Iberian *pugio,* itself in a similar scabbard.
22. A passage in the Byzantine compilation known as the *Suda,* discussing '*machaira*', believed to preserve a fragment of Polybius' *Histories,* known as Fragment 22. Translation provided by Graham Shipley, to whom I am also indebted for advice on the meaning of the passage.
23. Polybius 15.15.
24. 'With the shield they also carry a sword hanging down by their right thigh, which is called a Spanish sword. It has an excellent point, and can deal a formidable blow with either edge, because its blade is strong and unbending.' Polybius 6.23. Trans. adapted from E. S. Shuckburgh, 1889, *The Histories of Polybius,* London and New York, Macmillan.
25. Polybius 2.33. Trans. from E. S. Shuckburgh, 1889, *The Histories of Polybius,* London and New York, Macmillan.
26. Polybius specifically notes their swords' *suitability* for both (6.23).
27. Polybius 3.114.
28. Livy 30.36.10-11.
29. Rome lost 80,000 soldiers and 40,000 'servants and camp followers', according to a surviving excerpt of Livy's lost Book 67.
30. At the battle of Clastidium in 222 BC he killed the Gallic king Viridomarus with his own hand, becoming the third and last recorded winner of the *spolia opima* (Plutarch *Parallel Lives: Marcellus* 6–7). The first had allegedly been Romulus himself, the second A. Cornelius Cossus in the fifth century BC (Livy 1.10).

31. Whether the parade was officially a triumph or 'merely' an ovation, Marcellus behaved like a *triumphator.* The idea that third-century Rome was materially poor is a fiction of later Roman moralists; it was already materially rich and its art sophisticated, but statuary remained small-scale and largely terracotta. But in 211 BC the spectacle of large quantities of life-size Classical and Hellenistic Greek statuary of the finest quality in marble and bronze was a novelty which made a huge and lasting impression: McDonnell 2006.
32. Welch 2006 p. 17.
33. Polybius 10.40.
34. Appian *The Spanish Wars.* 34–36; MacMullen 1984 p. 454.
35. Polybius 1.7.
36. Trans. E. S. Shuckburgh, 1889, *The Histories of Polybius,* London and New York, Macmillan.
37. Chaniotis 2005.
38. Keppie 1984 pp. 33–35. Polybius 6.19–21.
39. Widely regarded as another essential asset in war: Sulla was nicknamed Felix, 'the Fortunate'.
40. Polybius 18.29–31.
41. Polybius 15.15. Trans. E.S. Shuckburgh, 1889, *The Histories of Polybius,* London and New York, Macmillan.
42. Polybius 18.30. Trans. E.S. Shuckburgh, 1889, *The Histories of Polybius,* London and New York, Macmillan.
43. Sekunda 2001. Generations later this adoption of Roman ways of war in the Hellenistic East would culminate with the Roman-style soldiers of King Deiotarus of Galatia simply becoming incorporated as an imperial legion, *XXII Deiotariana.*
44. The Royal Navy from the mid-eighteenth through the nineteenth century achieved a similar moral ascendancy over its foes: Rodger 2004 p. 272.
45. On European climate data, see Büntgen *et al.* 2011.
46. Polybius 2.38.

47. Sidebottom 2004.
48. Welch 2006 p. 7.
49. Plutarch *Parallel Lives: Titus Flamininus* 10.3–5.
50. Strabo literally says '10,000' daily (*Geography* 14.5.2), but it is likely that this implausibly high and round figure means 'very many': Trümper 2009 p. 32, fn 119.
51. Livy, 42.34.
52. Polybius 6.19.4.
53. Rosenstein 2004.
54. Terrenato 2007b.
55. Note 29.
56. Valerius Maximus 2.3.2. This roughly coincides with the recruitment of landless men who, not having hitherto been expected to serve as soldiers, perhaps typically had less prior weapons training anyway. See also Frontinus *Stratagems* 4.2.2.
57. Keppie 1984 pp. 59–68.
58. Although maniples (pairs of centuries) would last long into the empire for administrative purposes.
59. Keppie 1984 pp. 67–68; Pliny the Elder *Natural History* 10.4.
60. 'Social' from *socii*, 'allies'. Also called the Italian or Marsic War.
61. Appian *Civil Wars* 1.5.38–1.6.53.
62. Lendon 2005 p. 219.
63. Plutarch *Parallel Lives: Marius*, 7. 4–5. Campbell 1984 pp. 17–18, 32–58.
64. Suetonius *Twelve Caesars: Caesar* 67.
65. Polyaenus *Stratagems* 8.23.22.
66. Lendon 1997 pp. 240–42. Overplaying it would later help cost emperor Caracalla his life.
67. Ribera i Lacomba and Calvo Galvez 1995; Lacomba 2006.
68. Leach 1978 p. 48.
69. Rich 1993.
70. The Third Servile War: Plutarch *Parallel Lives: Crassus* 8–11, Appian *Civil Wars* 1.116–121.
71. Appian *Civil Wars* 1.120.
72. Although the distinctly unmilitary career of the 'new man' M. Tullius Cicero revealed that new ways of reaching the consulship were developing.
73. Keaveney 2007.

74. Plutarch *Parallel Lives: Sertorius*. Spann 1987 pp. 80–86.
75. Reddé 1996.
76. Plutarch *Parallel Lives: Caesar* 15.5.
77. Caesar, *Gallic War* 8.44, where Caesar is quite candid about his motives on this occasion.
78. Caesar, *Gallic War* 5.24–41, 6.34.
79. Examples from Port-Nidau, Switzerland: Wyss *et al.* 2002.
80. Brunaux 1999.
81. Caesar *Gallic War* 2.10.
82. Caesar *Gallic War* 1.18.
83. Commonly equated with the archaeological 'La Tène culture'.
84. The conquest and its aftermath meant that the Gauls became not only subjects of Rome, but clients of Caesar's descendants, the Julio-Claudian emperors, many families acquiring the family name Julius. Julius Indus was an auxiliary cavalry commander, while Classicianus became imperial procurator of Britain (*RIB* 12).
85. For an accessible modern account of the era, see Holland 2003.
86. Keppie 1991.
87. Nicknamed *x Equestris*, 'Knightly': Caesar *Gallic War* 1.42; Keppie 1984 pp. 83–84, 209.
88. Messer 1920.
89. Appian *Civil Wars* 3.94–95; Cassius Dio 46.47–49.
90. Chrissanthos 2001 p. 68.
91. Suetonius *Twelve Caesars: Julius Caesar* 69; Cassius Dio 41.26–35.
92. Chrissanthos 2001; Suetonius *Twelve Caesars: Julius Caesar* 70; Cassius Dio 42.52–55.
93. Chrissanthos 2001.
94. Plutarch, *Parallel Lives: Crassus* 24–25.
95. On 'globalization' of Roman culture, Hingley 1989.
96. Caesar *Civil Wars* 3.4.4, 103.5, 110.2.

### Chapter 3 'Our Weapons and Armour': The Earlier Empire
**30 BC–AD 167, pp. 116–175**

1. Becker *et al.* 2003.
2. *Clades Variana*: Cassius Dio 56. 18–24; Suetonius *Twelve Caesars: Augustus* 23, *Tiberius* 17–18. Kalkriese battlefield evidence:

Schlüter 1999; Schlüter and Wiegels 1999; Wells 2003.
3. Often memorably mistranslated as 'Herrmann the German'.
4. Trans. F. W. Shipley, 1924, *Velleius Paterculus*, Loeb Classical Library, London, Heinemann and Cambridge MA, Harvard University Press.
5. Suetonius *Twelve Caesars: Augustus* 26.
6. Lendon 2005 pp. 11–12.
7. Woolf 1998; Hingley 2005; Wallace-Hadrill 2008.
8. Cassius Dio 51.22. Pohlsander 1969.
9. Ulbert 1969.
10. Bishop and Coulston 2006 p. 78. Miks 2007 pp. 57–64, 436–37, Vortafel C. 1–7. Tafn 8–22.
11. Miks 2007 pp. 58–65.
12. E.g. the Fulham sword, now in the British Museum: Manning 1985 no. V2, 148–49, pl. XIX–XX. Miks 2007 p. 437. The commonest variant from Augustan times to the mid-first century AD was the curved-tapering 'Haltern-Camulodunum' form. The parallel-edged 'Wederath' variant, which appears in the AD 30s–40s, prefigures the familiar Pompeii form.
13. Bishop and Coulston 2006 p. 78.
14. Klumbach 1970; Walker and Burnett 1981 pp. 49–55. Miks classifies it as a 'Fulham' variant: Miks 2007 A465.
15. Bishop and Coulston 2006 pp. 34, 246.
16. Suetonius *Twelve Caesars: Julius Caesar*, 67.
17. Bishop and Coulston 2006 p. 78.
18. Miks 2007 pp. 77–80, 436.
19. Robinson 1975 pp. 45–61.
20. Beck and Chew 1991.
21. For example Miks 2007 A814 and A815, Fontillet blades from Zemplín, Slovakia, *c.* 730 and *c.* 770 mm in length respectively.
22. Bishop and Coulston 2006 pp. 107–9. Daggers, and perhaps swords, were attached to belts via 'frogs', i.e. supplementary loops linking scabbard rings to belt studs.
23. For example, Juvenal referring to

soldiers as 'armed and belted men' (using *balteus*): *Satires* 16.48.

24. Pliny the Elder *Natural History* 33.152.

25. Bishop and Coulston 2006 pp. 109–11.

26. Bishop and Coulston 2006 p. 110.

27. Bishop 2002 pp. 18, 20.

28. Franzius 1999 for the Kalkriese mask, its antecedents and parallels.

29. Reliefs on the tomb of Munatius Plancus built by 10 BC show the square-ended shield was in use by then: Fellmann 1957.

30. Speidel 1991.

31. Campbell 1984 pp. 164–65.

32. In the first century AD, legions may routinely have had specific bodies of *auxilia* formally attached to them; for example Tacitus reports a legion going to the east under Corbulo 'with its *alae* of cavalry and *cohortes* of foot' (*Annals* 13.35) and attests eight Batavian cohorts 'belonging' to *legio* XIV (*Histories* 1.59), both in the context of the AD 60s. However, later auxiliary units seem normally to have been more independent of specific legions, with units and part units brigaded flexibly for specific garrison duties or field missions.

33. The archaeologist Ian Haynes has observed that auxiliary foot were not really 'light' infantry, being equipped almost as heavily as the legions (pers. comm.). Rather they used different weapons and tactics.

34. Zahariade 2009.

35. Tacitus *Histories* 1.59.

36. Brunt 1974. See also note 32.

37. Demographic studies suggest about 40 per cent of Roman recruits would die before completing their twenty-five years, and up to 15 per cent more would leave the military early, through medical or dishonourable discharge, or desertion: Scheidel 1996, especially p. 124.

38. *Legio v Alaudae*: Suetonius *Twelve Caesars: Caesar* 24; legion recruited north of the Po: Caesar *Gallic War* 5.24.

39. The transformation was most likely

when Galatia was annexed as a province in 25 BC: Parker 1958 p. 89.

40. Mann 1983.

41. Speidel 1970, Connolly 1988a, 1988b.

42. MacMullen 1984 p. 441; Tacitus, *Annals* 4.4.2; 14.18. While many auxiliaries were conscripts, under the early emperors it seems most legionaries, at least, were volunteers, although conscription was used in wartime to get legions quickly up to strength: Brunt 1974; Goldsworthy 1996 p. 28.

43. http://classics.mit.edu/Virgil/ aeneid.html

44. The Great Wall already existed in early form. The Romans were dimly aware of China, and the rich wore its silks. Han China, it seems, was a society with bigger professional armies than the Romans; it may have been as well for Rome that the legions were never tested in battle against them.

45. Millar 1977.

46. Cassius Dio 62.17.16.

47. Whittaker 1994.

48. Roman legionaries reaching the Caspian: Jones 1992 pp. 156–57; Bosworth 1976 pp. 74–76.

49. Plutarch *Parallel Lives: Antony*, 42–51.

50. Becker *et al.* 2003; von Schnurbein 2003.

51. Wells 2003.

52. Tacitus *Annals* 2.88.

53. Creighton 2000, Creighton 2005; Henig 2002.

54. Millett 2001.

55. Trans. adapted from A. J. Church and W. J. Brodribb 1893, *The Agricola and Germania of Tacitus*, London, Macmillan.

56. Roymans 2004.

57. Tacitus *Histories* 1.59; Holder 1980 Appendix 3; Spaul 2000 p. 206.

58. The other being the later *cohors xx Palmyrenorum* (Kennedy 1994), many papyrus records relating to which were recovered at Dura-Europos, Syria.

59. Bowman and Thomas 1983; Bowman 1994; Birley 2009.

60. Speidel 1994.

61. The relationship between the British Army and the Gurkhas was so strong that it still retains battalions of these tough Nepalese soldiers sixty years after withdrawal from India.

62. On more recent parallels, see Van Driel-Murray 2002; Van Driel-Murray 2005; Abler 1999.

63. Lang 1988 p. 205.

64. The Fulham blade and 'Sword of Tiberius'; others may have been (Lang 1988 pp. 205, 208). On oil quenching applied to more delicate forgings, Pliny the Elder *Natural History* 34.144, 146, 149.

65. Lang 1988 p. 208.

66. A finer edge was given by an oil whetstone rather than water whetstone: Pliny the Elder *Natural History* 34.145.

67. A *spatha* from Augst also appears to have been treated in a similar way, for flexibility and strength: Bishop and Coulston 2006 p. 241; Biborski *et al.* 1985.

68. Lang 1988 pp. 205, 209–10.

69. Cassius Dio 69.12.2.

70. See page 30 and its note 71. On weapon inspection, Arrian reporting to Hadrian: *Guidebook to the Black Sea (Periplus)* 6.9.

71. *Gladiarius*: CIL 11.7125; 6.1952. *Spat[h]arius*: CIL 6.9043, 9898.

72. Bishop and Coulston 2006 pp. 233–40, *contra* MacMullen 1960 and Robinson 1975.

73. Bishop and Coulston 2006 p. 236; *P. Berlin* inv. 6765: Bruckner and Marichal 1979 no. 409.

74. Justinian *Digest* 50.6.7.

75. Bishop and Coulston 2006 p. 236; Justinian *Digest* 50.6.7.

76. Richmond 1943; Bishop and Dore 1988.

77. Bishop and Coulston 2006 p. 238.

78. CIL 13.6677. For inscriptions on weapons etc. see MacMullen 1960.

79. CIL 13.2828.

80. Tacitus, *Annals* 3.43.

81. *Notitia Dignitatum: Occidens* 9.33–34.

82. At Rheims and Amiens; the third was at Lucca in Italy: *Notitia Dignitatum: Occidens* 9.29, 36, 39.

83. Bishop and Coulston 2006 pp. 80–81.
84. Pompeii swords: Ulbert 1969. Herculaneum example: Miks 2007 no. A151: pp. 437, 577–78.
85. Miks 2007 pp. 65–68.
86. Bishop and Coulston 2006 p. 80. A variant of this 'classic' Pompeii type was the 'Putensen-Vimose' form with a 'Gothic arch' tip perhaps inherited from Gallic swords and prefiguring the form common on later imperial weapons. Miks 2007 p. 437.
87. Schoppa 1974.
88. Selzer 1988 no. 87.
89. It has a 650 mm blade, and is 33 mm wide. Planck 1975 pp. 183–84, pl. 79,3. Miks 2007 A617.
90. Curle 1911, p. 183, pl. xxxiv, nos 6 and 7.
91. One of these has a standard Roman bone grip and pommel, the others bronze guards decorated with native British ornament, a feature encountered quite widely on swords from Roman military sites in Britain, and which underlines the importance of cultural exchanges in arms. Curle 1911, p. 185, pl. xxxiv, 8, 10 and 13.
92. On a possible change in fighting style, see Bishop and Coulston 2006 p. 78.
93. This feature is seen not only on swords but also on a military dagger from Leeuwen, NL: Feugère 2002, fig. 171d.
94. *Dolabrae*, entrenching tools: Tacitus, *Annals* 3.43, 46.
95. Under the procurator Cumanus, AD 48–52: Josephus *Jewish War* 2.12.1 (224).
96. Suetonius *Twelve Caesars: Nero*, 49.
97. Goldsworthy 1996 pp. 84–92.
98. Yadin 1966, which should be read with Ben-Yehuda 2002. On the siegeworks, see Richmond 1962.
99. For an accessible overview of factors and events, see Millar 1993 pp. 337–86.
100. Josephus *Jewish War* 5.550–58.
101. Celebrated on reliefs on the Arch of Titus still visible in Rome.
102. Tacitus, *Histories* 2.88–89.

103. Tacitus, *Histories* 2.68, 2.88; Lendon 1997 p. 250.
104. Tacitus, *Histories* 1.64, 2.27,66,69; Lendon 1997 p. 250.
105. Trans. C. H. Moore 1925, *Tacitus, Histories, Books I–III*. Loeb Classical Library, Cambridge MA, Harvard University Press.
106. Tacitus, *Histories* 3.24.
107. Tacitus, *Histories* 3.33.
108. *Histories* 3.72 (description of events leading up to the destruction of the temple: 3.67–72). Trans. C. H. Moore 1925, *Tacitus, Histories, Books I–III*. Loeb Classical Library, Cambridge MA: Harvard University Press.
109. Trans. adapted from A. J. Church and W. J. Brodribb 1893, *The Agricola and Germania of Tacitus*, London, Macmillan.
110. Epictetus *Discourses* 3.13.9. See also Aelius Aristides *Oration* 26: Campbell 2002 p. 77.
111. Campbell 2002 p. 77: Dio of Prusa 1.28–29.
112. Heather 2005 p. 439.
113. Breeze and Dobson 2000.
114. Mann (1990) saw Hadrian's Wall as a piece of imperial rhetoric.
115. From a book of that title about the rise of American power: Boot 2002.
116. Luttwak's analysis of Roman 'grand strategy' (Luttwak 1976) was influential, but largely through prompting work that showed that he was mistaken. See rather Whittaker 1994 and, especially for the east, Isaac 1992.
117. Hanson and Haynes 2004.
118. Cassius Dio 68.32; Campbell 2002 p. 82. Perhaps curiously, given events before and after this time, Judea itself seems to have been little involved, although this may have been partly because of divergences between the communities of the Holy Land and those of the *diaspora*: Aubrey Newman, pers. comm.
119. Cassius Dio 69.14.
120. However, contrary to modern Jewish 'mythistory', the Romans did not expel the Jewish population *en masse*, beginning 'the exile'; this

is a modern invention: Sand 2009.
121. Grünewald 2004 p. 20.
122. Tacitus, *Annals* 3.43.
123. Krinzinger 2002; Kanz and Grossschmidt 2006.
124. Tacitus, *Annals* 14.17.
125. In Egypt 'sword bearers' and even a 'chief sword-bearer' are found assisting the *archephodoi*, the rural police, who were surely also armed: Alston 1995 pp. 92 and 224–25, fn 126.
126. Matthew 27.26–37; Mark 15.15–27; Luke 26.36–37, 47; John 19.1–3, 16–34.
127. There seems to have been a major massacre by Vespasianic troops suppressing unrest in Alexandria, and further atrocities there under Caracalla and Diocletian: Isaac 2002 p. 182.
128. In Pollentia under Tiberius: Suetonius, *Twelve Caesars: Tiberius* 37.3. Also in Puteoli under Nero: Tacitus, *Annals* 13.48; Isaac 2002 p. 182.
129. Isaac 2002 p. 190; *ILS* 6870 (AD 180–83); Campbell 1984 p. 252.
130. Isaac 2002.
131. Juvenal *Satires* 16.
132. *Tab. Vindol.* II 344: Bowman and Thomas 1994.
133. Apuleius, *The Golden Ass* 9, 39–42.
134. Epictetus, *Discourses* 4.1.79. Translation by Campbell 2002 p. 177.
135. Campbell 1984 p. 251. Such accommodation might be legally ordered by billeting officers, but these soldiers were making unsanctioned private demands.
136. Campbell 1984 p. 249.
137. Bennett *et al.* 1982 pp. 44–45.
138. Emperors spoke of *simplicitas militaris*, of the simple-mindedness of soldiers, for example as a means of excusing their failure to observe due legal forms in court actions, or drawing up their wills, which should be allowed to stand anyway. Justinian *Digest* 29.1.1, *Code of Justinian* 1.18.1.
139. Tacitus *Annals* 1.34.
140. Suetonius *Twelve Caesars: Caligula* 9.

141. Suetonius *Twelve Caesars: Claudius* 13.2; Cassius Dio 60.15.
142. Cf. the modern expression 'that's not my province', i.e. 'I have no expertise or authority in that'.
143. Corbulo in Armenia: Tacitus *Annals* 13.6–9, 34–36.
144. Phang 2008 pp. 201–48.
145. Speidel 2006 pp. 14–15, Field 30: translation adapted from Speidel's.
146. For example *Tab. Vindol.* II nos 225, 250.
147. Suetonius *Twelve Caesars: Augustus* 25.1.
148. Cassius Dio 68.8.2. Campbell 1984 pp. 45–46.
149. Campbell 1984 pp. 32–59; Lendon 1997 pp. 253–66.
150. Frontinus *Stratagems* 4.1.15.
151. The best archaeological evidence for republican military bases is found in the second-century sites around Numantia in Spain: Dobson 2006.
152. Some examples: *praesidium*: Tacitus *Annals* 13.36, Bishop 1999; Vindolanda 'auxiliary fort' as *hiberna*: *Tab. Vindol.* II no. 225; *castra*: Tacitus *Histories* 2.6; *castellum*: Tacitus *Annals* 15.17.
153. Military bases as unifying places: Driessen 2005.
154. Desertion: Campbell 1984 pp. 303–14; Goldsworthy 1996 pp. 30, 113; Romans deserting to join the defenders inside Jerusalem: Cassius Dio 65.5.4; Decebalus giving back deserters: Cassius Dio 68.9.5. Corbulo's severity to deserters: Tacitus *Annals* 13.35.
155. Pliny the Younger *Letters* 7.31.2. MacMullen 1984.

## Chapter 4 Deadly Embraces: The Middle Empire 167–269, pp. 176–221

1. Petersen *et al.* 1896; Ferris 2008.
2. Cassius Dio 74.11.2.
3. Dignas and Winter 2007 pp. 159–61.
4. For a study of the Roman military in the third century which, as here, emphasizes the role of Rome's changing enemies in Rome's crisis, but otherwise presents a more traditional military history of the 'Roman army' as an institution, devoting less attention to the roles of the soldiers as political agents within the empire, see Le Bohec 2009.
5. Bishop and Coulston 2006 p. 129.
6. Bishop and Coulston 2006 p. 144; James 2006.
7. Bishop and Coulston 2006 p. 173.
8. Bishop and Coulston 2006 p. 140.
9. Bishop and Coulston 2006 p. 179, Jørgensen *et al.* 2003 p. 322.
10. Bishop 2002.
11. Miks' 'Putensen-Vimose' and 'Hamfelde' variants respectively: Miks 2007 pp. 67–70.
12. Miks' confusingly named '"spatha"-type gladius, "Straubing" variant': Miks 2007 p. 72.
13. The equally confusingly named '"spatha"-type gladius, "Nydam" variant': Miks 2007 p. 73.
14. Pleiner 1993 pp. 142–43.
15. With the caveat that we currently know next to nothing about contemporary sword technology among groups such as the Sarmatians and Parthians, who influenced Roman arms, and swords in particular, in other ways.
16. Watson *et al.* 1982; Webster 1982.
17. Biborski *et al.* 1985 pp. 73–80. Maryon 1960; Rosenqvist 1968; Biborski and Ilkjaer 2007.
18. Peter Johnsson, pers. comm.
19. Bishop and Coulston 2006 p. 46; Miks 2007 pp. 135–39.
20. The apparent third-century resurgence of extremely short weapons in Fig. 8 largely represents a cache of curious examples found at Künzing (Schönberger and Herrmann 1968), which are most likely broken long-swords resharpened into makeshift daggers (they are of similar length to *pugiones* in the same hoard).
21. Perhaps known most widely as the 'Mainz-Canterbury' type.
22. Here I follow Miks' typology (Miks 2007). A quite different typology of middle and later imperial swords was presented almost simultaneously by Biborski and Ilkjaer in their magnificent publication of the Illerup weapons and their parallels (Biborski and Ilkjaer 2007); however, Miks' scheme has the virtues of being somewhat simpler, and of building more on type names already current in the literature, for example Ulbert 1974; Bishop and Coulston 2006 pp. 154–57.
23. Miks 2007 pp. 92–98, 444.
24. Miks 2007 pp. 80–92, 443–44; Ulbert 1974; Biborski 1994.
25. Miks 2007 pp. 177–87, 446. See Kellner 1966; Biborski 1994. Bishop and Coulston 2006 pp. 132–33.
26. Bishop and Coulston 2006 p. 157.
27. Referred to by Hadrian in a speech at Lambaesis: Speidel 2006 p. 13, Field 25.
28. Rectangular shields were retained in at least small numbers: a complete example (Pl. VI) and several fragments were buried at Dura-Europos in the 250s: James 2004 no. 629.
29. From Aquincum (Budapest): Bishop and Coulston 2006 p. 134, fig. 79.
30. When Severus cashiered the Praetorians, he confiscated their daggers: Herodian 2.13.10.
31. Bishop and Coulston 2006 p. 164. A number were found in a hoard in the fort at Künzing, Germany: Herrmann 1969 p. 133, Abb. 3.
32. Probably known as the *balteus* or *balteum*, contrary to much modern literature, which calls it the *cingulum*. Using literary sources and contemporary letters, Bishop and Coulston (2006 p. 106) make a strong case for *balteus* during the first and into the second century, with *cingulum* used in the third century. In the first century, two belts were often worn, one carrying the sword, the other the dagger.
33. Although other terms were used, such as *zona*: *Edict of Diocletian*, 10.8. *Balteus* may have been used in a generic sense for 'belt': Bishop and Coulston 2006 p. 226. It is not clear whether the 'silver gilt *balteus*' mentioned in *Augustan Histories*:

*Claudius Gothicus* 14.5 was a waist belt or sword-baldric. *Cingulum* was not an exclusively military term either. Romans used terminology more loosely and inconsistently than we might like!

34. *Augustan Histories: The Two Maximini*, 2.5; 3.4. Most FELIX VTERE mottos were on waist belts, but some are on cloak brooches (Fig. 83). A 'medallion' with this motto, belonging to Aurelius Cervianus (Bishop and Coulston 2006 pl. 3a) is a large baldric fastener (as Coulston suggests: Coulston 1990 p. 153, note 70), and so probably from a presentation baldric - and sword?

35. *Optime Maxime, conserva numerus omnium militantium*, which Allason-Jones (1986 pp. 68–69) translates as: '[Jupiter] Best (and) Greatest protect (us) a troop of fighting men all'.

36. For a splendid general survey of Roman weapon decoration and symbolism, see Künzl 2008.

37. Herodian 2.13.10.

38. Hornus 1980.

39. Speidel 1992; Vishnia 2002; MacMullen 1984 pp. 444–45.

40. MacMullen says *calones* were freeborn: MacMullen 1984 p. 444.

41. The future emperor Maximinus Thrax, before enlistment in the military, wanted to show his strength to Septimius Severus by wrestling soldiers, but to preserve military discipline (lest he win), Severus set him to wrestling with '*lixae* – all very valorous men, none the less': *The Augustan Histories: The Two Maximini*, 2.6; MacMullen 1984 pp. 444–45.

42. Speidel 1992.

43. Frontinus *Stratagems* 2.4.5–6.

44. Tacitus *Histories* 2.87.

45. Trans. C. H. Moore, 1931, *Tacitus: Histories, Books IV–V, Annals Books I–III*. Loeb Classical Library, Cambridge MA, Harvard University Press.

46. Second-century diplomas of citizenship for time-expired auxiliaries recognize that they were

in fact likely already to be married, and grant citizenship to a single wife, implying some soldiers practised polygamy. On soldiers' marriages, see Phang 2001.

47. Van Driel-Murray 1995; on 'female' artefacts and infant burials inside the fort of Ellingen, Germany, see Allison 2006.

48. Herodian 3.8.4.

49. Rostovtzeff *et al.* 1944 pp. 115–18, 166–67, and the texts on its walls, 203–65; possible military management: Pollard 2000 pp. 53–54, 188.

50. Pollard 2000 pp. 44–59, etc. The Dura base is subject to new fieldwork by the author: James 2007.

51. While most soldiers doubtless slept inside the base walls, so did some, perhaps many, non-combatants, and not just the families of commanders and centurions, but also military servants and perhaps some soldiers' families too (see note 47). Conversely, it is entirely plausible that some soldiers lived out in the extramural settlements in connection with their duties, or as a privilege.

52. Recruitment is unlikely to have kept up with attrition, especially in peacetime. MacMullen discusses previous estimates, the evidence and the various sources of uncertainty, and for the Severan era suggests actual strength was in the range 338,000–438,000: MacMullen 1980 p. 454. Le Bohec quotes another estimate of 456,000 as 'probably too high': Le Bohec 1994 p. 33.

53. *Tab. Vindol.* II, no. 118.

54. *P. Dura* 54; Welles *et al.* 1959 pp. 191–212.

55. Livy 2.19–21.

56. Harries 2007 pp. 33, 36; MacMullen 1986.

57. Justinian *Digest* 49.16; 18.1; Campbell 1984 p. 261.

58. In 177: Eusebius *History of the Church* 5.1.

59. *ILS* 8504. Trans. Campbell 2002 p. 176.

60. Grünewald 2004 p. 21.

61. *ILS* 1140, dating post-198, refers to *rebelles h(ostes) p(ublicos)* in Spain.

62. Grünewald 2004 p. 17. It was concerned with perceived threats to the state more than security of the people.

63. *Augustan Histories: Commodus* 16.2; *Augustan Histories: Pescennius Niger* 3.4; Herodian 1.10; Alföldi 1971.

64. Young Italian males denied access to careers as Praetorians turned instead to brigandage: Cassius Dio 75.2.5.

65. Grünewald 2004; Cassius Dio 76.7.1–3; 10.

66. Trans. Campbell 2002.

67. Petitions and complaints about soldier thefts and abuse: Robert 1943, Robert 1989, Millar 1977 p. 646.

68. Campbell 1984 p. 272; Campbell 1994 no. 301; *CIL* 3.12336.

69. *P. Dura* 55; Welles *et al.* 1959 pp. 213–17.

70. Cassius Dio 73.9.

71. Cassius Dio 80.4.1–5.1.

72. *Augustan Histories: Pertinax* 3; 11.

73. Shaw 1983 pp. 144–48.

74. Tacitus *Histories* 3.47; Sidebottom 2004 p. 12; Speidel 1984; Wheeler 1996.

75. Commodus, *fides exerc[ituum]* coins after revolt in Britain in 185; Gallienus, *fides militum*, 'loyalty of the soldiers', and also minted *fides, virtus, pax* and *concordia equitum*, reflecting the importance of his cavalry. Aurelian, *concordia militum*, 'harmony of the soldiers'.

76. Consolidated by Gallienus, whose military reforms included replacing senatorial legionary commanders with equestrian prefects, some of whom may have been promoted career centurions.

77. For a survey of the military in the third century, see Le Bohec 2009.

78. Ghirshman 1962; Colledge 1967; Campbell 1993; Kennedy 1996; Curtis 2000; Sheldon 2010.

79. A challenge to the notion that Parthians were essentially victims of the Romans, in what was largely

a 'Cold War': Wheeler 2002.

80. Cassius Dio 78.7.1–4, 18.1; Herodian 4.8.1.3.

81. How far the Sasanids really identified with, and intended to recreate, the Achaemenid empire, especially in the eastern Mediterranean, is unclear: Daryaee 2009, e.g. pp. 105–6. However, the prospect certainly frightened the Romans and the Sasanids knew it.

82. Attributed to General Bernard Montgomery.

83. Du Mesnil du Buisson 1936; Du Mesnil du Buisson 1944; Leriche 1993, James 2011.

84. Dignas and Winter 2007.

85. Dignas and Winter 2007 pp. 24, 27, 210–16.

86. Herodian 6.5.5–10.

87. See, most famously, Tacitus' *Germania*.

88. Being moved to remark that they were 'built quite carefully in Roman fashion': Ammianus 17.1.7.

89. Heather 2005 pp. 86–87.

90. Heather 1996.

91. Wells 1999; James 2005.

92. Gothic levies in the east in the third century: Parker 1986 pp. 129–31. A unit of Goths stationed in the east early in the third century: Speidel 1977 p. 712.

93. Heather 2005 p. 97.

94. Geschwinde *et al.* 2009.

95. Heather 2005 pp. 84–85.

96. For an overview, Ilkjaer 2000. The finds are being published in a series of large volumes. That on swords and scabbards: Biborski and Ilkjaer 2007.

97. Jørgensen 2001.

98. Storgaard 2001.

99. Kahaner 2007.

100. Under Marcus Aurelius the law expert Scaevola referred to the ban on weapons exports under the *lex Iulia maiestatis*, which probably goes back to 8 BC: Justinian *Digest*, 48.4.4.

101. Erdrich 1994.

102. As Hitler did in invading Russia in 1941, convinced of the weakness of a Communist regime that he despised on ideological grounds.

103. Whitmarsh 2005. On Caracalla's obsession with Alexander: Lendon 2004 p. 279. See also Arrian's second-century *Order of March against the Alans*, in which he, an ethnically Greek Roman commander, describes himself as 'Xenophon' after his hero and model the Athenian soldier, and uses antiquated Greco-Macedonian terms to describe his own Roman army: Lendon 2005 pp. 267–68.

104. Balty 1988 p. 101.

105. Batty 2007.

106. Trousdale 1975.

107. Bishop and Coulston 2006 p. 134.

108. Bujukliev 1986; Werner 1994.

109. Coulston 1991.

110. Certainly established by the early second century: note 27. Arrian records that in Hadrian's time there were Roman lance-armed cavalry who 'attack in the manner of the Alans and Sarmatians', *Tactical Handbook* 4.

111. Coulston 2003.

112. A thumbring was found in a Parthian context at Dura-Europos, and Roman-era arrows from the site appear to be fletched for shooting with a thumb-ring: James 1987.

113. Kennedy 1977.

114. Khorasani 2006 cat. nos 52–55, all from Dailaman in Gilan province bordering the Caspian in northern Iran. Two (nos 52 and 53) were excavated at Nowruz Mahalle, the others confiscated from plunderers at Rashi.

115. Pliny the Elder *Natural History* 34.145.

116. Tacitus *Annals* 12.16. *Milites* on the northwestern shores of the Black Sea: Maldur 2005; Roman garrisons in the Crimea: Sarnowski 2005.

117. The 'Antonine revolution' is also seen as 'not unconnected with the Marcomannic Wars' by Bishop and Coulston 2006 p. ix, etc.

118. Note 103.

119. Palmyrene gods with Roman swords: Louvre ao19801; Nabatean altar, Dmeir, Syria, AD 94 (Caubet 1990), no. 32.

120. Excavations of early imperial period graves in the region northeast of the Black Sea have produced Sarmatian bodies interred with iron mail armour reaching to the ankles: Goroncharovski 2006 p. 446 and fig. 3.

121. For example, via Roman troops deserting to the Sasanians under Severus Alexander: Cassius Dio 80.4.1–2.

122. For example the Gorgan Wall, which now seems to be later fifth century AD: Nokandeh *et al.* 2006; Rekavandi *et al.* 2007.

123. Cassius Dio 72.16.

124. Whittaker 1994.

125. Ilkjaer 2000.

126. A process known as 'cultural bricolage': Terrenato 1998a.

127. Arrian *Tactical Handbook* 33. Trans. by J. De Voto, 1993, *Flavius Arrianus, Techne Taktika (Tactical Handbook)*, Chicago, Ares.

128. Arrian *Tactical Handbook* 33.

129. Cassius Dio 75.2.6 Trans. E. Cary, 1927, *Cassius Dio, Roman History, Books LXXI–LXXX*, Loeb Classical Library, Cambridge MA, Harvard University Press; MacMullen 1984 p. 440.

130. Found in 1992: *AE* 1993, 1231; Wamser 2000 no. 137, Abb. 57.

131. This battle is one of several not mentioned in Roman sources, but attested by Sasanian texts, which in turn are silent on Sasanian defeats: Dignas and Winter 2007 pp. 77–80.

132. Latin rendering of German for 'All Men', and root of the French name for Germans, *les Allemands*.

## Chapter 5 Empire of the Soldiers: Forging the Dominate 269–376, pp. 222–260

1. The huge imbalance in scholarship between the effort to study the early imperial military and that expended on the later era can only in part be explained by differential survival of evidence to work on; much of it is down to the relative glamour and historical prestige of the two eras.

2. Vegetius *Epitome of Military Science*.
3. Paradoxically, because of his Enlightenment contempt for what he saw as a priest-ridden medieval society, the considerable attention Gibbon paid to Byzantine history has been blamed for undermining interest in it in subsequent centuries.
4. Ammianus 16.10.1–10. Trans. J. C. Rolfe 1935, *Ammianus Marcellinus, Books XIV–XIX*, Loeb Classical Library, Cambridge MA, Harvard University Press.
5. For example, in an official letter of AD 260 on a papyrus from Oxyrhynchus, Egypt: Parsons 2007 p. 119: *P. Oxy* 12.1411.
6. Dodgeon and Lieu 1991 pp. 126–27.
7. And quite possibly included some of each: Constantius had an exiled Sasanian prince with him (Ammianus 16.10.16), who likely had a personal retinue of Persian noble cavalry. Some quite senior Romans defected the other way, notably Antoninus, who served Shapur II: Ammianus 18.8.
8. Ammianus 16.12. Strasbourg and Adrianople are among the few fourth-century battles recorded in enough detail to reconstruct their shape with any confidence: Elton 1996 p. 250; Nicasie 1998 p. 219.
9. Ammianus 16.12.
10. Ammianus 16.11.1–14.
11. Serapio had acquired his Greco-Roman name because his father was long a Roman hostage in Gaul: Ammianus 16.12.25.
12. Ammianus 16.12.7–19. Nicasie argues that this was troops naturally wanting to 'get it over with' (Nicasie 1998 p. 223), but it was also symptomatic of Roman soldiers' unruliness, tendency to force the hand of commanders, and to get out of control, habits which contributed to disaster at Adrianople.
13. Ammianus 16.2.49 (trans. adapted from J. C. Rolfe 1935, *Ammianus Marcellinus, Books XX–XXVI*, Loeb Classical Library, Cambridge MA, Harvard University Press); see also

16.2.36: Roman 'sword-thrusts'.
14. Nicasie 1998 p. 232.
15. Some of them his own eyewitness testimony, especially of the Sasanian siege of Amida: Ammianus 18.9–10, 19.1–8.
16. For general surveys of the later Roman military, see Southern and Dixon 1996, and Le Bohec 2006.
17. Also called 'scorpion' by Ammianus: 19.7.6, 23.4.4.
18. Miks 2007 pp. 99–103, 453.
19. Miks 2007 pp. 453–54.
20. Khorasani 2006 cat. nos 61 and 62, both excavated at Niavol in Gilan province, near the Caspian in northern Iran.
21. Khorasani 2006 cat. no. 63, excavated at Amarlu in Gilan province, near the Caspian in northern Iran. The blade has a central midrib, and the handle is 310 mm (12¼ in) long.
22. Miks 2007 pp. 104–5, 454.
23. Miks 2007 pp. 132, 454.
24. Goethert 1996.
25. Germans recognizing Roman unit-specific shield devices: Ammianus 16.12.6. The unit shield designs drawn in the *Notitia Dignatatum* give a general idea, but appear garbled: Grigg 1983.
26. For example, fourth-century scale and mail from Trier; late fourth-century/early fifth-century mail from Weiler-la-Tour and Independenta: Bishop and Coulston 2006 p. 208; Zahariade 1991 p. 315.
27. Elton 1996 pp. 110–14.
28. Klumbach 1973. Further finds continue to be made, for example Lyne 1994.
29. Bishop and Coulston 2006 p. 214.
30. Ammianus 19.1.3.
31. James 1986.
32. Opposed animal heads feature on the back of a third-century helmet from Heddernheim (Robinson 1975 pl. 275), and on sculpture (as terminals on *tabulae ansatae* and *peltae*). For Parthian or Sasanian opposed animal head buckles, see James 2004 p. 251, fig. 141 D and E; Ghirshman 1979 pp. 176–82, pl. 4.

At Amida Shapur II wore a ram's-head helmet, reflecting the importance of animal imagery in Sasanian arms: Ammianus 19.1.3; James forthcoming.
33. *Edict of Diocletian* 10.8a.
34. Elton 1996 p. 156.
35. Trans. J. C. Rolfe 1935, *Ammianus Marcellinus, Books XX–XXVI*, Loeb Classical Library, Cambridge MA, Harvard University Press.
36. *CIL XIII*, 5980; Strasbourg Museum, Inv.Nr.20984 (this artefact was a victim of war, and only a cast now survives).
37. Ammianus 18.8–19.8.
38. Ammianus 19.6.7–12.
39. Ammianus 22.3.7–8.
40. Tacitus described the *barritus* as the German battle-cry in the early imperial period: *Germania* 3.
41. Ammianus 20.4.17–18. Raising leaders on a shield: Tacitus *Histories* 4.15; Nicasie 1998 p. 107.
42. Pohlsander 1969.
43. Early Christian attitudes to war and military service: Harnack 1981; Hornus 1980.
44. Ammianus 24.1.2; 24.6.4; 27.5.1.
45. Heather 2005 p. 215.
46. Libanius *Orations* 47.33. MacMullen 1963.
47. Recent 'revisionist' accounts: Elton 1996 and Nicasie 1998.
48. Heather 2005 p. 65.
49. Nicasie 1998 pp. 43–65.
50. Nicasie 1998 pp. 184–98.
51. Nicasie 1998 pp. 18–22.
52. A law of 372 sending inferior recruits to frontier units: *CTh* 7.22.8, Nicasie 1998 pp. 14–18; Treadgold 1995 p. 11.
53. For the literature on these and later developments, especially the presumed major reform which by the mid-fourth century saw many comitatensian units subdivided or duplicated into formations surnamed *seniores* and *iuniores*, see Nicasie 1998 pp. 40–42.
54. The 'Barbarian Conspiracy': Bartholomew 1984. Four regiments of *comitatenses* had previously been sent under Lupicinus in 360: Ammianus 20.1.2–3. The later

standing force under the *comes Britanniarum*: *Notitia Dignitatum: Occidens* 29.

55. Nicasie 1998 pp. 74–76 and Lee 2007 pp. 74–77 for literature and, perhaps inevitably, rather inconclusive discussion.

56. John Lydus, *On the Months* 1.27.

57. Agathias, *History* 5.13. Heather argues that the Sasanian threat required substantial increase in the scale of the Roman military, and appears to accept the largest figures: Heather 2005 pp. 62–64.

58. Ammianus 18.8.2.

59. See, for example, Britain's *legio II Augusta*, which in the second century required a 20-ha (50-acre) base at Caerleon, but by the late fourth century fitted into the 'Saxon Shore' fort at Richborough, not much over a tenth of the size: *Notitia Dignitatum: Occidens* 28.9.

60. James 1988.

61. James 1988. Imperial silver/goldsmiths, *barbaricarii*, were also involved in arms production, especially plating helmets.

62. James 1988 pp. 280–81.

63. Nicasie 1998 p. 8, citing Ferrill 1986 pp. 46–50.

64. Jones 1964; arguments summarized in Jones 1966, 362–70.

65. MacMullen 1990.

66. Ward-Perkins (2005) and Heather (2005).

67. And even then, much Roman culture (from landholdings and law to the Christian church) survived the fall of the western imperial regime during this period now known as 'Late Antiquity'.

68. Lactantius, as a Christian convert who became close to Constantine I, loathed Diocletian and Galerius in particular for their assaults on Christianity. He accused Diocletian of quadrupling the military: Lactantius *On the Deaths of the Persecutors* 7.2.

69. Drinkwater (1996) argues that multiple emperors were needed simply to control the armies, not because of external threats; for

example, the Alamanni were, in his view, for a long time more a convenient imperial construct and bogey-man than real danger: Drinkwater 2007.

70. Commonly cited as *Si vis pacem, para bellum*, a paraphrase of Vegetius' actual words, *Igitur qui desiderat pacem, praeparet bellum*, 'therefore, those who wish for peace, prepare for war', Vegetius *Epitome of Military Science* Book 3, preface.

71. Although by modern standards government remained small.

72. In part, these developments were also a continuation of the process of Severus' division of jurisdictions and increased mutual surveillance to make internal plots for the purple more difficult.

73. Heather 2005 pp. 102–3.

74. The extreme disparities of wealth in the late empire are staggering. The opulence of the tiny circle of super-rich and super-powerful is to be seen in the magnificence of the fourth-century senatorial palace at Piazza Armerina, Sicily, and in the historical record through cases such as the aristocrat Melania, who also owned a vast portfolio of estates in Sicily – and Italy, Africa and Spain. These brought her an annual income of 120,000 *solidi*, i.e. 660 kg (1450 lb) of gold, still placing her outside the top rank of late Roman senators who enjoyed fortunes around three times the size of this: Jones 1964 pp. 554–56.

75. MacMullen 1963 p. 61, on the bogus *cenatica superstatuta*, 'superstatutory food money': *CTh* 7.4.12, probably promulgated in 364.

76. On indications of undermanning in Roman imperial units, see Goldsworthy 1996 pp. 22–23.

77. Synesius *Letters* 132 (AD 405).

78. Synesius *Letters* 78 (AD 411), which records plans to appeal for the unit to be brought up to a strength of 200.

79. Ammianus 16.5.9; this from a passionate partisan of Julian, but

consistent with other indications.

80. Marmot 2004; Wilkinson 2005.

81. So especially Ward-Perkins 2005.

82. Heather 2005 p. 132, who vividly compares the experience of Rome to centuries of Soviet-style propaganda with no equivalent of the BBC or Voice of America to challenge it. Christianity was long feared as subversive, although rather than resistance to Rome it preached 'render unto Caesar…', facilitating its eventual co-option as an instrument of the state.

83. Constantinian state use of Christianity shows interesting confusions with the existing solar cult of *Sol Invictus*.

84. Heather 2005 pp. 122–23. Much of the religious violence that did occur after Constantine was based on Christian doctrinal in-fighting.

85. On widespread Jewish proselytizing preceding Christian expansion in the Roman world: Sand 2009 pp.128–89; Millar 1993 pp. 344–46.

86. The religious policy of the early Sasanian state and its Zoroastrian 'state church' varied between tolerance of other faiths (generally of its large Mesopotamian Jewish populations) and systematic persecutions (for example sometimes of Jews, Christians and Manicheans): Dignas and Winter 2007 pp. 28, 216, 218. Daryaee 2009 pp. 77–79.

87. Hopkins 1999 pp. 280–81.

88. Heather 2005 pp. 127–28.

89. Heather 2005 p. 140.

90. Harries 2007 p. 36: *Digest* 48.19.28.15. MacMullen 1986. Death by torture was officially forbidden, but still practised: Harries 2007 p. 41.

91. Lendon 1997 p. 6, especially fn.25.

92. Harries 2007 p. 116.

93. Alföldi 1971; Drinkwater 1984; Drinkwater 1989.

94. Heather 2005 pp. 114–15, 119, 134, 449.

95. Daryaee 2009.

96. Dignas and Winter 2007 p. 97.

97. The '*Savaran*': Farrokh 2007.

98. Farrokh 2007 p. 200.
99. Dignas and Winter 2007 p. 90.
100. Farrokh 2007 p. 205.
101. Heather 2005 p. 48.
102. Hunter 2005; Hunter 2007; Fraser 2009.
103. Adams 1996; Mattingly 2006 p. 452.
104. Heather 2005 pp. 84–85. On the Goths see also Heather 1996.
105. Heather 2005 p. 91.
106. Heather 2005 pp. 89–90.

## Chapter 6 Swords of God: Extinctions and Transformations 376–565, pp. 261–277

1. Trans. J. C. Rolfe 1939, *Ammianus Marcellinus, Books XXVII–XXXI*, Loeb Classical Library, Cambridge MA, Harvard University Press.
2. E.g. under Nero, in Moesia 'more than 100,000 of the number of Transdanubians' were brought into the empire 'for the payment of taxes, together with their wives and children or leaders and kings', *ILS* 986; Campbell 2002 p. 169.
3. Heather 2005 pp. 159–60.
4. Ammianus 31.12–13 for the primary account of the battle, discussed by Burns 1973 and Nicasie 1998 pp. 233–56.
5. Heather 2005 pp. 185, 189.
6. Heather 2005 p. 181.
7. Heather 2005.
8. The boundary in the Balkans is still roughly preserved in the line between Catholic lands using the Latin alphabet and Orthodox regions using Greek or derivative Cyrillic scripts.
9. Or possibly the year before, on 31 December 405: Kulikowski 2000.
10. Merrills and Miles 2010.
11. Heather 2005 pp. 146–51.
12. Ammianus (31.3.8) blames the Huns, who were rendering their homelands so insecure that Gothic groups decided to flee: Heather 2005 pp. 145–46, 153–54.
13. Heather 2005 pp. 202–3.
14. Heather 2005 pp. 194–95.
15. Heather 2005 pp. 173, 194–95.
16. Heather 2005 p. 333.
17. Heather 2005 p. 329.
18. Trans. J. C. Rolfe 1939, *Ammianus Marcellinus, Books XXVII–XXXI*, Loeb Classical Library, Cambridge MA, Harvard University Press.
19. Miks' 'Asiatic type spatha': Miks 2007 pp. 106, 454, Tafn 143–45, 282–85.
20. Heather 2005 pp. 156–58. Farrokh similarly turns to technological explanations for Hunnic success over the Sasanians (2007). For the archaeological evidence for Hunnic-era bows from Europe and Asia, see Bona 1991.
21. Heather 2005 pp. 303, 311.
22. The Huns included 'renegade' Romans, such as the Greek-speaking former merchant encountered by Priscus in Attila's camp. Taken at Viminacium in 441, he fought for the Huns, did well, and integrated: Heather 2005 p. 361.
23. For gold plating from a Hunnic-era bow from Jakusowice, Poland: Harmatta 1951; Laszlo 1951; Bona 1991 p. 259 and Abb 54.
24. Heather 2005 p. 369 note 40.
25. Heather 2005 p. 373–74.
26. Gregory of Tours, *History of the Franks* 2.8. Trans. adapted from O. M. Dalton 1927, *Gregory of Tours, History of the Franks*, Oxford, Clarendon.
27. Priscus, cited in Heather 2005 p. 320.
28. Unnamed soldier describing himself on his epitaph at Aquincum (Budapest): *ILS* 2814; Elton 1996 p. 141. Possible translation suggested by Graham Shipley.
29. Heather 2005 p. 247.
30. Elton (1996 pp. 152–54), on the other hand, argues that there is little evidence for the idea of manpower shortage requiring barbarian recruitment. However, dread of conscription was great enough to prompt some to prefer to amputate their thumbs, rendering themselves unfit to serve: Jones 1964 p. 618. Ammianus contrasts the more martial Gauls with thumb-cutting Italians (15.12.3).
31. Heather 2005 p. 296.
32. For example Hunnic contingents, shifting from serving for pay to demanding money with menaces: Heather 2005 p. 327.
33. Elton 1996 pp. 136–37, 144–45.
34. Ammianus 20.4.4; Elton 1996 p. 141.
35. Heather 2005 p. 177.
36. For example, the Alamannic king Vadomarius, kidnapped in Gaul, was later employed as a *dux* (general) in the east. Sasanians also served: Puseaus, a Sasanian officer who defected to Rome, was made a military tribune: Elton 1996 p. 135.
37. Elton 1996 pp. 145–52, 272–77.
38. Elton 1996 pp. 141–42.
39. Elton 1996 pp. 138–45.
40. Heather 2005 p. 450.
41. Heather 2005 p. 213.
42. Apparently from the fourth century, certainly later: Dignas and Winter 2007 pp. 34, 38.
43. Heather 2005 p. 344.
44. Heather 2005 pp. 397, 433.
45. Heather 2005 pp. 135ff, 421.
46. This is the cultural milieu of ' Late Antiquity', now seen as spanning the late Roman and earliest medieval ('Dark Age') world: Brown 1976; Webster and Brown 1997.
47. At Birdoswald, military granaries were succeeded by great wooden halls, likely home to a warband conceivably descended from the Roman garrison: Wilmott 1997 pp. 203–32, 408–9.
48. Trans. adapted from G. Robinson 1914, *The Life of St Severinus, by Eugippius*, Cambridge MA, Harvard University Press, and Oxford, Oxford University Press.
49. Eugippius *The Life of St Severinus* 27; Ward-Perkins 2005 pp. 17–20, 134–36.
50. *Notitia Dignitatum: Occidens* 35.24.
51. Trans. H. B. Dewing, 1919, *Procopius, History of the Wars, Books V and VI*, Loeb Classical Library, Cambridge MA, Harvard University Press and London, Heinemann. Passage cited by Casey 1992 p. 73.
52. Dignas and Winter 2007 pp. 34–37.
53. Dignas and Winter 2007 p. 35.

54. While noting that evidence is
lacking, Farrokh suggests Hunnic
success against the Sasanians was
substantially down to introduction
of the stirrup, a new two-point
sword suspension system, and
supposedly improved Hunnic-Avar
bow (Farrokh 2007 p. 218). This
is not very plausible; there is no
evidence of any sudden leap in
bow technology (rather than
refinements of a long-successful
design). Neither is there evidence
that the stirrup had yet arrived –
still less that this, either, really
revolutionized cavalry combat.
The long-established four-horned
saddle provided a very effective
platform for lance, sword and bow:
Connolly and Van Driel-Murray
1991; Herrmann 1989.

55. Claudian *Gothic War* 535–39;
James 1988 p. 285.

56. Cassiodorus *Letters* 18 and 19;
James 1988 pp. 282–85. In the east,
the *fabricae* existed until at least
the reign of Justinian: James 1988
pp. 281–82, 286–87.

57. Miks 2007 p. 454.

58. Bruce-Mitford 1978.

59. John Malalas *Chronicle* 14.23;
Dignas and Winter 2007 p. 135.

60. Dignas and Winter 2007
p. 135. These rule-bound Sasanian
combats are sometimes seen as
proto-'jousting'.

61. For example Farrokh 2007.

62. Treadgold 1995.

63. Procopius, writing of sixth-century
eastern armies, presents cavalry as
the leading arm, suggesting that the
tipping point away from the Roman
infantry tradition had already been
passed by then: Lee 2007 pp. 12–13.

64. Trousdale 1975 pp. 98–101, figs
79–86.

## Conclusion: Rome and the Sword, pp. 278–292

1. Trans. adapted from W. Whiston,
1895, *The Complete Works of Flavius
Josephus*, London, Nelson.

2. A view shared by Lendon 2004
p. 447.

3. Sand 2009.

4. For example Ward-Perkins 2005
pp. 87–88, etc.

5. Juvenal, *Satires* 10.81.

6. Attributed to Henry Fielding.

7. Grünewald 2004 pp. 17–18
expresses similar views.

8. Juvenal cited ridicule as the hardest
to bear of all the woes of 'luckless
poverty': *Satires* 3.147–53.

9. Marmot 2004; Wilkinson 2005.

10. The period examined was
1989–99: Marmot 2004
pp. 196–220.

11. The 'discrepant experience' of
Roman imperialism: Mattingly
1997.

12. Laughter as protective against the
prevalent powers of ill-fortune:
Clarke 2002 p. 156.

13. Ermine Street Guard:
http://www.erminestreet
guard.co.uk/
I have found their activities and
expertise enormously useful for
thinking about and understanding
the experience of Roman *milites*,
both in terms of successful
replication of some aspects, and
the undoubted contrasts between
re-enactment displays and original
brutal realities. With other serious
re-enactment or Living History
groupings in Europe, The Guard are
a vital asset to study of the Roman
military, and I am proud
to be an associate member.

14. By Deep-eeka Exports http://
www.deepeeka.com/armoury/
(accessed 24 January 2010).

15. This celebrated maxim appears only
in Matthew (26:51–52: translation is
the King James Version). Only John
(18.10–11) identifies the assailant and
victim by name; when Jesus tells
Simon Peter to sheath his sword, he
comments instead 'the cup which
my Father hath given me, shall I not
drink it?' Mark (14:47) has the sword
blow, but not Jesus' response; Luke,
himself a physician, reports Jesus
miraculously healed the injury
(22.49–52).

16. Heather 2005 ends on this
likelihood, also entertained by
others.

# Bibliography

**Classical sources**
Greek and Latin works used in the text, and guidance on the most accessible modern published editions. Loeb Classical Library, published by Harvard University Press, provides the most comprehensive range of authoritative parallel Greek/Latin and English texts, and Penguin Classics the broadest range of English translations (sometimes selections or abridgements). For less well-known authors not covered by Loeb or Penguin Classics, alternatives are suggested where available. At the time of writing many texts and translations are also available online, at: *http://www.perseus.tufts.edu/ hopper/collection?collection= Perseus:collection:Greco-Roman* and *http://penelope.uchicago.edu/ Thayer/E/Roman/Texts/home.html*

Aelius Aristides, *Orations* (*Complete Works* trans. C. A. Behr, Leiden: Brill, 1981–6)
Agathias, *History* (*Corpus Fontium Historiae Byzantinae* vol. 2A, trans. J. D. Frend, Berlin: de Gruyter 1975)
Ammianus Marcellinus, *History* (Loeb, Penguin Classics)
Appian, *Civil Wars* (Loeb, Penguin Classics)
Appian, *Punic Wars* (Loeb)
Appian, *Spanish Wars* (Loeb)
Apuleius, *The Golden Ass* (*Metamorphoses*) (Loeb, Penguin Classics)
Aristotle, *Politics* (Loeb, Penguin Classics)
Arrian, *Guidebook to the Black Sea* (*Periplus Ponti Euxini*) (trans A. Liddle, London: Duckworth 2003)
Arrian, *Order of March against the Alans* (*Flavius Arrianus, Techne Taktika [Technical Handbook], and Ektasis kata Alanon [Expedition against the Alans]*, trans J. G. De Voto, Chicago: Ares, 1993)
Arrian, *Tactical Handbook* (*Tekne Taktika*, aka *Ars Tactica*) (*Flavius Arrianus, Techne Taktika [Technical handbook], and Ektasis kata Alanon [Expedition against the Alans]*,

trans J. G. De Voto, Chicago: Ares, 1993)
*Augustan Histories* (Loeb)
Aulus Gellius, *Attic Nights* (Loeb)
Caesar, *Civil Wars* (Loeb, Penguin Classics)
Caesar, *Gallic War* (Loeb, Penguin Classics)
Cassiodorus, *Letters* (*Variae*) (*Cassiodorus: Variae* trans S. J. B. Barnish, Liverpool: University Press, 1992)
Cassius Dio, *Roman History* (Loeb, Penguin Classics)
Cato, *On Agriculture* (Loeb)
Celsus, *On Medicine* (Loeb)
Cicero, *Phillipics* (Loeb)
Cicero, *Tusculan Disputations* (Loeb)
Claudian, *Gothic War* (Loeb)
Columella, *On Agriculture* (Loeb)
Dio of Prusa (Dio Chrysostom) (Loeb)
*Diocletian, Edict on Maximum Prices* (text and trans by E. R. Graser in T. Frank, *An Economic Survey of Ancient Rome Volume v: Rome and Italy of the Empire*, Baltimore: Johns Hopkins Press 1940)
Diodorus Siculus, *Historical Library* (Loeb)
Dionysius of Halicarnassus, *Roman Antiquities* (Loeb)
Epictetus, *Discourses* (Loeb)
Eugippius, *The Life of St. Severinus* (trans G. W. Robinson, 1914, Cambridge MA: Harvard University Press and London: Oxford University Press)
Eusebius, *History of the Church* (Loeb, Penguin Classics)
Frontinus, *Stratagems* (Loeb)
Gregory of Tours, *History of the Franks* (Penguin Classics)
Herodian, *History of the Empire from the Death of Marcus* (Loeb)
Horace, *Epistles* (Loeb, Penguin Classics)
Horace, *Satires* (Loeb, Penguin Classics)
John Lydus, *On the Months* (no English translation available)
John Malalas, *Chronicle* (trans E. Jeffreys, M. Jeffreys, R. Scott and B. Croke, 1986, Melbourne: Australian Association for Byzantine Studies;

Sydney: University of Sydney)

Josephus, *Jewish War* (Loeb, Penguin Classics)

Justinian, *Code of Roman Law* (T. Kearley's online revision of F. H. Blume's 1943 *Annotated Justinian Code:* http://uwacadweb.uwyo.edu/ blume&justinian/Book%20I2.asp )

Justinian, *Digest of Roman Law* (Penguin Classics)

Juvenal, *Satires* (Loeb, Penguin Classics)

Lactantius, *On the Deaths of the Persecutors* (*de mortibus persecutorum*) (trans J. L. Creed, 1984, Oxford, New York: Clarendon Press)

Libanius, *Orations* (Loeb)

Livy, *History of Rome from the Foundation of the City* (Loeb, Penguin Classics)

Martial, *Book of Spectacles* (Loeb)

*Notitia Dignitatum* (W. Fairley's 1900 translation is available on http://www.fordham.edu/halsall/ source/notitiadignitatum.html )

Petronius, *Satyricon* (Loeb, Penguin Classics)

Plautus, *Pseudolus* (Loeb, Penguin Classics)

Pliny the Elder, *Natural History* (Loeb, Penguin Classics)

Pliny the Younger, *Letters* (Loeb, Penguin Classics)

Plutarch, *Parallel Lives* (Loeb, Penguin Classics)

Polyaenus, *Stratagems* (P. Krentz and E. L. Wheeler, eds 1994. *Polyaenus, Stratagems of War, text and translation,* Chicago: Ares)

Polybius, *History* (Loeb, Penguin Classics)

Suetonius, *Twelve Caesars* (Loeb, Penguin Classics)

Strabo, *Geography* (Loeb)

Synesius of Cyrene, *Letters* (trans A. Fitzgerald, 1926, Oxford, Oxford University Press)

Tacitus, *Agricola* (Loeb, Penguin Classics)

Tacitus, *Annals* (Loeb, Penguin Classics)

Tacitus, *Germania* (Loeb, Penguin Classics)

Tacitus, *Histories* (Loeb, Penguin Classics)

Valerius Maximus, *Memorable Doings and Sayings* (Loeb)

Varro, *On the Latin Language* (Loeb)

Vegetius, *Epitome of Military Science* (Loeb)

Velleius Paterculus, *History of Rome* (Loeb)

## Abbreviations

*AE l'Année Epigraphique,* 1888–

*CIL Corpus Inscriptionum Latinarum,* Mommsen, T. *et al.* eds (1863–), Berlin, Walter de Gruyter & Co

CTh *Codex Theodosianus. The Theodosian code and novels: and the Sirmondian constitutions. A translation with commentary, glossary, and bibliography,* by C. Pharr, with T. Sherrer Davidson and M. Brown Pharr, 1952, Princeton: Princeton University Press

*ILS Inscriptiones Latinae Selectae,* Dessau, H. ed., 1892–1916. Berlin, Weidmann

*P. Dura Excavations at Dura-Europos, Final Report Volume v, Part 1 The Parchments and Papyri,* C. B.Welles, R. O. Fink and J. F. Gilliam, eds 1959. New Haven: Yale University Press

*P. Oxy The Oxyrhynchus Papyri* 1898–2010. London, Egypt Exploration Fund/Egypt Exploration Society

*RIB Roman Inscriptions of Britain,* R. G. Collingwood, R. P. Wright *et al.* eds 1965–2009. Stroud, Alan Sutton and Oxford, Oxbow

*Tab. Vindol. 11 The Vindolanda Writing Tablets (Tabula Vindolandensis 11),* A. Bowman and J. Thomas 1994. London, British Museum Press

## Modern sources

Abler, T. S. 1999. *Hinterland Warriors and Military Dress: European Empires and Exotic Uniforms,* Oxford and New York, Berg

Ackroyd, P. 1998. *The Life of Thomas More,* London, Chatto & Windus

Adams, C. 1996. '*Hibernia Romana?* Ireland & the Roman Empire', *History Ireland* 4:2, pp. 21–25

Alföldi, G. 1971. 'Bellum desertorum', *Bonner Jahrbücher* 171, pp. 367–76

Allason-Jones, L. 1986. 'An eagle mount from Carlisle', *Saalburg Jahrbuch* 42, pp. 68–69

Allison, P. M. 2006. 'Mapping for gender: interpreting artefact distribution in Roman military forts in Germany', *Archaeological Dialogues* 13:1, pp. 1–48

Alston, R. 1995. *Soldier and Society in Roman Egypt: A Social History,* London and New York, Routledge

Anderson, B. R. 1991. *Imagined Communities; Reflections on the Origins and Spread of Nationalism,* London and New York, Verso

Anonymous 1993. *Hofkunst van de Sassanieden,* Brussels, Koninklijke Muse voor Kunst en Geschiedenis

Austin, N. J. E. and N. B. Rankov 1995. *Exploratio: Military and Political Intelligence in the Roman World from the Second Punic War to the Battle of Adrianople,* London and New York, Routledge

Balty, J.-C. 1988. 'Apamea in Syria in the second and third centuries AD', *Journal of Roman Studies* 78, pp. 91–104

Barnett, R. D. 1983. 'From Ivriz to Constantinople: A study in bird-headed swords', in R. M. Boehmer and H. Hauptmann, eds, *Beiträge zur Altertumskunde Kleinasiens 12, Festschrift für Kurt Bittel,* Mainz, pp. 59–74

Bartholomew, P. 1984. 'Fourth-century Saxons', *Britannia* 15, pp. 169–85

Batty, R. 2007. *Rome and the Nomads: The Pontic-Danubian Realm in Antiquity,* Oxford, Oxford University Press

Beard, M. 2007. *The Roman Triumph,* Cambridge MA and London, Harvard University Press

Beck, F. and H. Chew, eds 1991. *Masques de fer. Un officier romain du temps de Caligula. Musée des Antiquités Nationales, St. Germain en Laye, Paris, 6 nov. 1991 – 4 février*

1992, Paris, Réunion des musées nationaux

Becker, A., G. Rasbach and S. Biegert 2003. 'Die spätaugusteische Stadtgründung in Lahnau-Waldgirmes. Archäologische, architektonische und naturwissenschaftliche Untersuchungen', *Germania* 81:1, pp. 147–99

Ben-Yehuda, N. 2002. *Sacrificing Truth: Archaeology and the Myth of Masada*, Amherst NY, Humanity Books

Bennett, P., S. S. Frere and S. Stow, eds 1982. *Excavations at Canterbury Castle*, Canterbury, Kent Archaeological Society

Bersu, G. 1964. *Die spätrömische Befestigung 'Bürgle' bei Gundremmingen*, München, Beck.

Biborski, M. 1994a. 'Römische Schwerter im Gebiet des europäischen Barbaricum', *Journal of Roman Military Equipment Studies* 5, pp. 169–97

Biborski, M. 1994b. 'Typologie und Chronologie der Ringknaufschwerter', in H. Friesinger, J. Tejral and A. Stuppner, eds, *Markomannenkriege: Ursachen und Wirkunken*, Brno, Archäologisches Inst. der Akad. der Wissenschaften der Tschechischen Republik Brno, 1, pp. 85–97

Biborski, M. and J. Ilkjaer 2007. *Illerup Ådal, Die Schwerter Und Die Schwertscheiden : 11, Textband, 12 Katalog, Tafeln Und Fundlisten*, Moesgard, Jysk Archæologisk Selskab

Biborski, M., P. Kaczanowski, Z. Kedzierski and J. Stepinski 1985. 'Ergebnisse der metallographischen Untersuchungen von römischen Schwertern aus dem Vindonissa-Museum Brugg und dem Römermuseum Augst', *Gesellschaft pro Vindonissa*, pp. 45–80

Bidwell, P. 2007. *Roman Forts in Britain*, Stroud, Tempus

Birley, R. E. 2009. *Vindolanda: A Roman Frontier Fort on Hadrian's Wall*, Stroud, Amberley Press

Bishop, M. C. 1999. '*Praesidium*:

social, military and logistical aspects of the Roman army's provincial distribution during the early principate', in A. Goldsworthy and I. Haynes, eds, *The Roman Army as a Community*, Journal of Roman Archaeology Supplementary Series 34, Portsmouth RI, pp. 111–18.

Bishop, M. C. 2002. *Lorica Segmentata, Vol. 1: A Handbook of Roman Plate Armour*, Chirnside, Armatura Press

Bishop, M. C. and J. C. N. Coulston 2006. *Roman Military Equipment*, Oxford and Oakville CT, Oxbow

Bishop, M. C. and J. N. Dore 1988. *Corbridge: Excavations of the Roman Fort and Town 1947–80*, London, English Heritage Archaeological Report 8

Bona, I. 1991. *Das Hunnenreich*, Stuttgart, Konrad Theiss

Boot, M. 2002. *The Savage Wars of Peace: Small Wars and the Rise of American Power*, New York, Basic Books

Bosman, A. V. A. J. 1999. 'Battlefield Flevum: Velsen 1, the latest excavations, results and interpretations from features and finds', in W. Schluter and R. Wiegels, eds, *Rom, Germanien und die Ausgrabungen von Kalkriese*, Osnabruck, Universitätsverlag Rasch, 91–96.

Bosworth, A. B. 1976. 'Vespasian's reorganization of the north-east frontier', *Antichton* 10, pp. 63–78

Bowman, A. K. 1994. *Life and Letters on the Roman Frontier. Vindolanda and its People*, London, British Museum Press and New York, Routledge (1998)

Bowman, A. K. and J. Thomas 1983. *Vindolanda: The Latin Writing Tablets*, London, British Museum Press

Bowman, A. and J. Thomas 1994. *The Vindolanda Writing Tablets (Tabula Vindolandensis 11)*, London, British Museum Press

Bradley, R. 1998. *The Passage of Arms: An Archaeological Analysis of Prehistoric Hoards and Votive*

*Deposits*, Oxford, Oxbow

Breeze, D. J. and B. Dobson 2000. *Hadrian's Wall*, London, Penguin

Brewer, R. J., ed. 2002. *The Second Augustan Legion and the Roman Military Machine*, Cardiff, National Museums and Galleries of Wales

Brown, P. 1971. *The World of Late Antiquity*, London, Thames & Hudson

Bruce-Mitford, R. 1978. *The Sutton Hoo Ship Burial Vol. 11, Arms, Armour and Regalia*, London, British Museum Publications

Bruckner, A. and R. Marichal, eds 1979. *Chartae Latinae Antiquiores, Part x, Germany I*, Zürich, Urs Graf-Verlag

Brunaux, J.-L. 1999. 'Ribemont-sur-Ancre: Bilan preliminaire et nouvelles hypothèses', *Gallia* 56, pp. 177–283

Brunt, P. A. 1974. 'Conscription and volunteering in the Roman Imperial Army', *Scripta Classica Israelica* 1, pp. 90–115

Bujukliev, H. 1986. *La Necropole Tumulaire Thrace pres de atalka, Region de Stara Zagora*, Sofia, Izd-vo na Bulgarskata akademiia na naukite

Burns, T. S. 1973. 'The battle of Adrianople: a reconsideration', *Historia* 22:2, pp. 337–45

Campbell, B. 1984. *The Emperor and the Roman Army, 31 BC–AD 235*, Oxford, Clarendon Press and New York, Oxford University Press

Campbell, B. 1993. 'War and diplomacy: Rome and Parthia, 31 BC–AD 235', in J. Rich and G. Shipley, eds, *War and Society in the Roman World*, London and New York, Routledge, pp. 213–40

Campbell, B. 1994. *The Roman Army 31 BC–AD 337: A Sourcebook*, London and New York, Routledge

Campbell, B. 2002. 'Power without limit: "The Romans always win"', in A. Chaniotis and P. Ducrey, eds, *Army and Power in the Ancient World*, Stuttgart, Steiner, pp. 167–180

Casey, P. J. 1992. 'The end of garrisons on Hadrian's Wall: an historical-environmental model', *Institute of Archaeology Bulletin* 29, pp. 69–80

Caubet, A. 1990. *Aux Sources du Monde Arabe: L'Arabie avant l'Islam; Collections du Musée du Louvre*, Paris, Réunion des musées nationaux

Chaniotis, A. 2005. *War in the Hellenistic World: A Social and Cultural History*, Oxford and Malden MA, Blackwell

Chrissanthos, S. G. 2001. 'Caesar and the mutiny of 47 BC', *Journal of Roman Studies* 91, pp. 63–75

Clarke, J. R. 2002. 'Look who's laughing at sex: men and women viewers in the *apodyterium* of the suburban baths at Pompeii', in D. Frederick, ed., *The Roman Gaze*, Baltimore and London, Johns Hopkins, pp. 149–81

Clausewitz, C.v. 1832. *Vom Kriege*, Berlin, Dümmlers

Cloud, D. 1993. 'Roman poetry and anti-militarism', in J. Rich and G. Shipley, eds, *War and Society in the Roman World*, London and New York, Routledge, pp. 113–38

Colledge, M. A. R. 1967. *The Parthians*, London, Thames & Hudson and New York, Praeger

Collis, J. 2003. *Celts: Origins, Myths and Inventions*, Stroud, Tempus

Connolly, P. 1988a. *Tiberius Claudius Maximus the Cavalryman*, Oxford, Oxford University Press

Connolly, P. 1988b. *Tiberius Claudius Maximus the Legionary*, Oxford, Oxford University Press

Connolly, P. 1997. 'Pilum, gladius and pugio in the late republic', *Journal of Roman Military Equipment Studies* 8, pp. 41–57

Connolly, P. and C. Van Driel-Murray 1991. 'The Roman cavalry saddle', *Britannia* 22, pp. 33–50

Cornell, T. J. 1995. *The Beginnings of Rome: Italy from the Bronze Age to the Punic Wars (c. 1000–264 BC)*, London and New York, Routledge

Coulston, J. C. N. 1990. 'Later Roman armour, 3rd–6th centuries AD', *Journal of Roman Military Equipment Studies* 1, pp. 139–60

Coulston, J. C. N. 1991. 'The "draco" standard', *Journal of Roman Military Equipment Studies* 2, pp. 101–14

Coulston, J. C. N. 2003. 'Tacitus, *Historiae* I.79 and the impact of Sarmatian warfare on the Roman empire', in C. von Carnap-Bornheim, ed., *Kontakt – Kooperation – Konflikt: Germanen und Sarmaten zwischen dem 1. and 4. Jahrhundert nach Christus*, Marburg, Wachholz, pp. 415–33

Creighton, J. 2000. *Coins and Power in Late Iron Age Britain*, Cambridge and New York, Cambridge University Press

Creighton, J. 2005. *Britannia: The Creation of a Roman Province*, London and New York, Routledge

Cumont, F. 1923. '"Le sacrifice du tribun romain Terentius" et les Palmyréniens a Doura', *Monuments et Mémoires publié par l'Academie des Inscriptions et Belles Lettres* 26: 1–46

Curle, J. 1911. *A Roman Frontier Post and its People. The Fort at Newstead*, Glasgow, J. Maclehose

Curtis, J., ed. 2000. *Mesopotamia and Iran in the Parthian and Sasanian Periods: Rejection and Revival c. 238 BC–AD 642: Proceedings of a Seminar in Memory of Vladimir G. Lukonin*, London, British Museum Press

Dalrymple, W. 1994. *City of Djinns: A Year in Delhi*, London, Flamingo

Daly, G. 2002. *Cannae: The Experience of Battle in the Second Punic War*, London and New York, Routledge

Daryaee, T. 2009. *Sasanian Persia: The Rise and Fall of an Empire*, London and New York, I. B. Tauris

Dignas, B. and E. Winter 2007. *Rome and Persia in Late Antiquity: Neighbours and Rivals*, Cambridge, Cambridge University Press

Dobson, M. 2006. *The Army of the Roman Republic: The 2nd Century BC, Polybius and the Camps at Numantia, Spain*, Oxford and Oakville CT, Oxbow

Dodgeon, M. H. and S. N. C. Lieu 1991. *The Roman Eastern Frontier and the Persian Wars, A.D. 226–363. A Documentary History*, London and New York, Routledge

Driel-Murray, C. van 1995. 'Gender in Question', in P. Rush, ed., *Theoretical Roman Archaeology: Second Conference Proceedings*, Aldershot, Avebury, pp. 3–21

Driel-Murray, C. van 2002. 'Ethnic soldiers: the experience of the Lower Rhine tribes', in T. Grünewald and S. Seibel, eds, *Kontinuität und Diskontinuität: Germania Inferior am Beginn und am Ende der Römischen Herrschaft*, Berlin and New York, De Gruyter, pp. 200–17

Driel-Murray, C. van 2005. 'Imperial soldiers: recruitment and the formation of Batavian tribal identity', in Z. Visy, ed., *Proceedings of the 19th Congress of Roman Frontier Studies, Pécs 2003*, Pécs, University of Pécs, pp. 435–39

Driessen, M. 2005. 'Unifying aspects of Roman forts', in J. Bruhn, B. Croxford and D. Grigoropoulos, eds, *TRAC 2004: Proceedings of the Fourteenth Annual Theoretical Roman Archaeology Conference*, Oxford, Oxbow, pp. 157–62

Drinkwater, J. 1984. 'Peasants and Bagaudae in Roman Gaul', *Classical Views* NS 3, pp. 349–71

Drinkwater, J. 1989. 'Patronage in Roman Gaul and the problem of the Bagaudae', in A. Wallace-Hadrill, ed., *Patronage in Ancient Society*, London and New York, Routledge, pp. 189–203

Drinkwater, J. 1996. '"The Germanic threat on the Rhine frontier": a Romano-Gallic artefact?' in R. W. Mathiesen and H. S. Sivan, eds, *Shifting Frontiers in Late Antiquity*, Aldershot, Variorum, pp. 20–30

Drinkwater, J. 2007. *The Alamanni and Rome 213–496. Caracalla to Clovis*, Oxford and New York, Oxford University Press

Eckstein, A. M. 2006. *Mediterranean Anarchy, Interstate War, and the Rise of Rome*, Berkeley CA, University of California Press

Elton, H. 1996. *Warfare in Roman Europe, A.D. 350–425*, Oxford, Clarendon Press and New York, Oxford University Press

Erdkamp, P. 1998. *Hunger and the Sword: Warfare and Food Supply in Roman Republican Wars (264–30 BC)*, Amsterdam, J. C. Gieben

Erdrich, M. 1994. 'Waffen in Mitteleuropäischen Barbaricum: Handel oder politik', *Journal of Roman Military Equipment Studies* 5, pp. 199–209.

Erdkamp, P., ed. 2007. *A Companion to the Roman Army*, Oxford, Blackwell

Farrokh, K. 2007. *Shadows in the Desert: Ancient Persia at War*, Botley and New York, Osprey

Fellmann, R. 1957. *Das Grab des L. Munatius Plancus bei Gaeta*, Basel, Verlag des Institutes für Ur- and Frühgeschichte der Schweiz

Ferrill, A. 1986. *The Fall of the Roman Empire: The Military Explanation*, London and New York, Thames & Hudson

Ferris, I. M. 2008. *Hate and War: The Column of Marcus Aurelius*, Stroud, History Press

Feugère, M. 2002. *Weapons of the Romans*, Stroud, Tempus

Foster, J. 1980. *The Iron Age Moulds from Gussage All Saints*, London, British Museum

Franzius, G. 1999. 'Maskenhelme', in W. Schlüter and W. R. Wiegels, eds, *Rom, Germanien und die Ausgrabungen von Kalkriese*, Osnabruck, Universitätsverlag Rasch, pp. 117–48

Fraser, J. E. 2009. *The New Edinburgh History Of Scotland Vol. 1 – From Caledonia To Pictland*, Edinburgh, Edinburgh University Press

Geschwinde, M., H. Hassmann, P. Lönne, M. Meyer and G. Moosbauer 2009. 'Roms Vergessener Feldzug: Das neu entdeckte Schlachtfeld am Harzhorn in Niedersachsen', in S. Berke, S. Burmeister and H. Kenzler, eds, *2000 Jahre Varusschlacht: Konflikt*, Stuttgart, Konrad Thiess, pp. 228–32

Ghirshman, R. 1962. *Iran: Parthians and Sassanians*, London, Thames & Hudson

Ghirshman, R. 1979. 'Le ceinture en Iran', *Iranica Antiqua* 14, pp. 167–96

Goethert, K.-P. 1996. 'Neue römische Prunkschilde', in M. Junkelmann, ed., *Reiter wie Statuen aus Erz*, Mainz, Von Zabern, pp. 115–26

Goldsworthy, A. 2003. *The Complete Roman Army*, London and New York, Thames & Hudson

Goldsworthy, A. K. 1996. *The Roman Army at War 100 BC–AD 200*, Oxford and New York, Oxford University Press

Goroncharovski, V. A. 2006. 'Some notes on defensive armament of the Bosporan cavalry', in M. Mode and J. Tubach, eds, *Arms and Armour as Indicators of Cultural Transfer: The Steppes and the Ancient World from Hellenistic Times to the Early Middle Ages*, Wiesbaden, Reichert, pp. 445–52

Grigg, R. 1983. 'Inconsistency and lassitude: the shield emblems of the Notitia Dignitatum', *Journal of Roman Studies* 73, pp. 132–42

Grünewald, T. 2004. *Bandits in the Roman Empire: Myth and Reality*, London and New York, Routledge

Hallett, J. P. and M. B. Skinner, eds 1997. *Roman Sexualities*, Princeton, Princeton University Press

Hanson, W. S. 2007. *A Roman Frontier Fort in Scotland: Elginhaugh*, Stroud, Tempus

Hanson, W. S. and I. P. Haynes, eds 2004. *Roman Dacia: The Making of a Provincial Society*, Journal of Roman Archaeology Supplementary Series 56, Portsmouth RI

Harmatta, J. 1951. 'The Golden Bow of the Huns', *Acta Archaeologica Hungaricae* 1, pp. 114–49

Harnack, A. 1981. *Militia Christi: The Christian Religion and the Military in the First Three Centuries*, Philadelphia, Polebridge Press Westar Institute

Harries, J. 2007. *Law and Crime in the Roman World*, Cambridge and New York, Cambridge University Press

Harris, W. V. 1985. *War and Imperialism in Republican Rome, 327–70 BC*, Oxford, Clarendon Press and New York, Oxford University Press

Heather, P. 1996. *The Goths*, Oxford and Cambridge MA, Blackwell

Heather, P. 2005. *The Fall of the Roman Empire: A New History of Rome and the Barbarians*, London, Macmillan and New York, Oxford University Press (2006)

Henig, M. 2002. *The Heirs of King Verica. Culture and Politics in Roman Britain*, Stroud and Charleston SC, Tempus

Herrmann, F. R. 1969. 'Der Eisenhortfund aus dem Kastell Künzing', *Saalburg-Jahrbuch* 26, pp. 129–41

Herrmann, G. 1981. *The Sasanian Rock Reliefs at Bishapur: Part 2, Bishapur IV, Bahram II receiving a delegation; Bishapur V, The Investiture of Bahr am I; Bishapur VI, the enthroned King*, Berlin, Dietrich Reimer Verlag

Herrmann, G. 1983. *The Sasanian Rock Reliefs at Bishapur: Part 3, Bishapur I and II, Sarab-i Bahram, Tang-i Qandil*, Berlin, Dietrich Reimer Verlag

Herrmann, G. 1989. 'Parthian and Sasanian saddlery', in L. de Mayer and E. Haerinck, eds, *Archaeologia Iranica et Orientalis. Miscellanea in Honorem Louis Vanden Berghe II*, Ghent, Peeters, pp. 757–809

Hingley, R. 1989. *Rural Settlement in Roman Britain*, London, Seaby

Hingley, R. 2005. *Globalizing Roman Culture: Unity, Diversity and Empire*, London and New York, Routledge.

Holder, P. I. 1980. *The Auxilia from Augustus to Trajan*, Oxford, British Archaeological Reports International Series 70

Holland, T. 2003. *Rubicon: The Triumph and Tragedy of the Roman Republic*, New York, Little, Brown

Hopkins, K. 1999. *A World Full of Gods: Pagans Jews and Christians in the Roman Empire*, London, Weidenfeld & Nicholson and New

York, Free Press (2000)

Hornus, J.-M. 1980. *It Is Not Lawful for Me to Fight: Early Christian Attitudes Toward War, Violence and the State*, Scottdale, PA, Herald Press

Horvat, J. 1997. 'Roman republican weapons from Šmihel in Slovenia', *Journal of Roman Military Equipment Studies* 8, pp. 105–20

Hunter, F. 2005. 'Rome and the creation of the Picts', in Z. Visy, ed., *Proceedings of the 19th Congress of Roman Frontier Studies, Pécs 2003*, Pécs, University of Pécs, pp. 235–44

Hunter, F. 2007. *Beyond the Edge of Empire: Caledonians, Picts and Romans*, Rosemarkie, Groam House Museum

Ilkjaer, J. 2000. *Illerup Ådal – Archaeology as a Magic Mirror*, Højberg, Moesgård Museum

Isaac, B. 1992. *The Limits of Empire: The Roman Army in the East*, Oxford, Clarendon Press and New York, Oxford University Press

Isaac, B. 2002. 'Army and power in the Roman world: a response to Brian Campbell', in A. Chaniotis and P. Ducrey, eds, *Army and Power in the Ancient World*, Stuttgart, Steiner, pp. 181–91

James, S. T. 1986. 'Evidence from Dura-Europos for the origins of late Roman helmets', *Syria* LXIII, pp. 107–34

James, S. T. 1987. 'Dura-Europos and the introduction of the "Mongolian release"', in M. Dawson, ed., *Roman Military Equipment; The Accoutrements of War*, Oxford, British Archaeological Reports International Series, 336, pp. 77–83

James, S. T. 1988. 'The fabricae: state arms factories of the later Roman empire', in J. C. N. Coulston, ed., *Military Equipment and the Identity of Roman Soldiers*, Oxford, British Archaeological Reports International Series, 394, pp. 257–331

James, S. T. 1999. *The Atlantic Celts: Ancient People or Modern Invention?*, London, British Museum Press and and Madison,

University of Wisconsin Press

James, S. T. 2002. 'Writing the legions: the development and future of Roman military studies in Britain', *Archaeological Journal* 159, pp. 1–58

James, S. T. 2004. *Excavations at Dura-Europos, Final Report Vol. VII, The Arms and Armour, and other Military Equipment*, London, British Museum Press

James, S. T. 2005. 'Large-scale recruitment of auxiliaries from Free Germany?' in Z. Visy, ed., *Limes XIX: Proceedings of the XIXth International Congress of Roman Frontier Studies, held in Pécs, Hungary, September 2003*, Pécs, Hungary, University of Pécs, pp. 273–79

James, S. T. 2006. 'The impact of steppe peoples and the Partho-Sasanian world on the development of Roman military equipment and dress, 1st to 3rd centuries AD', in M. Mode and J. Tubach, eds, *Arms and Armour as Indicators of Cultural Transfer: The Steppes and the Ancient World from Hellenistic Times to the Early Middle Ages*, Wiesbaden, Reichert, pp. 357–92

James, S. T. 2007. 'New light on the Roman military base at Dura-Europos: Interim report on a pilot season of fieldwork in 2005', in A. S. Lewin and P. Pellegrini, eds, *The Late Roman Army in the Near East from Diocletian to the Arab Conquest*, Oxford, British Archaeological Reports International Series, 1717, pp. 29–47

James, S. T. 2011. 'Stratagems, combat and "chemical warfare" in the siege-mines of Dura-Europos', *American Journal of Archaeology* 115: 69–101

James, S. T. forthcoming. 'Roman: Partho-Sasanian martial interactions: Testimony of a cheekpiece from Hatra and its parallels', in L. Dirven, ed., *Hatra. Politics, Culture and Religion between Parthia and Rome*

Johnson, A. 1983. *Roman Forts of the 1st and 2nd Centuries in Britain and*

the German Provinces, London, A & C Black

Jones, A. H. M. 1964. *The Later Roman Empire. A Social, Economic and Administrative Survey*, Oxford, Oxford University Press and Norman, University of Oklahoma Press

Jones, A. H. M. 1966. *The Decline of the Ancient World*, London, Longman

Jones, B. W. 1992. *The Emperor Domitian*, London and New York, Routledge

Jørgensen, L. 2001. 'The "warriors, soldiers and conscripts" of the anthropology in Late Roman and Migration Period archaeology', in B. Storgaard, ed., *Military Aspects of the Aristocracy in Barbaricum in the Roman and Early Migration Periods*, Copenhagen, National Museum of Denmark, pp. 9–19

Jørgensen, L., B. Storgaard and L. G. Thomsen, eds 2003. *The Spoils of Victory: the North in the Shadow of the Roman Empire*, Copenhagen, Nationalmuseet

Kahaner, L. 2007. *AK-47: The Weapon that Changed the Face of War*, Hoboken, NJ, Wiley

Kanz, F. and K. Grossschmidt 2006. 'Head injuries of Roman gladiators', *Forensic Science International* 160:2–3, pp. 207–16

Keaveney, A. 2007. *The Army in the Roman Revolution*, London and New York, Routledge

Keegan, J. 1988. *The Face of Battle: A Study of Agincourt, Waterloo and the Somme*, London, Barrie & Jenkins

Kellner, H.-J. 1966. 'Zu den Römischen Ringknaufschwerten und Dosenortbandern in Bayern', *Jahrbuch des Römisch-Germanischen Zentralmuseums*: 13, 190–201

Kennedy, D. L. 1977. 'Parthian regiments in the Roman army', in J. Fitz, ed., *Limes. Akten des XI Internationalen Limeskongress*, Budapest, Akadémiai Kiadó, pp. 521–31

Kennedy, D. L. 1994. 'The cohors xx Palmyrenorum at Dura Europos', in E. Dabrowa, ed., *The Roman and Byzantine Army in the East*, Krakow, Uniwersytet Jagiellonski, Instytut Historii, pp. 89–98

Kennedy, D. L. 1996. 'Parthia and Rome: eastern perspectives', in D. L. Kennedy, ed., *The Roman Army in the East*, Journal of Roman Archaeology Supplementary Series 18, Portsmouth, RI, pp. 67–90

Keppie, L. 1984. *The Making of the Roman Army from Republic to Empire*, London, Batsford and Totowa, NJ, Barnes & Noble

Keppie, L. 1991. 'A centurion of *legio Martia* at Padova?', *Journal of Roman Military Equipment Studies* 2, pp. 115–21

Khorasani, M. M. 2006. *Arms and Armor from Iran: The Bronze Age to the End of the Qajar Period*, Tübingen, Legat-Verlag

Klumbach, H. 1970. 'Altes und Neues zum "Schwert des Tiberius"', *Jahrbuch des Römisch-Germanischen Zentralmuseums Mainz* 17, pp. 123–32

Klumbach, H. 1973. *Spatrömische Gardehelme*, Munich, Beck

Krinzinger, F., ed. 2002. *Gladiatoren in Ephesos: Tod am Nachmittag*, Istanbul and Vienna, Österreichisches Archäologisches Institut

Kulikowski, M. 2000 'Barbarians in Gaul, usurpers in Britain', *Britannia* 31, pp. 325–45

Künzl, E. 1996. 'Gladiusdekorationen der frühen römischen Kaiserzeit. Dynastische Legitimation, Victoria und Aurea Aetas,' *RGZM Jahrbuch* 43: 383–474

Künzl, E. 2008. *Unter den goldenen Adlern: Der Waffenschmuck des römischen Imperiums*, Regensburg/Mainz, Schnell Steiner/Verlag des Römisch-Germanischen Zentralmuseums

Lacomba, A. R.i. 2006. 'The Roman foundation of Valencia and the town in the 2nd–1st centuries B.C.' in L. A. Casal, S. Keay and S. R. Asensio, eds, *Early Roman Towns in Hispania Tarraconensis*, Portsmouth RI, Journal of Roman Archaeology Supplementary Series 62, pp. 75–89

Lang, J. 1988. 'A study of the metallography of some Roman swords', *Britannia* 19, pp. 199–216

Laszlo, G. 1951. 'The Golden Bow of the Huns', *Acta Archaeologica Hungaricae* 1, pp. 91–106

Laubscher, H.P. 1975. *Der Reliefschmuck des Galeriusbogens in Thessaloniki*, Berlin, Mann

Le Bohec, Y. 1994. *The Imperial Roman Army*, London, Batsford

Le Bohec, Y. 2006. *L'Armée Romaine sous le Bas-Empire*, Paris, Picard

Le Bohec, Y. 2009. *L'armée romaine dans la tourmente. Une nouvelle approche de la crise du troisième siècle*, Paris and Monaco, Rocher

Leach, J. D. 1978. *Pompey the Great*, London and Totowa NJ, Croom Helm

Lee, A. D. 2007. *War in Late Antiquity: A Social History*, Oxford and Malden MA, Blackwell

Lendon, J. E. 1997. *Empire of Honour: The Art of Government in the Roman World*, Oxford, Clarendon Press and New York, Oxford University Press

Lendon, J. E. 2004. 'The Roman Army now', *Classical Journal* 99, pp. 441–49

Lendon, J. E. 2005. *Soldiers and Ghosts: A History of Battle in Classical Antiquity*, New Haven and London, Yale University Press

Leriche, P. 1993. 'Techniques de guerre sassanides et romains à Doura-Europos', in F. Vallet and M. Kazanski, eds, *L'Armée Romaine et les Barbares du IIIe au VIIe siècle*, Rouen and Saint-Germain-en-Laye, Association Française d'Archéologie Mérovingienne and Musée des Antiquités Nationales, pp. 83–100

Lewis, M. E. 2007. *The Early Chinese Empires: Qin and Han*, Cambridge MA and London, Harvard University Press

Luttwak, E. N. 1976. *The Grand Strategy of the Roman Empire from the First Century AD to the Third*, Baltimore and London, Johns Hopkins University Press

Lyne, M. 1994. 'Late Roman helmet fragments from Richborough', *Journal of Roman Military Equipment Studies* 5, pp. 97–105

MacMullen, R. 1960. 'Inscriptions on armour and the supply of arms in the Roman empire', *American Journal of Archeology* 64, pp. 23–40

MacMullen, R. 1963. *Soldier and Civilian in the Later Roman Empire*, Cambridge MA, Harvard University Press

MacMullen, R. 1980. 'How big was the Roman Imperial Army?', *Klio* 62:2, pp. 451–60

MacMullen, R. 1984. 'The legion as a society', *Historia* 33, pp. 440–56

MacMullen, R. 1986. 'Judicial savagery in the Roman empire', *Chiron* 16, pp. 147–66

MacMullen, R. 1990. *Corruption and the Decline of Rome*, New Haven, Yale University Press.

Maldur, V. 2005. 'L'armée romaine entre Prut et Nistru I–IIIe siècles (à la recherche de nouvelles frontières)', in Z. Visy, ed., *Proceedings of the 19th Congress of Roman Frontier Studies, Pécs 2003*, Pécs, University of Pécs, pp. 121–29

Mann, J. C. 1974. 'The frontiers of the Roman principate', in H. Temporini, ed., *Aufstieg und Niedergang der Römischen Welt II.i*, Berlin and New York, Walter de Gruyter, pp. 508–33

Mann, J. C. 1983. *Legionary Recruitment and Veteran Settlement during the Principate*, London, UCL Institute of Archaeology Publications

Mann, J. C. 1990. 'The function of Hadrian's Wall', *Archaeologia Aeliana* 5th series 18, pp. 51–54

Manning, W. 1985. *Catalogue of the Romano-British Iron Tools, Fittings and Weapons in the British Museum*, London, British Museum Press

Marmot, M. 2004. *Status Syndrome: How Your Social Standing Directly Affects Your Health*, New York,

Times Books and London, Bloomsbury

Maryon, H. 1960. 'Pattern-welding and Damascening of sword-blades, Parts 1–2', *Studies in Conservation* 5, pp. 25–60

Mattingly, D. J., ed. 1997. *Dialogues in Roman Imperialism. Power, Discourse and Discrepant Experience in the Roman Empire*, Journal of Roman Archaeology Supplementary Series 23, Portsmouth, RI

Mattingly, D. J. 2006. *An Imperial Possession: Britain in the Roman Empire*, London and New York, Penguin/Allen Lane

Mattingly, D. J. 2010. *Imperialism, Power and Identity: Experiencing the Roman Empire*, Princeton, Princeton University Press

McCarthy, M. 2002. *Roman Carlisle and the Lands of the Solway*, Stroud and Charlston SC, Tempus

McDonnell, M. 2006. *Roman Manliness: Virtus and the Roman Republic*, Cambridge and New York, Cambridge University Press

Merrills, A. and R. Miles 2010. *The Vandals*, Oxford and Malden MA, Wiley-Blackwell

Mesnil du Buisson, R. du 1936. 'The Persian mines', in M. I. Rostovtzeff, A. R. Bellinger, C. Hopkins and C. B. Welles, eds, *The Excavations at Dura-Europos, Preliminary Report of Sixth Season of Work, October 1932–March 1933*, New Haven, Yale University Press, pp. 188–205

Mesnil du Buisson, R. du 1944. 'Les ouvrages du siège a Doura-Europos', *Mémoires de la Société Nationale des Antiquaires de France, 9th Series* 1, pp. 5–60

Messer, W. S. 1920. 'Mutiny in the Roman Army. The Republic', *Classical Philology* 15, pp. 158–75

Miks, C. 2007. *Studien zur römischen Schwertbewaffnung in der Kaiserzeit*, Rahden, Westphalia, Leidorf

Millar, F. 1977. *The Emperor in the Roman World*, London, Duckworth

Millar, F. 1993. *The Roman Near East, 31 BC–AD 337*, Cambridge MA and

London, Harvard University Press

Millett, M. J. 2001. 'Roman interaction in north-western Iberia', *Oxford Journal of Archaeology* 20:2, pp. 157–70

Mommsen, T., P. Krueger and A. Watson, eds 1985. *The Digest of Justinian*, Philadelphia, University of Pennsylvania Press

Motta, L. and N. Terrenato 2006. 'The origins of the state *par excellence*: power and society in Iron Age Rome', in C.C. Haselgrove, ed., *Celtes et Gaulois, l'Archéologie face à l'Histoire, 4: les mutations de la fin de l'âge du Fer. Actes de la table ronde de Cambridge, 7–8 Juillet 2005*, Glux-en-Glenne, Bibracte, Centre archéologique européen, pp. 225–34

Navarro, J. M. de 1972. *The Finds from the Site of La Tène: Vol. 1, Scabbards and the Swords Found in Them*, London, Oxford University Press, for the British Academy

Nicasie, M. 1998. *Twilight of Empire. The Roman Army from the Reign of Diocletian until the Battle of Adrianople*, Amsterdam, Gieben

Nokandeh, J., E. Sauer, H. O. Rekavandi, T. Wilkinson, A. A. Ghorban, J.-L. Schwenninger, M. Mahmoudi, D. Parker, M. Fattahi, L. S. Usher-Wilson, M. Ershadi, J. Ratcliffe and R. Gale 2006. 'Linear barriers of Northern Iran: The Great Wall of Gorgan and the Wall of Tammishe', *Iran* 44, pp. 121–73

Parker, H. M. D. 1958. *The Roman Legions*, Cambridge, Heffer and New York, Barnes & Noble

Parker, S. T. 1986. *Romans and Saracens: A History of the Arabian Frontier*, Winona Lake IN, American Schools of Oriental Research

Parsons, P. 2007. *City of the Sharp-Nosed Fish: Everyday Life in the Nile Valley, 400 BC–350 AD*, London, Weidenfeld & Nicolson

Peddie, J. 1994. *The Roman War Machine*, Stroud, Alan Sutton and Philadelphia, Combined Books

Péristiany, J. G. 1966. *Honour and Shame: The Values of*

*Mediterranean Society*, Chicago, University of Chicago Press

Petersen, E., A. von Domaszewski and G. Calderini 1896. *Die Marcus-Säule auf Piazza Colonna in Rom*, München, Bruckmann.

Phang, S. E. 2001. *The Marriage of Roman Soldiers (13 BC–AD 235): Law and Family in the Imperial Army*, Leiden and Boston, Brill

Phang, S. E. 2008. *Roman Military Service: Ideologies of Discipline in the Late Republic and Early Principate*, Cambridge and New York, Cambridge University Press

Pitts, L. F. and J. K. St Joseph 1985. *Inchtuthil: The Roman Legionary Fortress Excavations 1952–65*, London, Society for the Promotion of Roman Studies

Planck, D. 1975. *Arae Flaviae I. Neue Untersuchungen zur Geschichte des römischen Rottweil*, Stuttgart, Landesdenkmalamt Baden-Württemberg

Pleiner, R. 1993. *The Celtic Sword*, Oxford, Clarendon Press and New York, Oxford University Press

Pohlsander, H. A. 1969. 'Victory: the story of a statue', *Historia: Zeitschrift für Alte Geschichte* 18:5, pp. 588–97

Pollard, N. 2000. *Soldiers, Cities, and Civilians in Roman Syria*, Ann Arbor, Michigan University Press

Purdue, B. N. 2000. 'Cutting and piercing wounds', in J. K. Mason and B. N. Purdue, eds, *The Pathology of Trauma*, London, Arnold and New York, Oxford University Press, pp. 123–40

Quesada Sanz, F. 1997. '*Gladius hispaniensis*: an archaeological view from Iberia', *Journal of Roman Military Equipment Studies* 8, pp. 251–70

Rapin, A. 2001. 'Des épées romaines dans la collection d'Alise-Sainte-Reine', *Gladius* 21, pp. 31–56

Reddé, M. 1996. *L'Armée romaine en Gaule*, Paris, Éditions Errance

Rekavandi, H. O., E. Sauer, T. Wilkinson, E. S. Tamak, R. Ainslie, M. Mahmoudi, S. Griffiths, M.

Ershadi, J. J. Van Rensberg, M. Fattahi, J. Ratcliffe, J. Nokandeh, A. Nazifi, R. Thomas, R. Gale and B. Hoffmann 2007. 'An imperial frontier of the Sasanian empire: further fieldwork on the Great Wall of Gorgan', *Iran* 45, pp. 95–132

Ribera i Lacomba, A. and M. Calvo Galvez 1995. 'La primera evidencia arqueológica de la destrucción de Valentia por Pompeyo', *Journal of Roman Archaeology* 8, pp. 19–40

Rich, J. 1993. 'Fear, greed and glory: the causes of warmaking in the middle republic', in J. Rich and G. Shipley, eds, *War and Society in the Roman World*, London and New York, Routledge, pp. 38–69

Richmond, I. 1943. 'Roman legionaries at Corbridge, their supply base, temples and religious cults', *Archaeologia Aeliana, Series 4* 21, pp. 127–224

Richmond, I. 1962. 'The Roman siege works of Masada', *Journal of Roman Studies* 52, pp. 142–55

Robb, J. 1997. 'Violence and gender in early Italy', in D. L. Martin and D. W. Frayer, eds, *Troubled Times: Violence and Warfare in the Past*, Amsterdam, Gordon and Breach, pp. 111–44

Robert, L. 1943. 'Sur un papyrus de Bruxelles', *Revue de Philologie* 17, pp. 111–19

Robert, L., ed. 1989. *Opera Minora Selecta, Épigraphie et Antiquités Grecques, Tom.6*, Amsterdam, Hakkert

Robinson, H. R. 1975. *The Armour of Imperial Rome*, London, Arms and Armour Press and New York, Scribner

Rodger, N. A. M. 2004. *The Command of the Ocean: A Naval History of Britain, 1649–1815*, London, Allen Lane and New York, W. W. Norton

Rosenqvist, A. 1968. 'Sverd med Klinger med Figurer; Kopperlegeninger fra Eldre Jernalder; Universitetets Oldsaksamling', *Universitetets Oldsaksamlings Arbok 1967–68*, pp. 143–200

Rosenstein, N. 2004. *Rome at War: Farms, Families and Death in the Middle Republic*, Chapel Hill and London, University of North Carolina Press

Rosenstein, N. 2009. 'War, state formation, and the evolution of military institutions in ancient China and Rome', in W. Scheidel, ed., *Rome and China: Comparative Perspectives on Ancient World Empires*, Oxford and New York, Oxford University Press, pp. 24–51

Rostovtzeff, M., A. Bellinger, F. Brown and C. Welles, eds 1944. *The Excavations at Dura-Europos, Preliminary Report on the Ninth Season, 1935–1936, Part 1: The Agora and Bazaar*, New Haven, Yale University Press

Roth, J. P. 2006. 'Siege narrative in Livy: representation and reality', in S. Dillon and K. E. Welch, eds, *Representations of War in Ancient Rome*, Cambridge and New York, Cambridge University Press

Roymans, N. 2004. *Ethnic Identity and Imperial Power: The Batavians in the Early Roman Empire*, Amsterdam, Amsterdam University Press

Sabin, P. 1996. 'The mechanics of battle in the Second Punic War', in T. Cornell, B. Rankov and P. Sabin, eds, *The Second Punic War: A Reappraisal*, London, Institute of Classical Studies, pp. 59–79

Sand, S. 2009. *The Invention of the Jewish People*, London and New York, Verso

Sarnowski, T. 2005. 'Die Römer bei den Griechen auf der südlichen Krim neue Entdeckungen und Forschungen', in Z. Visy, ed., *Proceedings of the 19th Congress of Roman Frontier Studies, Pécs 2003*, Pécs, University of Pécs, pp. 741–48

Scheidel, W. 1996. 'The demography of the Roman imperial army', in W. Scheidel, ed., *Measuring Sex, Age and Death in the Roman Empire: Explorations in Ancient Demography*, Journal of Roman Archaeology Supplementary Series 21, Portsmouth RI, pp. 95–138.

Schlüter, W. 1999. 'The Battle of the Teutoburg Forest: archaeological research in Kalkriese near Osnabrück', in J. D. Creighton and R. J. A. Wilson, eds, *Roman Germany: Studies in Cultural Interaction*, Journal of Roman Archaeology Supplementary Series 32, Portsmouth RI, pp. 125–59

Schlüter, W. and R. Wiegels, eds 1999. *Rom, Germanien und die Ausgrabungen von Kalkriese*, Osnabruck, Universitätsverlag Rasch

Schnurbein, S. von 1979. 'Eine holzerne Sica aus dem Romerlager Oberaden', *Germania* 57, pp. 117–34.

Schnurbein, S. von 2003. 'Augustus in Germania and his new "town" at Waldgirmes east of the Rhine', *Journal of Roman Archaeology*, 16:1, pp. 93–108

Schönberger, H. and F.-R. Herrmann 1968. 'Das Römerkastell Kunzing-Quintana', *Jahresbericht der Bayerischen Bodendenkmalpflege* 8/9, pp. 37–86.

Schoppa, H. 1974. 'Ein Gladius vom Typus Pompeji', *Germania* 52: 102–8

Schüle, W. 1969. *Die Meseta-Kulturen der Iberischen Halbinsel. Mediterrane und Eurasische Elemente in früheisenzeitlichen Kulturen Südwesteuropas*, Berlin, De Gruyter

Scullard, H. H. 1981. *Festivals and Ceremonies of the Roman Republic*, London, Thames & Hudson and New York, Cornell University Press

Sekunda, N. 2001. *Hellenistic Infantry Reform in the 160s BC*, Lodz, Oficyna Naukowa MS

Selzer, W. 1988. *Römische Steindenkmäler: Mainz in Römischer Zeit Landesmuseum Mainz, katalogreihe zu den Abteilungen und Sammlungem Begründet und herausgegeben von Berthold Roland, Band 1*, Mainz, Von Zabern

Shaw, B. D. 1983. 'Soldiers and society: the army in Numidia', *Opus* 2, pp. 133–57

Sheldon, R. M. 2005. *Intelligence Activities in Ancient Rome: Trust in* the Gods, but Verify, New York and London, Cass

Sheldon, R. M. 2010. *Rome's Wars in Parthia*, London and Portland OR, Vallentine Mitchell

Sidebottom, H. 2004. *Ancient Warfare: A Very Short Introduction*, Oxford and New York, Oxford University Press

Siebert, G. 1987. 'Quartier de Skardhana: la fouille', *Bulletin de la Correspondance Hellenestique* 111, pp. 629–42

Skinner, M. B. 2005. *Sexuality in Greek and Roman Culture*, Oxford and Malden MA, Blackwell

Smith, C. J. 2006. *The Roman Clan: The Gens from Ancient Ideology to Modern Anthropology*, Cambridge and New York, Cambridge University Press

Southern, P. and K. R. Dixon 1996. *The Late Roman Army*, London, Batsford and New Haven, Yale University Press

Spann, P. O. 1987. *Quintus Sertorius and the legacy of Sulla*, Fayetteville, University of Arkansas Press

Spaul, J. E. H. 2000. *Cohors 2*, Oxford, British Archaeological Reports International Series

Speidel, M. P. 1970. 'The captor of Decebalus: a new inscription from Philippi', *Journal of Roman Studies* 60, pp. 142–53

Speidel, M. P. 1977. 'The Roman army in Arabia', in *Aufstieg und Niedergang der Römischen Welt* II:8, pp. 687–730

Speidel, M. P. 1984. '"Europeans" – Syrian elite troops at Dura-Europos and Hatra', in M. P. Speidel, ed., *Roman Army Studies I*, Amsterdam, Gieben, pp. 301–9

Speidel, M. P. 1991. 'Swimming the Danube under Hadrian's eyes', *Ancient Society* 22, pp. 277–82

Speidel, M. P. 1992. 'The soldiers' servants', in M. P. Speidel, ed., *Roman Army Studies II*, Stuttgart, Steiner, pp. 342–52

Speidel, M. P. 1993. 'The *fustis* as a soldier's weapon', *Antiquites Africaines* 29, pp. 137–49

Speidel, M. P. 1994. *Riding for Caesar:*

*The Roman Emperors' Horse Guards*, Cambridge MA, Harvard University Press

Speidel, M. P. 2006. *Emperor Hadrian's Speeches to the African Army – A New Text*, Mainz, Romisch-Germanisches Zentralmuseum Mainz

Stead, I. M. 2005. *British Iron Age Swords and Scabbards*, London, British Museum Press

Stiebel, G. 2004. 'A Hellenistic *gladius* from Jericho', in E. Netzer, ed., *Hasmonean and Herodian Palaces at Jericho, Final Reports of the 1973–1987 Excavations, Vol. II*, Jerusalem, Israel Exploration Society: Institute of Archaeology, The Hebrew University of Jerusalem, pp. 229–32

Storgaard, B., ed. 2001. *Military Aspects of the Aristocracy in Barbaricum in the Roman and Early Migration Periods*, Copenhagen, National Museum of Denmark

Terrenato, N. 1998a. 'The Romanization of Italy: global acculturation or cultural *bricolage*?' in C. Forcey, J. Hawthorne and R. Witcher, eds, *TRAC 97: Proceedings of the Seventh Annual Theoretical Roman Archaeology Conference, Nottingham 1997*, Oxford, Oxbow, pp. 20–27

Terrenato, N. 1998b. '*Tam firmum municipium*: the Romanization of Volaterrae and its cultural implications', *Journal of Roman Studies* 88, pp. 94–114

Terrenato, N. 2001. 'A tale of three cities: the Romanization of northern coastal Etruria', in S.J. Keay and N. Terrenato, eds, *Italy and the West: Comparative Issues in Romanization*, Oxford and Oakville CT, Oxbow, pp. 54–67

Terrenato, N. 2007a. 'The clans and the peasants: reflections on social structure and change in Hellenistic Italy', in P. Van Dommelen and N. Terrenato, eds, *Articulating Local Cultures: Power and Identity Under the Expanding Roman Republic*, Journal of Roman Archaeology Supplementary Series 63,

Portsmouth RI, pp. 13–22

Terrenato, N. 2007b. 'The essential countryside: the Roman world', in S.E. Alcock and R. Osbourne, eds, *Classical Archaeology*, Oxford and Malden MA, Blackwell, pp. 139–61

Tomlin, R. S. O. 1999. 'The missing lances, or making the machine work', in A. Goldsworthy and I. Haynes, eds, *The Roman Army as a Community*, Journal of Roman Archaeology Supplementary Series 34, Portsmouth RI, pp. 127–38

Treadgold, W. 1995. *Byzantium and its Army, 284–1081*, Palo Alto CA, Stanford University Press

Treherne, P. 1995. 'The warrior's beauty: the masculine body and self-identity in Bronze-Age Europe', *European Journal of Archaeology* 3, pp. 105–44

Trousdale, W. 1975. *The Long Sword and Scabbard Slide in Asia*, Washington, Smithsonian

Trümper, M. 2009. *Graeco-Roman Slave Markets: Fact or Fiction?*, Oxford and Oakville CT, Oxbow

Ulbert, G. 1969. 'Gladii aus Pompeji', *Germania* 47, pp. 97–128

Ulbert, G. 1974. 'Straubing und Nydam. Zu römischen Langschwerten der späten Limeszeit', in G. Kossack and G. Ulbert, eds, *Studien zur Vor- und Frühgeschichtlichen Archäologie. Festscrift für Joachim Werner zum 65. Geburtstag*, München, Beck, pp. 197–216

Vishnia, R. F. 2002. 'The shadow army – the Lixae and the Roman legions', *Zeitschrift für Papyrologie und Epigraphik* 132, pp. 265–72

Wainwright, G. J., ed. 1979. *Gussage All Saints: An Iron Age Settlement in Dorset*, Department of the Environment Archaeological Reports No. 10, London, HMSO

Walbank, F. W., ed. 2002. *Polybius, Rome and the Hellenistic World: Essays and Reflections*, Cambridge and New York, Cambridge University Press

Walker, S. and A. Burnett 1981. *Augustus: Handlist of the Exhibition and Supplementary Studies,*

London, British Museum

Wallace-Hadrill, A. 2008. *Rome's Cultural Revolution*, Cambridge and New York, Cambridge University Press

Walters, J. 1997. 'Invading the Roman body: manliness and impenetrability in Roman thought', in J. P. Hallett and M. B. Skinner, eds, *Roman Sexualities*, Princeton, Princeton University Press, pp. 29–43

Wamser, L. 2000. *Die Römer zwischen Alpen und Nordmeer. Zivilisatorisches Erbe einer europäischen Militärmacht*, Mainz, Von Zabern

Ward-Perkins, B. 2005. *The Fall of Rome and the End of Civilization*, Oxford and New York, Oxford University Press

Watson, J., J. Anstee and L. Biek 1982. 'The swords and pieces of equipment from the grave: scientific and technological examination', in P. Bennett, S. S. Frere and S. Stow, eds, *Excavations at Canterbury Castle*, Canterbury, Kent Archaeological Society, 1, pp. 188–90

Webster, G. 1982. 'The swords and pieces of equipment from the grave; description', in P. Bennett, S.S. Frere and S. Stow, eds, *Excavations at Canterbury Castle*, Canterbury, Kent Archaeological Society, 1, pp. 185–88

Webster, G. 1985. *The Roman Imperial Army of the First and Second Centuries*, London, A & C Black and Totowa NJ, Barnes & Noble (3rd edn).

Webster, L. and M. Brown, eds 1997. *The Transformation of the Roman World AD 400–900*, London, British Museum Press and Berkeley, University of California Press

Welch, K. E. 2006. 'Introduction', in S. Dillon and K. E. Welch, eds, *Representations of War in Ancient Rome*, Cambridge and New York, Cambridge University Press, pp. 1–26

Welles, C. B., R. O. Fink and J. F. Gilliam, eds 1959. *Excavations at Dura-Europos, Final Report Vol. v, Part 1 The Parchments and Papyri*, New Haven, Yale University Press

Wells, P. S. 1999. *The Barbarians Speak: How the Conquered Peoples Shaped Roman Europe*, Princeton, Princeton University Press

Wells, P. S. 2003. *The Battle that Stopped Rome: Emperor Augustus, Arminius and the Slaughter of the Legions in the Teutoberg Forest*, New York and London, Norton

Werner, J. 1994. 'Chinesischer Schwerttragbügel der Han-Zeit aus einem thrakischen Häuptlingsgrab von Catalka (Bulgarien)', *Germania* 72, pp. 269–82

Wheeler, E. L. 1996. 'The laxity of Syrian legions', in D. L. Kennedy, ed., *The Roman Army in the East*, Journal of Roman Archaeology Supplementary Series 18, Ann Arbor MI, pp. 229–76

Wheeler, E. L. 2002. 'Roman treaties with Parthia: *Völkerrecht* or power politics?' in P. Freeman, J. Bennett, Z. T. Fiema and B. Hoffmann, eds, *Limes xviii: Proceedings of the xviiith International Congress of Roman Frontier Studies held in Amman, Jordan (September 2000)*, Oxford, British Archaeological Reports International Series 1084, pp. 287–92

Whitmarsh, T. 2005. *The Second Sophistic*, Oxford and New York, Oxford University Press

Whittaker, C. R. 1994. *Frontiers of the Roman Empire: A Social and Economic Study*, Baltimore, Johns Hopkins University Press

Wilkinson, R. G. 2005. *The Impact of Inequality: How to Make Sick Societies Healthier*, London, Routledge and New York, New Press

Wilmott, A. 1997. *Birdoswald: Excavations of a Roman Fort on Hadrian's Wall and its Successor Settlements: 1987–92*, English Heritage Archaeological Report 14, London, English Heritage

Wyss, R., T. Rey and F. Müller 2002. *Gewasserfunde aus Port und Umgebung*, Bern, Bernisches Historisches Museum

Woolf, G. 1998. *Becoming Roman: The Origins of Provincial Civilization in Gaul*, Cambridge and New York, Cambridge University Press

Yadin, Y. 1966. *Masada*, London, Weidenfeld & Nicholson

Youtie, H. C. and J. G. Winter 1951. *Papyri and Ostraka from Karanis, Papyri in the University of Michigan Collection, Vol. 8*, Ann Arbor, University of Michigan Press

Zahariade, M. 1991. 'An early and late Roman fort on the lower Danube limes: Halmyris (Independenta, Tulcea County, Romania)', in V. Maxfield and M. J. Dobson, eds, *Roman Frontier Studies 1989: Proceedings of the xvth International Congress of Roman Frontier Studies*, Exeter, Exeter University Press, pp. 311–17

Zahariade, M. 2009. *The Thracians in the Roman Imperial Army from the First to the Third Century AD, 1 Auxilia*, Cluj-Napoca, Mega

# Sources of Illustrations

All drawings and photographs are by Simon James unless otherwise noted.

Numbers refer to Figures and Plates.

# Index

Vegetius, writer 223, 234, 237
Veii 40–41, 57, 62
*velites* 25, 89
vendettas 54
Vercingetorix, Gaulish leader 104–5
Vespasian, emperor 154–57
*Victoriatus* coins 77
Vietnam War 11
violence 28, 54, 121, 163–66; in civil
    society 163–66; historical
    representations of 7–8, 9–10; illicit
    soldierly 26; kin-based 54; martial
    17–18, 53, 55, 58, 66, 283; and the *pax
    Romana* 15–16, 288; political 256;
    state control of 57, 65–66
Visigothic, Visigoths 264, 270
Vitellius, emperor 21, 155–57
Volscians 57, 60

waist belts 124, 190–91, *215*, 234
War of the Deserters 199
warcries 242
whips 18
wives of soldiers 194
wolf standards and insignia
    24–28, 237
wooden training swords 33
World War I 6, 10–11

Xanthippus, general 72
*xiphos* 48–49, *48–49*, 81, 83, 213

Yemen 141

Zama, battle of 74, 76, 78–79, 85, 90
Zealots 155
Zenobia, queen of Palmyra 227